AL SMITH:

Hero of the Cities

A Political Portrait
Drawing on the Papers
of Frances Perkins

Books by Matthew Josephson

Galimathias
Zola and His Time
Portrait of the Artist as American
Jean-Jacques Rousseau
The Robber Barons
The Politicos
The President Makers
Victor Hugo
Empire of the Air
Stendhal: or the Pursuit of Happiness
Sidney Hillman: Statesman of American Labor
Union House, Union Bar
Edison: A Biography
Life Among the Surrealists: a Memoir
Infidel in the Temple
Al Smith: Hero of the Cities

Books by Hannah Josephson

The Golden Threads
Aragon, Poet of the Resistance
   (with Malcolm Cowley)
Al Smith: Hero of the Cities

AL SMITH:

Hero of the Cities

*A Political Portrait
Drawing on the Papers
of Frances Perkins*

MATTHEW AND
HANNAH JOSEPHSON

Illustrated with Photographs

Thames and Hudson
London

First published in Great Britain in 1970 by
THAMES AND HUDSON LTD, LONDON

Copyright © 1969 by Matthew Josephson, Hannah Josephson, and Susanna Coggeshall

All rights reserved. No part of this book may be reproduced or transmitted in any form by any means, electronic or mechanical, including photocopying and recording, or by any information storage or retrieval system, without permission in writing from the publisher

Printed in the United States of America

ISBN 0 500 53008 4

"Al Smith . . . has attained national prestige, partly by his honesty and his ability, but mainly owing to his origins . . . in the slum quarters of New York . . . The enormous mass of immigrants rightly look upon him as their mouthpiece, for he is Catholic, though not the tool of the Church; a man of the people in every fibre and yet not an extremist; and above all he proclaims a new Americanism in which the Nordic Protestant tradition counts for nothing. In spite of his crudeness, this Irish-American stands for the best in the non-Anglo-Saxon community, and the foreign population feels for the first time that he gives them access to power and honours."

André Siegfried

America Comes of Age (New York: Harcourt, Brace & World, 1927). Quoted by permission of the publishers.

Preface

IT SEEMS VERY FITTING to take the opportunity which the publication of the present volume affords to express a satisfaction I believe I must share with all who, as children in the 1920's and 30's, were domiciled with parents then regarding themselves as liberal or progressive. This will apply especially to such of those children as were living in New York, many of whom attended Lincoln, Horace Mann, Birch Wathen or other "progressive" schools.

Al Smith, to our childish hearts, was a personage not a little divine, and with the engaging manners of a Robin Hood. We knew that the millennium would be at hand were he to worst the venal Sheriffs of Nottingham who seemed to have occupied the seats of power. We looked forward to this nearly impossible day with as much excitement and wonder as to the moment when, in a fairy story, the total stranger may manage to utter the secret password and come into his own kingdom, the emblems of which had been locked away by a wicked witch of his grandfather's generation.

The note of expectancy, struck then, continues still to murmur, "not yet, but sometime," in a half-forgotten corner of our consciousness. And this murmur is swelled by the account which the Josephsons have given, the memories they have evoked and enlarged of those battles won and lost when we were very young. Whether the welling waters of nostalgia, thus replenished, can bring a green cover to the landscape of our present world is doubtful. That prosperity, once envisaged for the good of all, appears now to have engulfed nearly all in a mass of infertile anxiousness. But it is good to be reminded of how it all started — with a noble, compassionate impulse.

Frances Perkins had undertaken to recall in print the substance of the Al Smith era and struggled with the problem for some years. This work was left unfinished at her death. I believe she would now have been thankful that perceptive observers have been able to accomplish the task which she, as a onetime participant, toward the end of her life, could not and would join me in applauding the Josephsons for their accomplishment in recalling to some and presenting to others, whose memories' span is shorter, the glory which, lacking the encumbrance of excessive power, has probably remained all the brighter.

We loved Al Smith, and we are happy to hear the story told.

SUSANNA W. COGGESHALL
LITERARY EXECUTOR
June, 1969

Foreword

THE VARIOUS LEGENDS surrounding Governor Alfred E. Smith, one of the great regional leaders in the America of his time, to whom many attributed a genius for democratic politics, would seem to be reason enough to attempt a new and comprehensive account of his career for the public of today, which remembers his name, but has somewhat forgotten his good works. There are other reasons: Al Smith was a hero figure fifty years ago to the new urban masses, whose sheer weight of numbers was already changing the country's old face and way of life. Smith was not only a man of the people, but a man of the big-city people who stemmed from the more recent immigrations and the minority religious-ethnic groups. Too often these groups found that as citizens they were denied their full voice in the affairs of government. Ours was a government by consent, but in its traditional structure there were many built-in prescriptive devices, including electoral rotten boroughs at the state level, under control of the county machines that worked to frustrate the will of the city folk. In his heyday Smith was a great destroyer of rotten boroughs in his own state and in the national party system. By the 1920's the new urban culture pressed steadily against the residual culture embodied in the Americans of older stock, and thrust the man from the sidewalks of New York up into leadership in the national theater. The elevation of Smith, Roman Catholic and "Irish," to the role of Democratic Party candidate for the Presidency constituted a sort of peaceful insurrection, as Walter Lippmann described it at that period: "for with him the millions of half-enfranchised Americans are making their first bid for power." They were destined to make renewed bids, and it is certain that the spectacular campaigns waged by Smith prepared the way for the eventual victory of John F. Kennedy.

United States history has in good measure been the story of the prolonged struggles of successive groups of immigrants or other disadvantaged groups against discrimination and intolerance practiced upon them by the descendants of earlier immigrants. A few generations ago the Irish, who for years had been neglected and ill-used in our society, won their fight for "Irish power" in New York and Massachusetts, and after that other white ethnic minorities strove for a place in the sun. The unrest of today, epitomized by the call for "black power," is but another phase of this recurring battle for civil rights for all men.

It must be remembered that in the days when he ruled as party leader in New York State, Smith was an ardent progressive and innovator in politics. At an early stage of his career this son of Tammany Hall came under the influence of a group of outstanding intellectuals and social workers, several of whom were women. By joining forces with them he forged his unique coalition of reformers and machine politicians that made his long gubernatorial regime at

Albany at once so practical and so creative. In those days the Federal Government, except in wartime, was one of limited powers — it was the states that were concerned with the general welfare, only the states could control the conditions under which people worked, or were transported to their jobs, only the states could set standards for housing or sanitation or the care of dependents. In all these fields Smith performed pioneer work in the nation's most important and most populous state. And since much of this reform legislation was copied by other states, his vigorous sponsorship of humane social laws had a profound effect on the everyday life of millions of plain citizens all over the country. There were to be sure some western states that were also in the vanguard in certain areas, but in New York you could find the beginnings of the Welfare State which was to reach full bloom later in its federal form under the New Deal Administration of Franklin D. Roosevelt.

If he was an intuitive master of the art of democratic rule, it was also true that Smith was a superb teacher of the craft of popular politics. Franklin Roosevelt himself acknowledged that he was Smith's admiring disciple, and served as one of his lieutenants in the party hierarchy for many years. It was Smith, moreover, who chose Roosevelt to succeed him in the Governor's chair at Albany. The New Deal, in its turn, was an alliance of reformers and professional politicians, quite like Smith's original model; it even drew for its Brain Trust on members of Smith's "privy council" and carried over to Washington some of that group's program for social security and human welfare planning.

Despite the resistance of politicians, the use of experts or specialists had been coming into vogue for some years, and it was a distinctive feature of Smith's setup at Albany. One of the ablest of his aides was the former social worker Frances Perkins, who served under him as a member of the Industrial Commission for all his four terms, as under Governor Roosevelt afterward. Appointed by Roosevelt as the first woman member of the national Cabinet, she was one of America's most famous career women. Miss Perkins's perceptive memoir, *The Roosevelt I Knew*, showed affection for as well as keen understanding of the "patrician" President. Nevertheless she was more deeply attached to Smith, the man from the East Side tenements, whom she encountered at a formative period of her own life, and with whom she collaborated even more closely, over a longer period.

After her book on Roosevelt was published Miss Perkins undertook to write a biography of Smith. Although she was by then in ripe old age she carried on her researches for many years in intervals between other tasks, but at the time of her death in 1965 she had completed only a rough draft of three brief chapters on the boyhood and youth of the Governor, and some additional pages of commentary on the 1928 presidential campaign. However, she left a mass of notes, including a thousand pages of tape-recorded reminiscences of Smith and his circle, which were deposited in Columbia University Library's Oral History Collection.

It was Mrs. Susanna Wilson Coggeshall, Miss Perkins's daughter and literary executor, who invited us to complete her mother's unfinished work, a proposal in which she was joined by Houghton Mifflin Company. It soon appeared, however, that the problem was not one of "finishing" another author's posthumous work, but of writing it ourselves from beginning to end. The gaps in Miss Perkins's unfinished manuscript left out virtually the entire public career of the subject from 1900 on, and his later years in private life as well. We were fortunately able to avail ourselves of Miss Perkins's extensive notes and tape-recorded recollections, but they composed only part of the raw material for the book, to which we added the results of our own researches in Smith's papers, official records, the newspaper files over a span of forty years, and personal interviews with his surviving associates.

Miss Perkins's posthumous papers form a historical document of the highest interest, for they contain the reminiscences of an intelligent eyewitness and participant in many of the events recorded here. Besides her other services for Governor Smith she took the stump for him in 1928, and so was able to record her own testimony on that turbulent presidential contest and its embittered religious controversies. Her tapes also contain many shrewd insights into Smith's modus operandi, the master politician that he was, and into the operations of Roosevelt, along with comments on the rupture between the two longtime political friends. Her searches into the vital records of New York City have also helped dissolve the mystery about Smith's forebears and racial origins, which has been preserved in half a dozen earlier and incomplete biographies.

Since, unfortunately, Miss Perkins did not live to accomplish more than a brief beginning of her project, it has turned out that the preparation and writing of this book has been almost wholly our own work; moreover we have also been obliged to verify and correct many of her reminiscences, recorded when she was almost eighty years old. We felt therefore that we ought not to name her as our co-author, that it would not be proper to hold her responsible for opinions and interpretations with which she might have differed in some respects. Our book, at all events, gives some account of Miss Perkins's remarkable character as well as of her achievements. She was the first American woman to attain national cabinet rank, and the most famous career woman of her day. In short she has been a silent partner in this enterprise and a most valued one, and that is well reflected, we hope, in our text.

We are greatly indebted to the Oral History Office of the Columbia University Library for having recorded in tape the reminiscences of Miss Perkins, and for providing us with transcripts of them. We owe thanks to the Oral History directing staff, Dr. Louis Starr and Mrs. Elizabeth Mason, for their courtesies.

Mrs. Susanna Coggeshall not only encouraged us to complete the biography of Smith, but also furnished us with planning notes and correspondence of her mother.

Mrs. Emily Smith Warner, daughter of Governor Smith, is given thanks for permission to use the Governor's scrapbooks of newspaper cuttings, and for furnishing us with reminiscences of both her parents.

We are under obligation to various friends, associates, and aides of Governor Smith for having given us their recollections of the Governor; among these are Commissioner Robert Moses and former New York Supreme Court Judge Joseph M. Proskauer, Lindsay Rogers, Burgess Professor of Government, Columbia University (retired), John A. Coleman, the Governor's friend and co-worker in his later years, and Carlos Israels, son of Mrs. Belle Moskowitz, who was Governor Smith's political adviser from 1918 to 1932. Others who kindly granted us interviews were former New York Supreme

Court Judge Samuel I. Rosenman, Mrs. Henry Goddard
Leach, Mrs. Vanderbilt Webb, Miss Pauline Newman, and
Miss Rose Schneiderman.

To Mrs. Anne N. Barrett of the Houghton Mifflin editorial
staff we wish to express our gratitude for her long-continued
interest in this project and for the sustaining help of her good
counsels.

We are also under special obligation for his generous aid
and encouragement to Dr. Isador Lubin, of the Twentieth
Century Fund, longtime assistant to Miss Perkins at the U.S.
Labor Department, as well as to President Roosevelt and
later to Governor Harriman of New York. To be sure none of
these persons are responsible for the opinions expressed in
this book.

MATTHEW JOSEPHSON
HANNAH JOSEPHSON

Contents

Illustrations

Al Smith in Indianapolis, 1928

Al Smith with Governor Roosevelt in Albany, 1929

Al Smith, c. 1930

Colonel Edwin Halsey, secretary of the U.S. Senate; Nancy Cook of Hyde Park, N.Y.; and Secretary of Labor Frances Perkins, snapped at the evening session of the Democratic National Convention in Philadelphia, June 23, 1936. Courtesy of ACME

Mayor La Guardia, Smith, Katie, and Robert Moses at the dedication of the Belt Parkway, Brooklyn, June 29, 1940. Courtesy of Robert Moses

(Unless otherwise credited, the photographs are reproduced through the courtesy of the Museum of the City of New York)

AL SMITH:

Hero of the Cities

A Political Portrait
Drawing on the Papers
of Frances Perkins

CHAPTER I

Encounter at Albany

THE FIRST TIME Frances Perkins set eyes on Al Smith was in the winter of 1910 in the State Capitol at Albany. A young social worker, then undertaking one of her first important assignments, she had arrived there the day before to represent the New York Consumers' League as lobbyist for a bill to limit the working week of women and children to fifty-four hours. Joseph Hammett, Albany representative of the Citizens' Union of New York, a good-government association, had offered to show her the ropes, beginning with a tour of the Victorian-Gothic and red-plush Assembly Chamber of the Capitol.

As they stood behind the brass rail closing off the Assembly floor from visitors, they saw no more than half a dozen men in the Chamber that morning, most of them on their feet passing to and from committee meetings in session. Hammett pointed out the only one of them who was sitting and working at his desk, Alfred Emanuel Smith, Assemblyman from the Second Assembly District of New York City. Miss Perkins noticed that he was youthful and personable, and remarked to Hammett that he seemed to be deep in his studies.

"Yes," said Hammett, "he's reading the bills that were pre-

sented last night. When he first came to the Assembly he
used to read every bill that was introduced and send out to
the Legislative Reference Library for the law it amended."
In that way, according to Hammett, he mastered the business
of the Chamber, unlike most of his colleagues, who voted as
their party leaders instructed them without giving it further
thought. Hammett also allowed that Smith was intelligent
and conscientious, and seemed well disposed toward the social welfare bills Miss Perkins was interested in. But, he
added with a sigh, "It's a pity he's a Tammany man."

At that period Miss Perkins's acquaintance with Tammany
men was rather limited. She asked Hammett if he would
introduce her to this well-intentioned young lawmaker who
appeared so different from her idea of a city machine politician. As they waited behind the rail for Assemblyman Smith
to come out to the lobby, they were joined by Robert Benkard, Secretary of the City Club of New York, who was well
known to many of the Albany legislators, and he ventured
to attract Smith's attention by leaning over the rail and calling out in a loud stage whisper, "Al." The Assemblyman
turned and, recognizing Benkard, came up the aisle to shake
hands.

Smith bowed and smiled when Hammett introduced Miss
Perkins as the lobbyist who would be in Albany that winter
to promote the Fifty-four-Hour Bill. "Do you vouch for her,
Joe?" asked Smith quizzically. Hammett started to say that
he did, though he was unfamiliar with the bill whose passage
she urged, when Benkard, breaking in, said with warmth,
"She's all right, Al; she's level-headed, and you can trust her."

"Very well," said Smith, "Jackson's got the bill. It's still in
committee and not moving very fast. Better ask for a hear-

ing." And with that he left them and returned to his desk.

It was typical of Smith that his first words to a newcomer should have been both friendly and of practical help, for as Miss Perkins learned later, if no one asked for a hearing there would be none. Moreover his remark conveyed the suggestion that Jackson, who had himself introduced the bill, was not moving as rapidly in its support as might have been expected from its sponsor. No one knew better than Smith how a man might win standing among his constituents by championing a measure which was unlikely to be passed.

"So it was," wrote Miss Perkins long afterward, "that I met Alfred Emanuel Smith, one of the most colorful figures in the history of American politics, a man who was to go forward to be majority leader and then Speaker of the Assembly, and later was to be Governor of New York State for four terms, and in 1928 a candidate for President of the United States."

At their first meeting Smith, then aged thirty-seven, had already come a long way from the East Side of New York where he was born and grew up. Obliged to go to work at the age of twelve, without formal education, but with extraordinary natural gifts, he had learned how to learn, and also how to communicate with people of every social stratum. He was then at the threshold of a career which even to a man of his sanguine temperament must have seemed unimaginable. Frances Perkins, stemming from old New England stock, and having the advantages of a protected childhood and a college education to boot, was then just turning thirty. After some years of intermittent teaching and of pursuing advanced studies, she had found her calling; she had opted for social work and loved it. She too was reckoned by her associates as a promising person, seeking her career in an almost uncharted field, and devoting herself to the problems of working people and of the poor.

The brief encounter between the professional politician and the social worker during the Albany legislative session of 1910 — although their two roles seemed so incongruous — turned out to be a momentous one; each had something valuable to contribute to the development of the other, and each later, in his own way, gave recognition to that fact. The Capitol at Albany was still in the brass spittoon era of our politics, and one could really smell it in that rambling palace, whose elegant corridors were littered with rubbish and cigar butts. Miss Perkins's first feelings were of ladylike revulsion at the whole place which she later came to know so well. But the Democratic Party was changing, the movement for woman suffrage was gathering force, the reformers all about were raising their heads, and Assemblyman Smith, the "gentleman from Tammany," as he used to be called, was changing his ideas. Miss Perkins was by no means the first or only social worker engaged in lobbying for welfare laws before the practical men of state politics, and Al Smith would be meeting others like her far more often than he would have believed likely in the past. Their encounter signified something relatively new: the alliance of the rising machine politician with one of the social reformers in New York was to prove a fruitful partnership in which both worked for the public weal with mutual trust and without any real conflict during long years.

In the course of the next four years Miss Perkins came to know Smith very well as politician and lawmaker, for in addition to meeting with him frequently in connection with her lobbying activities, she worked as an investigator for an important legislative commission of which he was vice-chairman, and journeyed all about the state in his company. One day (it was probably in 1911, as she remembered) she also had an opportunity to see him in his home in New York City, and to judge the manner of man he was in private life.

Mrs. Charles Dana Gibson, wife of the artist, had asked Miss Perkins to accompany her on a visit to Assemblyman Smith, whose support she was seeking for the Widows' Pension Bill soon to be voted on in Albany. Irene Gibson, one of the famous Langhorne sisters of Virginia (another was Lady Astor), was a beautiful and vivacious member of New York society in those days; the original model of the "Gibson girl" crusaded not only for woman suffrage but also for various social welfare measures designed to improve the condition of the poor. The Widows' Pension Bill, her favorite project at the time, provided for state aid to enable widows to keep their young children at home instead of sending them away to orphanages. The bill had other sponsors, among them Sophie Irene Loeb, well-known "sob sister" writing for the Hearst press, who carried on a tireless campaign for its passage. But Hearst's two newspapers in New York were held in contempt as sensation-seeking journals. Mrs. Gibson, as an active board member of several philanthropic agencies, wanted it to be known that the bill had more serious backers than the Hearst papers. She was also eager to see that the bill was properly drawn up, with provisions for supervising money allotments so that orphaned children would be well protected.

The two ladies, escorted by Paul Kennaday, Director of

the American Association for Labor Legislation, rode down
to the City Hall station on the subway and took a taxi to
the corner of Oliver Street on the lower East Side of Manhattan, since none of them was confident of finding their way
in the district. In that area of teeming tenements Oliver
Street proved to be a respectable, middle-class oasis; it was
lined with neat, three-story red brick houses built before
the Civil War, with high stoops and trim iron railings. Number 25, where the Smiths lived, was well kept, with steps
and sidewalk swept clean and spotless white curtains at the
shining windows. When Paul Kennaday rang the bell the
door was opened by a pretty young woman in a dark dress
with a little white apron tied about her waist. Miss Perkins
noted that her curly hair was neatly arranged and that her
only adornment was a string of beads around her neck. Smiling and friendly, Mrs. Smith informed them that her husband
had not yet returned from Albany but that he was expected
momentarily. Would they come in and sit down? Shown
into the parlor on the first floor, they found it a cheerful,
pleasantly furnished room, with a clock and knickknacks on
the mantel, a large rug on the floor, and a general air of comfort and neatness. There were children in the house, running
up the stairs and poking their heads in the door, then disap-
pearing when Mrs. Smith told them, "No, your father hasn't
come home yet." As the visitors chatted with Mrs. Smith,
mostly about the children, they found her amiable, well-
mannered, conscientious as a mother and a housewife.

Soon the front door was heard to open and Mrs. Smith
ran to greet her husband. When he kissed and embraced
her Mrs. Gibson whispered to Miss Perkins, "Oh, he *loves*
her." Then the children came flocking up the stairs again

to welcome their father, and it was clear that the whole family was united in affection, and unashamed to show it. Smith then turned to his visitors and asked what he could do for them. He was obviously accustomed to having members of his constituency drop in at all hours to tell him their troubles when he came home for the weekend. Mrs. Gibson stated very briefly what she had in mind about the Widows' Pension Bill, and it was evident that she made a favorable impression on him. He made a deep impression on her as well, for she became his fast friend from then on, and an ardent worker in all his campaigns.

Meeting Smith in his own home, Frances Perkins saw the man who inhabited the politician: a doting husband and father, loved in return by a happy little family, living in as respectable a middle-class American situation as could be found in any small town from Maine to California. All very commonplace in a way, but the man himself was not commonplace. He was a tough-minded politician, she knew, as energetic in defense of Tammany's purposes as he would be in backing a bill for widows' pensions, and like many others in her time, she responded to his warmth and charm while wondering what forces had made him what he was.

CHAPTER II

Origins and Childhood

"AFTER THIS VISIT," Frances Perkins wrote many years later, "I began to think of him in a much more personal way, and from time to time gathered up crumbs of information about his background, who his people were, his schooling, his occupation before he became Assemblyman. Little by little, either in his words or in those of his acquaintances and friends, one formed a picture of what the realities of his life were."

Smith once said to her: "My mother was a widow when I was pretty young, and I had to go to work to help support the family a little earlier than she would have liked to have me." To Miss Perkins this seemed one of the prime reasons for his success, quite in the American tradition of rags-to-riches, or canal-boy to President. Many a man employing young boys had told her, "I'd sooner take a boy who is a widow's son than anyone else because he's likely to be serious-minded and reliable. He has to be."

In his Oliver Street days Smith used to remark on how close were his ties with the quarter where he lived, and how long-rooted they were: "I was born within a stone's throw of where I now live; and my grandfathers and grandmothers, my father and mother, me and my wife and my children have all lived in the old Fourth Ward." In truth they had all resided within a few blocks of one another and within a few minutes' walk from the house near the waterfront where Smith's maternal grandparents, the Mulvehills, first settled in 1841 when they came off the ship that brought them from Ireland. Theirs had been a rough passage of sixty days on a clipper ship of the Black Ball Line, as the Governor had often been told; his grandmother, moreover, arrived carrying a three-months-old baby. As the ship docked at South Street, at the foot of Beekman, the Mulvehills picked up their baggage and walked just three blocks along the river until they came to a house with the sign out, "Rooms to Let," at the corner of Dover and Water Streets. Here they found a flat on the third floor of a small tenement whose lower floors were occupied by a family of German immigrants. The Mulvehills "took the rent," as they used to say, and remained for many years. There Smith's mother, Catherine Mulvehill, and a number of other children were born. In talking of his origins Smith used to say to Miss Perkins playfully, "You see what an old family we are!" He was possibly unaware of the fact that his paternal grandfather had settled in New York earlier than the Mulvehills, in the 1820's.

Thomas and Maria Mulvehill had come to the United States from Westmeath County, near Dublin, several years before the massive exodus of the Irish to America began in 1846, as a result of the potato blight and the famine. The want of land, the prevailing poverty of workers and peasants, the unremitting oppression of the English had already caused many of Ireland's young people to migrate to these shores. Here their labor was in strong demand; indeed, many

of them were lured here by immigration agents for the shipping lines who promised that all English-speaking persons
would find work at good wages. For Thomas Mulvehill and
his young wife there were additional motives that prompted
them to emigrate. Mulvehill, a tailor by trade, and a Roman
Catholic, had formed an attachment to Maria Marsh, who
was of Protestant English stock and of a higher social station
than he. Her father was reputed to have been a well-to-do
barrister of Westmeath County, where he owned a property
in the village of Moate called, appropriately, "Marshland."
Deeply in love, Maria determined to change her religion in
order to marry young Mulvehill, an act that earned the disapproval of the parents of both. In later years Maria Marsh
Mulvehill was described by her American descendants as
"ladyborn," one who had received the education of a gentle-
woman in a time when the British barred all schooling for
the Catholic Irish. Even as an aged woman living in New
York's East Side she was known to do beautiful embroidery
and needlework, as Alfred Smith's sister related. She also
wrote letters in an elegant hand for many of her neighbors
who could not read or write, letters telling of their safe arrival in the new world, of the jobs they had found, and declaring their undying affection for their parents and for old
Ireland.

Within a few days of debarkation Thomas Mulvehill found
work with the tailoring firm of Brooks Brothers, which had
just that year opened its shop in Catherine Street. There he
was to be employed for the rest of his life, a steady and
skillful craftsman earning a fair living wage. To him and
Maria six children were born, one of the younger ones being
Catherine, the mother of Alfred Smith. Two of the sons

grew up to be solid and useful citizens of the "Old Neighborhood," as the Fourth Ward used to be called; one of them, Peter, became a member of the New York City Fire Department; another joined the Police Department. A younger sister, Delia, who remained a spinster, came to live in Catherine's household after Catherine was married and bore children.

The Mulvehills were faithful attendants at the parish church, the St. James, on James Street and the New Bowery. This was an imposing edifice in Federal style, with a portico of heavy Doric columns, which had been acquired by the Roman Catholic diocese from the Episcopal Church as early as 1827, when the native-born Protestants began to retreat uptown before the flood of immigrants. The Mulvehills were active in the church socials and formed lasting friendships with many of their fellow parishioners.

Catherine, who was educated at the school for girls run by St. James Church, grew up to be a handsome young woman with strongly marked features and a long face that was not "typically Irish," it was said. Her nose, incidentally, was fairly large, and her son's was to be even larger. When she was eighteen she met a young man of the neighborhood named Alfred Emanuel Smith, who was also a communicant of St. James Church. In fact, for a year or so, when he was eight or nine years old, Smith had been a student at the boys' school of the church, before Catherine was born. Now in his early thirties, he owned a small trucking business consisting of two trucks and four or five horses, and employing a helper, thus a man of substance for those days. The truckman was tall and powerfully built; he was dark complexioned, dark-haired, and wore a bushy moustache.

The old East Side quarter of those days was strong on neighborliness, as Governor Smith used to recall. On summer evenings the local families would sit out on the front steps of their tenements and greet the passersby; the policeman on his rounds regularly stopped to exchange the time of day with the local residents. Alfred Smith Senior's horses were stabled in Dover Street, a few steps from the Mulvehill house, which he passed morning and night. Thus the truckman and the Mulvehills struck up an acquaintance, for he was not only a familiar figure but one whose manner was friendly to all. His interest in Catherine Mulvehill was marked; indeed he courted her for a whole year. The fact that he was a widower with an infant daughter and fifteen years older than Catherine may have raised some questions in her parents' minds, but the couple knew their own minds, and in the late summer of 1872 they were married in St. James Church and went to live nearby in South Street.

At the time the Mulvehills knew very little about the origins of their daughter's husband; it would seem that his reputation as a responsible character and a churchgoer was what made him acceptable as a suitor. All that was definitely known was that he had been born and raised in this same villagelike community, and that he had been baptized in their own parish church. Long afterward, when his son brought his own first-born to be baptized in St. James Church as Alfred Emanuel Smith the priest asked him where he had found such an outlandish name as "Emanuel," which was not traditionally Irish. "I got it right here in this church," said Smith firmly, "and so did my father before me."

Old-timers in the Fourth Ward remembered that Alfred Emanuel Smith Senior had been the son of a man bearing the same name who was said to have kept a boardinghouse for sailors on South Street at one time. The Governor's father had had but little schooling, and his parents were by no means rich, for he had gone to work as a boy of ten, performing light manual labor around the docks and warehouses before becoming a teamster. It was known also that he had long been a member of the city's volunteer firemen's corps, and that during the last two years of the Civil War he had served in the Union Army. After the war he had married a Miss Donnelly, of a respectable Brooklyn family, and when she died he had sent their infant daughter to be reared by her grandmother. For the rest some mystery as to his background has prevailed, a mystery his son did little to dispel, for in his autobiography he wrote, "I do not remember ever hearing him tell where his parents came from."

In 1926, during one of Governor Smith's lively election campaigns, a report was circulated by his opponents to the effect that he was in reality no Irishman, that his father was a German whose name originally had been "Schmidt." This charge outraged the Irish members of Tammany Hall, but it was soon stigmatized as a base canard. The Governor's family produced an old certificate, dating from 1857, evidencing his father's membership in a volunteer fire company under the name of Alfred E. Smith. It was admitted, however, that the father might well have had Italian forebears.

Much of the confusion about the senior Smith's ancestry has finally been cleared up in recent times by Frances Perkins's searches of old city records as well as by her probing interviews with Governor Smith's younger sister, Mrs. Mary Glynn. Mary must have listened more intently to the talk of her elders, or was perhaps more interested in the family history than her brother, for her impressions were vivid and revealing. When asked what part of Ireland her father's people came from she shook her head, adding that when his friends used to engage in heated arguments over the "Irish question," he would say, "Well, thank God I haven't got a bit of Irish in me. I've got no Irish in my blood."

Mrs. Glynn also remembered that her father had once shown her an old silver key ring that bore the initials, "A. E. S.," which he said stood for "Alfredo Emanuelo Smith," his father's name. Thus she was given to understand that her grandfather was of Italian origin. Another detail that stuck in her mind was her father's boast, "I have an uncle who is Bishop of Naples." And on still another occasion he was quite agitated when some of his Irish neighbors ranted against the "dagos" who were then arriving in New York in large numbers. To the charge that the Italian immigrants were good-for-nothing bootblacks who "spoiled the neighborhood," he replied hotly, "Don't talk like that! They're good people, and they have a right to come here just the same as you!"

The death certificate of the Governor's father, dated 1886, provides the clue from which the origins of the family on the paternal side can be traced. It gives his name as Alfred Emanuel Smith; his place of birth, New York City; his age, fifty-one; his father's name, Emanuel; his father's birthplace, Italy; his mother's name, Magdalena; and his mother's birthplace, Germany.

Going back to the New York City Directories, one finds the name Emanuel Smith listed every year from 1842 to 1859 (when he is presumed to have died), at various addresses in the Fourth Ward, in Oliver Street from 1842 to 1846, and at 31 Hamilton Street from 1857 to 1859. In 1860-61 his widow, Madelaine (another form of Magdalena) is listed as residing at the last address.

In the New York State Census of 1855, generally regarded as the most reliable of the period, the family is reported as living in the Fourth Ward, Third Assembly District, and consisting of the following members:

Emanuel Smith: age, 42 years; born, Genoa
    Resident of New York for 30 years
    Occupation: Mariner
    Naturalized citizen
Magdalena: age, 39 years; born, Germany
    (Wife) Resident of New York for 18 years
Teresa (Daughter):   age, 13 years; born, New York
Alfred (Son):   age, 15 years; born, New York

In these sparse records of obscure immigrants the actual Italian surname of Emanuel does not appear. From the dates indicated he was twelve or thirteen years old when he landed in this country. Could he have been a cabin boy who jumped ship? It is likely that the immigration officer could not understand Italian, and that the lad could not write his name. For all we know it might have been Schiaccio, or Cecchi, or even da Vinci. The officer no doubt had recourse to a common practice, and handed him an entrance card with the name Smith, as who should say, "Man."

Madelaine Smith was remembered by Governor Smith's uncle Peter Mulvehill as a "blond German woman" who in old age was employed to do the housekeeping and bedmaking at the firehouse in the neighborhood where he was stationed. When she died in 1863 her son, the Governor's father, bought a plot in Old Calvary Cemetery where she was

buried, and where he in his turn was interred in 1886. Of
the daughter Teresa Mrs. Glynn knew only that she had
died young.*

Concerning the Governor's father, however, the official
records have been definitely located; moreover his children
recalled the chief incidents of his life as told by him in
stories that represent him as a simple and worthy man,
whose life was laborious and whose character seems to have
been humane as well as courageous. Among the tales they
remembered was one of his exploits during the Draft Riots
in the third year of the Civil War. As a volunteer fireman
it was his duty not only to help put out the fires that destroyed about a hundred buildings in the city during that
week of terror, but also to try to calm the rioters who had
come into the Fourth Ward and persuade them to disperse.
The violence was initially provoked by resentment against
the conscription law, which permitted the better-heeled
young men to buy a substitute for three hundred dollars;
but the presence of large numbers of Irish immigrants among
the rioters was no doubt due to their long-smoldering anger
at the Know-Nothing "nativists" who for years had manifested strong prejudice against them, and had sometimes
clashed with them in the streets. The immigrant population
was also agitated over the influx of emancipated Negroes
who came North during the war to perform casual labor as
dockworkers, hackdrivers, waiters, or house servants, these

---

* Thus the records are fairly clear, although the dates given are not always
reliable. The death certificate of the Governor's father, for example, gives
his age as 51 in 1886, which would have made the year of his birth 1835,
instead of 1840, as indicated in the New York State Census. Neither do
Magdalena's age and length of residence tally exactly. But these discrepan-
cies may have arisen because the grandparents were illiterate.

being the categories of work usually allotted to white folk from Europe or Ireland. The rioters therefore turned their fury on the few Negroes found in the vicinity, pursuing them relentlessly and lynching them when caught.*

The Governor's father related afterward that on one day he had arrived in time to cut down a Negro who had just been strung up by the mob, and had borne him away to safety. On another occasion he managed to save two other Negroes who were being chased and stoned by hiding them in barrels and carrying them in his truck over the ferry to Brooklyn where they could find shelter. "They are children of God," he is said to have declared, "and they have a right to live."

Later in 1863 the elder Smith volunteered for service in the war by joining a regiment of Zouaves, whose colorful uniforms consisted of baggy red trousers and vests, along with a tasseled fez, modeled after those of French Algerian troops. Recruited largely in New York City, many of the Zouaves were Irish, and some of them, like Smith, were volunteer firemen. While he gave his children no account of his regiment's combat service, he did recall one hazardous adventure that occurred while he was stationed temporarily in Washington. A hotel there caught fire, and Smith was among those sent to the rescue of people caught in the burning building. The most daring exploit of the day was performed by the stalwart teamster who, climbing out of an upper-story window of the hotel and hanging head downward with his feet gripped by comrades above, managed to

---

* It has been estimated that more than a thousand persons of both colors were killed in that tumultuous week in July, 1863, and eight thousand wounded.

reach down and draw up by sheer strength a man trapped
at the window of the floor below.

After the war Smith's affairs seemed a little more flourish-
ing than before. Could he have gained a little capital from
bounties paid to volunteer soldiers or substitutes? At any
rate the carts and draft horses he owned were worth a tidy
sum, several hundreds of dollars. He was able to marry, rent
a five-room flat in a tenement at 174 South Street for fifteen
dollars a month, and begin raising a family. After his first
wife died of a sudden illness, he waited two years before
he was married again, to Catherine Mulvehill.

On December 30, 1873, his second wife bore him a son
who was baptized Alfred Emanuel Smith, a boy fair-com-
plexioned, light-haired, blue-eyed, closely resembling his
mother. Two years later to the day a second child was born
to the Smiths, a girl whom they named Mary. Mary, or
"Mamie," as she was called, was dark-haired and olive-com-
plexioned, her cast of features, as some noticed, suggesting
her father's Italian forebears.

So the third generation Alfred Emanuel Smith, who was
to be regarded for long years as this country's most famous
Irish-American, was after all not a "pure" Irishman at all, but
a fine mixture of Italian, German, English, and Irish strains,
a true product of the melting pot of New York. But for
the whimsical intervention of an immigration officer, his surname might never have been Smith. It was the ethnic mixture in his makeup, Frances Perkins believed, which accounted for qualities approaching genius — a view which
accorded with some of the racial theories of her era. Like
all Americans he was the descendant of immigrants; he was
not, however, the child of recent immigrants, but of a family

established in the same urban corner of the United States since the early nineteenth century, and of a father who had served his country as a soldier. Neither he nor his parents ever regarded themselves as belonging to the immigrant class. Nor did he grow up in poverty or neglect, as many were led to believe by the myths about him in later years. His people were actually of the lower middle class, and were able to offer him as many educational and social advantages as the great majority of Americans then enjoyed. "We never felt poor, or thought we were poor," his sister told Miss Perkins. "We had good food and good clothes, and we even had toys, and toys weren't so common in those days." The Smith children could judge how well-off they were by contrast with a family on their street whose children wore no shoes, except on Sundays to go to church. There was, to be sure, a period of hardship for two or three years, when their father fell ill of a terminal disease, but even then they did not suffer actual want.

Alfred Smith's boyhood was passed in one of the most populous quarters of the big city, a community in itself, where most people were acquainted with one another and flocked together for birthdays or wakes or parish gatherings. It was not unlike the small-town world of New England or upstate New York. Until he was quite grown up he almost never ventured north of Canal Street, or at farthest Fourteenth Street. It was the special urban environment of the seaport metropolis, with its ever-changing street scene and its grand orchestration of cries and sounds that perhaps molded his personality more than anything else.

In the decades immediately following the Civil War New

York City was still largely a collection of villages each of which maintained its identity even as they were growing together. The "Battery District" in the old Fourth Ward, which ran from the southern tip of Manhattan to Chatham Square and extended to the East River, contained mostly Irish residents. To the north, along the Bowery, East Broadway, Delancey, and Grand Streets, the population was dominantly German; only in the 1890's were these almost wholly replaced by Russian Jews. Farther uptown were Greenwich, Chelsea, Gramercy, and Bloomingdale, and still farther up-island Yorkville and Harlem.

The Lower East Side community where three generations of Alfred E. Smiths resided still boasted many private homes in the old style, relics of the district's aristocratic past, with large shade trees fronting them. (These were later cut down because they impeded the work of the fire companies.) By the seventies most of the older American families had moved uptown, but the main business and shopping centers were still located in the region of lower Broadway and Nassau and Pearl Streets, as for example the big merchant establishments of Lord & Taylor, Hearn's, and Brooks Brothers.

The neighborhood possessed considerable portside charm, and resembled in no way the grimy slum or ghetto quarter into which it was transformed during the 1890's. Already the huge towers of Brooklyn Bridge, in course of construction since 1869, loomed over the whole district and constituted its dominant physical landmark. Indeed its great steel cables were suspended almost directly above the Smiths' house on South Street. As the docks along the street were not covered by warehouses, the people living nearby could take the air at the river's edge, which harbored ships from every nation, ships that still carried sail for the most part, and whose high bowsprits extended well across the broad thoroughfare. The waterfront was in fact a forest of spars and rigging, but the horizon was wide. Since the business structures at the lower end of the island were then at most eight or ten stories high, one could see the whole sweep of the tidal river from the upper floors of dwellings on the East Side.

The Smiths' flat at 174 South Street was on the third floor of a narrow brick house with two windows both front and back. They also had the use of an attic above their quarters, and in afteryears the Governor used to recall with what joy he would gallop through the rooms, stopping at the windows to peer out at the ships, the horses, the carriages, or sometimes the itinerant German bands in the street below. His mother remembered that a doctor who came to pay a call once commented, as he looked out of their front window, "This is like a view from an ocean liner."

But the boy's preferred playground, from which he could never stay away for long, was the eye-filling waterfront, where he would climb up and dangle from the bowsprits of the ships whenever the weight of the cargo brought them within reach. Other favored spots were a boat-building shop owned by one John T. Smith, a good friend of his father's, and the base of the towering New York pier of the Brooklyn Bridge. For him, as for many poets and artists, the bridge was more than a giant structure, it was a symbol, evoking emotions which the boy could hardly define. Later he wrote of it, "The Bridge and I grew up together. I have never lost the memory of the admiration and envy I felt for the men swarming up, stringing the cables, putting in the roadways, as the bridge took shape." It dominated his boyhood as it did the city skyline, for it was fourteen years in the building, and it was made "by hand," as he remarked perceptively. His mother used to tell him in a tone of awe about the many workers who had died while struggling to sink its caissons into the river. "Perhaps if they had known," she said, "they would never have built it."

Here at the harborside there were no gardens or parks, there was only the street as playground for the boy. And South Street was not only exciting visually; it was earsplitting. With traffic heavier than the main thoroughfares of larger cities such as Paris and London, the clatter of carts, carriages and horses' hooves on the cobblestones, the shouts of sailors and roustabouts, the ringing of ships' bells, the cries of hawkers, the rattle of hammers all made a roaring cacophony. Here Alfred and his friends ran about among the crates and trucks, almost under the feet of the great draft horses, or scrambled onto the docks where bags of tea or coffee or fragrant spices from all over the world were unloaded. At the nearby Fulton Fish Market he would go aboard the fishing smacks that tied up there every morning. The fishmongers' stalls had tanks where live fish and green turtles were kept fresh, and in the summer after the fish had been removed the jovial traders would drop the small boys of the neighborhood into the tanks to paddle and splash about.

The East River in those days was relatively clean. On hot summer afternoons the inhabitants of the quarter refreshed themselves by diving off the docks and enjoying a saltwater swim. Alfred's father, a fine swimmer, and a noted oarsman, kept a little bathhouse down near the tower of the Brooklyn Bridge, where he and his friends used to change for their evening dip. He taught his son to swim in the good old-fashioned way, by tying a rope around his waist and dropping him into the water. The boys all swam naked, the Governor recalled; they would have ridiculed any boy who used a bathing suit, like the older men, as "stuck up."

Alfred's father was nothing if not indulgent with his children, to whom he usually devoted his one day of rest. His son said of him, "He certainly gave us a good time when we were children," and his daughter reflected the same feeling; "We had everything we wanted," she told Miss Perkins. Alfred was allowed to keep innumerable pets: dogs, cats, sometimes a monkey or a goat in the attic above their flat. It was his delight to gather up stray dogs and bring them home, until the pack became so numerous that his mother insisted that he kennel them down in his father's horse stable.

The boy long remembered the Sunday walks he and his sister took with their father to the Battery, then full of lilac bushes, or to City Hall Park, where a brass band played just as on the greens of country towns. They also accompanied him to the Atlantic Gardens on the New Bowery, a German beer garden favored for family parties, where an all-female orchestra played. Longer excursions were made to Prospect Park in Brooklyn, or to Coney Island, or across the Upper Bay to Staten Island, a rustic place where they visited a roadhouse kept by a friend of their father's.

The most memorable adventure shared by father and son was a walk across Brooklyn Bridge before the road surface was completed and pedestrians were allowed to pass over. At this time the elder Smith was employed as a sort of guard to keep unauthorized people off the bridge, and "he gave himself permission to take Alfred across," as Mrs. Glynn

related, when as yet only the catwalk for workers slung between the piers was passable. Alfred often described this
hazardous journey to the Brooklyn side and back, made when
he was nine years old, as the most thrilling experience of his
boyhood. His sister, declaring that his accounts of this outing were in no way embroidered, exclaimed to Miss Perkins,
"My heavens, that was real! I remember mother sitting at
home, saying ten rosaries all the time they were gone! But
my father was determined to take the boy across the bridge
so he could say he crossed it before it was built."

The boy also remembered all his life the day of the formal
opening of the bridge, on May 24, 1883. The great span was
the pride of all New York, and tens of thousands attended
the celebration and fireworks. Six days later, on Decoration
Day, there was an even greater throng of visitors, along with
several regiments of the National Guard. Now there had
been much discussion in the newspapers about whether the
bridge — then the largest suspension bridge in the world,
6000 feet long and 329½ feet above the river — was really
safe, and whether the rhythmic movement of large numbers
of people or horses, or even strong winds, might not cause
the cable structure to sway or perhaps collapse. Suddenly
the promenading crowd heard a cry of alarm at the New
York end of the bridge, where a number of people had
tripped and fallen on the steps leading up to the higher level
of the roadway. Alfred was with a group of boys who hurried to the bridge terminal at Park Row when they heard of
the accident, and crowded as close to it as the police would
allow. They could see hats, coats, parasols, umbrellas, and
pocketbooks dropping from the bridge into the street. "I
seem to remember," Smith said many years later, "that some-

one in the crowd yelled that the bridge was falling. There was a rush for the New York end." Hundreds of people tried to get away from the suspended roadbed and climb up the masonry tower which they thought would be a place of safety. "Those rushing from the bridge," Smith continued, "met the crowd coming from Park Row," and in the melee that followed twelve persons were trampled to death, and thirty-five wounded. "That was my first view of a great calamity," he said. "I did not sleep for nights."

Alfred Smith used to speak of his father as a brave man and one of generous spirit. His sister described him as proud, and at the same time gregarious and hospitable. After his long hours at work he loved to gather with friends at the end of the day over a pot of beer. Often he would bring his fellow teamsters or navvies home for supper, even though Mrs. Smith sometimes lamented at the inroads into her larder. But food, especially fresh fish, was cheap, and there was generally enough to go around. The elder Smith would say that he wanted "the boys" who lived in boardinghouses to taste some of the good fare his wife and Aunt Delia prepared. One of his favorite sayings was "A man who can't do a friend a favor is not a man."

On the second floor of the South Street house, just below the Smiths' flat, there was a barbershop much frequented by the Sandy Hook pilots, a group of seafaring men who had formerly served as officers of merchant ships. Mr. Smith held these men in great esteem and occasionally invited them to share a meal. They were well-spoken, and their talk ranged over places they had visited in four continents and seven seas, while the children listened open-mouthed.

Other friends of the family were Irishmen who discussed

the Irish question with passion. One of these was the elder
Smith's closest friend, Henry Campbell, a prosperous grocer
who lived nearby in Madison Street. During Smith's last
illness, Campbell helped pay the doctor's bills, and after his
father died Alfred, too, found the man a warm friend and
counselor.

Like all small boys Alfred was captivated by the fire
wagons of Liberty Hose Company Number 10, at Pearl and
Dover Streets, of which both his father and his uncle Peter
Mulvehill were volunteer members. Uncle Peter later became a salaried member of the city's Fire Department and
drove a truck for Engine Company Number 32 at John Street
for thirty-five years. Mr. Smith had a superb uniform, consisting of a blue and red coat, long gum boots, a brass helmet, and a long pike, and thus accoutered he appeared not
only at fires, but also at holiday parades and political processions. Volunteer firemen enjoyed status in the community
because, as we have seen, they served as an auxiliary police
force to keep order in times of danger or riot.

The elder Smith was extremely proud of his certificate of
membership in the Volunteer Fire Corps which for many
years hung in the parlor of his flat. The document was illustrated with a steel engraving showing Neptune, unclothed,
holding a trident, in company with a goddess supposed to
be Minerva, and two disconsolate-looking women, presumably the victims of a fire. The children remembered the engraving well, but as they began to grow up it was taken
from the wall by Mrs. Smith and stored in a bureau drawer,
for she shared the prudery of other women of her time.

There is every evidence that Alfred Smith and his little
sister were closely guarded by their parents, as well as by

the parish priests. Though the father was lenient with the children, their strong-willed mother, on the contrary, was wary of the dangers to which they were exposed, and exercised a firm authority over their behavior. Not only was she solicitous for their physical well-being, she was also deeply religious, and brought them up in a strict pattern of virtue and piety. For another boy this might have had an unfortunate effect, making him rebellious or hostile, but although Alfred was playful enough, he was also tractable and tenderly submissive to his mother. Having been trained in infancy to kneel before her and receive her blessing every night before going to bed, he repeated this ritual as a grown man whenever he visited her, and did this as much out of love and compassion as out of habit.

The children were taught always to behave with decorum, Alfred's sister told Miss Perkins. They had to mind their manners and were often reminded of them. They must wash up and slick down their hair before meals; they must fold their hands on the edge of the table when they sat down and wait until their elders had given the signal before they began to eat. They must say "please" and "thank you"; they must not interrupt. Mamie must not cross her legs because "it's not ladylike." On Sundays they were dressed in their "best clothes"; they wore their second best for school. From an early age Alfred was fussy about his clothes, and his mother and Aunt Delia extended themselves to sew neat little suits for him, if only out of his father's outworn garments. As Oscar Handlin observed, many poor immigrants living in the populous, crime-infested quarters of our cities made prodigious efforts to bring up their children as respectable citizens, and were surprisingly successful. The Smith family, living in a dominantly immigrant quarter, were under the same compulsions to keep their good name.

For temptations lay all about them. Mrs. Smith preferred to have the children play in the attic of the South Street house, where the boy kept his toys and animal pets, rather than in the swarming streets. Alfred had so many friends from the neighborhood and school that his sister could not keep track of them, but his mother did; she knew which were the good boys and encouraged these to come to their home to play. Nevertheless they could not always be confined indoors and often played in the street up to a late hour on fine summer evenings. But here their other guardians took over. When nine o'clock struck Father John Kean, pastor of St. James Church, would put his head out of the rectory window and call out, "Everybody home!" and the children would obey, however reluctantly. It was a kind of curfew, Mamie said.

Protected and sheltered in a close-knit family though he was, nothing could prevent the boy from seeing all that went on around him, and this in the impressionable years of childhood and boyhood. In the street he had sometimes to face the rude challenges of young dockrats, who were quick with fists or stones, and he had to learn to survive. Though he was a child of gentle, even sentimental nature, and really disliked fisticuffs, he acquired certain tough-minded traits of the New York street urchins: their quickness of tongue and racy slang, their sauciness, their teasing manner.

Alfred Smith grew up in a district which in the seventies and eighties embraced human elements of the most astonishing diversity in character, language, and station in life. While predominantly Irish since the 1840's the old Fourth

Ward during his boyhood came to hold an increasing proportion of Germans, Italians, Jews, Spanish-speaking immigrants, and even a small Chinese community in Pell Street. In their occupations and social mores the people also showed striking differences: on the one hand there were the decent, laborious, God-fearing folk who probably constituted the majority of the twenty thousand souls in this mile-long sector of Manhattan at the time; on the other there was a numerous drifting population of casual maritime workers and sailors, several thousand of whom congregated around the docks, warehouses, and shabbier tenements or boardinghouses. For the diversion of these mostly unattached men there were about six hundred saloons in the quarter, including many of the cheaper dives bearing signs "ALL OUR DRINKS 3 CENTS" established in basements along the grimy portside streets. Cockpits and gambling dens were also to be found in the dark narrow alleys. As part of the area became notorious, it attracted a carefree, sometimes dissolute and lawless breed from all over the city, so that it was as much as your life was worth to walk through some of the streets there at night.

Mrs. Glynn told Miss Perkins that she and Alfred were always warned to keep away from a certain block in Water Street, and they learned early that the painted girls sitting out on the stoops of the houses there were "an invitation to sin." There were other streets too, where, as in all great seaports, houses of ill fame flanked each other in solid rows, advertised by the unmistakable red lamps. Water Street was only a block away from where the Smiths lived, and here drunken sailors would go reeling by, while women, often described as "hideously painted and bedizened," passed in and out of the local pothouses.

Large numbers of homeless children swarmed through the streets, dodging the horse-drawn carts, playing before the swinging doors of the saloons or beer dens. Indeed the downtown sector of the city was well remembered by visitors for its gangs of ragamuffins, those bold, half-wild, abandoned or orphaned children who survived by selling newspapers, blacking boots, or running errands for disreputable characters, and who slept under the docks, in cellars, or in decaying warehouses.

As fantastic as anything else were the places of refuge for alcoholic derelicts known as Gospel Missions, which were run by evangelistic rescue workers. One of these, called MacCauley's Helping Hand for Men, was located in one of the focal centers of prostitution, on Water Street. A woman worker in one of these missions, reporting on her years of service among the outcasts of the district, declared that "only a Zola could describe adequately what any eye may see in this locality."

Indeed the old Lower East Side of New York City was transformed during the period of Alfred Smith's youth into a Dantesque region, a kind of nether world, in the eyes of observers like Jacob Riis. In addition to prostitutes and pimps, who plied their trade under the friendly protection of the police with the full knowledge of the city's ruling political machine, directed from Tammany Hall, other criminal elements were centered here, or nearby, as in the Five Points Quarter above Chatham Square, where even the police dared not enter. In the bleak tenements as many as eleven persons slept in one room, with a single water pump and one toilet in each of the yards to serve the needs of the inhabitants. From the streets one could hear harsh voices in furious quarrels, the sound of crashing stove lids being hurled about, or a voice crying out, "Mike, give me a dollar for the childer!" to which the only reply would be a drunken oath. And throughout this teeming, noisome community, turning into a vast slum as the nineteenth century drew to a close, were thousands of the industrious poor, men and women and children, working long hours in the tenement sweatshops to make hats, envelopes, artificial flowers, dresses, pants, and even cigars.

During two generations much publicized crusades to clean up the region and drive out the strumpets and the habitual criminals were undertaken by reform politicians, among them Theodore Roosevelt who, as Police Commissioner, used to prowl the streets of the East Side by night in evening dress and conduct raids on unsavory premises, when Alfred Smith was a youth. Later District Attorney William Travers Jerome leaped into the headlines by indicting a number of grafters, pimps, and errant police officers. Later still the sensation-loving Charles H. Parkhurst sounded the alarm in his column in the Hearst press, but, like his predecessors, to little avail.*

It is true that Alfred Smith grew up safe and sound under the guidance of his intelligent mother and in the charge of the ministers and instructors of his church, from whose parochial school he received his elementary education. But it would not be correct to say that he grew up in innocence

---

* The growth of urban crime frightened the country then as now. The incidence of homicide and murder in New York increased by 325 per cent from 1881 to 1898. A cordon sanitaire guarding the Wall Street community from suspected criminals was established at Fulton Street by the police in March, 1880. (Cf. Arthur M. Schlesinger, Sr., *The Rise of the Cities; 1878–1898*, New York, MacMillan Company, 1933, pp. 94–95.)

or ignorance of his surroundings. One of his newspaper
friends who knew him well in his early political career wrote
in a sketch of his boyhood, based on Smith's own candid
reminiscences:

> His youth was spent in the streets. The waterfront was lined
> with saloons, and policemen in that time were picked for their
> ability to hold their own with inebriated sailors. His earliest
> memories are dotted with pictures of fighting men and scream-
> ing women being dragged through the streets to the police
> station. As a toddler ranging away from the doorstep of his
> house he heard and was curious about the tinkle of piano music
> and the shuffle of dancing feet behind windows painted red
> and screen doors that swung continuously during the long
> summer evenings. Thousands of rigidly respectable families
> in the Fourth Ward lived in that environment, but at the same
> time far apart from it. Things were just that way and few
> people thought of changing them in the world of tenements,
> stables, old brick row houses.

And from many spontaneous remarks that escaped him in
conversation long afterward it is evident that the street
scene of New York held an unending attraction for him.
Here was his school for life; here he witnessed a drama of
infinite variety, now absurdly comic, now tragic, always sensational. This was the real world of the giant city, where
things happened fast, and never a dull moment. Afterward
he could never understand how anyone could prefer to live
in the country. And when he was approached in later years
by those who urged that something be done about vice and
corruption, or about the conditions of the poor in the slums,
he responded quickly. He knew a great deal about the
problem; he knew it in his bones.

CHAPTER III

Schooling

IN THE FALL of 1880, when he was not quite seven years old, Alfred began to attend St. James Parochial School at the corner of James Street and the New Bowery. This grammar school, adjoining the parish church, had been established some forty years earlier; indeed Alfred's father had studied there for a year or so, and his mother had attended its classes for girls at a later period. The continuous functioning of the school and church remind us how village-like was the character of this parish. Not long before Alfred's enrollment, however, Father John Kean, at the start of his service there, had persuaded the order of the Christian Brothers to take over the work of instruction in order to improve the scholastic standards.

In those days New York public schools were few; their classes were overcrowded, and the teachers more often than not lacked normal school training. By comparison the schools run by the Christian Brothers, a lay order specially trained for the vocation of teaching, were superior to most of the city's free public schools. To have brought the Christian Brothers to the parochial school of his parish was quite a coup for the enterprising Father Kean. He was a well-spoken man, with a beautiful singing voice, dignified and somewhat severe, compared with some of his more easygoing predecessors. Indeed, his flock stood somewhat in awe of him.

St. James School for boys was considered hard by its pupils, and its curriculum included some subjects now taken up in junior high school. All children of that era were taught mainly by rote, which meant that they were given portions of text to commit to memory so they could repeat them verbatim. This old army method of fixing items of knowledge in the memory was reinforced by drills, reviews, and spelling contests. The Christian Brothers were known for their firm but kind discipline. Corporal punishment was routine, to be sure, but it was then not unknown in other schools either. Pupils were trained to give the right answers, not to raise interesting questions or debate with their instructors; and this emphasis might explain why the mettlesome young Alfred did not become a shining star of the classroom. No foreign languages were taught, and almost nothing of science, but there was plenty of English grammar, with readings of approved classics, as well as elocution, geography, and some history. American history, then and for decades later, in most schools, went no further than the Civil War. Finally there was a daily class in Christian Doctrine, whose precepts had to be memorized word for word, along with collateral reading in the lives of the saints and bowdlerized versions of biblical tales. The boys had little access to books for home reading; all their reading was done in the classroom.

Though there were some outstanding teachers at St. James School, some of whom, like Brother Baldwin Peters, were much attracted to Alfred, their habitual mode of instruction was calculated to discourage the enjoyment of books. The case of the nondenominational schools was not much better: many of their students who were forced to read and recite Shakespeare found that long years passed before they could learn to read him with pleasure. At St. James School the daily sessions ran from eight-thirty in the morning until three-thirty in the afternoon, and the boys were wild to be at large afterward. Books were what you were done with, thank Heaven, when you escaped from the classroom for the day. "I never read a book for entertainment in my life," Alfred Smith used to say in later years, thus unwittingly contributing to the myth that he was an undereducated waif of the city slums. In reality he had been strictly tutored by men who were probably better educated than teachers in other schools. Because teaching methods of the time were not designed to stimulate mental curiosity or powers of observation in young minds, many an able American boy finished grammar school with only a passing grade, like Alfred's, or even less, although he might actually have had a considerable potential that would show itself later.

That Alfred was lively and prankish as a schoolboy was the distinct recollection of his sister Mamie. Mamie told Miss Perkins that one of his teachers, Brother Edwards, asked her one day to tell her mother that Al was "a great mischief," and that "it was useless to keep the boy in school any longer." Quite pleased to "tell on" her brother, Mamie duly reported what the teacher had said, but her mother simply would not believe her. To Catherine Smith, who was no fool, the boy could do no wrong. (Nevertheless he teased his sister unmercifully for tattling.) What is also worth noting here is how much the mother worked to give her son confidence in himself.

If he sometimes vexed his teachers with his playful ways, he managed, however, after his second or third year, to gain a ranking position among his high-spirited Irish classmates by virtue of his gift of gab and his ready wit, for he was never a shrinking violet. One schoolmate remembers that he used to be quicker than anyone else at looking up words in the big dictionary they had at school, and sometimes stunned his fellow students by the impressive vocabulary he used. Another of his school friends recalled that the boys of St. James School were in general "rough-and-ready and more than ordinarily scrappy. You might say that a boy had to fight his way through school and then through youth in order to get anywhere. But outside of some harmless school-boy scuffles, I don't think that Al ever had a fight. He didn't have to fight." How did he manage this? It seems that even at that early age he was "a smooth kid," a sort of "boy diplomat."

> He could talk louder and faster than any boy in the ward, and as he grew up his voice increased in volume and his dexterity with words also. If anybody made a hostile demonstration against Al — and many did because he had a caustic tongue and used sarcasm — he would talk that hostile party into a pacific state of mind. I saw him do it dozens of times. His humor was our kind of humor. A boy or man can't fight and laugh, at the same time, and Al Smith could make anybody laugh.

There was one occasion, however, when Alfred was inspired to use his fists with such effect that he became the hero of the ward. He was then no more than thirteen, and

the family was living in Dover Street, where Mrs. Smith ran
a little fruit and candy store in the basement of their house.
While she was busy in the shop, and Alfred and his sister
were playing in the street, a neighbor's boy came running
to tell him that a burglar had broken into their flat. Alfred's
chief concern was for his first suit of long pants, which had
just been given him; he dashed into the house and inter-
cepted the thief in the hallway. The intruder proved to be a
full-grown young man, but Alfred laid on to such good
effect that he cut and ran, leaving behind the boy's new suit
and other articles, as well as some cash stolen from Mrs.
Smith's purse.

At his mother's wish he undertook to serve as an altar boy
at the age of ten, and for many years discharged his duties
faithfully, which endeared him to her more than ever. Awakened at 5:15 A.M. for the early Mass, he would stop at Cherry
Street on his way to the church to call for Johnny Keating,
who served with him. One day Johnny slept so soundly
that Alfred's lusty calls could not wake him; they did, however, rouse up a neighbor in an upper story, who emptied
the contents of a slop pail in the general direction of the
waiting Alfred. After that Johnny had to get to church without assistance.

Mrs. Smith, like many another pious Catholic mother,
would have liked her boy to become a priest, but she did
not insist, and he felt no call. Nevertheless during his boyhood he learned the sound and beat of the great medieval
Latin liturgy, which stayed with him all his life. Miss Perkins
recalled that when he was a grown man "he could often be
heard at his early morning shaving concerts intoning in his
deep baritone the responses of the Mass and even the priest's

part." (But often this sacred music would be intermingled with snatches of sentimental Irish airs, like "Kathleen Mavourneen.") Alfred had an imagination attuned to the beauty and symbolism of orthodox ritual; yet though he had had plenty of Christian Doctrine drilled into him, and though his faith was deeply rooted, he used to say in later years that he knew nothing of theology. "I know only the Ave Maria and the Mass," he admitted.

Among the subjects that the Christian Brothers taught with good effect were civics and extemporaneous speaking. These really aroused Alfred's interest, and he seems to have memorized the Declaration of Independence — which he often cited in later years — and the Preamble to the Constitution, among other major documents. There were also historic speeches by the Founding Fathers or leaders in the struggle over secession and slavery which he was encouraged to commit to memory, and which he liked to recite in boyhood. His appetite for political recitation may have been sharpened at home, where there was much talk of politics, his father being a devoted supporter of the Tammany Democracy. While he made not much more than passing grades in most of his studies, he was clearly outstanding in reciting from memory and public speaking. At the age of eleven he represented his class in an oratorical contest held for the juniors of all the New York parochial schools, winning first prize and a silver medal for his delivery of an oration on the death of Robespierre. Another St. James boy won the senior class medal, which speaks well for the training in elocution provided by the Christian Brothers.

The pastor of St. James Church was highly regarded in the district not only for his dedicated spirit, but also for

the special interest he showed in the social activities of his
flock, which he channeled into numerous auxiliary societies
designed for their entertainment and improvement. In all
there were fifteen of these, including the St. James Union, the
St. James Rifle Guard, a ladies' sodality, a Longshoremen's
Protective Society, and a so-called Literary Society. The last
was actually a dramatic club which met at the union's building on Henry Street, where the younger people rehearsed
for concerts and amateur theatricals. An old Wells Fargo
order book used by Alfred as a scrapbook contains a program
listing a recitation he gave at a St. James Union concert when
he was but ten. Very possibly he recited Poe's "The Bells,"
one of his favorite poems. Other recitations at which he ex-
celled were said to have been "The Night Before Christmas"
and "Old Grimes is Dead." He also loved to give comic
impersonations of certain immigrant types such as the one
that ran

Hans Breitman giff a pardy.
Vere ees dot pardy now.

The St. James Literary Society staged various children's
plays and Alfred took part in them with enthusiasm; he
would also call his friends together in the attic of the South
Street house to act in plays of his own improvisation. Recitations and theatricals made a powerful appeal to his imagination; learning came more easily to him this way, and where
other boys might have been timid or confused on a stage, he
was bold and ever eager to shine or hold forth before his
fellows. Nothing fazed him, neither the collapse of a piece
of the scenery, nor the contrariness of an improvised curtain.
After he left school, and while still in his teens, he continued

as a leading spirit in the St. James group of amateur players, showing marked gifts of mimicry and impersonation.

Though cheeky and playful in disposition, this spark of a boy grew responsible and dutiful as the years passed. Father Kean, in his reserved way, showed a real liking for Alfred, and sometimes relied on his help in keeping order among the more unruly youths of the parish Union. The priest was long remembered in the district for his severe enforcement of correct moral conduct among his parishioners. For five years he hounded one of the local tavernkeepers because the man permitted women to frequent the back room of his saloon, until the place was closed up. On another occasion — the episode probably dates from the time when Alfred was sixteen or seventeen — Father Kean learned that a couple of his young men, following a church social, had taken a girl to a saloon for a glass of beer, and he insisted that the youths be expelled from the St. James Union. This summary action aroused the anger of most of the boys in the players' group, who were ready to oppose the priest, but Alfred calmed them down, arguing that the Union was "part of the Church; we cooperate with the Church, and it cooperates with us." Father Kean had his way.

Despite his lack of higher education the boy was not unlettered. He had what was for those days an average schooling, since in the 1880's the great majority of American youths never went beyond grammar school. There were then but two high schools in all of New York City, and the percentage that enjoyed higher education in the colleges was tiny. One of Smith's admirers in later years said of him that "he had a first class mind unspoiled by formal education." If he had not learned to enjoy books, he read newspapers avidly and

kept himself informed; he had learned, moreover, how to find
out what he needed to know. The random recollections of
his contemporaries and the sparse records we have of his
school days tell us clearly that in point of personality and
self-command he would have been regarded by instructors
of a later day as a most promising individual.

Frances Perkins once spoke to Smith about his being a
dropout, and asked him why he had not continued his schooling at night, as other poor boys had done. Smith answered
that he didn't know. "I remember one of the Brothers, when
I had to leave school, recommended that I go to Cooper
Union at night, but I never got started. I had to work pretty
hard and pick up extra money working at odd jobs nights.
We had quite a family to feed: Aunt Delia couldn't go to
work but kept house and sewed; my mother worked very
hard but wasn't strong and couldn't keep it up; and Mamie
my sister was too young. She went to work later and helped
in the store too. But I never seemed to have the time," he
ended with a sigh, "and too soon I began enjoying the life
I had." A contemporary of Smith's, Robert F. Wagner, who
did make the effort to gain higher education at night school,
once rounded upon an interviewer who seemed to find poverty for America's lower classes acceptable, because there
were opportunities to escape from it, and exclaimed with
anguish, "My boyhood was a pretty rough passage. I came
through it, yes. That was luck, luck, luck. Think of the
others!"

"Of course everything was different after my father died.
We really had a pretty hard time then," Alfred Smith wrote
later. In fact his father was nearly two years dying of a

lingering illness which might have been cancer. At the beginning of 1885, feeling himself too weak to lift heavy loads into his carts, he hired a man to replace him while he found lighter work as a watchman. At no time had he shown a sharp mind for business, or earned more than a tolerable living, and now he had no reserves left with which to face the disaster of a terminal disease. He was forced to sell first one horse, then the other and all his gear. The family was obliged to move into cheaper quarters, first at 316 Pearl Street, and then at 12 Dover Street, and when Alfred was little more than eleven years old he took on a newspaper delivery route as well as other odd jobs, earning in all about two dollars a week. The papers he sold were the *Evening News,* the *Sunday Democrat,* and the *Leader,* a famous penny daily edited by Henry George, the Single Tax advocate, who was to make a strong race for election as Mayor of New York in 1886. Alfred used to bring home a free copy of the *Leader* which his mother and father liked to read, and which he also read regularly.

On Election Day in November, 1886, Alfred Emanuel Smith, Sr., went to cast his last vote for the Tammany ticket. By then he had been confined to his home for several months, and his limping off to vote was a measure of his courage and party loyalty. Descending the two flights of stairs with the support of his friend Campbell, he made the polling station several blocks away, but on arriving back at his house he was so exhausted that he sank down on the steps before the door. Mrs. Smith propped him up with some cushions and he sat there for a long while; then after he was rested she and Campbell between them carried the sick man upstairs in a chair. To his old friend he said, "I guess this is the last ballot I'll ever cast. I've distributed the ballots my party printed to every polling place in this area for many years, but I guess I'm through now."* He died only a few days later, on November 11.

The Smiths had used up every penny they had left. Several family friends — Campbell, John T. Smith, the boat builder, and one of the Sandy Hook pilots — together made up a purse to pay for the funeral. As the son related long afterward, their situation was desperate, "but my mother was very brave, and when we three came back from the grave in Old Calvary Cemetery on the night of his burial, I built a fire in the stove and mother made a hot supper for us, and then she went to see the forelady of an umbrella factory, whom she knew, and she got herself a job, where she began to work the next day." Alfred's sister remembered that the boy, who was not yet thirteen, had said to his mother, "I'm here. I can take care of you," but Mrs. Smith wanted him to continue his schooling as long as possible, and bade him accompany her on that dark night when she went out to find work to support her family. If the widow had not been strong enough or sufficiently skilled to find employment, and if the children had been a little younger, they might have been taken away by a police officer to some dreary orphanage, in compliance with the laws of the time; the family would have been broken up. It was the fear of this that drove Catherine Smith back to the umbrella shop where she had worked before her marriage, and her earnings of four or five dollars a week for an eleven-hour day, supplemented by sewing she took home at night, and Alfred's contributions, kept her little brood afloat and together.

After a year, however, the long hours proved to be too

---

* A loyal Tammany man all his life, and well known to the district leaders, Alfred's father obtained only this small commission from the local bosses.

much for her strength. She then rented a small store in the
basement of the Dover Street house and set herself up in
business selling candy and groceries. The children were able
to help her in the afternoons, and the little shop, while never
very profitable, enabled them to go on with their education
a while longer. But despite the hardships of that period, it
was not all work and penury for the growing boy. The com-
munal spirit of the old East Side, as he said repeatedly,
showed itself on such occasions; his father's cronies, along
with Uncle Peter Mulvehill, Father Kean, and even the
Democratic ward boss, all kept a friendly eye out for the
widow and her charges. Even in that grim time, Alfred remembered, he enjoyed all sorts of skylarks, as, for example,
during the historic blizzard of March, 1888, when he woke
up to find the little shop in the basement completely buried
in snow. It was midday before they were able to dig their
way in, and what worried the boy more than the condition of
the stock or the loss of business was the fact that he had a
Scotch terrier and four puppies locked up in back of the
store. After the blizzard came the deep cold snap, when
the East River froze over for the first time in the memory of
living men. With some of his buddies he slid down the
side of Pier 28 and walked across the mile-wide river to
Brooklyn and back, just before the ice broke. The streets
were impassable; schools were closed; and as there was
great danger of fires getting out of control Alfred, a fire buff,
or "Buffalo," as they were then called, stood by to help at
Engine Company No. 32.

About this time Mrs. Smith fell ill, and the family crisis
deepened. Although Alfred was then only fourteen years old,
in the eighth grade at school, and within a month or so of
graduating, he decided it was time for him to take on a full-

time job in order to provide for his family. Whatever achievements her son might boast of in the years that followed were as nothing to the mother beside the fact that at the time of his father's death — as she related afterward to Frances Perkins — "He told me he would take care of us, and he always did. Alfred was always a little man."

It was no doubt through friends of his father that he found employment as a "truck chaser" at three dollars a week. This entailed running up and down the waterfront streets all day, hunting up his employer's carts, giving the teamsters their orders, and taking their messages back to the office. Before telephone service became widespread many small business firms relied on runners like Alfred for rapid communication with their helpers. But within a year or two his mother was obliged to close the little shop, and Alfred saw that he would need to earn more money to keep the family going. To be sure their food bill was not high: "With a couple of dollars and a big basket my mother could go into the market and get enough provisions to keep the family a week," he told an interviewer in 1922. "I might also add mention that we ate quite a lot of fish." Still there was the rent to be paid, and coal to be bought, and occasionally clothing.

Looking about for a better-paying job, he soon found one as a shipping clerk and handy boy for the kerosene oil firm of Clarkson & Ford, in Front Street, at eight dollars a week, fairly good pay for a teen-ager at the time. After two years, again desiring to improve his position, he managed to land a job at the Fulton Fish Market as clerk and all-around man for the wholesale commission house of Feeney & Co. The hours were long, the work was arduous, but the salary — twelve dollars a week to begin with, later increased to fifteen

— was excellent pay for a youth of eighteen. With his mother's careful management, and the help of Mamie, who had found a job addressing envelopes, the Smith family was now assured of a decent livelihood. In his teens Alfred was a cocky fellow, full of the New Yorker's sass and ginger, and one, moreover, who was not going to be put off by anything he had to face. From age sixteen he was, in fact, quite a good provider for those times, and was even able to allow himself a few modest extravagances. There was within him, along with his strong sense of responsibility, the eagerness of a young blade to shine among his companions as a nifty dresser. He now used a little of the money he earned to brighten up his wardrobe, a matter of prime importance to him in his salad days and forever after.

At the Fulton Fish Market, that teeming waterfront site, he was required to do a bit of everything, although his position was nominally that of bookkeeper. The key to success in the business, he used to explain, was to estimate correctly the size of the catch for the day before the boats docked. It was one of his duties to climb to the roof of the fish market shed at dawn and "use a pair of strong marine glasses to pick out the fishing smacks of my employers as they turned out of the Buttermilk Channel into the lower East River." If the boats lay low in the water it meant they had a big catch; if they rode high the cargo was light. A big catch generally implied lower prices, and vice versa. Knowing the different boats and where they habitually fished — if they came from the New Jersey coast they brought bluefish, if from New England, mackerel — he would quickly prepare to bid for or offer fish in the market in accordance with his advance estimate. Hurrying downstairs he would perch on a crate and begin trading among the crowd of hotel and restaurant buyers or retail dealers already gathered there. In this trade his stentorian voice served him well. The grand object was to clean out the batch before it could spoil or become too "high."

That he enjoyed his labors among the products of the sea, then the pride of New York's tables, is shown by his frequent reminiscences of the two years he spent in the Fulton Fish Market. The central market of a great city is a world in itself, full of movement and color, crowded with people from every walk of life. There were the old salts off the boats, the teamsters, the sharp-trading commissionaires, the fishmongers in their soiled smocks, the poor, the thievish, even rich women arriving in their carriages to shop for great households. From his platform in the market Smith exchanged quips all day with the fish dealers and held his own with men wise in the ways of the world. He absorbed their dockside language, and years afterward would describe persons he disliked as having "an eye as glassy as a dead cod," or as giving one the feel of "shaking hands with a frozen mackerel." It was a great place, in short, to learn about human beings as well as fish, and in later years he declared seriously that the old fish market was one of his "universities." Gregarious by temperament, he loved to mingle with people and find ways to make them like him. In certain apt observations he made later on the craft of the political leader in a democracy he laid stress on the fact that such a man "must really know people, and know how to work with them."

The fame of the Fulton Fish Market was spread by Al Smith himself, after he entered politics, when in public speeches he recalled his employment there in accents of pride. It was as if he wanted to stress his climb from one of the humblest stations in life. In truth the Fulton Market in the 1890's was a thriving place, and Al at eighteen to twenty was already earning half again more than most skilled workers of similar age and relative experience; he was even then quite a success. After two years at the market he tried other clerical jobs, but seeing that they earned him too little, he went on to another position requiring heavy manual labor. As shipping clerk at the Davison Steam Pump Company in Brooklyn he made a little more money handling machinery and pipe, but it was dull work compared with the daily drama of the fish market, and in afteryears he retained scarcely any memory of it.

All through his youth — even when he had to rise at 4:00 A.M. to go to the Fulton Market, or later at 5:00 A.M. to take the early ferry to his Brooklyn job — Alfred was in constant attendance at the St. James Literary Society, the amateur dramatic club of his church. Of the several players' groups associated with the larger Catholic parishes of the city, the St. James Players were considered to have the best talent. Smith became a member of the Players when he was about eighteen, and was soon awarded leading parts in their productions. Rehearsals must have taken up a good deal of his free time, for during the winter season the group gave benefit performances of popular melodramas and sentimental comedies that ran from one to four weeks. As a rule they played in the basement auditorium of the St. James School, but they also traveled to other city parishes, and sometimes out of town.

Smith often confessed that for a long time he was "dead

stuck on acting," and, in view of his manifest success as an amateur, confidently expected to go on to a career in the commercial theaters on the Bowery one day, like several other members of the St. James Company. He had a flair for histrionics, like many another popular political leader; he enjoyed the costumes, the footlights, and the responses of his high-spirited audience. His roles were varied: a sinister character in *The Confederate Spy*, the gentle hero of Boucicault's Irish fantasy, *The Shaughraun,* a long-winded American politician in *The Mighty Dollar*, and others. In one of the Irish comedies much favored by his neighbors one scene showed uniformed English soldiers trying to collect rent from the rebellious farmers of Ireland, with attendant scrimmages that kept the audience in a state of ecstasy, for the farmers always wound up sitting on the chests of the Redcoats.

One of Smith's favorite stories of his days in the amateur theater suggests that he sometimes experienced all too much audience participation. In one version he related to a newspaperman:

> I was playing the hero and was in a death struggle with the villain. He was armed with a knife [in other versions with a pistol] with which he was trying to stab me to the heart. In our struggle he dropped the knife. This wasn't in the play; we hadn't rehearsed that possibility. If we stopped struggling long enough to pick up the knife it would be noticed by the audience. I thought that I was about to allow myself to be killed. We were wrestling around whispering to each other to frame up a plan of action, when a little boy who had been sitting popeyed in the front row solved the problem. In a couple of jumps he was over the footlights and on the stage. Picking up the knife he rushed toward me crying: "Here, Al, stick him."

Once he acquired some experience he was occasionally hired as a supernumerary at the old Windsor Theatre on the Bowery where he appeared as a Roman soldier in *The Fall of Rome,* and again as a Russian peasant in the melodrama entitled *Siberia.* For such labors he received a dollar a night; but what was more important to the stagestruck youth was that he strode the boards in the company of such famous professionals as Blanche Walsh and Melbourne McDowell.

One of the men who used to coach the St. James Players remarked afterward that the experience of acting gave Smith a poise and presence of mind vis-à-vis an audience that stood him in good stead in later years. He knew when to execute a full dramatic pause; he knew how to hold his public. Old newspaper clippings treasured by him and preserved in his scrapbook contain flattering comments on his acting performance, such as, "Alfred E. Smith, as Honorable Bardwell Slote [in *The Mighty Dollar*] was very amusing and rendered the speeches of that voluble Member of Congress from the Kohosh district with good effect," while others referred to him as "the leading man of the St. James Lyceum Company." *The Mighty Dollar,* that long-popular farce written for the famous Irish-American comedian who called himself William Florence, presented the unsavory Congressman Slote as a monumental bluffer given to absurd and windy lucubrations. Smith played the part in the vaudeville manner of Florence, all smart-alecky and bantering, rendering it as satire of the political calling with which, even in his earliest youth, he was familiar, at least in its local form.

Though the nightly rehearsals and performances left him but little time for sleep or rest, these appearances in the amateur theater afforded him the brightest hours of his laborious youth. When he played a hero's role, he took the applause as his due, but he did not enjoy the hisses or derisive whistles of the audience when he played the part of the villain. His lines as Jim Dalton, the "heavy" in *The Ticket-of-Leave Man,* called on him to press his suit on the pretty young heroine who stubbornly rejected him, and when he snarled at her, "You will yet be mine!" the gallery resounded with catcalls. On one occasion he rebelled against this inhospitable reception, and vowed he would no longer play the villain. At reports of this defection Father Kean called him in; taking off his glasses in a characteristic gesture, he placed his hand on the young man's shoulder and said gravely, "Alfred, we have over two hundred little orphan girls next door. It is getting harder every year to feed and clothe those girls." Of course Al relented and returned to play the detested role.

Then, as in later years, an appeal to his generous nature could always win a response. The St. James Players performed not only for the sake of high art, as Father Kean reminded him, but for Christian charity. Meanwhile it is worth noting that as a very young man he disliked being hissed or whistled at, though a trained actor would have taken such hostile manifestations as a compliment to his rendition of the part. For Alfred Smith from his earliest years wanted above all to be liked by people, to be admired by them, and when he failed to win his public as he customarily did by the power and charm of his personality, he appeared at a loss.

The tradition has persisted that Al Smith as a youth was virtuous and pious, the sort the Irish call an "altar boy." True enough, his mother communicated to him some of her

spirit of puritanism. It seems that she herself considered the
theater sinful and never went there; at first she only allowed
her Alfred to attend matinees with his sister. But he was in
fact no Little Lord Fauntleroy. His love of the theater trans-
cended the straitlaced views of the ultrarespectable. He
frequented the Old Miner Theatre on the Bowery at night —
though it cost him his sleep — to see not only famous dramatic artists but also the Can-Can girls. He also haunted the
vaudeville theaters of the downtown district and found the
happy-go-lucky Harrigan and Hart irresistible. Moreover he
used to make his way into the wings and the greenrooms of
the commercial stage to mingle with popular actors and
actresses.

At twenty we also find him joining one of the convivial
East Side political clubs, and dropping in regularly at the
saloon at Oliver and Dover Streets owned by Tom Foley,
one of the district leaders of the Democratic Party, where
he drank his beer and puffed a cigar, a man among men. He
not only enjoyed making himself known in the Fourth Ward
as an amateur actor, but also liked to call attention to himself
through his studied elegance of dress. A photograph of him
taken at that time shows him as slim and personable, his nose
not quite so prominent as it came to be later on, his eyes then
as always expressive, on the whole a winning young man and
brimming with self-confidence. Going to church on Sundays,
or calling on friends, he would sometimes appear in a cutaway coat, striped trousers, a stand-up collar and cravat, and
a high-crowned derby, the very model of a dapper New
Yorker of the gay nineties. One old resident, a Mrs. Rofrano
of Oliver Street, recalled to Miss Perkins that even at the age
of nineteen he would turn up looking quite the dandy, in a

fancy waistcoat, a red necktie, and tight trousers. This neighbor also remembered that he was no shrinking violet with the ladies at church socials or dances. As she described him,

> He was talking all the time, at parties, reciting, or dancing. He was quite a boy at jigs, and he thought he could sing too. One day some of us girls were making plans for a picnic. For some reason we hadn't invited Alfred — no one called him Al in those days — but while we were talking it over he happened along and chimed in. "You haven't been asked to go," one of us said. "Oh, you'll ask me," he answered. "You won't be able to get along without the talent."

CHAPTER IV

Ward Politics

IN AL SMITH's boyhood and youth, and up to the early years
of the twentieth century, Tammany Hall conducted the popular politics of New York City with a splendid eye-and-
stomach-filling pageantry. The voting populace was inspired
to turn out in grand fraternal and democratic festivals, made
all the more joyous by rivers of free beer and mountains of
free sandwiches. Those happy, artless folk fiestas have been
quite lost to us in these days of electronic viewing and com-
mercialized spectacles. The parades and political picnics
were usually held on certain holidays, such as St. Patrick's
Day, Decoration Day, Independence Day, or Thanksgiving;
their organizers were the ruling district satraps of the city's
Democratic Party, and the guests ran into the hundreds and
even the thousands, including not only voters but their wives
and children. In fine weather they would all form in a procession, bearing the banners of their fraternal and church
societies, and to the music of a brass band, march up Park
Row and East Broadway to East Twenty-third Street where
a boat would be waiting to take them to the picnic grounds
at Coney Island or College Point in the Bronx.

Alfred Smith remembered one such outing he attended

with his father which was sponsored by Big Tim Sullivan, East Side leader and lieutenant to Boss Croker. His father marched in the uniform of the Volunteer Firemen, who paraded in a group, along with the members of the St. James Riflemen and the Hudson Rangers, also in uniform, and other local associations and trade unions. One year as many as 6000 men, women, and children from all parts of the city embarked on two river steamers to take part in a monster "chowder breakfast" held at Sulzer's Harlem River Park. There were parades, games, fireworks, and political speeches galore; free carousel rides for the children; fried clams and beer, ice cream for the nourishment of the young, as well as barbecued oxen for more manly appetites. On such occasions Alfred heard some of Tammany's silver-tongued orators, such as Congressman Bourke Cockran, or State Senator Tom Grady, who had been to the St. James School as a boy. He used to clip out the extracts of their speeches in the newspapers and paste them into his scrapbook, sometimes committing passages to memory.

From his earliest youth Alfred, like his father and even his mother, ate, drank, and breathed local politics. The more or less benevolent despotism of Tammany Hall operated through its branches or local clubs to lead, control, and, when needed, help the common man, while gathering in his vote. Tammany was as close to the people of the East Side Irish quarter as Pat Divver, the district leader, could make it in election seasons. Around the corner from the Smiths' house was the saloon of the genial, broad-beamed, moonfaced Tom Foley, the former blacksmith, who had been Divver's adjutant for twenty years. Henry Campbell, the friend of the elder Smith, was also a close friend of Foley's, and like him a member of the New York County Democratic Committee, which equated Tammany Hall. Foley's friendship was worth cultivating, for through his influence in Tammany he might win a young man an appointment to the police force or the fire department, or as a clerk in some city bureau. These secure positions then paid more than manual labor and were much sought after by the Irish, who had long been barred from public service in the old country. Moreover a man like Foley could be of help to fellows who got into little scrapes with the law, and he could be expected to distribute food or coal to the needy at Thanksgiving and Christmas, and even provide a few dollars for a poor devil's funeral. It was Foley who gave Alfred's father the little commission to haul bundles of ballots to the polling booths on the eve of election days, and Alfred himself enjoyed some small patronage at the age of twelve or thirteen through being employed to fold ballots at so many pennies per thousand.

The boss system was the same in all the great cities, whether the machine was run by the Democratic Party, as in New York and Boston, or by the Republicans, as in Philadelphia. However righteously it was deplored by the so-called better element among the citizenry, it is now acknowledged that it had its social usefulness. Whereas the law often worked in a coldly impersonal way to inconvenience or punish the small man (who could not afford the services of a lawyer), and made redress through courts or legislatures seem an abstraction, the machine and its boss tended to cushion the law's severities, and offered a modicum of relief to the little fellows, if the recipients of these favors could be relied on to vote as they were told. The men who directed the affairs of Tammany Hall compromised representative government, but they were human; they understood the frailties of the common man and kept in close contact with him.

To be sure, even in the old Fourth Ward there was some discussion of the charges of graft in the city bureaus, or of the sale of influence, and of the grant of indulgences by the police to illicit taverns, gambling places, and houses of ill fame. But many of these complaints were thought to be inspired by rich uptown people, the ultra-respectable reformers whose sole remedy for the evils of corrupt government was to prohibit beer drinking on Sundays, and to staff the civil service and police force with right-thinking men. These kid-glove reformers generally had little contact with the common people and did nothing for them. They were ineffectual when in office, and their awkward efforts were greeted with laughter by the customers of Tom Foley's saloon.

From about the age of twenty, Al Smith regularly frequented Foley's bar, which was an informal center of local political action. As a boy he had seen Foley often give pennies to the children in the street — "and when it was a nickel he gave us it was like Sunday," he wrote later. Now that Smith was approaching manhood Foley would sometimes ask him to perform some small errands — called "contracts" in the Tammany lingo of the time — such as delivering a message to someone about a job in the street-cleaning department, or inquiring about a neighbor who was in trouble. Foley had a number of young men like Alfred who assisted him in their spare time. Brief-spoken and reserved himself, he expected his informal aides to carry out his orders loyally and discreetly, in return for which, it was understood, he would eventually reward them with some political favor. Smith began to function in his ward's politics in a small way, and evidently to the satisfaction of Tom Foley.

Early in the autumn of 1894, although he was two months short of twenty-one, he attended his first political meeting at the district Democratic Club in Grand Street where Divver held sway, and not long afterward he made his first political speech. It has often been said that Smith began his career as an unquestioning follower of the Tammany machine, but the truth is that his first venture into politics happened to be a manifestation of independence of the Hall during a local conflict. He joined then with a group of Democratic insurgents in his district, led by Foley, who were opposing the high command at Fourteenth Street, then in the hands of the ineffable Richard Croker.

For a period of years the Lower East Side constituency had been represented in Congress by a man named Timothy J. Campbell, who lived in the district and was popular among its residents. One day in 1894 Boss Croker decided to supplant Timothy Campbell with a Mr. Miner, owner of the popular theater in the Bowery bearing his name that Al Smith attended. But though his theater profited from the patronage of the local people Miner himself lived uptown on Madison Avenue and was personally unknown to them. Deeply incensed at the nomination of a rank outsider, a "carpetbagger," Foley called for rebellion and undertook a fight to reelect the incumbent, rallying to his side Henry Campbell (no relative of Congressman Campbell) and the grocer's young friend Alfred Smith. Smith made his maiden speech to promote the candidacy not of the regular Tammany candidate, but of one rejected by Tammany.

It was one of the rare instances when several of the local district leaders bolted the Democratic organization. Their action led not only to the defeat of Croker's candidate for Congress but also helped the Republicans elect William L. Strong Mayor of New York City on a fusion ticket. That year Tammany was beset by scandals, thanks to the revelations of the Lexow Committee, an investigating committee of the State Legislature, one of whose attorneys was William Travers Jerome. The New York City police were shown to have been demoralized by their extra-legal "licensing" of illicit saloons, gambling resorts, and brothels, which, it was estimated, yielded more revenue than the legitimate licensing activities of the state and city governments combined. Boss Croker had let things go too far; amid the disasters that befell Tammany that season he retreated to Ireland with his cash-filled tin box, promising to return when the people had need of him.

By leading the insurrection in his precinct, Tom Foley had taken a big step toward party leadership in the old Fourth Ward, challenging the rule of Pat Divver. The affair had not been entirely bloodless, for there had been some rough collisions on Grand Street between Divver's toughs, armed with shillelaghs, and Foley's supporters. Alfred Smith was not involved in any of the physical clashes, but had to withstand noisy interruptions as he spoke at several East Side clubs for his candidate, a task for which he was well qualified because of his stout pair of lungs.

His services were not forgotten. Once the Strong administration took office, Henry Campbell, who had given much help in the campaign for the fusion ticket, prevailed upon his (temporary) Republican allies to appoint his young protégé as a process server for the Commissioner of Jurors at a salary of eight hundred dollars a year. This white-collar job relieved Smith at last from the heavy labor and long hours at the pump works; it also placed him, as a minor official of the municipal court system, close to City Hall, and finally it offered prospects of advancement. With this change in his fortunes it is no wonder that he now discovered, as he wrote later, that he had a fondness for politics and thoroughly enjoyed the excitement of public life.

The Irish, it used to be said, with their gift of gab, had a passion for politics. They had always been good intermediaries for the immigrant masses in the cities, mostly Catholics too, who did not speak English. But in the 1890's it was also true that the best-rewarded places in business — because of the prevailing religious prejudice — were not generally open to the Catholic Irish. One might say that Al Smith chose politics because, like Skeffington, the anti-hero of Edwin O'Connor's novel of city politics, *The Last Hurrah,* he knew that "it was the quickest way out of the cellar and up the ladder."

Within a year or two he began to cut quite a figure on the local political scene, as is indicated by several clippings preserved in his scrapbook, one of which, dated 1895, describes a weekend outing of young Democrats at Far Rockaway "under the leadership of Alfred E. Smith, one of the most prominent Democrats in the District." Another press notice, dating from 1896, and probably inspired by him, reflects his growing appetite for political glory:

Alfred E. Smith, the orator of the Seymour Club of the Second Assembly District, was a hard worker during the last two campaigns. He is ambitious to become a member of the [state] legislature and is looking for the nomination in his district. He has announced that he will take the stump for Timothy J. Campbell next year if he is not involved in a personal canvas.

In one of the clippings there is also the hint that his aspirations were being nursed by friends, who could have been no other than Henry Campbell and Tom Foley. Campbell was president of the Seymour Club on Madison Street, an active Democratic group, and by 1896 Smith had become its secretary. He continued to help Foley with political chores in the district, thus acquainting himself with the needs and problems of the residents, and in addition began to prepare himself for larger responsibilities by close reading of the newspapers for developments in the city and state governments. He felt he had reason to hope that his devotion to the local organization would lead to his advancement in the political hierarchy.

His prospects were slim, however, while dissension raged among the leaders of the Fourth Ward. Tom Foley would, no doubt, have been the last man to arrogate to himself the virtues of a reformer, yet he had come perilously close to this in heading an uprising against Boss Croker and Pat Divver. For a Tammany man to bolt the party organization was a cardinal sin. Nor was Alfred Smith easily forgiven for having joined the bolters. After a year or two, when the latest scandal over Tammany Hall had died down, Croker returned from Ireland to his old throne on Fourteenth Street, and moved to compose the strife among the city Democrats. By working harmoniously together, he argued, they would seize power once more. He was aided in this program by the ineptitude of the reform administration, whose Police Commissioner, Theodore Roosevelt, alienated most of the workmen in the city by enforcing the Raines Law, which called for Sunday closing of saloons. Men who wanted to enjoy their beer in peace on their one day of rest were indignant at the heartless reformers and at the next election voted en masse for the Democrats.

This meant that Croker's old lieutenant Divver was reinstalled as district leader, a post he clung to for years, despite Foley's efforts to dislodge him. Neither Foley nor Smith could go forward during the years that followed, until, in 1901, a fresh wave of scandal broke upon Tammany Hall. Croker fled the country again, this time for good. It was only then that Foley took power as undisputed leader of the Second Assembly District and was able to further the ambitions of his followers, notably those of Alfred Smith.

Meanwhile that irrepressible young man was expanding his horizons in the office of the Commissioner of Jurors. Having bought a bicycle he pedaled all about the city to serve notice on people chosen for jury duty, discovering streets and whole areas he had never seen before. It was a busy life, and he often suffered a rude welcome or downright abuse from citizens who were inclined to shirk their civic obligations. After some months he was promoted to the post of investigator for the Commissioner of Jurors, with authority to pursue the shirkers. Now he learned more about the meaner aspects of human nature than he had known before.

There were prospective jurors who tried to win immunity from serving by hoodwinking him about their status as property owners, or by feigning some physical disability. But the sharp young investigator was not to be taken in easily by such folk. On one occasion a Wall Street financier, when called to serve as a talesman, submitted a doctor's certificate showing that he was deaf, and therefore unqualified. The leading actor of the St. James Players thereupon appeared at the broker's office apparently suffering from a fearful cold in the head, unable to speak above a hoarse whisper, and posed as a man seeking advice on securities he was considering for investment. The supposedly deaf financier, miraculously cured, heard every whispered word and responded to every question. Reporting the case to his superior, Smith made arrangements to compel the man to serve as juror, but was overruled by the weight of political influence the broker brought to bear on the case.

A compelling reason for Smith's decision to become a city officeholder around this time was the fact that he had fallen in love, and felt that he must improve his standing in the community before he could be accepted as a desirable suitor. The girl he was courting lived far uptown in the Bronx, but even when he was working at the fish market or at the pump works in Brooklyn he regularly made the long journey to 170th Street by the Third Avenue Elevated and several changes of horsecar to see her. Now that he was on the staff of the Commissioner of Jurors his hours were shorter than before, and his duties occasionally brought him to the Bronx. Even so it is related that he would return home quite late, and stagger in to work the next morning with eyes heavy from lack of sleep. Yet he was always "the life of the office," his associates recalled long afterward. Tired as he was he would find the strength to stick a feather duster in his hat and go prancing around the back room of the office while bellowing the "Toreador Song" from *Carmen* in his strong baritone.

In Alfred Smith's old scrapbook, among the newspaper clippings he pasted there, one finds the program of an amateur concert held in 1895 at the St. James School Auditorium, with these words underlined: "Songs — Miss K. Dunn." He had first met Miss Catherine Dunn (known to her friends as Katie) the year before, when an old school friend who was related to her family asked Alfred to accompany him on a visit to the Dunns in the Bronx. The Dunns had formerly lived on Cherry Street in the Lower East Side, where the head of the family ran a sailors' supply store, but they had risen in the world, and when Katie was ten years old they had moved up to the Bronx and into their own home. The girl had been educated at a convent, and when Smith first laid eyes on her she was a shy, gently bred maiden, with a shapely figure, dark curly hair, delicate features, and large blue eyes. He saw her and a roof-tile fell on his head; he was in love.

The courtship was not easy or smooth, for in addition to the arduous trips to the Bronx to see his beloved, Smith had to face the disapproval of her father, who was now a successful building contractor, and seemed to think that his charming daughter deserved a more brilliant match. As a widow's son Alfred was obliged to support his mother, and he gave no promise of being able to provide for a wife and children as well. Moreover young Smith talked too freely of his theatrical ambitions, which to Katie's father indicated that he was a lightheaded, harum-scarum fellow, certain to come to a bad end.

Mr. Dunn, however, failed to take into account the persistence of the young man, or the state of his daughter's affections, which were soon wholly engaged by her suitor. There is no record of Smith's ever having formed so strong a connection with any other girl, or in fact of his ever having taken another girl out.

In New York in the 1890's the games of love were pursued

by members of the respectable middle class, among whom
Alfred figured, with a decorum that our young persons of
today would find comic or downright intolerable. Alfred
wooed his well-protected Katie at her home, save for an
occasional church social or dance, when he would appear
in rented tails and top hat, bursting with pride to have that
lovely young woman on his arm. In the parlor of the Dunn
house she would play and sing the saccharine ballads of the
time in a voice he found entrancing, such songs as "Sweet
Violets," "After the Ball," or "Say Au Revoir but Not Goodbye." For his part the rituals of the courtship required him
to sing along with her, execute a jig, or give one of his humorous impersonations. But there was no doubt in her mind
of the earnestness of his professions, and it was not long before he received her modest assurances that she returned his
feelings. They were pledged to each other, which was a
comfort to the warm-blooded swain, but the engagement
was prolonged year after year while his responsibility to his
mother and the opposition of her father made the prospect
of marriage dim.

"Things can't go on like this!" the young Irish used to
complain when finding themselves in such a plight, for long
engagements were often the rule among the Irish, and Irish-
Americans as well. Only after five years were the obstacles
to the union removed. Alfred announced his definite aban-
donment of a theatrical career, although some alluring professional opportunities, he claimed, had just then been offered him by none other than Charles Frohman. At the same
time his salary at the Commissioner of Jurors' office was advanced a little, so that he could now hope to support a wife.
Then, with his sister's marriage to patrolman John Glynn,

his mother decided to go and live with Mamie in Brooklyn Heights. She took this step, as Miss Perkins gathered in talk with her, out of consideration for what she thought were her son's wishes. He, of course, continued to contribute to her support all her life. At last the way was clear, and the long-delayed marriage of Alfred Emanuel Smith and Catherine Dunn took place on May 6, 1900, at the Church of St. Augustine in the Bronx. Father Kean, who had always refused to officiate at services beyond the boundaries of his parish, made an exception to his rule in the case of one of his favorite communicants, journeying uptown to 167th Street to conduct the rites.

After the ceremony the newlyweds traveled by ferry and streetcar to Bath Beach in Brooklyn, where they stayed for the summer season before returning to Manhattan to live in a flat on Madison Street. Smith never dreamed of moving to the Bronx, as many of his friends did, to find lower rents and greater space in the new apartments sprouting up all over that borough. He preferred to live near the bureau where he worked and the East Side political clubs. His wife had been born on Oliver Street, "and I brought her back," he declared, "to the ward she was born in."

As a wife Katie came up to his every expectation; cheerful, unselfish, and uncomplaining, in the early years she did all the housework unassisted, cooking and washing and caring for the children as they came along. After a year their first child was born, a son whom the father named Alfred Emanuel Smith, the fourth of his line; next came a daughter named Emily. Soon their first flat became too cramped, and almost every year they moved to larger quarters, until in 1903 they wound up in a roomy old-fashioned place of the type Smith liked most, at 9 Peck Slip, by the river, at the edge of the Wall Street financial district. The young father undertook additional work in a small real estate office nearby to provide for his growing family. On his return home, often at a late hour, Katie was there to greet him with an unaffected warmth he always found moving. "I never dreamed of the happiness that was to come into my life," he wrote later, "when I made that accidental visit to the Bronx." He took great joy in his children, and was from the beginning a doting father, unashamed to play with them exuberantly. One service he performed for them became a weekly ritual: every Saturday night he would bathe them all, and he continued to do this with his three boys even when they were in their teens, at the Governor's Mansion in Albany, amid tremendous commotion.

In his late twenties, Alfred Smith was one of the most sanguine and energetic young men in all the town. He had married a belle of the East Side and the Bronx, who was the joy of his life, and who bore him five fine-looking children. He was established in the solid middle class, well-connected with the city's political hierarchy, and brimming over with ambition to climb the ladder. He had known how to fend for himself in the harder days of his youth, and now he knew where he was going: he was going up, and if he failed, it would not be for want of self-confidence and derring-do.

For a year or more he had been urging his superiors in the Democratic Party organization to help him gain the nomination for the State Assembly, or even for a seat in Congress. Foley was heard to say that Alfred "might go far some day," but still made no move to give him a leg up; indeed in 1902 Foley passed him over for the nomination for Assemblyman in favor of a schoolmate of Smith's who had become a lawyer. At the time of his struggle with Divver and Croker, Foley had publicly vowed that he would stop sending saloonkeepers to the legislature, but would work to elect able and intelligent younger men. The new chief of Tammany Hall, Charles F. Murphy, with whom Foley was now closely allied, apparently favored such improved standards. The young man Foley chose in 1902, however, disappointed him by neglecting to help with the district's political chores, and the local boss decided to replace him with someone more obliging.

At last, late in the summer of 1903, Smith heard from Henry Campbell that his name was under serious consideration by the district convention for the Assembly seat. The party's choice meant certain election, but there were several rival aspirants, so he could not be sure of success up to the last hour. Then, "to his great surprise," as he claimed, an emissary came to his office to break the news. "Is that the only suit you've got?" asked the man. "Hurry home and get it pressed." Smith did as he was told, and while he was still in the kitchen, clad in his wife's apron, pressing his only presentable summer suit, a delegation from the district convention arrived to give him formal notice of the nomination.

There were no decent meeting halls in the district at that time, and if there were, he could not have afforded to hire them. From the back of a truck Smith harangued his public in the streets in a ringing voice that could easily be heard above the din of the horsecars. He might have spared his lungs; the Republican candidate didn't have a chance, as the quarreling factions of Democrats were now united in support of Foley's man, and the voters marched to the polls in droves to do the party's bidding. Smith won his first election con-

test by an overwhelming majority of about 5000 votes to
1472.

His chief at the Office of the Commissioner of Jurors, an
elderly Republican judge who was kindly disposed toward
him, had advised him not to run for the Assembly, which in
his chief's view might be a dead end, but to stay and advance
himself slowly. Flushed with victory after the election, however, Smith felt that he had made the right choice, as shown
by the jubilant statements he issued in an interview with a
reporter for the *Morning Telegraph:* Yes, he had formerly
aspired to become a professional actor, he confessed, but
politics had proved even more entertaining than the theater,
and besides it paid better than the "wig-paste profession."
The recent contest had been as easy as rolling off a log; he
could have sat at home and won, but he took the stump because he liked it. Now he could claim to be a politician, and
he airily ventured the prediction that someday he might
really "bask in the political limelight."

In Albany, once the elation had worn off, the ebullient
Smith conducted himself with more discretion. Moreover,
in New York's historic and tradition-bound capital the press
correspondents, like the legislative leaders, coldly ignored
him as a crude novice in the halls of state.

CHAPTER V

"My University"

HIS FIRST IMPRESSIONS of the capital were highly discon-
certing. As the year 1904 was ushered in a cold wave blew
in from Canada down the valley of the Hudson, bringing
icy winds to the steep streets of Albany. Together with another Tammany politician, Tom Caughlan, who represented
the First Assembly District, Smith trudged up the hill from
the station to a cheap old-fashioned hotel on State Street,
the Keeler, that was much frequented by the lesser politicians. In the lobby fireplace the guests had worked up such
a huge log fire that the new arrivals feared the whole wooden
structure might be set ablaze, recalling a recent fire in a
Chicago hotel where many lives had been lost. That night,
in the seventh floor room they shared, Smith and Caughlan
stayed awake playing pinochle until dawn in order to be
ready at any moment to take flight.

The Capitol to which he came the next morning to take
up his duties was no ordinary structure. Conceived as a suitable monument to the great Empire State, it loomed atop
the hill above State Street like a fortress. Its general design,
however, was that of a Renaissance palace, with Italian,
French, Gothic, and Arabic features, including gables, dorm-

ers, turrets, balconies, and a great flight of steps going up to
the second story, the diverse elements having been contributed by a succession of architects at different periods. Begun
in 1867, it had been declared officially completed only a few
years before Alfred Smith's arrival, at a cost of some $25,000,-
000, a vast sum for those days, and one that gave rise to
repeated charges of graft and mismanagement. It was fashionable not too long ago to dismiss the edifice as an architectural monstrosity, but time has softened this appraisal. As
a famous wit among artists, Marcel Duchamp, once remarked, "All buildings are beautiful after fifty years." The
interior reveals many handsome areas, such as the Senate
Chamber on the third floor, a room of elegant proportions,
decorated with splendor, but not forbidding, and the Executive Chamber on the second floor, with the scale, warmth,
and dignity befitting the Governor's office. These two rooms
were the work of the noted architect, Henry H. Richardson,
who also had a hand in the exterior. But most impressive
of all is the monumental inner staircase of red freestone that
rises one hundred and nineteen feet from the ground floor
to the skylights, a neo-Gothic fantasy replete with arches,
balustrades, and stone sculptures representing birds, beasts,
flowers, children, persons of note, and a few politicians of
bygone times thrown in for good measure.

Unaware of the architectural oddities of the place, and
also ignorant of the existence of an elevator, Assemblyman
Smith on his first day climbed all the way up the "million
dollar staircase," as it was called, to the Assembly Chamber
on the third floor, a long ascent because the ceilings were
so high. Although its original dimensions had been altered,
making the proportions of its great columns somewhat incon-

gruous, it was still a spacious room with seats in concentric rows running down to a well in the center, where the Speaker's dais stood. There the oath of office was administered in routine fashion to Smith as to the other novice legislators, and he took his assigned seat on the Democratic side of the central aisle, the Republicans occupying the other side. At first his place was so far back that he felt almost as if he were out in the lobby, which was separated from the Chamber proper only by a brass rail. At all events the Speaker, S. F. Nixon, a Republican veteran, accorded no recognition to the new members; in fact he did not know the name of the member from the Second District, one of New York's most populous, until three days before the session ended. Moreover the parliamentary usages peculiar to this Assembly seemed both arcane and ritualistic to newcomers; as the purpose of the many bills introduced was almost never stated, their legal phraseology was for a long time completely mystifying to Alfred Smith.

He was also troubled by the air of cold formality that marked certain social occasions. To a reception held by Governor Benjamin Odell at the Executive Mansion he came dressed in the spiketail coat and top hat which Henry Campbell had bought for him after the election, in company with a party of his New York colleagues, only to find matters so arranged that he was ushered into the house, presented to the Governor and his wife, and ushered out again by a military aide, all within the space of three minutes. Instead of providing an opportunity for the Governor and the legislators to become acquainted, it was a purely mechanical gesture, an exercise in the expeditious admission and ejection of hundreds of guests, about as sociable as a subway turnstile in the rush hour.

But life in Albany had its more frivolous aspects too. The lawgivers, who hailed from all parts of the state, had to spend three or four months of the year in the capital, away from home, and often sought distractions that might have caused criticism in their hometowns. The high-spirited element among them not only liked their beer and whiskey after hours, but also whiled the time away with gambling, or at boxing matches. A certain section of the town called "The Gut" was known for its taverns with professional women on hand or in nearby houses of prostitution. There was at that period a veteran Sergeant-at-Arms of the Assembly who knew just where to find certain members whenever the speaker or floor leader needed their votes, and had no hesitation in having them rudely apprehended and hauled back to the Chamber in whatever state of disarray they happened to be. For Alfred Smith, however, these pastimes of bachelors afforded no pleasure. Though a moderate social drinker, he found prizefights repugnant, and had no taste for gambling. When far from home he pined for Katie and the children, to whom he returned by train every weekend during the legislative session. A parochial New Yorker, he missed the bustling metropolis and all its noise and light. In his first years in Albany he was lonely and bored, unable to break through the indifference with which the ruling group usually treated the green men of the Assembly.

He suffered also the stigma of his origins and his party affiliation. The men who ran the Legislature and the state government were in the main upstate Yankees, most of them Republicans and Protestants, serving rural districts or small towns. The Democrats were in a minority, even though they represented the huge city that held more than half of the state's population, and also districts of Buffalo, Albany, and

Troy.* The Republicans, moreover, manifested strong prejudice against the politicians from New York City, which
reflected their abiding fear that the one "little corner" of the
Empire State would dominate all the rest of its territory unless held in check. In their view the great metropolis was
a city of the plain, and its spokesmen were invariably evil.
They were supported in this opinion by respectable authors
of national renown, such as Mark Sullivan, who argued that
New York was not an American city at all; it was in his
opinion a polyglot conglomeration of Irish, Germans, Italians, and Jews. Native Negroes were also reckoned as aliens.
Hamlin Garland too wrote at this time, "Seen from the West
and the South, Manhattan is a city of aliens who know little
and care less for American traditions." Since these aliens
were supposed not to understand republican institutions, the
ruling Republicans had for long years given them lessons
in the democratic process by gerrymandering Senate and
Assembly districts so thoroughly that the masses in the cities
enjoyed only minority representation. Meanwhile the Republican bosses were not averse to making political deals
with the Tammany contingent whenever it suited their book.

From the very beginning Smith was made aware of the

---

* The people of the cities of New York State were in large part disfran-
chised by the state's constitution, which set aside sixty-two seats of the one
hundred and fifty in the Assembly to represent each of the sixty-two counties,
leaving New York City's five counties with, at best, a poor representation
in Albany.

On the other hand, the denizens of the huge metropolis looked down upon
the people of the hinterland. "The New Yorker was already famed for his
provincialism, his proud ignorance of the rest of the country and lofty con-
descension toward cities of lesser note," according to one observer writing in
1901. (See Arthur M. Schlesinger, Sr., *The Rise of the Cities*, pp. 84–85.)

tensions between the county people and the big-city folk; it was a problem not always discussed openly, but he would confront it all his life and address himself to it more and more seriously as time went on. He was city-bred, Roman Catholic, and half-Irish, and he had his pride, his sense of his own worth and decency, and the knowledge that he had acquitted himself well thus far. He was also by nature friendly, outgoing, and candid, and he was well-liked by all sorts of men, whether in his own neighborhood or in the shops and offices where he had worked. Although in his published recollections he does not directly mention the fact that he was made to feel himself an outsider during his first two terms in Albany, the suggestion of it is there between the lines. On various occasions in later years he showed his resentment at having been snubbed by certain of the old families of Albany who regularly entertained members of the Legislature at their homes without including him. This was a point on which he was unusually sensitive: as a talented amateur actor he enjoyed holding sway over people, and when for some reason he found he could win no positive response he was taken aback. Of course his spirits were more resilient in his young days, when he endured the rough and tumble of local politics very well and he was not so thin-skinned as in the later years.

Part of his frustration came from the fact that when he first went to Albany he was wholly ignorant of the functions and procedure of a legislative body. His wise counselor and patron, Foley, had warned him to watch his step; "Don't speak until you have something to say. Men who talk just for the pleasure of it don't get very far." And so he remained mum day after day through his first two terms (having been reelected easily in 1904), while voting regularly with the caucus of the minority party. New laws were steamrollered through committees and the printed bills were heaped on the desk of the new Assemblyman every morning while he sat there in silence. The Republicans, often small-town lawyers, paraded their legal learning as they defended their pet projects, some of them pretty shady too, while offering scant explanation of the purpose or usefulness of their measures, or of curious amendments to them. The whole process seemed so baffling to Smith that he said afterward, "I did not at any time during the [first two] sessions really know what was going on."

He held no committee posts, and there seemed to be little he could do on his own. The newspapers carried no dispatches about him to impress his constituents. Indeed his insignificance was brought home to him when the Albany correspondents held their annual dinner, and he was seated in a far corner of the room, under the gallery. The stout and opulent-looking Governor Odell, accompanied by his retinue, all rigged out in gold lace, figured as the leading actor in this affair. "That's the way to come to these dinners," Smith remarked enviously to the friend who had wangled the invitation for him.

In an effort to learn more about what was going on in the Legislature he began to take home copies of the printed bills and struggled to understand them. How could a novice tell what appropriation bills were simply pork-barrel affairs for certain localities, or which measures had been drawn up only for their nuisance value (as "strike bills") for which the notorious Black Horse Cavalry hoped to be paid off before they were permitted to die in committee? In vexation

Smith exclaimed to his friend Caughlan that in his Fulton
Market days he had always known "the difference between
a hake and a haddock," but in this business he could not
tell one from the other.*

In 1905, during his second term in the Assembly, Robert
F. Wagner, a newly elected Assemblyman from the Yorkville
district of Manhattan, also sponsored by Tammany Hall, arrived in Albany and became Smith's friend and roommate.
Wagner had immigrated to New York from Germany as a
boy, but unlike Smith he had managed to acquire an education at City College and at law school, by studying at night
while working for his living during the day. Thanks to his
legal training Wagner found no mystery in the various bills
under consideration, and he did much to help Smith understand their ostensibly occult terms. Now he who had never
read a book for pleasure, as he said, put himself through a
rigorous course of study, training himself to comprehend
the legal terminology and real intent of bills on which he
was required to vote. Thus he began to know what he was
voting for during his second and third terms in the Assembly, when bills favoring lower gas rates, regulating old-law
tenements, and enforcing certain safety and sanitary conditions were presented. Though Tammany, to be sure, usually
favored legislation benefiting the numerous poor, Smith's
own predilections would have led him in the same direction.

But despite his growing intelligence of the legislative
process, he was still uncomfortable in Albany. In 1905 he
was appointed to two committees, one on banking and the

---

* The nomenclature of Black Horse Cavalry was applied during the late
nineteenth century to the rings of legislative grafters who accepted bribes
from interested parties to vote for or obstruct various bills before the New
York Legislature.

other on forestry, but he had hardly ever seen the inside of a bank, as he remarked, except once or twice to serve a jury notice, and he had never been in a forest. The key committees were then virtually closed to a young follower of the Tammany Democracy; they were controlled by the county fellows from upstate who won appropriations for their districts by logrolling tactics. The Democrats, unable to gain any favors for their own constituents, usually avoided serving on these committees. Smith's first exposure, then, to the representative system of government was quite disenchanting. "I was still seated in the last row," he recalled, and at the time he told his friend Robert Wagner that he was resolved to quit the Assembly at the end of his present term. There seemed to be no future here for an ambitious young man of thirty with a rage to do things and go places.

In the spring of 1905 the disgruntled Assemblyman returned to New York to air his discontents. Meeting Foley at the Seymour Club, he pointed out that his family was increasing; there would soon be six mouths to feed, and he could not manage on his small salary. In response to this Foley, whose influence in the "new" Tammany Hall had grown considerably, invited him to breakfast together with the newly installed Democratic Mayor, George B. McClellan, at Holtz's Restaurant on Franklin Street. The appointment of a city Superintendent of Buildings was under consideration at the moment, and Smith's name had been proposed to the Mayor as that of a deserving Democrat. It would have been a more lucrative, if politically hazardous, office; moreover Foley had enough influence to get him the appointment. Smith was inclined to accept it, arguing that the Assembly was too much for him, but his old friend pleaded with him to stay on in Albany. "I need you there," he is reported to have said, and after some reflection Smith agreed to go back to the Assembly again.

In order to help him make ends meet a little real estate business in connection with court bankruptcy proceedings was passed on to him by the city machine. Financial assistance also came from his mother-in-law, Mrs. Dunn, who contributed a little money for his election campaign, and even from his mother, who turned over to him her small savings accumulated from the sums her son had given her for her support. While he had been beset by self-doubt, the women in his life, his mother, his mother-in-law, and of course his Katie, all believed fervently in his political future.

The year 1906 found him back in the State Legislature, now hard at work reading all the bills that came before the Assembly. Perhaps one consideration leading to his return was that he hated to admit he had failed to understand the legislative system others had mastered. He was determined now to learn the rules of the game. It was a more mature Alfred Smith who regularly came back to the Chamber after his supper to get on with his studies. The image of him at his desk remained in the memory of many denizens of the Capitol. Frances Perkins caught her first glimpse of him, as we have noted, in that pose. In those years only a small minority of the state legislators ever bothered to read the many bills presented to them; most of them voted by order of their party bosses, as he had done at the beginning.

And now Smith began to make progress; the more he learned the more interesting he found the proceedings, and he began to believe he might yet do something worthwhile

in the Assembly. Where at first he had been somewhat over-
awed by the legal vocabulary of the measures presented, he
now came to realize that their objects were quite transparent
and material. The annual appropriations bill, for example,
was a document of some six or seven hundred pages covering thousands of items. He toiled through it, and thanks to
his powerful memory, retained a good deal of its factual
material in his mind. As he reduced the work of the Legislature to its simplest terms he found that only a few matters
that were actually "political" ever came before the Assembly. Nearly all the bills involved spending the state's money
for one purpose or another, and more often than not were
designed to serve some local interest, such as a bridge over
a creek in Chenango County, or the repair of a road in Erie
County. It was all a question of business, of the public's
business, and he wondered why it could not be managed in
a nonpartisan spirit, and with fewer emissions of hot air by
the orators of the Assembly.

Smith was a man who grew slowly, and had to learn
things in his own way, but he had a clear head, a fund of
common sense, and a down-to-earth realism in speech that
caught the attention of his peers when he first began to
speak in committee or from the floor. In fact he had turned
himself into a legislative expert: not only did he remember
a multitude of laws on the statute books, but amendments
to them as well. His winning personality also began to make
itself felt after the first season or two, when he had seemed
only the usual big-city product. There was something
straightforward and unaffected about his talk that impressed
many of his colleagues, who found him quite different from
what a Tammany man from the sin-loving metropolis was

supposed to be; and he willed to be different. Nearly twenty years later in a talk before the Friendly Sons of St. Patrick he recalled how often in his public career, as a Catholic of Irish descent, he had met "the foul breath of prejudice," and he went on to observe, "We are watched a little more than anybody else. We have to be just a little better than the other fellow. Let us do all we can to keep Irish names off the police calendars and divorce courts . . . Let each of our business transactions be above the breath of suspicion."

Even though he had not yet caught the attention of the bigwigs in the Assembly, he made friends among the newer arrivals, like Wagner, and even among the country squire Republicans. Despite their stubborn suspicion of Irish Catholics from New York, and of persons of Jewish or Italian descent, many found it hard to resist liking the "Assemblyman from the Bowery" as Smith was sometimes called in Albany. During the 1905 session James W. Wadsworth, a freshman Assemblyman, sat across the aisle from him in the back row. Wadsworth, scion of the old Genesee, New York, family that had figured prominently in American history in war and peace since the eighteenth century, had brains, charm, money, and social position. Different though their backgrounds were, Wadsworth and Smith became good friends. Wadsworth confessed later that he had learned a good deal from Smith, who by this time had begun fraternizing with both sides of the house, and whose talented story-telling made him the best of companions.

Unlike Smith, however, Wadsworth was destined by the Republican hierarchy, on orders that came from high up in Washington, for immediate promotion; only one year after he took his seat in the Assembly he was named Speaker. In

this role, young as he was, he distinguished himself by rulings that were of benefit to both parties. Long afterward
Smith wrote that Wadsworth's practice of requiring members to set forth clearly the purposes of the bills they were
presenting contributed a great deal to clarification of the
Assembly proceedings. Smith had further reason to be grateful to the new Speaker. Encountering Smith one day soon
after the session opened in 1906, Wadsworth asked him if he
had received any interesting committee posts. Smith admitted sadly that he had been passed over, so far as the important committees were concerned, even by the Democrats.
Thereupon Wadsworth, though officially the leader of the
opposition party, used his authority as Speaker to name his
friend to the Committee on Insurance, which that year became the most important committee in the Assembly. Taking part in the insurance committee hearings yielded Smith
new insights into the affairs of state. Those hearings, in fact,
constituted the most important "course" he had yet taken in
his "university."

Smith knew full well that the Tammany element, which
dominated the state's Democratic organization, was strongly
addicted to what was termed "little graft," principally city
jobs for their followers, from whom small money contributions were regularly collected. But he soon discovered that
the Republican politicians from upstate had county machines
more blatantly corrupt than the city organizations. While
Tammany's district captains were accused of buying immigrants' votes with free beer, the Republican county bosses
virtually "robbed the graveyards" for ballots during election
contests. In the State Legislature, Smith perceived, the Republican bosses carried on graft on such a large scale —

doing business with giant corporations, with the gas, light, and traction interests, and the insurance companies — that they put the petty Tammany grafters in the shade.

During the autumn of 1905 Charles Evans Hughes, the formidable counselor of the Governor's special commission, had begun inquiries into the conduct of insurance and banking corporations in the state. Questioning his witnesses in a cool, soft-spoken manner that concealed his thorough competence, Hughes extracted evidence of nepotism, financial favoritism, and corrupt practices involving some of the most prominent members of the financial community. The state's insurance companies, which held the savings of millions of people, were shown to have become convenient reservoirs of capital used to manipulate the stock market by their directors, big financiers such as the partners of J. P. Morgan, or Kuhn, Loeb & Company, or lone wolves of Wall Street like Thomas Fortune Ryan. Testimony proved that unlawful loans to favored persons had been made in violation of state insurance laws, and millions of dollars had been spent for the purchase of favorable legislation under the head of "legal expenses." Lobbying activities of insurance companies had included the maintenance of a "House of Mirth" (so the newspapers promptly dubbed it) where the state's legislators were lavishly entertained, while their voting record was closely checked. It was found that most of those who had sold their votes for an evening's pleasure were Republicans. The two United States Senators from New York, both Republicans, Chauncey Depew and Thomas C. Platt — the latter being also the state boss — were shown to have received large annual retainers as legal "consultants" to the insurance companies. As a result of the Hughes investigation, which created a tremendous public scandal, several high insurance company executives were indicted; others took flight to Europe.

It was on the presentation of Hughes's completed report to the Legislature that the Committee on Insurance began to hold hearings early in the 1906 session. Smith took an active part in its deliberations, and in discussion of the specific reforms proposed by Hughes and his aides. The bills that were written into law and passed in April, 1906, provided for drastic changes in the conduct of the insurance business, eliminating stock speculation, mutualizing life companies, limiting salaries, prohibiting donations to political chests, adding protection to policyholders, and prescribing standard forms of policies.

The insurance company scandals made 1906 a year of misfortune for the Republicans of New York, who were able to salvage the Governorship only by nominating Hughes himself for the office. The Democrats, though not yet in the majority, were returned to the Legislature in greater force than before, while winning all of the state ticket except for the Governorship. Smith and his fellow Democrats began to take hope. Returning to Albany for his third term in the Assembly in 1907, Smith in fact found that he was beginning to enjoy his life and his work there. Around this time he started the practice of holding weekly dinner gatherings at Keeler's Restaurant on State Street, usually inviting four or five of his colleagues, among whom were often men from distant parts of the state. The menu was simple but hearty: corned beef and cabbage, boiled potatoes, rye bread, and dark imported beer, and after the food was out of the way Smith's guests would sit back in their chairs at the round table in Keeler's to listen and laugh as he regaled them with anecdotes or impersonations drawn from recollections of his youth on the East Side. The Fulton Fish Market was a rich source for many of these tales, but if someone brought up the subject of horses and horse racing he would declare that "the only kind of horses I knew were truck horses," and he would then take off on incidents he had witnessed when he was a teamster's chaser. Often a knot of men from other tables would gather around as he acted out his stories, which came to be repeated all about town until an embryonic fame attached itself to Assemblyman Smith. These contacts meanwhile gave him an opportunity to improve his acquaintance with the men from the rural districts and to acquire some knowledge of their local problems. They on the other hand, warmed by the beer, the food, and the talk, found some of their prejudice against the big-city politician dissolving. In one of his early interviews Smith said,

> I pick up ideas from the back country fellows. They don't have a hell of a lot to think about when they are at home and their thinking is generally pretty straight and to the point. I don't blame them for trying to use the power of the majority for the benefit of their own communities in a legitimate way. But when they try to use their power for the benefit of an influential or wealthy individual or institution then I am going to try to stop them.

In 1907 he was appointed a member of the committee set up to recommend revisions of the charter of the City of New York. This was an assignment that enlisted all his enthusiasm, for he deeply resented the injustices suffered by the taxpayers and voters of his native city under the state charter. In the two years that followed he gave close study to the problem of the relations between the city and state governments, as well as to the need for reapportionment of local and congressional districts.

Long years ago, as he used to protest before the Assembly, the State Legislature had been rigged against the city voters by constitutional law. In accents of passion he would gird against those (meaning the "county" Republicans) who contended that the city people were more ignorant of democratic processes than the rural voters, and that "the man of the tenements was not as 'good' as the man on the farm." His opponents aired their age-old fears of submitting the entire State of New York to "the tyranny of a huge seaport." He retorted that the city dwellers accounted for most of the state's population and industry, and paid seventy-five per cent of its taxes, and in time of war the men of the tenements were considered in no way inferior to others in being accorded the privilege of fighting and dying for their country.*

His warm advocacy of home rule, his ardent defense of the plain people from the city streets, made him something of a hero to his hometown toward 1908. He was beginning at last to figure frequently in newspaper dispatches from the state capital. In the summer of that year, too, he met Charles F. Murphy for the first time, at a picnic on a Long Island beach. The former streetcar driver and saloonkeeper, now chairman of the New York County Democratic Committee, the boss of Tammany Hall, was sufficiently impressed with the young Assemblyman from the Second District to entrust him with added political work.

* Smith reflected the conviction that the Catholic and Irish machine politicians also worked to indoctrinate the immigrants with American principles of equality and justice as understood by the non-Anglo-Saxon city folk, according to André Siegfried.

After his third term Smith emerged as one of the most active members of the Tammany group in the Assembly, introducing as many as fifteen bills in one year, some of them, to be sure, of a perfunctory character, such as one calling for a state tax on advertising posters. This was the sort of bill he himself later held up to derision. As he had previously performed little "contracts" for Foley in the Second Assembly District, so now he labored to win passage of measures sponsored by Tammany's new chief, Murphy. A typical bill favored by Tammany provided for Sunday baseball, a measure his own constituents would warmly approve. Another called for the establishment of a statewide holiday in honor of Christopher Columbus, a bow to Italian voters in the city. Still another, showing Tammany's serious bid for popular support, provided for a lowering of telephone rates.

Few of his speeches in the Assembly of that earlier phase of his career have been recorded. But one passage that gives the flavor of his impromptu talk, and has the stamp of his frank character, has often been cited and is attributed to an afternoon session of the Legislature in 1911. He had the floor and was discussing points in a bill before the Chamber, when a member asked permission to interrupt the proceedings by announcing news he had just learned by telephone that the intercollegiate boat races at Poughkeepsie had been won by Cornell. "And I am an alumnus of Cornell," he added with pride. "That means nothing to me, I'm a Yale man," put in another, while a third declared that he too was indifferent, as he was a Columbia graduate. Smith then asked for the floor again and said, according to one of many reported versions, "Mr. Chairman, if my old alma mater had been represented in the race we would have won. Boats and boating were necessary adjuncts to my alma mater. We were, and I say it without boasting, strong on the water." "What is your alma mater, may I ask?" queried the Cornell man. "F.F.M.," replied Smith; "I'm an old F.F.M. man." "And where's that, Al?" asked another Assemblyman. "The Fulton Fish Market," Smith replied. "That's where I got my higher education after leaving school."

His words provoked laughter — and yet there was in them a serious undertone that more than one of his fellow members sensed. They realized that whereas another man might have tried to conceal the lowly station from which he had risen to the State Legislature, Al Smith recalled his humble origins frankly and with pride, and this trait won him the respect of his fellows.

On another occasion it is recorded that he reverted to the theme of his fishmongering days when someone questioned his competence on the subject of fishing and game laws. "Mr. Speaker," he exclaimed,

> If all the fish I handled in Fulton Fish Market were put into the Capitol Building, they would pry the roof off, bulge out the windows, cover the lawn and cascade down State Street hill to the Hudson River in a stream fifteen feet deep. I am the only member of this Assembly who can talk the fish language.

Another instance of his happy improvisations occurred in the course of debate over a proposed workmen's compensation law, when a certain Republican Assemblyman named Pratt, who often assailed him in sarcastic terms, asked him what purported to be an embarrassing question: "Mr. Tammany leader [so he regularly called him], what good is the Workmen's Compensation Act to the three hundred and fifty thousand men that are out of work on account of President Wilson?" Smith later told of his rejoinder:

> Mr. Speaker, I was walking down Park Row, and a man came up and hit me on the shoulder and said: "Hello, Al. Which would you rather be, a hammock full of white door knobs, a cellar full of stepladders or a piece of dry ice?" I said, I would rather be a fish, because no matter how thick plate glass is you can always break it with a hammer.
>
> Whereupon Pratt sprang to his feet and said, "I don't get the point of the gentleman's answer."
>
> I replied, "There is just as much point in my answer as there is to your question."

After four or five years of experience in Albany, he was a man to be reckoned with on the floor of the Chamber, and the most effective debater on the Democratic side. His racy language, his horse sense, his resonant voice, and his actor's flair for the dramatic punch line offered the Assemblymen, and the news reporters also, some entertainment in the course of what were usually dreary parliamentary proceedings. It was noticed, incidentally, that his speech was not only fluent but rhetorically correct, although, as one who often heard him remarked, he probably did not know why. But he had been taught long ago at the St. James School to speak in complete sentences, and moreover he seemed to have an innate sense of the right word to use, especially when the wrong one might change the whole purport of a bill; and no pundit could catch him out in this area of knowledge. In one exchange with an opposing member about Smith's substituting "or" for "and" in a certain passage, his adversary, a lawyer, asked him upon what authority he based his opinion. Was it Webster's Dictionary? Could he cite it?

Only for a moment did Smith appear flustered; then he answered briskly, "I will refer the gentleman from Buffalo to the grammatical rule that says, 'When a pluperfect adjective precedes a noun, insert a plus!'"

Smith's corned beef and cabbage dinners, according to certain skeptical observers in Albany, were designed to win support for the bills sponsored by Tammany Hall. On the other hand he was winning commendation nowadays from independent and reform groups such as the Citizens' Union of New York. As early as 1906, in its annual bulletin, this nonpartisan organization observed that Assemblyman Smith was "intelligent and active, somewhat above the average of the machine men who follow Tammany's orders." A year later the same group called him "the best Democratic representative from New York City," and by 1908 they judged him to be "very much above average . . . in intelligence and usefulness . . . though still inclined to follow the machine."

But though the friends of good government found reason to hope for better things from Assemblyman Smith, he was as yet following the party line rather than setting it. At this time liberals in both parties were agitating for a direct primary law sponsored by Governor Hughes, which was expected to eliminate the power of the machine over nominating conventions. Smith went all the way with Tammany in opposing such a bill in the Assembly. Partly out of personal conviction, he also worked against "dry" measures urged by the Prohibitionists. In 1909 a bill forbidding the sale of liquor or beer at establishments located within two hundred feet of a church was introduced in the Legislature and passed. Since Tammany collected regular donations from saloonkeepers and the liquor interests, the Democrats pressed for an amendment to this law, which bore particularly hard on the Hotel Gotham in New York City, a large, fashionable hostelry close by the Fifth Avenue Presbyterian Church. Despite Smith's best efforts the desired amendment failed to pass, and the Hotel Gotham's management was reduced to all sorts of subterfuges to keep its clients from perishing of thirst.

His ties with the Tammany organization were deep-rooted. That Tammany collected for its tin box from place holders all around town he knew well, but he knew too that the Republican bosses were involved in truly large-scale graft, as shown in the insurance scandals. Tammany's district bosses were generous and charitable men, like Big Tim Sullivan, who annually distributed 2000 pairs of shoes to the poor children of his ward, or Tom Foley, who gave away most of the money he handled to his co-workers, and was destined to die a relatively poor man. Smith felt obliged to play the game, work with his team, with the people he had grown up with and who had helped him. He used to say that he would sooner quit public life than break his word to his friends. If compromise was called for, he would accept that, as he had promised his party. "By God, I hate a buck passer," he used to say.

He drew the line, however, as Frances Perkins testifies, against personal involvement in any of the petty graft that was so widespread in both parties. His proud mother had imposed strict standards of behavior on her children; no lying or cheating was ever tolerated. Smith, to be sure, gave and received favors involving political influence; he made bargains or compromises as part of the strategy of legislative power; but none of his enemies who afterward combed his record thoroughly were able to find that any money gained by misconduct in office ever came to him. His associates, including his Republican opponents, knew him as a square shooter, honest in speech and action. Some of his friends even thought there was a core of innocence in Alfred Smith, an astonishing trait in a man engaged in politics for most of his mature life. To tell the truth was not only a moral obligation; it had its practical compensations as well, he discovered. Before he went to Albany for his first term in the Assembly his old mentor Tom Foley had warned him not only to keep a tight rein on his lip, but also never to

> promise anything that you are not perfectly sure you can deliver. Most people who come to public men are not looking for the truth. They like to be jollied. The safest practice is to tell them the truth, and after they have tried out a dozen other people, they will come to the conclusion that you were right in the beginning.

Smith never forgot this advice.

In the autumn of 1910 the Republican machine that had long reigned in Albany was wholly repudiated at the polls. Their leaders in the Legislature had worked to frustrate the good intentions of their own Governor Hughes, who went to the Supreme Court in 1910; the GOP was split further when the restless ex-President, Theodore Roosevelt, made war on the conservatives in his own party. A Democratic Governor was carried into office in New York State, and both legislative houses came at last under control of the Democrats. In view of his signal services to his party, it was not surprising, therefore, that Alfred Smith should be desig-

nated by Boss Murphy as Majority Leader of the lower
house (the dominant part of the Legislature), as well as
chairman of its Ways and Means Committee. In the session
that began in January, 1911, Smith was the most powerful
Democrat in the Legislature. In a shrewd review of his
early career Tom Foley told a newspaperman in 1922:

> Al went to Albany on his first trip to the Assembly just as cock-
> sure of himself as he has ever been in his life. He didn't cut
> much of a figure in the first two or three terms, but there was
> a reason for that, and if he won't tell, I will.
>
> He was too smart to be a morning glory. The secret of his
> success is that he never mingles in anything that he doesn't
> know all about. He played a minor part in the Assembly until
> he was thoroughly familiar with the rules and procedure and
> with state legislation and finance. When he was sure of his
> ground he walked out, and it wasn't very long before he was
> the dominating figure in a legislative body hostile to him and
> his political organization.

Smith remembered that legislative session in which he
served as majority leader as one of the most protracted and
turbulent he had ever known. Finding themselves at long
last in full control of the state government, the machine
Democrats were bent on legislating out of existence as many
Republican officeholders as possible, while supplanting them
with deserving members of their own party. This was not
always as easy as might be expected, for as is often the case
with a majority group, cleavages soon appeared to threaten
the solid front. In the midst of a fierce battle between organization Democrats and an insurgent group, a fire broke out
in the Capitol building, causing so much damage to the
Assembly Chamber that the lower house was obliged to

move its deliberations to the Albany City Hall for a period.

As he entered upon his duties as Majority Leader of the Assembly Smith was still, above all, a strict Tammany man. Early in January of that year Boss Murphy came to Albany to hold conferences with the Democratic county bosses and with his young legislative leaders, Smith and Robert Wagner, Wagner having been named Majority Leader of the Senate. One of the prizes of victory that fell to the Democrats that year was the office of United States Senator, then chosen by vote of the Legislature. Following Murphy's visit to Albany the Democratic caucus moved obediently to nominate his choice, William F. ("Blue-Eyed Billy") Sheehan, for the Washington post. Sheehan was an old party stalwart who had formerly held office as Lieutenant-Governor, but recent disclosures had revealed that he was closely associated in his law practice with Thomas Fortune Ryan, the arch corruptionist and Wall Street manipulator who had been involved in the insurance scandals a few years earlier.

Sheehan's name was no sooner put forward than a little bloc of upstate Democrats bolted from the party caucus and voted with the Republican minority to prevent action on the United States Senatorship. Their leader was a young State Senator from Dutchess County named Franklin Delano Roosevelt. Roosevelt was then the very antithesis of Alfred Smith. Member of an aristocratic New York family, he was independently wealthy and represented a rich farming community; he had been educated at Groton and Harvard and had taken his law degree at Columbia. Tall, handsome, but looking younger than his years, he affected a pince-nez and held his nose in the air. The top-lofty attitude of this fledgling politician did not endear him to his party associates.

Smith and Wagner tried persuasion, in the interests of party unity, on Roosevelt and the other rebels, but in vain. Privately Smith dismissed the new Senator from Dutchess County as a brash young man and a "damn fool." In his recollections he remarked that Democratic reformers such as Roosevelt (in those days) showed more interest in civil service reform than in social legislation for the benefit of the common people.

Roosevelt's demonstration against Tammany rule brought him a flurry of front-page notices in the New York press, but after several weeks of deadlock the insurgent group was outsmarted by Murphy; they were obliged to drop their own undistinguished candidate for the Senate and accept Justice J. A. O'Gorman, Tammany's alternate choice. Murphy also managed a double play by injecting his son-in-law, Daniel F. Cohalan, into O'Gorman's former place on the New York Supreme Court. (The choice of Cohalan did Murphy no credit, for at the very beginning of his career on the bench Cohalan came under a cloud.) Thus Roosevelt's first political venture ended in inglorious compromise. He was possessed, however, by towering ambitions. For a long period the Democratic professionals underestimated the energy and tenacity of this amateur, who, in time, thoroughly mastered the rules of their game.

From 1911 on Smith conferred regularly with Boss Murphy at the weekend luncheon gatherings held at Delmonico's restaurant in New York, where the party's strategy was mapped out. Smith has testified that Murphy was no autocrat, but rather a good listener, a sort of committee chairman, one might say, who strove for unity among his lieutenants before taking action. Murphy also supported welfare legislation, not so much on principle, as to win the votes of the masses. At that time it was frequently asserted in the metropolitan press that he had the whole Legislature of the Empire State in his pocket. Once when a newspaperman asked him his view of certain pending bills Murphy answered dourly that he was not a member of the Legislature and had nothing to say. The newspaper's editor then asked Smith if Murphy did not exert influence on the lawmakers, and Smith replied solemnly, "I do not believe Mr. Murphy is any more concerned in the deliberations of the Legislature than any other good Democrat." But when Franklin Roosevelt was approached for comment on Murphy's declaration of innocence, he remarked drily, "I thought he was said to be without a sense of humor."

As Majority Leader in 1911 Smith directed the fight in the Assembly for measures demanded by the machine, of which the "ripper" bills affecting officeholders were first in order of importance. To Tammany partisans this meant only "taking back stolen goods." Repeal of a law curbing race track gambling was also pushed through under Smith's guidance, as well as various bills opposing local-option "dry" laws urged by the Prohibitionists. Faithful to the party line, he continued to block a bill providing for the direct primary (which all progressives then favored), contending that it would have little effect on the operation of political parties — an accurate prophecy. Several years later, however, he was to change his mind about this issue, as if with a bow to fashion.

In another area of legislation he had to satisfy himself with a compromise. The Democrats, with the state's legislative and executive branches both in their control, had a

glittering opportunity to enact an improved charter for the
City of New York such as Smith had long advocated. What
they brought forth, in fact, was a patchwork affair. Although
it provided for a somewhat increased measure of home rule,
the law had several features that the "goo-goo" groups, like
the Citizens' Union, looked on with considerable disfavor.
Through "Murphy's Charter," as it was called, the city's
budgeted expenditures were greatly increased and a larger
number of officeholders came under the control of the Democratic machine. As the party whip in the Assembly Smith
had to drive hard to win passage of the bill for the new
charter. Many members of his own party, reluctant to cast
their votes for this dubious measure, hid in the corridors
of the Capital or took refuge on the scaffolding where workmen were repairing the building after the fire of April, 1911,
but Smith sternly sent the Sergeant-at-Arms to haul them
back to the Chamber, and be counted. When the battle was
over he maintained, somewhat lamely, that the charter was
"the best that could be obtained at the time."

There was nothing to apologize for in another measure
that came up for debate: the Workmen's Compensation Act,
one of the most important bills to be passed in 1911, and
one to which Smith was deeply committed. Under a previous
law covering injuries to workmen the burden of proof of
negligence fell upon the injured. In order to claim damages
an injured man was obliged to show that the accident had
not been caused by the mistakes of fellow workers in the
same plant. Moreover he had to pay for the services of a
lawyer who could be a match for his employer's lawyers and
the casualty insurance experts. All this was changed by the
new law sponsored by the Democrats, which placed respon-

sibility for occupational accidents largely on the employers.

To oppose this bill a crowd of corporation lawyers and high-powered lobbyists flocked to Albany, presenting what would seem nowadays the most absurd objections to its passage, the gravamen of their argument being the charge that workmen in great numbers would intentionally lose their limbs in order to collect a thousand dollars or two in compensation! Smith sat on the committee to which the bill had been referred, and worked day by day to frustrate the opposition's schemes for taking the heart out of it by seemingly innocent amendments. The bill was passed in the form stipulated by the Democrats, and contributed much to Smith's lasting popularity among trade unionists in New York from 1911 on.

Still, despite his effectiveness in obtaining the enactment of the Workmen's Compensation Act, Smith was not yet regarded with unquestioning approval by the good government fellows. In reviewing the work of the Legislature in the autumn of 1911 the New York *World* maintained that the Democratic Party's leaders such as Smith and his lieutenant, State Senator James J. Walker, had shown themselves indifferent to the interests of the people and subservient to the will of the Tammany boss. The *World* therefore called on an "aroused electorate" to eliminate these men from public life at the forthcoming elections. The Citizens' Union also castigated Smith as one of the principal agents of the Tammany plunderbund, charging him with being all the more culpable because he was so clever at manipulating the Chamber.

Smith, so well loved in his district, could never be unseated. Popular discontent, however, caused a slight pendular swing in the overall vote which cost the Democrats control of both houses, reducing Smith to the role of Minority Leader in the 1912 session, and putting Boss William A. Barnes and his Republican followers in the saddle again. The local politics of those times were scarcely edifying, and Smith himself sometimes showed a certain lack of interest in carrying out merely partisan tasks. The trouble with most politicians, he used to say, was that they "had no ideas"; he would like to get them to "think," instead of engaging in the scramble for offices or appropriations for their own bailiwicks.

Even as the *World* and the Citizens' Union were calling for his defeat, change was beginning within him. The furor for reform was in the air of America then; progressive and humanitarian ideas were becoming contagious. Events, too, played their part in changing his course. A tremendous catastrophe in New York City in the spring of 1911 had a profound effect on him, directing his attention to new fields of action, and offering fresh and inspiring opportunities for public service, which his parliamentary experience had by now prepared him to grasp.

The State Legislature at Albany reflected fully the immense wealth and power of the Empire State and the well-organized interest groups working within it. Here famous governors, and six Presidents of the United States, were groomed, not to speak of others who became national political leaders or presidential candidates. The stakes were very high in this body; giant corporations and their sharp-witted attorneys were always on the scene, and the politicians here were ever engaged in the shrewdest competition.

During many years Alfred Smith came to love the activity of the Assembly, the thrust and parry of debate, the everlast-

ing struggle to pass or defeat bills. He had said that the
Fulton Fish Market had been his "university"; the State
Legislature was also a school, though of another sort, in
which he learned a great deal. Many years later when he had
reached a much higher office, he appeared in the old Chamber and spoke of the place itself in moving words:

> This is the sixteenth time I have taken the oath of allegiance
> in this room. I have a deep and abiding affection for the As-
> sembly Chamber. It has been my school and my college; in
> fact the very foundation of everything that I have attained was
> laid here.

This eloquent statement reminded Frances Perkins of how
Winston Churchill described himself. "I am a House of
Commons man," said Churchill. "Alfred Smith too," wrote
Miss Perkins, "was a parliamentary man, an Assembly man.
He thought and felt and reasoned in terms of that body.
What he learned there from 1904 to 1915 was the very basis
of a deep understanding and knowledge of the trade of a
politician — a political leader in a democratic society."

CHAPTER VI

"He Read a Book": Frances Perkins

THE YEAR 1910 had ushered in one of America's periodic waves of reform, incidental to which the Democrats had won majority power at Albany. In that year the insurgents in Congress, led by young George Norris of Nebraska, finally unseated the autocratic Speaker "Uncle Joe" Cannon, a key man among the Republican standpatters. Senator La Follette, espousing the "Wisconsin Idea" of liberal improvement, now hastened to launch the National Progressive League; Colonel Theodore Roosevelt, promoting the New Nationalism, opened fire on the "bad trusts" in business and the machines in politics, while at the same period Louis D. Brandeis, the "people's lawyer," led the conservationists as in holy war against the Taft Administration. Labor conflicts spread all about the country and that autumn centered in New York City where thousands of underpaid women factory workers maintained a strike of desperation for long months. From Oregon to New Jersey the liberals of politics clamored for the direct primary and the popular referendum; the women carried on a powerful agitation for suffrage. Among them there was a new breed of political and social workers who had begun to be heard in the land, women who went to live among and help the poor in the slums, or who carried on a powerful propaganda for state laws setting up improved labor standards in factories.

Assemblyman Smith, in the line of duty, met some of the women social workers who came to Albany on behalf of their philanthropic organizations. Though most machine politicians disliked women social workers and held goo-goos in contempt, he was increasingly drawn to them. He wanted new ideas, as he said, and they brought them to him; he wanted to know the facts and their experts gathered them. His encounter with Miss Perkins was very important for him, for it came at a time when he felt a growing interest in social welfare legislation; moreover he found there was much he could learn from her. His acquaintance with this pertinacious little spinster soon ripened into one of his closest and longest associations with the women then entering the political field. By 1911, when circumstances began to throw them together more frequently, he sensed that he had been too long occupied with dreary chores for Tammany, such as ripper bills and other political jobs, while it did not escape him that by championing a reform measure also urged by the goo-goos — home rule for his native city — he had won some acclaim in the metropolitan press. He was, in short, morally and intellectually prepared to break into new ground.

Many years later Frances Perkins overheard a man asking one of the Tammany sachems where Smith got all his information. "He read a book," said the Tammany man. "What did he read?" "He knew Frances Perkins and she was a book." Miss Perkins was certainly full of her special subject, and she has repeatedly described, as have others, how Smith acquired his extensive factual knowledge of public affairs by extracting it orally from persons who were experts in their fields. He read little but played by ear, had a keen sense of what questions to ask, and was often able to fish up information that those questioned were unaware they possessed.

Miss Perkins, for her part, was deeply impressed by Smith's knowledge of the inner workings of the Legislature as well as by his parliamentary skills. He could tell her with authority whether a bill she supported stood a chance of passage or not at a certain time, and suggest that it would be wise to try again at a later session. They saw a great deal of each other in 1911, when Smith was Majority Leader of the Assembly, and they worked together on an important legislative committee of inquiry, the Factory Investigating Commission. On either side it proved to be a fruitful relationship; together they were to pioneer in untrodden areas of the law.

Frances Perkins was destined to take office as the first woman Cabinet member in United States history, but she never forgot that she owed her advancement to Smith, as he owed something of his growing social consciousness to her. A character in her own right, she deserves her niche in the annals of our regional politics as well as in the larger theater of the nation's capital.* No two persons united in a common cause could have been more different. Frances Perkins was Protestant, Yankee, of comfortable middle-class origins,

---

* She was one of a group of women who contributed to the shaping of his character and to his education, a sisterhood that included his mother, his wife, and one other who, thanks in part to Miss Perkins, was also to play a leading role among his advisers at the height of his career.

and well educated by the standards of the time. As a government official Miss Perkins always showed a stubborn reticence about revealing to the press the facts about her domestic life, her husband, and her child. She had her private sorrows which she strove always to conceal, holding that they affected in no way her professional career. Of her New England lineage, however, she used to speak freely and with pride. The first Perkins in Massachusetts Bay Colony had come from England in the mid-seventeenth century, and she could also claim for her family a collateral relationship with James Otis, the Revolutionary patriot. The Perkinses, occupied in farming and shipbuilding, were among the early settlers of the Maine coast: the site of the ancestral home at New Castle, on the Damariscotta River, which once included a busy brickworks, is still marked on maps as "Perkins Point." In New Castle Miss Perkins's father, Frederick W. Perkins, was born, being one of three brothers. He received a secondary school education in Maine, then went to Boston, where one of his brothers had established himself as a lawyer. In the 1870's he was employed for some years in the department store of Jordan Marsh, and after that managed a small shop of his own. His marriage to Susan Bean, of Bethel, Maine, was followed by the birth of a first child at their home in Boston on April 10, 1880, a girl who was christened Fanny Coralie.* When the child was about two, her parents moved to the nearby city of Worcester,

---

* Miss Perkins in later life unfortunately gave the year of her birth as 1882, which led one scurrilous pamphleteer, during the New Deal, to charge her with being an immigrant of Jewish origin, since the Boston birth records listed no child of Frederick and Susan Perkins born in that year. Anti–New Deal newspapers gleefully seized on the story, to which Miss Perkins issued a dignified answer, stating that if she had been Jewish she would have been proud to acknowledge it, and describing her family tree in some detail.

where Mr. Perkins conducted a business in wholesale stationery.

Far from wealthy, though comfortable enough, the Perkinses lived in a succession of unpretentious frame houses in a quiet residential quarter of Worcester. There Fanny Coralie grew up, attending public school and the Congregational Church where her family worshiped. Of her very early years she recalled one episode with horror; on a visit to Boston, when she was perhaps six years old, she happened to witness a street fight between some Irish boys and a larger band of Yankees; the Yankees, giving shouts of "Paddys! Paddys!" threw stones at the Irish who were driven to flight. Such incidents were not uncommon in the Boston of the 1880's. Happier memories were associated with summer vacations at the Perkins farm in Maine, which was run by one of her uncles. As her relatives died off it was she who eventually took possession of the old brick house at the inlet of the sea, which she used as her summer home in later years.

Fanny's parents were by disposition undemonstrative, and her upbringing was strict. There was only one other child, a younger sister, and as Fanny had almost nobody to play with she applied herself to books and became a great reader from the age of eight; it was then, she relates, that her father taught her the rudiments of Greek. At the Worcester Classical High School she studied Greek and Latin and showed some taste for the sciences.

College education for girls was rather rare then, especially in families of modest means. But even at eighteen, though her scholastic record at high school was not outstanding, Fanny gave evidence of a lively mind and considerable intellectual curiosity. Her father foresaw that college training would lead to professional employment, probably at teach-

ing, and agreed to let her enter Mount Holyoke, one of the
leading women's colleges, in the fall of 1898.

College was good for Fanny; she found studying physics
and chemistry stimulated her mind, and she enjoyed exposure to English and German literature. She was also a
normal and fun-loving girl who made numerous friends, and
took delight in extracurricular activities such as kiteflying in
the spring, and sleighing in winter. She was, moreover, pro-
ficient at amateur theatricals, and it is remembered that she
played creditably a man's role in a burlesque musical of
Julius Caesar and again in a skit based on a poetic drama
by Browning. In later life she was to be called upon often
and again to play what used to be considered a man's part.

While Miss Perkins did not rank among the leading scholars
of the college — she had but an average record — her major-
ing in the sciences helped her, after graduation, to win teaching jobs. Yet for her college mates she was a success; they
considered her clever, vivacious, and strong on college spirit;
affectionately they nicknamed her "Perky," designated her
in her senior year as "the Girl Who Has Done Most for Her
Class," and elected her class president. There was an idealis-
tic and religious vein in Fanny Coralie, shown by her heading the Prayer Meeting Committee and by her faithful attendance at the YWCA chapter. In her youth she had the
feeling she was waiting for a "call" to her true vocation, but
for years it was not discovered, and she sometimes feared
there would be none for her.

One of her college courses, however, was to have a greater
effect on her development than she realized for some years
to come. In her senior year she studied under Annah May
Soule, professor of political economy, whose methods seem to
have been considerably in advance of her time. Professor

Soule taught the principles of economic theory according to the orthodox economists of the nineteenth century, and reviewed the history of industrial society in England and America, but also required her students to "visit a factory . . . during the semester, or previous summer, and make a formal report to the class." Mount Holyoke was not far from Chicopee Falls and other mill towns in the Connecticut Valley where the industrial process could be observed at first hand in large textile and paper mills. Later on Miss Perkins remarked that Miss Soule's course had first opened her mind "to the idea that there were some people poorer than other people . . . and that the lack of comfort and security was not solely due to the fact that they drank," as her parents firmly believed.

There was a letdown after college ended, and while waiting for something to turn up she helped her mother keep house in Worcester, an occupation that never held much attraction for her. A post as a substitute in a secondary school came up but did not last. While waiting for something more permanent she undertook some volunteer social service among the young factory workers in her city, forming a club of girls from fourteen to sixteen years old, with whom she met in the evenings for gymnasium exercises and games. In addition she put in some time at a Gospel Mission affiliated with her church, teaching homeless women and girls how to sew, an art in which she herself was little practiced. Gradually she was coming to know an aspect of society but dimly glimpsed in her girlhood years. One of the girls in her club, for example, had her hand cut off by an unguarded machine in a candy factory, and Miss Perkins exerted herself prodigiously to win compensation of one hundred dollars for the terrible injury. There was food for thought in this gruesome story, with implications of a possible career for the young college graduate, but she was not yet prepared to act on it.

At length an attractive teaching offer came to her from Ferry Hall, a girls' preparatory school in Lake Forest, Illinois, near Chicago. Bent on winning her independence and seeing a bit of the world too, she accepted with enthusiasm and took up her duties in the fall of 1904. Chicago was not only a metropolis famous for its glittering shops, theaters, and other amusements; it was alive with new departures in education, literature, and above all in social work, thanks to the settlement houses where original ideas were being applied in attacking the social problems of the modern industrial city. Introduced by a fellow teacher to Dr. Graham Taylor, head of the Chicago Commons, Miss Perkins undertook to spend her Christmas holiday in 1905 as a resident there.

"I never got so many ideas in my life as I did in those three weeks," she wrote exuberantly to her college friends. "I'm more interested than ever in settlement work." Dr. Taylor was the first to explain to her the social meaning of trade unionism, which in the view of her family was the work of the devil. Where the workers were organized, he pointed out, as among the printers, the unions saw to it that they received the wages agreed upon, whereas unorganized women in the needle trades often failed to get even the poor pay due them. One of her assignments at the Chicago Commons was to help collect overdue wages for the "bundle women" who worked in their tenement homes for the clothing industry.

It was strong stuff the young teacher was absorbing in Chicago, and she was to be exposed to more of it the next

season when she came as a temporary resident to Hull House,
soaking up what she could from those great women who
made it a center of light: Jane Addams, Ellen Gates Starr,
Grace Abbott, and many others. Sometimes she accompanied one of the district nurses of the settlement on missions to Chicago's blighted areas, witnessing scenes of misery
and degradation beyond all imagining. She found herself
possessed of unexpected reserves of courage and a strong
stomach as well when called on to help the Hull House nurse
attend the alcoholic wretches of the neighborhood. Deeply
moved, as if by a religious experience, she came to believe
firmly that her vocation was to be social work. It was for her
an instance of what might be called the Florence Nightingale
syndrome, which affected many women of the educated
middle class, and even of the wealthy class at that period,
and drove them to contend against the horrors of America's
industrial centers. At about this same time Miss Perkins
underwent another religious experience; having been brought
up as a Congregationalist, she became a communicant of the
Episcopal Church, to which she adhered for the rest of her
life. Another departure, slight though not insignificant,
marked this period: she dropped her given names and thereafter became Frances Perkins.

Casting about for a position in her new vocation in 1907,
she learned from a friend of an organization being formed
in Philadelphia for the protection of working girls, applied
for the post of general secretary, and was appointed almost
immediately. Immigrant girls from Europe and Negro girls
from the South were then arriving in Philadelphia in considerable numbers to look for work. Commercial agents

would meet them at the railroad terminals or docks, lead
them to lodginghouses where they were charged exorbitant
rates, and thence to shady employment offices recruiting candidates for the brothels of Philadelphia and nearby industrial
towns. The Philadelphia Research and Protective Association of which Miss Perkins became general secretary was
founded to protect the immigrants from these predatory
operators, while also bringing pressure on the city authorities
to pass corrective ordinances. Its backers were church people
and philanthropists, but she constituted most of the paid
staff, and in fact had to set up the project, improvising
methods of investigation and counseling in an area where
few before her had had experience. She began by making
a systematic study of rooming houses in the low alleys of the
City of Brotherly Love, often in decayed mansions where
working girls and prostitutes were mingled indiscriminately.
Incidental to her work for the society she compiled an independent report on the industrial and living conditions of self-
supporting women in Philadelphia for the Intermunicipal
Research Bureau, the first of its kind made in America.
While doing this she ran across two immigrant girls working
in a factory for five dollars a week, and paying half of that
for a small dark room in a basement to sleep in. "How much
do you use for food, and what do you eat?" Miss Perkins
asked. Good-humoredly one of the girls replied in broken
English, "Bread and bananas. It fills you up so you don't feel
hungry."

The spunky Miss Perkins soon served warning that she
would have the law on the shady immigrants' agents and
crooked employment offices. A Negro woman, assisting her
in meeting girls who came up from the South, was subjected

to so much harassment that she had to appeal to the police for protection. Miss Perkins herself was followed one rainy night by two Negro procurers whom she had threatened to put out of business. As they began to close in on her, she dodged around a corner, then wheeled around and thrust her umbrella point-blank at one of the men pursuing her, at the same time screaming for help and calling out his name. At that period people were not indifferent to a cry of terror in the night. Windows were flung up, heads popped out up and down the street, and the two ruffians took flight. Several crooked employment agencies were closed down as a result of the incident, and patrolmen were sent out to the docks and railroad stations to protect the immigrant girls on their arrival. A new ordinance requiring the licensing of lodging-houses was also drafted with the help of the Research and Protective Association, but Miss Perkins observed that the police and the city fathers had done nothing to remedy the situation until she brought them complaints signed by influential citizens.

All this was part of her education, which she began to feel was being advanced without much knowledge of the theory of social organization. While she was in Philadelphia therefore she enrolled at the Wharton School of Finance and Commerce of the University of Pennsylvania to study economics and sociology, and found to her surprise that she was enjoying it. "I discovered my mind at that time. I never knew before that I had a mind," she said later. At the Wharton School she encountered one of the foremost scholars of the time, Professor Simon Patten, who inspired her to go on with her postgraduate studies, and recommended her for a fellowship at the New York School of Philanthropy in 1909. In his letter of recommendation to Professor Samuel McCune Lindsay, Patten described her as "a remarkably good executive . . . I believe she will acquire through her energy and brains an important position among social workers . . ."

Entering the New York scene under these pleasant auspices, she took full advantage of the larger theater, working for her master's degree at Columbia's Teachers College at night, and by day surveying Hell's Kitchen for a study under the direction of Miss Pauline Goldmark, head of the School of Philanthropy. In Philadelphia she had already had some useful contacts with district political bosses, who there functioned as part of a Republican city machine; in New York when she needed help she went to the Tammany leader of her district, The McManus, a State Senator, whose authority in Hell's Kitchen was, as she put it, "only a little less than that of the angels." A family in deep distress came to her attention in the course of her study of the area: a mother with two small daughters and a son, her sole support, who had been arrested for some petty crime. The local charity bureau refused to donate funds because the mother was supposed to be not quite respectable, and the son had a previous police record. Miss Perkins repaired to the district Tammany club and applied to Boss McManus for aid, explaining that the boy's mother and sisters would starve if he were imprisoned. "I'll see what I can do," said The McManus. "Come around tomorrow afternoon." The next day she learned that the boy was to be released. She could have had no more striking illustration of the fact that where the impersonal force of the law and the pharisaical rules of charity bureaus lacked compassion, the intervention of the machine boss as a humane agent could help to bridge the gap. A pragmatic thinker, Miss Perkins was forced to revise many of the notions she had held about machine politics. The fact that Smith was Tammany's man from the Fourth Ward did not deter her, when she met him about a year later, from applying to him on behalf of the sweated women workers. As for Senator McManus, he proved to be one of her staunchest allies in pressing for social welfare laws.

A while later Miss Perkins took up residence at Greenwich House, the settlement in Greenwich Village established by Mrs. Mary Kingsbury Simkhovitch. That charming and philanthropic woman attracted to her settlement house a wide social circle, not only of welfare workers and church leaders, but of cultivated men and women from every walk of life. Among them were doctors like Hans Zinsser, philosophers like John Dewey, historians such as James Harvey Robinson and James T. Shotwell, and in addition a whole train of writers and artists. Dining out with her new friends, attending art exhibitions, the theater, the opera, sometimes talking at street corner rallies for woman suffrage, Miss Perkins was living the New York life to the full. She bloomed in this lively milieu, where her eager intelligence won her the respect and affection of many gifted and accomplished contemporaries. With her wavy hair, her expressive brown eyes, and her beautiful hands she was by no means unattractive and looked younger than her thirty years. Sometimes she even thought of marrying — "to get it off my mind," as she used to say jocularly.

In 1910 she was appointed to the responsible position of Secretary of the New York Consumers' League. The League was one of several welfare agencies established in the late

nineteenth century. A group of indomitable women had
been active in this movement, notably Mrs. Josephine Shaw
Lowell, who had founded the Charity Organization Society
in New York in 1882. This society coordinated the efforts of
many well-meaning groups and by undertaking more me-
thodical research helped to raise the professional standards
of charity workers.

At about the same period settlement houses began to appear in the blighted sections of the great cities, the two
best-known being Hull House in Chicago, headed by Jane
Addams, and the Henry Street Settlement in Alfred Smith's
old neighborhood in New York, started by Lillian Wald. In
a further move the resourceful Mrs. Lowell organized the
Consumers' League to spread propaganda about harmful industrial conditions and lobby for social welfare laws before
city and state bodies. The League was also designed to maintain close liaison with all the other welfare institutions, and
thus Frances Perkins, through her office, had wide contacts
with other workers in related fields. Another association with
which she cooperated, for example, was the Women's Trade
Union League, founded by two heroic union organizers,
Leonora O'Reilly, and Rose Schneiderman of the Shirtwaist
Makers' Union. Headed successively by two philanthropic
sisters, Margaret (Mrs. Raymond Robins) and Mary E.
Dreier, this group also publicized intolerable conditions
among women workers and lobbied for reform laws.

When Frances Perkins went to the New York office of the
Consumers' League its national director was Florence Kelley,
a brilliant figure in the galaxy of notable American women.
Daughter of the ironmaster William F. ("Pig Iron") Kelley,
a well-known Republican leader in Congress in the 1870's,

Mrs. Kelley (who reassumed her maiden name after marriage and a divorce) had been educated in leading universities of America and Europe; in 1894 she also took a law degree at Northwestern University. She was associated for many years with Jane Addams at Hull House, where she made pioneer studies of slum conditions and labor problems. Later she acted as an adviser to the liberal Governor Altgeld, and was appointed by him as Chief Inspector of Factories for the State of Illinois, the first woman to serve in such an office. It was Florence Kelley who set up a model program for reform of working conditions: she would make painstaking, highly documented inquiries into abusive practices in industry, employing doctors, engineers, and other experts to aid her; next she would have remedial legislation drafted, carrying on propaganda and lobbying for its passage; and then she would keep close check on how it was administered. As head of the National Consumer's League after 1899 Mrs. Kelley recruited and trained dozens of young women social workers, including Josephine Goldmark, who helped write the "Brandeis brief" for the Oregon Eight-Hour Law for women, and her sister Pauline, founder of the New York School of Philanthropy. One of her ablest pupils was Frances Perkins, who was destined to rise higher in public office than all the others.

Mrs. Kelley, to whose influence Frances Perkins paid handsome tribute, was both an inspirational character and a driving leader. When there was something "impossible" to be done, she would exclaim, "Frances, you're *got* to do it!" Under Mrs. Kelley's direction the Consumers' League investigated working conditions in the consumer industries and drew up a "White List" of concerns that maintained humane standards. These would be awarded a label for their merchandise to guide thousands of women shoppers in their purchases. Miss Perkins was detailed to make a study of cellar bakeries, where most of New York's bread was produced. But Mrs. Kelley had other tasks for her too. New York then stood behind some other states in restricting working hours for women and children, although Oregon's Eight-Hour Law had already been sanctioned by the United States Supreme Court in a famous decision of 1908 argued by Louis Brandeis. A far more moderate law, calling for a fifty-four-hour week, had, however, been set aside by the New York State Court of Appeals in 1909. Mrs. Kelley labored tirelessly to have the law rewritten in language that would overcome the court's objections, and she now directed her young associate to go to Albany to lobby for passage of the revised bill. It was on this, her first visit to the state capital, in January, 1910, that Miss Perkins first met Alfred Smith.*

She was not to see her bill passed in that session, nor yet in the next, whatever her efforts. Meanwhile she was assigned to a new study: the causes of accidents to women workers in industry, an inquiry stimulated by a factory fire in Newark, New Jersey, in December, 1910, in which twenty-five girls died and many more were injured. Miss Perkins made a careful investigation of this and another fatal fire in the same industrial area, aided by an engineer and two independent fire prevention experts. Her reports showed that there was a certain pattern in fires resulting in casualties: there was no fire fighting equipment available, inflammable

---

* Child labor is reported to have increased from approximately 1,000,000 workers to 1,750,000 between 1880 and 1900. The increase of women workers was correspondingly large in the cities.

material was spread all over the plants, no fire drills were held, and finally there was as a rule only one exit available, and that exit blocked!

From this she went on to study laundries, textile mills, and clothing shops, where women's hands and arms might be caught in unguarded mangles or in the wheels and gears of machines, or where when their hair was caught girls were literally scalped. These grim facts were being assembled, and recommendations were being patiently drawn up by Miss Perkins and her associates, when the Triangle Shirt-waist Company fire suddenly burst upon them and gave their studies a terrible relevance.

CHAPTER VII

New Directions

LATE IN THE afternoon of Saturday, March 25, 1911, strollers in Washington Square observed smoke rising from one of the upper stories of the large loft building at Washington Place and Greene Street, just to the east of the little park. Moments later, as related by a newspaperman who happened to be passing by, a great tongue of flame shot out of an eighth-story window. A policeman reassured a knot of spectators who had gathered quickly; the fire did not look serious, he said; it was "a modern fireproof building, pretty hard to burn." Nevertheless a first fire alarm was sent in. The policeman had scarcely finished speaking when jets of flame began pouring from the windows of the eighth floor, one of three at the top of the ten-story building occupied by the Triangle Shirtwaist Company. For a while still no sign of life could be discerned high up in the burning loft. Suddenly, as the reporter described it,

something that looked like a bale of dress goods was hurled from an eighth floor window. Were they trying to save bundles of valuable cloth? Another seeming bundle came down through the same window; this time the breeze tossed open the cloth and from the crowd, now of 500, came a cry of horror! The form of a girl was disclosed shooting to instantaneous death on the stone sidewalk. Before the crowd could realize the full meaning of what was happening another girl sprang up on the window ledge, her hair and clothing all aflame. She stood poised for a moment and then down she came.

The horrifying death leaps continued, the girls' hair streaming up in flames as they jumped, their bodies thudding against the pavement "like drums beating a tattoo," forming heaps on the ground where here and there a limb stirred or a moan was heard. Among the gathering crowd of onlookers many turned their heads away; women fainted and had to be carried off.

At last the firemen arrived, one group scrambling up the stairway of the building with hose, another spreading nets to catch those still jumping from the windows. But the drop of one hundred and ten feet was too great for the nets to break the force of the falling bodies, one of which hit a heavy plate-glass protective covering over part of the sidewalk and broke it into a thousand pieces. The firemen inside the building, when they reached the upper floors, found scores of the dead who had been burned or suffocated on the eighth and ninth stories heaped up against locked doors. One elevator in three had continued to operate for a time and had brought down several hundred persons who managed to find their way out, but when it was forced to stop, many of the maddened victims threw themselves down the open shaft. Those who had been working on the tenth floor climbed up to the roof and were helped to escape to the adjacent building, which housed the New York University Law School, by students who had seen the blaze from their classrooms. It was all over in half an hour.

The toll of the dead came to one hundred and forty-six, most of them girls; many of these were recent Jewish immigrants from the East European ghettos, only fifteen or sixteen years old. Lacking space elsewhere for such a purpose, the police used the Municipal Charities Pier at East 26th Street as a gigantic morgue, where grief-crazed relatives and friends tried to identify the remains of bodies burnt or mangled beyond recognition.

Frances Perkins by chance had been an eyewitness of the Triangle Company fire. She had been taking tea, as she recalled, with some friends that Saturday afternoon at the home of Mrs. Gordon Morris on North Washington Square, west of Fifth Avenue, when the clangor of fire engines broke into their conversation. Hostess and guests went to the door, and, seeing clouds of smoke issuing from the top of the building across the square, hastened to join the crowd of onlookers. Miss Perkins remembered seeing girls hanging out of the windows by their hands, then plummeting down toward the net that could not save them. The horror of that spectacle, that aimless slaughter of the innocents, would stay with her all her life.

It was the greatest tragedy by fire in the history of New York, which had known so many fearful disasters in the past. The city was convulsed with emotion, and a general cry arose for the authorities to fix the guilt for this holocaust. Some of the reasons for the great loss of life became known quickly: the exit doors on the eighth and ninth floors had been locked on order of the proprietors of the factory, Isaac Harris and Max Blanck; there was but one fire escape, exit to which had also been barred; no fire drills were held; piles of cloth, paper patterns, and waste material covered the floors, where the sewing machines occupied so much of the available space that the aisles between them were almost impassable; and in amongst all the inflammable material cigarette smoking was permitted. Whose responsibility was it to check on such matters? The city's Fire Department or Building Bureau, the state's Factory Inspection Division of the Labor Department? All could claim limited jurisdiction, limited funds, and insufficient personnel to make proper investigations. Another macabre feature of the tragedy was that the building itself was fireproof, or at least fire-resistant, and suffered little structural damage. But people, it seemed, were not fireproof.

In the universal attempt to fix responsibility for the disaster the strongest and most telling accusations were made by the trade unionists and the social workers who knew something about conditions in the burned-out loft. During the preceding year a local union of shirtwaist makers, affiliated with the International Ladies' Garment Workers, and also with the Women's Trade Union League, had gone on strike for shorter hours and better working conditions. Led by organizers still in their teens, like Rose Schneiderman and Pauline Newman, the shirtwaist makers came out of the shops in force, set up their picket lines in defiance of the police, and carried on their fight for recognition despite mass arrests. Among those who suffered arrest were some of the well-to-do women crusaders, such as Mary E. Dreier, head of the Women's Trade Union League.

The strike was won in most of the city's shops, although not at the Triangle Shirtwaist Company. Inez Milholland, the suffragette, reported after the fire that she had called on Mayor McClellan with a delegation to complain about the

overcrowded and dangerous conditions there, but that he had
refused to see them. Mary Dreier also testified that she had
been induced by Mr. Blanck to send the girls back to work
in his plant without an agreement, on his promise that he
would effect improvements voluntarily. But not only had he
failed to keep his promise; he had also arranged to fire the
former strikers, once the pressure of unfilled orders for goods
was relieved. Various witnesses testified that the loft's doors
were generally kept locked during working hours, presumably to prevent thievery, but in reality to keep the union's
walking delegates out.

So much damning evidence was reported in the press that
public emotion over the affair was maintained at a high pitch
for days on end. On Sunday evening, April 2, a memorial
meeting was held at the Metropolitan Opera House, not only
to mourn the dead but also to plan corrective measures. The
huge theater was filled to the topmost galleries; the stage
was occupied by civil leaders, clergymen, philanthropists,
and social workers. Moving sermons were given by Bishop
David H. Greer, Rabbi Stephen Wise, and Father William J.
White; Dr. Henry Moskowitz, speaking for the Joint Board
of Sanitary Control of the cloak and suit industry, described
the many hazards to life reported to exist in various factories, and told how recommendations for improvement had
been ignored. The philanthropic banker, Jacob Schiff, as
head of an improvised relief committee, appealed for funds
to aid the families of the victims. But the most eloquent
speech of the evening, perhaps equaling passages of the
famous music dramas shown in that house, was delivered
by tiny Rose Schneiderman, who looked like a child but had
led the Shirtwaist Makers Union in their recent strike:

I would be a traitor to these poor burned bodies [she said] if I came here to talk good fellowship. We have tried you good people of the public and found you wanting. The old Inquisition had its rack and its thumbscrews and its instruments of torture with iron teeth. We know what these things are today: the iron teeth are our necessities, the thumbscrews the high-powered and swift machinery close to which we must work; and the rack is here in the firetrap structures that will destroy us the minute they catch fire.

This is not the first time girls have been burned alive in the city. Every week I must learn of the untimely death of one of my sister workers. Every year thousands of us are maimed. The life of men and women is so cheap and property is so sacred. There are so many of us for one job it matters little if 143 are burned to death . . .*

You have a couple of dollars for the sorrowing mothers and brothers and sisters by way of a charity gift. But every time the workers come out in the only way they know to protest against conditions which are unbearable the strong hand of the law is allowed to press down heavily upon us.

Public officials have only words of warning — that we must be intensely peaceable and intensely orderly, and they have the workhouse back of their warnings . . . I can't talk fellowship to you who are gathered here. Too much blood has been spilled. I know from my experience it is up to the working people to save themselves. They can only save themselves by a strong working-class movement.

There was no applause when Miss Schneiderman sat down. Many persons in the audience, however, could scarcely control their emotions. Frances Perkins, who attended that meeting, remembered Miss Schneiderman's impeachment of the shirtwaist manufacturers and of officialdom as the most moving speech she had ever heard.

* This figure was a preliminary estimate; a later count made it 146.

One more public demonstration of grief and compassion took place on April 5, when a great funeral procession for the unidentified victims was held. Under gray skies and a persistent rain a silent crowd of enormous size — estimated by the police as 400,000 — lined the streets to watch the file of mourners. The marchers included members of the Shirtwaist Workers and many other unions, as well as citizens from every walk of life. At their head were the women labor leaders, Mary E. Dreier, Rose Schneiderman, and Leonora O'Reilly; accompanying them were other women eminent then or later, such as Jeanette Rankin, destined to be the country's first Congresswoman, Harriet Stanton Blatch, Mary Beard, and Helen Marot. There were no banners and no sounds of music, only that of marching feet in the rain — and but one cry from the watching crowd, when Rose Schneiderman was seen to falter as if in a faint. She was helped to her feet, and went on.

And now the social workers went into action. After several preliminary meetings to coordinate their activities they agreed on April 10 to form a "Committee on Safety," whose purpose was "to conserve the lives and health of working people, especially in their places of employment . . . to investigate existing conditions, to recommend standards of safety and health . . ." R. Fulton Cutting, the New York philanthropist, guaranteed $10,000 to finance the work of the committee, and, in order to avoid duplication of effort it was decided to merge its membership with that of the temporary committee chosen for the same purpose at the Metropolitan Opera House meeting. As it was finally set up Henry L. Stimson was chosen President, and the Executive Committee consisted of Cutting, Mary Dreier, Henry Morgenthau, Sr.,

Daniel Harris, Dr. Henry Moskowitz, and Anne Morgan. Among other agencies from whom the Committee sought counsel was the Consumers' League, whose Secretary, Frances Perkins, had already made some studies of the fire hazards in factories. Because of her experience the Committee on Safety engaged her services immediately; a little later she became its Executive Secretary.

As soon as the Committee was set up it sent a delegation to Albany to lay a petition before Governor Dix, the delegation including John Kingsbury (of the Association for Improving the Condition of the Poor), Dr. Henry Moskowitz, and Miss Perkins, among others. The Governor declared himself in full sympathy with their purpose; on his advice the delegation then went to call on the two Democratic leaders of the Legislature, Smith and Wagner, who were in a position to initiate some action.

Smith, as Miss Perkins learned, had already been talking with fellow members of the Legislature on the train going up to Albany the day after the fire. He was deeply moved, remembering that his mother had been a factory worker and might have been killed in the same way as those girls. If this could happen in New York City he reasoned there must be danger spots all over the state. The public was so highly aroused that party lines were forgotten; Republicans and Democrats alike were convinced that they had to "do something."

When the Committee on Safety representatives met with Smith, Miss Perkins noticed the close attention he gave to their plea for corrective action. "Politics" must be kept out of this affair, they urged; only the "finest and ablest" citizens should be called in. Characteristically he said, "We've got to know the facts," and, he added, these could best be ascertained by a Legislative Commission armed with the power to subpoena and examine witnesses, and backed by an appropriation. Those "finest citizens" the social workers wanted, he pointed out, would prove to be too busy to help. The state legislators would also be more likely to act on recommendations presented to them by their own political associates or appointees.

Here we find Smith combining the spirit of charity with opportunism: he was not above trying to make political capital for his party out of this crisis, although in an honorable way. As a machine politician as well as a man of conscience he was ready to jump in with both feet and work for reform in cooperation with the aroused social workers.

A bill setting up the Factory Investigating Commission was promptly presented in the Senate by Robert Wagner; strongly backed by Smith, as Majority Leader and chairman of the Ways and Means Committee, it was passed in the Assembly without opposition, becoming law on June 30. Wagner, then President of the Senate, was named chairman of the Commission, and Smith vice-chairman; four other members of the Legislature, drawn from both parties, were to serve with them. In addition the Governor was empowered to appoint four private citizens to the Commission, and his choice fell on Mary E. Dreier, of the Women's Trade Union League, Samuel Gompers, head of the AFL, Robert Dowling, a leading real estate operator, and Simon Brentano, the well-known publisher and bookseller.

The scope of the Commission's inquiries was probably as broad as that of any yet undertaken in the field of private industry by a governmental body in the United States. It was empowered to examine the conditions causing fires in factories, methods of fire prevention, dangers arising from unguarded machinery, as well as from unsanitary conditions and occupational diseases; determine how existing legislation could be better enforced; and draft new laws to prevent industrial accidents and dangers to life and health created by the greed or ignorance of employers. It was a large program indeed.

The Triangle factory fire had the effect of a watershed in United States history. It had thrown a sudden glaring light on the human problems of the industrial society in America, wholly unplanned and unregulated as it then was. The day before it occurred the state's Court of Appeals had struck down as unconstitutional a workmen's compensation act passed by the Legislature. But in the four years that followed the fire one measure after another was to be passed, and upheld by the courts, measures to protect the lives and preserve the health of workers in factories and shops, to limit the hours of labor of women and children, and to compensate the victims of accidents incurred at their places of employment. Alfred Smith's work on the Factory Investigating Commission, along with his successful campaign for enactment of the bills originating from its surveys, constitutes one of his greatest political achievements. By sponsoring needed social legislation, which the state's Republican Party had for so long studiously ignored, he redeemed the good name of the Democratic Party in New York State.

The Commission began its work in July, 1911, with Abram I. Elkus, noted New York lawyer, philanthropist, and (later)

Ambassador to Turkey, as its counsel. His assistant, a public-spirited young lawyer named Bernard Shientag, was to become Smith's intimate aide for many years. Dr. George Price, a sanitation expert who had made many studies of conditions in the New York City sweatshops, served as director of investigations, with a staff of experienced social workers, among whom was Frances Perkins. The Commission carried on its inquiries for more than three years, winning additional funds from the Legislature as needed, up to February, 1915. Public hearings were held in New York City, Troy, Schenectady, Syracuse, Utica, Rochester, and Buffalo — in addition to numerous executive sessions — in which the conduct of some 1800 establishments in twenty different industries was surveyed.

In this heartening situation the social workers, as Frances Perkins recalled, were "happy as clams." For long years they had been making their own inquiries on the slimmest of budgets, without authority even to gain entrance where they sought it, and without assurance that their reports would be given any attention. Now, as the only group trained for such work, they had the power of the state government backing them as they went about their field surveys, and were assured of a respectful hearing instead of being dismissed as impractical idealists or meddlers.

They did not, however, go unchallenged by certain powerful property interests, and of these the real estate people were the most obstructive. When Frances Perkins, for example, was called on to testify about cellar bakeries on November 4, 1911, a real estate operator named Stewart Brown came storming down the aisle at the Aldermanic Chamber in New York City, where the hearing was being held, to protest that she was unqualified as a witness. As she remembered the incident, Smith asked her a few pertinent questions about her recent study of the bakeries, the number she had visited and the records she had made, and briskly qualified her as an expert. She then offered her testimony, backed up by photographs, of the filthy underground basements where bread was baked in New York City, of all the dirt and water accumulating there, of cats lying on the rising dough, of the bakers in their soiled clothes resting on the boards where the dough was kneaded. No citizen could read that testimony and eat his daily bread in comfort thereafter.

Miss Perkins appeared as a witness before the Commission on three other occasions in the following year, once to testify on home work in the tenements, and twice on fire hazards and prevention. Her presentation of the case for the fire hazard bills on December 4, 1912, was so brilliant that it won a vote of commendation by the commissioners. After months of study under the foremost fire prevention experts in the country, she had arrived at certain conclusions which she expressed with great clarity. These could be boiled down to two main principles: one, the horizontal exit and fire wall, and two, measured occupancy and provision for units of exit in exact proportion to the number of occupants to be evacuated in case of fire. She had been taught, and she was able to teach the commissioners, that every floor and every part of every floor must be emptied in less than three minutes, in case of fire, or you could not save lives.

On the issue of measured occupancy — that is, limiting the number of workers on every floor to the number that could make their escape within three minutes — the real estate interests were for long unyielding. Robert Dowling, their representative on the Commission, held out against any legislation that would limit the return for landlords. On one occasion he cited the small percentage of people who died in factory fires each year, saying that they formed only "an infinitesimal proportion of the population." At this the handsome Miss Dreier opened wide her fine blue eyes and exclaimed, "But Mr. Dowling, they were men and women! They were human souls! It was a hundred per cent for them!" These words Smith warmly applauded, saying to Dowling, "Good Catholic doctrine, Robert!"

The real estate interests indeed showed poor diplomacy in opposing the Commission's recommendations. One Sunday morning a wealthy young realtor named Charles F. Noyes drove his flashy yellow Stutz downtown and parked it in front of 25 Oliver Street. When no one answered the bell at the Smith home he inquired of the neighbors where Smith could be found. According to Miss Perkins the neighbors showed themselves curious both about the splendid racing car and the man's business with Smith. Returning from Mass a few minutes later, Smith demanded what Noyes's errand was. "I came to see you about the Factory Commission report" was the answer. "I don't like the testimony that Miss Perkins is bringing before you. She's got a lot of cranks testifying, and if the Commission takes their advice you'll be wrecked, and I'll see to it that you don't get returned from this district." Smith looked him straight in the eye and barked, "What do you mean by coming down to my house with that great big fancy car? You'll ruin my reputation forever in this neighborhood. If you've got anything to say to me you come down before the whole Commission and say it. Don't you try to approach me in any private or secret way. This is where I live. Goodbye."

For Smith his service on the Factory Investigating Commission was the most broadening experience of his life thus far; as he told Miss Perkins, it marked a great advance in his education. Up to that time his knowledge of New York State had been limited more or less to a few blocks of New York City and what could be seen from the window of the train between Manhattan and Albany. Now, thanks to the Commission's investigations in various parts of the state, he came to know almost all of it well, its landscape, its people, its industries, even its history, as revealed in its monuments and public works.

On many trips he saw the great plains of the central New York area with its rich farms along the Cherry Valley; on the banks of the Mohawk River he observed a way of life quite different from his own; in the lower regions of the Adirondacks he saw the splendor of the mountains; he came to know the Great Lakes area, the Southern Tier with its strange glacial Finger Lakes; he watched the busy barges on the Erie Canal, perceiving how much De Witt Clinton's "big ditch" had done for the development of the State of New York; he beheld the growing cities: Buffalo, Rochester, Syracuse, Utica, Rome, places whose names until then had merely stood for districts from which his colleagues in the Assembly had come. He heard it explained that the reason why so many of the towns bore classical names was that a wandering schoolmaster, employed as a surveyor after the Revolution, could not pronounce the Indian place-names, and substituted for them names out of ancient history and literature.

New York was truly an imperial state, its terrain highly

varied, and the old upstate Dutch and Yankee towns with their white churches and green commons had their sound traditions and their famous centers of learning. How different were the forms of local government in the villages from those of the crowded city! St. Lawrence County, with its sparse population, was an astonishment to him, no less than the miners' village of Chateaugay, where workers lived in old, dilapidated houses without any sanitary conveniences. He was impressed by the salt mines south of Syracuse, as by the great chemical works of the Solvay Company. One day he visited the grimy plants of Lackawanna Steel in Buffalo, and another, the spic and span buildings of the Eastman Kodak Company in Rochester.

Together with his fellow commissioners he also had occasion to question the proprietors and managers of the different establishments, as well as the people employed there. Some of the factory owners he met were quite unaware of the hazards to health and life in their plants; others were surly and uncooperative, unwilling to spend a dime to improve their plants; still others were forward-looking, or eager to know what safety precautions might be taken. The workers, largely unorganized, were for the most part so driven that they gave little thought to the factory standards, although they testified freely as to their personal experience of them.

Frances Perkins accompanied the Commission as an investigator on many of its journeys around the state, and several of these left a lasting impression on her mind also. The canneries in the country south of Auburn, for example, were said to make broad use of child labor. Prior investigations had indicated that children worked in most of the canneries during the busy season, but because their work was intermittent,

it was difficult to obtain actual evidence. According to Miss
Perkins, the Commission members started out at four o'clock
one morning in two Model-T Ford cars, each approaching
the cannery to be investigated by a different route. One
carload, consisting of Smith, Miss Dreier, and Miss Perkins,
went directly to the sheds where the vegetables were being
prepared; the other group, including Wagner, entered the
factory proper through the front door. The first party found
about a dozen children, ranging from five to twelve years old,
sitting beside their mothers on little stools and shelling peas.
The manager was quite embarrassed to explain the presence
of the children and said that the cannery did not hire them,
but that their mothers couldn't leave them at home, so they
brought them along. When questioned the mothers agreed
with this interpretation, but added that the children's earnings, though not entered on the books, were a welcome incre-
ment. A woman working a twelve-hour day, with the help
of her children, might earn twelve or fourteen dollars a week
in season.

In the city of Auburn Miss Perkins conducted the commissioners to a ropeworks where the men's wages on the day shift
were so low that their women had gone to work on the night
shift to supplement their income. Smith managed to turn
up at the factory's gate at 6:45 A.M., just before the shifts
changed; at 7:00 he saw the women filing wearily out, stopping for a moment to greet their husbands who were coming
in for the day shift. Along with Miss Perkins and Miss
Dreier, Al Smith followed one of these women to her home;
there they were invited to come in and have a cup of coffee.
According to Miss Perkins, this was too much for the soft-
hearted Smith. "Look here," he said, "we ought to get *you*

a cup of coffee. You sit right down there and put your feet up on the other chair." The children came bouncing in from another room in their nightclothes and found strangers preparing coffee for their mother, "an unusual sight, I dare say," wrote Miss Perkins.

The mother then excused herself to get the children dressed and fed before they went off to school. When they were gone she sat down again and described the routine of her day, the housework, the meals, the few hours of sleep, and then the return to the factory. She was used to it, she said, and they needed the extra money, what with three children and prices rising all the time. Her folks had been strictly temperance people, but some of her neighbors needed a drink to start the day. It was not a pretty picture, and it left Smith, according to Miss Perkins, quite shaken. From then on, she claimed, he was firmly opposed to night work for women.

The commissioners visited many other factories: a candy factory in Buffalo, where almost every health and safety hazard was in evidence — the Gloversville cottage workshops, where the sweatshop conditions of the New York City tenements were repeated in a rural setting; they went into large, modern clothing plants in Rochester, but found that the "finishing" of suits was done in crowded tenements outside the factories. Miss Perkins recalled that Smith was full of pity and grief at the sight of so much human misery. But then, she added, "The lighter side of his nature came into play to save him from brooding. It was characteristic of him that he would turn a gloomy meeting into a sunshine club not merely by jokes but by a kind of spontaneous gaiety."

Fortunately there were plants and factories so well de-

signed and conducted that they were able to serve as models.
In Buffalo the commissioners inspected a shop making pearl
buttons where the precautions against fire were exemplary,
the sanitary arrangements commendable, and where also the
dust from the cutting and polishing of the pearl — a serious
occupational hazard — was drawn off by ventilators. At the
Eastman Kodak plant near Rochester they found the management fully aware of the risks in the manufacture of films
and strict in the application of precautionary measures. No
smoking was permitted in the building; no one was allowed
to carry matches on his person.

As the commissioners and investigators came to the door
of the film-drying gallery, the official accompanying them
said, "This is the most dangerous operation in the building.
The rule is 'only one person at a given moment in there.' I
recommend that you agree on one only to go and I'll chance
it with him." He went on to say that the slightest spark from
friction might cause an explosion. It was agreed that Smith
should be the one to go in. As he was advised to do, he removed his shoes, watch, and chain, and other metal objects
in his pockets, handed them to Bernard Shientag, and with
a jolly "Remember me!" proceeded on the tour of inspection.

Frances Perkins was of the opinion that the Triangle Shirtwaist fire and his years on the Factory Investigating Commission changed Smith's life, his outlook, the whole direction
of his career. One of the more interesting side effects of this
experience was a gradual alteration in his attitude toward
members of the opposite sex. At no time had his bearing
toward women been anything but respectful, and toward the
women he knew best — his mother, his wife, his sister — he

was most affectionate. He had never felt that they were lesser creatures for not having the right to vote or limiting themselves to work in their homes. But he had long ago absorbed the social traditions of the lads in Tom Foley's saloon, who looked with scorn at Prohibitionists, do-gooders, suffragists, and silk-stocking reformers alike; only recently Smith himself had spoken out against votes for women. Now he became well-acquainted with several of the most intelligent, courageous, and public-spirited women of his time; he found himself deeply impressed by them, and, more and more, came to rely upon their help. They, in turn, found him nothing like the roughhewn machine politician they expected, but a man of great personal charm, with an uncommon intelligence and talent for public service. Within a few years, by 1918, exposure to these women social workers brought Smith to the point where he announced his full conversion to the cause of woman suffrage.

But notwithstanding his new appreciation of the do-gooders he continued to stress the importance of working through political channels to achieve desirable goals, for his experience confirmed him in the opinion that only through politics could remedial measures be secured. And his notion of politics was highly sophisticated; it involved a seismographic responsiveness to waves of public sentiment, as well as an understanding of the need for artful manipulation of party groups and special interests. He was able to "sell" Boss Murphy and Tammany Hall on welfare legislation as a means of winning votes on the one hand, and on the other he could bide his time or accept a compromise when those opposed to his program were too strong for him to win a quick victory.

It was during the life of the Factory Commission that

Smith developed the pattern of thinking that he was to apply so brilliantly during his years as Governor. "What are the facts?" he would ask. What do experts propose to remedy the situation? How can their proposals be carried out? In ferreting out the facts he used his lifelong method of learning, the simplest method of the autodidact: he listened. Frances Perkins remarked that he was a keen judge of the credibility and disinterestedness of people he talked with, and was not easily taken in. He would ask the kind of question that required a clear answer; he could fairly dig information out of you. If you offered him conclusions, he would want to know the ground on which they were based. "What did you see? What did you learn? Where did you learn it?" And he listened attentively, never taking notes, but seemingly never forgetting what you had said, filing every little fact away in his mind to be drawn out when needed.

Having heard the proposals of the experts, the Commission's next step was to prepare reports for the Legislature, along with recommended legislation. By the end of the first year of its life, 1912, when Smith was Minority Leader of the Assembly, eight bills dealing with factory regulation were passed, and by 1914 thirty-six had been enacted into law. Many of these dealt with the registration of factories, standards of construction, fire prevention, and sanitary regulations. Far more important was the reorganization of the Labor Department, which had previously been so poorly managed that its head had been unable to provide the Commission with a list of the factories in the state, and lacked the power to enforce compliance with such safety laws as were already on the books.

The newly reorganized Labor Department was to consist

of an Industrial Commission of five members, appointed by the Governor and approved by the Legislature, vested with broad administrative and judicial powers. Among the experts who had been consulted on its composition and duties was Professor John R. Commons of the University of Wisconsin, the highly informed labor historian. Abram Elkus and Bernard Shientag put his proposals for safety regulation and enforcement into legal form. In 1915 the act was amended to give the Industrial Commission power to permit variations from the rules where practical difficulties or unnecessary hardships were involved. The rules and regulations of each industry were known as "codes," and since they could be modified by the Industrial Commission as new technological advances were made, they provided an elastic system of administrative law that worked admirably. These safety codes, set up after public hearings in which representatives of labor, the employers, and the public participated, were the forerunners of the industrial codes established by the Federal Government under the NRA in 1933.

While the Legislature was debating the new labor bills Smith was called upon again and again to explain details of the measures under consideration. To accomplish the reforms to which he was committed he was not above making shrewd bargains with conservative Republican leaders with whom he was on friendly terms, such as Ed Merritt or John Yale; in fact the program could not have been put over without their compliance. Frances Perkins remarked, moreover, that he was struck by the support the reform measures won from organizations and private persons all over the state. Two special trains were needed, for example, to accommodate the visitors attending an open hearing before a joint committee of the Senate and the Assembly, one starting from New York City and the other from Buffalo, both converging on Albany with their hundreds of social workers, university professors, architects, engineers, labor leaders, and businessmen. Smith never forgot how much popular support the reform proposals generated among the voters; in addition, as Tammany's legislative specialist in the Assembly, he found it highly significant that the testimony of outside experts carried great weight with an influential part of the public. Before his time most politicians had little business with technical experts. He was to utilize this discovery with much profit when he became Governor, having learned how to "use" people for the public good in a way that flattered their self-esteem, while at the same time swelling the ranks of his followers by his policies.

The final report of the Factory Investigation Commission was presented to the Legislature in 1915, with only one of the Commission's members dissenting from its conclusions. His was the voice of the real estate interests; he had come into the Commission late (having replaced Dowling) and had heard none of the testimony and visited none of the factories. Yet he vigorously opposed the standards and codes for factory buildings recommended, characterizing Miss Perkins as "a professional agitator" who alarmed the public without cause. Smith remarked later that men of this sort were "always declaring themselves in favor of the principle [involved] but could invariably find a way of explaining that . . . the proposed measure would not bring the result desired."

Another member, Samuel Gompers, raised objections to the Commission's recommendation that a Minimum Wage

Board be set up with power to fix wages for women. Gompers contended that the labor unions wanted no governmental interference in the matter of wages, which they preferred to handle through direct bargaining with employers. According to Miss Perkins, Smith was surprised to find a labor leader taking such a stand. He undertook to win Gompers over, addressing him with the utmost tact, and persuaded him that the minimum wage for women was intended to prevent their earnings from falling too low to sustain life, and as "a health measure, pure and simple." Gompers admitted that he had been looking at it solely from the economic point of view, but since Smith put it on humanitarian grounds, he would go along with the majority. Miss Perkins, recalling their discussion, said of Gompers, "I'm sure he agreed because he wanted to agree with Al Smith as so many others did."

Inspired by the epoch-making Factory Commission, the New York Legislature during three years made seven-league strides in enacting labor and welfare laws, whose beneficial effects were felt by the whole nation, for many states proceeded to study and imitate the new statutes. Meanwhile another historic reform measure, the Fifty-four-Hour Bill, for which Frances Perkins and other social workers had lobbied for years, was made into law at the same period, thanks to the powerful sponsorship of Smith and Wagner.

The bill was actually passed by a very narrow margin, after a breathtaking contest in which Miss Perkins demonstrated that she had learned much under the tutelage of Alfred Smith about the art of legislative maneuver. Assemblyman Edward Jackson of Buffalo, a former railroad laborer, and a bighearted fellow, had introduced the bill back in 1910, but thereafter Miss Perkins had vainly pursued the legislative committees in charge of it with her pleas to hold public hearings. The local statesmen, using the age-old arts of delay, repeatedly frustrated her hopes. Senator McManus, the boss of Hell's Kitchen, tried to help in the next session by introducing the same bill in the Senate, but through Smith Miss Perkins learned that the bill would not be reported out of committee. In his helpful, though hard-boiled manner, he explained to her that while the Democrats had endorsed the measure at their last convention, it was done only as a "show of action." They had assumed that they could rely on the Republicans to hold up the Fifty-four-Hour Bill.

After the furor over the Triangle Shirtwaist fire in New York City in late March, 1911, she felt new hope the bill would be presented and passed, but a smaller fire that began in the library of the Capitol adjacent to the Chamber turned the place into a shambles for several weeks, creating much confusion as the legislative session came to a close. In 1912 the persistent social worker went into battle again. At the time she gave a "cliff-hanger" account of how the Fifty-four-Hour Bill was maneuvered to final passage in the last hours of the 1912 session to her friend Leroy Scott, who published it in the *Metropolitan Magazine* for July, 1912.

She had counted the noses of the twenty-six senators whose votes were pledged for the bill, or enough to pass, when suddenly one of the lawmakers arose to offer four amendments in swift succession, and "fair, plausible amendments" they appeared to be, as she said. But their effect would be to kill off the bill for that session. McManus led the Democratic majority in voting them down, then moved for final passage. But a Republican Senator whose heart bled for the shirt and collar manufacturers of Troy broke in with a set speech on how much the women of his city preferred to work in the mills to staying at home. At this Big Tim Sullivan, a product of the Tammany machine in New York City, stepped in to compliment the preceding speaker in sardonic fashion: sure, and it was a fair sight to see the women and girls working in those bright, airy shops. "But it's a far finer sight at noontime," he said, "to see the fine big upstanding men fetching around the women's dinner pails!" Amid the laughter created by this sally, the roll call was taken, and the bill was passed.

There was still the hurdle of the Assembly Chamber, however. There the companion bill drawn by Jackson differed from the McManus Bill by exempting all cannery workers from such regulations. The pretext was that canning was a seasonal industry requiring long hours for a short period to avoid spoilage. They were at the last day before adjournment. Smith took the floor to oppose exemption of the cannery workers, in what was probably his shortest speech on record, yet long remembered. He was reported to have said:

> I have read carefully the commandment, "Remember the Sabbath Day, to keep it holy"; but I am unable to find in it any language that says, "except in the canneries."

Nevertheless the bill was passed as written.

To have opposed the provision exempting the canneries from control to the bitter end — as the Consumers' League might have desired her to do — would have meant the loss

of the measure for that year. But Miss Perkins quickly calculated that only a few thousand women and girls were at the
canneries in the season of a few months, while the Fifty-four-
Hour Bill would protect some 400,000 women workers all
year. There was no time left to reconcile the two versions.
Therefore she went at once to The McManus in the Senate,
and proposed that he resubmit the Jackson bill in place of
his own. He agreed, and, amid much tumult, the substitu-
tion was made.

Even so, danger loomed again in the very last moments.
Big Tim Sullivan and another Tammany regular had cast
their votes in advance, while the roll call was still to be completed, so that they might catch the night boat to New York
City. Two of the downstate Senators she had relied on, seeing that Big Tim was gone, changed sides and voted to defeat the bill. The McManus was still there. What were they
to do? he asked. "Move to reconsider," she cried. In frantic
haste she had a page boy telephone to the boat, which had
not yet left, to call Big Tim Sullivan. He came roaring back
up the hill to the State House, arriving just before the end
of the roll call to cast his vote again, and also to force the
two deserters into line once more. And thus the day was
won.

She felt no little panic, however, as she returned to New
York City to report to Florence Kelley, at the Consumers'
League, that the canneries had been exempted from the provisions of the law. "I went back in fear and trembling, thinking I'd probably lost my job," she recalled. Instead of rebuking her, Mrs. Kelley gave way to tears of joy and embraced her. At last they had got some limitations on the
hours of labor for women. Later they would work to

strengthen the law and eliminate night work, but they had made a great beginning.

It did not escape Alfred Smith that Frances Perkins had tough-minded qualities of her own as he observed her in action; he did not forget her as he rose in the political hierarchy. From that time forward he found it worthwhile to work with her and other pertinacious women who had taken up political action and whose entire sex, all the millions of them, now at last stood at the threshold of political equality with men.

CHAPTER VIII

Growth in Leadership: 1912-15

DURING THE FOUR years that followed his rise to the post of Majority Leader, Alfred Smith continued to gain in stature before the public, while his party shifted in and out of power, according to the momentary fortunes of war. He had become the legislative expert of the New York Democrats and a most useful member of their party machine, but despite his close working relations with Tammany Hall, his constructive achievements at Albany were winning him many admirers even among the civic reformers.

In the elections of November, 1912, the Democrats were carried back to power in New York State. Smith had already attended Democratic National Conventions as a delegate in 1904 and 1908. At Baltimore in 1912, he went down the line with the Tammany bloc from New York in opposing the nomination of Wilson, in favor of Champ Clark — though he learned to admire Woodrow Wilson. He heard William Jennings Bryan, still heroic on the platform, deliver himself of a sensational tirade against Tammany, whose chieftain, Murphy, headed the New York delegation, and against its alleged Wall Street allies, Thomas Fortune Ryan and August Belmont, also present among the New Yorkers. In effect,

Bryan, by his attack on the Tammany machine, helped
stampede the convention into the Wilson camp. The three-
cornered race that followed — when Theodore Roosevelt's
Progressive Republicans bolted from their party — made for
an easy Democratic victory in New York as in most other
states. As a consequence, Tammany's choice for the Governorship of New York, William Sulzer, a popular and progressive Congressman from New York City, was elected in
a Democratic sweep that won control of both legislative
houses.

One of the incidental effects of the Democratic triumph
of 1912 was to lift Alfred Smith to an office he had scarcely
hoped to attain, that of Speaker of the State Assembly. In
his recollections Smith remarks that hitherto it was customary for the New York City Democrats to select upstate
Protestants for the key offices of Majority Leader and
Speaker, in tacit recognition of the prevailing prejudice
against Irish Catholics from the metropolis. The same strategy of appeasement, as William V. Shannon has noted, was
followed by the predominantly Irish Catholic Democratic
machine in Boston, which for many years backed Yankees
for high office in Massachusetts. Thus Tammany had chosen
Dix, a Protestant from Albany, for the Governorship in 1910,
and Sulzer, likewise a Protestant, in 1912; Sulzer's running
mate, Lieutenant-Governor Martin H. Glynn, although a
Catholic, came from upstate. An exception to the general
rule had been made in 1911, when Smith was named Majority Leader, but when he was elected Speaker in 1912, as he
himself stated, it was the first time a man from New York
City, and, moreover, a Tammany man, had been chosen by
the Democrats for the office.

Smith still lived in the old East Side quarter in which he

had been born, but as his family increased in size he had moved to more spacious quarters. From 28 Oliver Street where they had resided for several years they had crossed the street to Number 25; there the family enjoyed the use of the basement and two floors above it. The birth of his youngest son Walter in this house in 1909 had brought the number of his children to five, three boys and two girls. The Oliver Street block, with its low-rise red brick houses, was then still a middle-class island in what had become a region of badly crowded six-story tenements. The local Democratic Club was around the corner on Madison Street, a place where anybody who had need of him might call to see Assemblyman Smith, everybody's good friend.

His domestic routine had taken on a pleasant pattern: when the Legislature was in session he would hurry back to New York toward the end of the week, to be met by Katie and the older children at Grand Central Station; then in company with several close friends the Smith couple would dine at some favorite restaurant and go to the theater to see a popular play or musical comedy. Besides his political work at the district clubs and his regular conferences with the wise men of Fourteenth Street, he occasionally had some routine real estate business to look after. This earned him a little extra money, much needed, for he was always hard up in those days. On Sundays, after Mass, he would walk across Brooklyn Bridge to Middagh Street in Brooklyn Heights, accompanied by members of his family and two dogs on leash, and call on his aging but still lively mother. During the week she would have read all the newspaper dispatches from Albany and would be ready with a volley of questions about what he had been up to.

On the great occasions in his career he loved to have his

family share his triumphs. And so as he took the oath of office as Speaker, at the beginning of the legislative session in January, 1913, he stood on the dais, ruddy-faced and beaming, flanked by his mother, his wife, and his five children. Striking his gavel against the lectern to open the proceedings, he spoke with much feeling of his long association with the Chamber, even as he seemed to be saying, "These are my people. It is my family, as well as myself, that you have chosen to honor."

In the turbulent session of 1913 that followed, Smith directed the transactions of the lower house with great energy, pressing with equal vigor for the passage of welfare bills and of measures increasing the patronage of his party. An indication of Tammany's new concern for progressive and pro-labor legislation was an improved Workmen's Compensation bill, introduced in January by Murphy's other son-in-law, Senator James A. Foley. A whole series of Factory Code bills, the first fruits of the labors of the Investigating Commission, were pushed through and signed by the Governor, despite the obstructive tactics of real estate and manufacturing lobbyists.

It was reported in the press that Smith was running the Assembly single-handedly, firmly, and with dispatch. "There is nobody else," wrote one reporter. "Nobody has to put their hands to their ears to hear what he is saying. His powerful voice is at times almost sinister." Another unfriendly witness described him as performing like a barker at Coney Island, yelling in a hoarse, raucous voice, and pounding his gavel repeatedly to get on with the business of the day. During the late sessions he would send out for food and sit munching sandwiches in the Speaker's chair, shouting out his rulings with his mouth full of food. "At times bills on the cal-

endar are rushed through at the rate of eight a minute," this
same observer wrote, to the accompaniment of roars from
the throne: "Read the last section!" "Call the roll!" "The bill
is passed!" He had long observed how bills could be rail-
roaded through the Legislature at the end of a session. Having been shelved in committee for months, they would be
brought out as emergency measures just before adjournment,
with the Governor's permission, thus evading the usual re-
quirement that they be printed three days preceding a vote.
Smith commanded many such last-hour raids on behalf of
the party organization, which he himself was later to describe as highly improper.

But the partisan action in which he took least pride in
later years was the impeachment of Governor Sulzer by his
own party at this time, an episode that he passed over
quickly in his memoirs, and one that caused his hagiogra-
phers some embarrassment. Sulzer was an odd character,
almost a caricature of a crusading politician, with his string
tie and waving forelock, his fervid and long-winded oratory,
his Bryanesque attitudes. While a member of Congress he
had played a part in the famous Pujo Committee Investigation of the "money trust," and along with Samuel Untermyer,
the committee's counsel, and Woodrow Wilson himself, had
urged breaking up the great banking and financial monopoly
in the interests of free competition.

It should therefore have caused no surprise when, early
in his term as Governor, he sponsored a bill to regulate the
New York Stock Exchange, which had always conducted
itself as a private club. It was a bill of which Smith, at first,
expressed his approval. In the past such bills had seldom
gone beyond the stage of debate, or had died in committee,
and this measure was to have a similar fate. The members

of the Stock Exchange, however, viewed the proposal with profound alarm, and their Republican friends in Albany joined them in the uproar against the Governor.

Having outraged his partisan opponents Sulzer now proceeded to alienate his supporters in Tammany Hall by coming out strongly for another measure then considered radical, the direct primary bill, which would eliminate the function of the party convention in the nomination of candidates for elective office. What was worse, the Governor denounced a bowdlerized version of a direct primary law that had been introduced by the Tammany Assemblyman Aaron J. Levy — and which Smith admittedly helped to write — as "a fraud and betrayal of the people." In short Sulzer, Tammany's own choice for the Governorship, bit the hand that fed him, and Murphy decided to show him who was master. Bills sponsored by the Governor were blocked in the Legislature by his own party, with Smith and Wagner leading the interference. Sulzer responded by denying appointments to Tammany followers. A similar manifestation against boss rule by Wilson in New Jersey — after the bosses had picked him to run for Governor — had won him national fame, and "Wild Bill" Sulzer was now charged with ambition to succeed Wilson in the White House. This was really too much. Murphy became implacable, and directed his henchmen in Albany to begin an investigation of Sulzer's conduct in the recent election campaign. The evidence uncovered led to the filing of charges in the Legislature that the Governor had diverted campaign funds to his own use. Articles of Impeachment were introduced and, amid furious debate, quickly passed.

Smith was quite aware that the Governor's cardinal sin

had been to turn against his political friends, those who had supported him in office for more than twenty years. The amount of campaign funds said to have been diverted was in fact relatively modest; other candidates had committed similar irregularities without suffering such cruel retribution. Smith's statements to the newspapers at the time indicate that he was ill at ease in the role of a leader of the execution squad. He was reported to have advised Murphy to drop the inquiry into Sulzer's campaign finances in order to avoid a public scandal that would injure the Democratic Party.

There was in fact dirty work on both sides. The evidence of Sulzer's misconduct was unmistakable, and made him unfit to rebuke Tammany Hall for its own sins. In his desperation he formed an alliance with William Randolph Hearst, who for some time had been trying to win for himself a leading role in the New York political scene. The Hearst newspapers published ferocious attacks on the Tammany organization, while defending Sulzer as an "innocent" who had been "framed." Hearst also employed detectives to trail Smith, Wagner, and other Tammany stalwarts, in the hope of uncovering some wrongdoing on their part, but without success. Sulzer was on his way out, ingloriously. He did not even take the stand in his own defense before the Court of Impeachment, which was made up of a body of legislators and the judges of the Court of Appeals. On their verdict of guilty, Lieutenant-Governor Martin Glynn succeeded to the office of Governor, and the boss of Tammany was appeased.

The unsavory Sulzer affair, however, occurring at the same time as a sensational scandal involving the New York City police force, made it fairly certain that the local Democrats would come to grief in the 1913 elections. In July, 1912, a professional gambler named Herman Rosenthal had been killed on the street in the middle of Manhattan in broad daylight, and his murderers had escaped from the scene while seven policemen looked on. Charles S. Whitman, then District Attorney of New York County, made a searching investigation of the city's police department, and was able to prove that the dead gambler had been forced to accept the partnership of Police Lieutenant Charles Becker, who took large payoffs in return for "protection." When Rosenthal one day threatened to squeal, Becker gave the order that he be eliminated. Whitman produced evidence of a widespread protection ring in the police department exacting tribute not only from gamblers but also from the operators of disorderly houses masked as hotels. After a prolonged trial in 1913, Becker was condemned to death, and the ambitious District Attorney became the Republican Party's successful candidate for Governor in the next year's elections.

All these unpleasant revelations, meanwhile, had stimulated the growth of a strong reform movement in the city itself. An impromptu political organization called The Committee of One Hundred and Seven, sponsored by the Citizens' Union and the City Club, put up a Fusion ticket to try to capture the principal city offices in 1913. John Purroy Mitchel, an independent, progressive Democrat, headed the slate, and in a three-party contest won the election for Mayor with only a minority of the total vote, although Tammany retained control of the Board of Aldermen. The "accidental Mayor," as he was called, was the hero of the anti-Tammany crusade that season. Pledged to establish the merit system for city employees and bring order into the budget, Mitchel also committed himself to clean up the

police and other departments with the help of a board of
strategy composed of civic reformers, social workers, and
university intellectuals, most of whom were wholly ignorant
of practical politics. There was to be much confusion as a
result of the clash between the Mayor and the city's en-
trenched officeholders, backed by the Board of Aldermen,
who worked to obstruct or delay the program of the Fusionists. The professionals grimly waited for the reform wave
to ebb, although some among them were growing sensitive
to the desire for a change among a large section of the electorate.

In November, 1913, Tammany lost not only its great
stronghold in New York City, but also the legislative majority
it had enjoyed in Albany, and in the following year the Democrats would lose the Governorship as well. Truly Tammany
was in deep trouble. Its councils were loud with dissension,
and Murphy himself was almost unhorsed. The crassness of
the New York Democratic machine — leaving aside its fraternal and charitable activities — derived from its self-limit-
ing character as an office-seeking association. It had no ide-
ology, no platform beyond satisfying the appetites of the
spoilsmen. In this shady company two men stood out un-
touched by scandal, Smith and Wagner, although they owed
their advancement in regional politics to the machine and
felt bound to support its partisan measures. By this period
both men had begun to show signs of looking beyond mere
office-grabbing toward a program of social welfare. In the
heyday of Wilsonian liberalism Smith and Wagner constituted the reform wing of the New York Democratic Party.
Both had worked hard to frame the new factory laws; both,
especially Smith, had been instrumental in securing passage

of the Workmen's Compensation Act. Vulnerable though he was on the score of his loyalty to the machine, Smith was steadily winning honors from outside the party organization as a legislator with humane ideals.

He was turning forty; he had served in the State Legislature for ten years now with increasing distinction; and he was a poor man still. The newspapers cited rumors that he had been marked for nomination to higher office, such as Borough President of Manhattan, or even Mayor of New York City. Indeed Murphy had made some vague promises to that effect at the time when Smith had been elected Speaker. Recently, however, Tammany had been taking some rude blows, and there was no certainty that such promises would be implemented. Perhaps to put pressure on his patrons, Smith began hinting to Foley and Murphy that he planned to quit the State Legislature at an early date and take some business position in which he could earn a decent living for his family. There was another post he thought he could fill, according to his intimates in the Assembly. Over several years, as Speaker or as Majority Leader, he had paid repeated visits to the spacious Executive Chamber on the second floor of the Capitol, and had come to understand thoroughly the operation of the Governor's office. But as a Catholic, a follower of Tammany Hall, and a man, moreover, from New York's East Side, he was not supposed to give this any serious thought.

Those were lean years for the Democrats, yet Smith, serving once more as Minority Leader in the Assembly, rose to new heights of achievement as he led the opposition to the Republican machine. The minority party in a legislative body, stripped of its power to win offices and feed at the pork barrel, can generally take a high moral position on measures affecting the public welfare. When the Democrats had enjoyed topheavy majorities, Smith and Wagner had given much of their time to promoting the partisan bills advanced by their political friends. Now, heading the opposition, they made a concerted onslaught on the ruling party which was working to emasculate the social welfare laws passed earlier, and this they could do in good conscience, for they had been largely instrumental in getting those laws on the statute books. Smith distinguished himself as the Democrats' most forceful public speaker; to the press his was a more colorful personality than Wagner's. When it was known that he would rise to speak newspaper reporters and members of the public would crowd into the galleries to hear him.

The Republicans in the Legislature were under the firm command of William A. Barnes of Albany County, once described by Smith as "probably as reactionary a man as I ever met." Assailing the Democrats for having sponsored what he called "socialistic legislation," Barnes promptly set to work to remove the teeth from the recently enacted welfare measures. Like its Democratic counterpart, the Republican machine also pushed through various ripper bills designed to relieve Democrats of their offices and replace them with deserving Republicans. They appropriated twice as much money for highways as their own Governor Whitman recommended, and, with the arrogance of power, reapportioned the aldermanic districts of New York City in order to strengthen the thin ranks of Republicans in that benighted metropolis.

In these days Smith was constantly embroiled with his parliamentary opponents. Indeed, he now carried the war beyond the Chamber in Albany, directing his appeals to the public at large through the press. For two years he had espoused a bill to provide a pension for widows left with small children. In 1915 the Republican majority threatened to prevent its passage, as before, on the ground that it would encourage pauperism. Smith gave one of his most forceful speeches, and one that was extensively reported in the New York newspapers, in defense of the bill, contending that the obligation of the government to protect the weak and poor was absolute. Using what was to become one of his favorite analogies, he pointed out that just as men had begun of late to understand the need to conserve the state's natural resources, such as forests, streams, and the soil, so they must also grasp the need to conserve the human resources of the state. The title of this bill, he said, should read, "An Act to Conserve the Family Life of the State." As he went on to plead for its enactment, he was inspired, no doubt, by the memory of his own widowed mother's plight when his father died:

> We are simply fixing and determining in time to come what is to be the policy of the State. Under the old system the widow-mother goes to the Police Court or to the charity organization when her husband dies, and her children are committed to an institution . . . What must be her feelings? What must be her idea of the State policy when she sees those children separated from her by due process of law, particularly when she must remember that for every one of them she went down into the valley of death that a new pair of eyes might look out into the world? What can be the feelings in the hearts of the children themselves separated from their mothers by what they must learn was due process of law in after years . . . ? That is the old system. That is the dark day we are walking away from.

The State of New York under the provisions of this act reaches out its strong arms to that widow and her children and says to them: "We recognize in you a resource to the State and we propose to take care of you, not as a matter of charity but as a matter of government and public duty."

Here the Minority Leader of the Democrats was using a homely rhetoric of his own device, charged with old-fashioned Irish sentimentality, but carrying a powerful appeal for decent and kindly citizens up and down the state. The women representatives of the various welfare bureaus listening in the Chamber, as Frances Perkins relates, were often moved to tears on hearing his speeches for the measures they urged.

When the 1915 session of the Legislature adjourned in April, the Assembly Chamber in Albany became the scene of a long-awaited convention summoned to draw up a revised constitution for the State of New York, one more in accord with changing administrative practices and the requirements of a new day. It was at that time the rule to hold such a constitutional convention once every twenty years; the last one had been held in 1895, and the urgency of revision had become apparent to all those who had cause to examine the old charter, or plan legislation within its restrictions. This cumbersome document, a dense thicket of legal provisions and prescriptive devices, reflected the unplanned structure of the state government; the assumption by the government of new powers had created one hundred and fifty-two administrative departments and agencies where there had been only about sixty ten years earlier, and some of the constitution's articles made fraud easy, malfeasance in office likely, and political deals inevitable.

The one hundred and sixty delegates to the convention represented the two parties in the ratio established at the last state election, thus giving the Republicans a two-thirds majority. Most of them were members of the Legislature, but the Governor had also appointed several Republicans who were experts in constitutional law or otherwise distinguished in public life, such as United States Senator Elihu Root (chairman of the convention), former United States Attorney-General George W. Wickersham, the eminent lawyers Henry L. Stimson, John Lord O'Brian, and Louis Marshall, as well as Jacob G. Schurman, President of Cornell University, and Seth Low, formerly Mayor of New York City and at one time President of Columbia University. The nominal leader of the Democratic delegation was Morgan O'Brien, a noted jurist, but from the first it was apparent that their bright star was to be Alfred Smith.

It was one of several turning points in Smith's life, a moment of revelation as much to himself as to others. He emerged as a shrewd expert in legislative affairs, who also knew well the administrative processes of the state departments and the duties attached to the Governor's office. Moreover he was given to plain talk, to calling things by their right names, and doing this with much good humor and wit. In his talks during the five months of the sessions he ranged widely over the problems of the state government, and seemed ready, at every turn, to bolster his arguments with precise details, figures, dates, without once referring to notes or books or other authorities. Almost from the beginning he was called on for advice, or for the actual facts in a case. He knew the reasons why certain bills were passed, and why they had been drawn up in such a way as to evade constitutional limitations. He knew the history of many parts of the old constitution, and of the various amendments tacked on to it to enable the Legislature to take such action as it deemed fit at a particular time.

The number of subjects he discussed was fantastic: the salaries of members of the Legislature, the role of emergency messages in procuring undesirable legislation, home rule for cities, the budget and appropriation bills, apportionment of seats in relation to population, the role of special privilege, impeachment methods, bond issues, and taxation. Also the short ballot, reorganization of the state departments, the minimum wage, education, waterpower and conservation projects, civil service, and many others.

Although he could use legal or formal language when it was called for, his speech was more often studded with homely illustrations of the points he wanted to stress. The proposal to raise the salaries of members of the Legislature led him to explain why the fifteen hundred dollars a year they had earned since 1894 was not enough. He urged that Assemblymen be paid a living wage to keep them honest, and not be driven to rely too much on their "lulu" (legislative slang for "in lieu of expenses"); then he added ruefully, "We can't be seen coming out of the Essex Lunch," a reference to the low-priced cafeteria near the Capitol on State Street.

Out of his own experience he denounced the emergency bills as a source of much skullduggery in the Legislature, leading to eleventh-hour padding of appropriations. In a frank confession of his own role in such schemes he remarked,

I do not say it has been done by any one party any more than
the other. I was Chairman of the Committee on Ways and
Means for long and stormy sessions. I was the Speaker for
another . . . and had something to say about when appropriations bills were to pass, and I myself directed that they should
wait until the last moment because it was easier. Now that is
the truth about it. If you do away with the emergency message, you will compel the majority leader, you will compel the
Committee on Ways and Means, the men that are responsible
for the legislation, to have their program ready and put it
through, and they can do it.

There is another class of bills that the emergency message
has been very useful in passing . . . the bills that give rise to
dispute between the two houses. The Senate does not agree
with . . . the Assembly . . . and vice versa, and finally in the
last days . . . when the flags are flying from the Capitol and
the band is playing and everybody feels happy over the last
$250 draw [of salary] and a good time for the summer — they
will patch up their differences and say, "Well, go downstairs
and get a message [emergency message from the Governor]
and put it right through," and they do it.

He could treat some subjects with humor, provoking
laughter with his anecdotes, but he was also capable of expressing honest passion on matters such as home rule for
cities. The Republicans in the convention, under the influence of their liberal members, such as Stimson, Wickersham,
and editor Herbert Parsons of the New York *Tribune*, offered
a few extensions to the existing home rule provisions in the
new constitution, but these still required that a city wishing
to make changes in its own charter, affecting its local authority, must first obtain the approval of the State Legislature
before such changes could become effective. In defense of
these restrictions one of the Republicans argued that "the

new people" congregating in great cities like New York had no knowledge of democratic institutions and were easily manipulated by crooked political bosses. The same speaker went on to say that the voting cattle of the big cities must be kept under control by the "upstate . . . Anglo-Saxon and Protestant element." In the course of this debate Smith scoffed at the notion that corruption was limited to big cities:

Now we have heard an awful lot about fraud at elections, and the men who proclaim [complain?] the loudest about the manner in which elections are conducted in the thickly populated centers come from districts where if fraud is not committed, there is abundant opportunity to commit it . . . They say . . . "Why in the little country districts everybody knows his neighbor; there cannot be anything wrong there." One member of the House said: "Yes, and he even knows his neighbor's horse when he goes down the road," and somebody forthwith suggested that possibly the horse might answer for him on election day if he was away.*

When President Schurman of Cornell argued that the state must place some restrictions on its local subdivisions, just as the Federal Government had in the case of the Philippines, then a colony, Smith bridled at the parallel implying that the citizens of New York City were entitled to only those liberties "Washington was satisfied to give to the half-civilized Filipinos." He vigorously attacked the idea that the will of five million people should be overruled by a little conclave in Albany whose power was grounded on rotten boroughs. "Take that foolishness out!" he exclaimed. "If

---

* According to some scholars, county politics was the largest field of political fraud in the United States.

the people are adopting the charter, let it be their charter."
To a delegate from Ossining (site of a state prison) who had
urged a literacy test that would exclude foreign-language-
speaking immigrants from the ballot he suggested caustically
that not all persons who read and wrote English well were
qualified to cast an honest vote. The district of the gentleman from Ossining, he said, contained "people who could not
only sign their own name but that of others as well."

One bone of contention between the Republicans and
Democrats was the reapportionment of aldermanic districts
in New York City. The party in power always tried to re-
draw the district lines to gain an advantage at the polls,
professing always to be acting in the interests of justice, a
myth that Smith rejected with vehemence. In one talk he
recalled how the constitutional convention of 1895, dominated by the Republicans, had readjusted the boundaries
of a senatorial district on Manhattan Island. Beginning at
Fourteenth Street their committee had marked off a strip of
territory running along the gold coast of Fifth Avenue to
Ninety-Sixth Street three miles long and two miles wide.
This was done, he wound up sardonically, "so that the candidate for Senator . . . could on registration days and election days just walk up Fifth Avenue, look up and down the
side streets and see if the district captains and poll clerks
were absolutely Republican, and thereby assure them of at
least one State Senator on Manhattan Island."

He mocked at the pretention that reapportionment could
be carried out impartially. "Apportionments have always
spelled politics," he exclaimed. The majority party changed
boundaries with calculation. In a frank attempt to get a
Fusion or anti-Tammany Board of Aldermen for the second

two years of Mayor Mitchel's term, a Republican-dominated
Legislature had "made all the Republican districts this way
[hands held a short distance apart] and the Democratic districts that way [hands held far apart]. The Mayor said he
would like to sign the bill," Smith added, "but it was too
raw, it was more than he could stand."

He showed a knowledge of the state's finances that created
surprise among the members of the convention. After listening attentively while Stimson delivered a carefully
drafted report on the Executive Budget, which contained
proposals for eliminating extravagance in the departments,
he asked for the floor and presented his own analysis of the
problem, as seen from "the practical side rather than the
theoretical side." Stimson's recommendations did not go
half far enough, he observed. The real source of waste was
the logrolling of the legislators for local improvements in
their home districts. Such appropriations generally came to
twice the amount originally called for in the different departmental budgets at the beginning of each legislative session,
and the additional appropriations were usually obtained
through those emergency bills passed at the last hour which
he had criticized earlier. One Republican delegate protested that this was a gross exaggeration, that only one such
bill had been passed in the last session, and it had been
vetoed by the Governor.

Smith: Will the gentleman yield?
Hinman: Yes.
Smith: There were seventeen of them . . . Seventeen became
law.

Asked by the chairman to supply the facts in the case, Smith,
without notes, rattled off the list:

Senator Wicks' bill for a canal bridge; Assemblyman Maier's Waterloo Bridge, $3,000; a footbridge at Seneca Falls, $5,000; reconstruction of the Potsdam School, $100,000; to fix up the wall of the canal feeder, Oneida, $4,000; Senator Brown's Minett Bridge bill, $50,000, with an additional $300,000 for the Lyons Falls Bridge . . .

And he went on to name all seventeen emergency bills which at the last hour of the recent session had increased the cost of local improvements by some $700,000. It was an amazing feat of memory.

Then he offered his own suggestions for changes in Executive Budget procedures. Department heads, he proposed, should be required to submit their estimates under oath, as a means of persuading them to treat the matter less lightly, and making it more difficult to obtain supplemental appropriations. Specifications for local improvements should be spelled out clearly, and submitted in good time so that they could be subject to careful scrutiny. Stimson was so impressed with Smith's comments that he accepted several of his recommendations without further argument.

Smith's enlightened views on legislative methods and administrative procedures did not, however, indicate any break with the party system or with Tammany Hall at that time. Stimson and other liberal Republicans, clinging to the belief that merely by placing honest men in office most political ills would be cured, proposed an amendment that would extend the term of office of the Civil Service Commissioner to overlap that of the Governor, and thus help reduce party pressure on appointments. Smith then voiced the skepticism of the Tammany men toward all such goo-goo schemes, arguing that in any case party pressure would be brought to bear on appointments, and that the Governor ought to be held responsible for the performance of his own Civil Service Commissioner. Moreover, he observed shrewdly, the Republicans seemed eager to reform the civil service only while they held control in the state. The proposed amendment would enable them to retain their appointees in office and freeze out the Democrats even should the opposition party regain power. These arguments had a specious ring, and it is worthy of note that Smith later underwent a change of heart on this question, and did much to raise the standards of the state's civil service system.

Although he usually kept a jump ahead of his opponents in the debate, while regaling them with his humorous sallies, the opposition leaders, such as Barnes, repeatedly tried to bring him to heel. On one occasion, while explaining the workings of the Legislature, he recalled that when he was Minority Leader of the Assembly, he had given a friendly welcome to the lone Socialist elected to the Legislature that year, a man from Schenectady. He had described the proceedings in the Chamber to the newcomer, and had even prevailed on Speaker Merritt to appoint him to several committees. "When he found that the debate was open and unrestricted, and he was able to participate freely in the discussion," Smith continued, "and he found that seventy-six votes and only seventy-six votes did anything in this chamber, he went immediately down to the Ten Eyck Hotel barbershop and got a haircut — " At this point Barnes interrupted him with a point of order on the ground that he had exceeded his speaking time. Smith pleaded with the presiding officer, "Mr. Chairman, I wish the gentleman from Albany had let me get out of the barbershop; I don't like to finish there."

The convention made serious efforts to deal with the problem of reorganizing the state's sprawling executive departments. After studying the Republicans' proposals Smith pointed out that some of them made for more, rather than fewer offices, and for more jobs and payouts. In the course of his rebuttal, one of the Republican delegates, Frederick Tanner, taxed Smith with taking his orders from Tammany Hall when he went down to New York for the weekend, and hinted that that was the case in the weekend just passed. Smith took the floor and avowed that he liked to go to New York and "find out what they think of things there," but that by chance he had happened to spend the last weekend in Saratoga with his family. His confession continued: while in Saratoga he had received a long-distance call from someone at Tammany Hall. And what did his Tammany Hall friend want to know? He wanted information about a bill providing for a new state office. And who had sponsored it? "I said: 'A gentleman named Tanner, the Republican state chairman.' 'Read him page five of the Governor's last message to the Legislature,'" said the person at the other end of the telephone. In that message, Smith concluded with his widest grin, Governor Whitman, a Republican, to be sure, had severely criticized those who contributed to "the increase, on an unprecedented scale, in the number of state offices."

Smith gave one hilarious instance of how bureaucratic redundancy frustrated the efforts of the Legislature itself to bring order into the proliferating departments. He told of how the members had tried to remove the Surveyor of Adirondack Lands, an official who had absolutely no functions to perform, by cutting off his salary and denying him the use of office space in the Capitol. The Superintendent of Public Buildings then assigned the man to a little attic room "where all the brooms and mops and pails were kept, and there was no window or air." Nevertheless the official brought up his sign and hung it over the door, and, said Smith, "He then sued the State of New York in the Court of Appeals, which finally ordered his salary appropriated as fixed by the statutes previously."

In the closing days of the convention there was a rousing debate over the merits of the various social welfare measures enacted under Democratic sponsorship between 1911 and 1913. Determined to undo this legislation, the Republican boss Barnes introduced a constitutional amendment that would serve as a declaration of permanent policy, banning forever what he called socialistic and class legislation. The language of the amendment was general; it forbade "granting to any class of individuals any privilege or immunity not granted equally to all members of the State," and Barnes defended it in the hallowed rhetoric customarily employed by the extreme right in American politics. This amendment, he said, was a means of protection "for the true principles of individual freedom, without the interference or regulation of the state," and would help preserve "the American theory of life . . . the traditions of our country . . ."

Even George Wickersham objected that Barnes was going a bit far, that such an amendment would tie the hands of the Legislature too rigidly, so that any future laws for the benefit of working people would require a constitutional amendment. But Wickersham knew that the cause of social legislation had a more ardent advocate present than himself; though he had been given a half hour to speak, he limited

himself to ten minutes, then yielded his remaining time to
Smith, because, as he said, "I think he can do better with the
argument than I can."

Smith then rose to give one of his most famous extempore
speeches, speaking for almost an hour and striking off sentences that should have been cast in bronze and mounted
in public places for the people of the state to remember. He
offered a definition of democracy quite at variance with the
conception of Mr. Barnes:

> The gentlemen around this chamber would lead us to believe
> that law in a Democracy is the expression of some Divine or
> eternal right. I am unable to see it that way. My idea of law
> and democracy is that it is the expression of what is best, what
> fits present-day needs of society, what goes farthest to do the
> greatest good for the greatest number.

He denied that fire and safety laws for factories, or compensation for injury in industry, constituted a privilege or immunity for any class. In a passage reminiscent of his speech
on the Widows' Pension Bill he exclaimed,

> Labor laws are enacted for the preservation of the health of
> the men of the State, because after all what is the State?
> Green fields, and rivers and lakes and mountains and cities?
> Why not at all. It is the people, all the people of the State,
> and anything that tends to make the members of the State
> strong and vigorous helps to make the State so, and every one
> of these enactments has been for the general good and could
> in no way be described as a privilege.

In his conclusion he pointed out that because of its own
strength and power wealth could protect itself, and added,

> The great curse in poverty lies in the utter helplessness that
> goes with it. Having that in mind, may I ask you, is it wise,

is it prudent for this Convention to do what it can to reduce
the basic law to the same sharp level of the caveman's claw,
the law of the sharpest tooth and the angriest brow, and the
greediest jaw? I respectfully but firmly suggest that we should
not favorably report this . . .

In another phase of the debate, a little earlier, he had
taken up the question of the minimum wage, which had been
recommended by the Factory Investigating Commission but
had never come to a vote. This was opposed by Barnes and
other Republicans on grounds similar to those used for the
amendment on social legislation: minimum wage laws would
spread pauperism, render employers unequal vis-à-vis labor,
and discourage thrift and self-reliance. These spurious arguments gave Smith the opportunity to go into the history of
the Factory Investigating Commission and describe its findings with regard to wages paid to women and child workers.
He recalled what the Commission had uncovered in the way
of sweatshops, overworked mothers, of children employed
for sixteen hours a day for sixty cents, of the many who went
without breakfast or meat for weeks on end in order to buy
a pair of shoes. "There has been a great deal of talk against
the Factory Commission," he said:

> There has crept into the minds of some people a little jealousy
> about the great work done by the Factory Commission. But
> after careful . . . study of testimony the Commission has come
> to the conclusion that the State is justified in protecting under-
> paid women and minors in the interests of the State and society.

Whereas women were almost entirely unorganized, he
added, and hence powerless to win concessions from their
employers, men were able to obtain a minimum wage
through the strength of their unions. Then he struck a note
of pathos, echoing perhaps the arguments of his social worker

friends, as he discoursed on the critical health and moral problems of a girl working long hours for wretched pay. Would she not be tempted into a life of sin? Would she not be inclined to ask

> "Shall I not sell myself to make more than $6 a week?" But the absence of amusement, the barrenness and ugliness of life, the whole thing combined with unemployment does tend powerfully in that direction . . . In the end they become charges upon the State.

Smith, in short, worked tirelessly to place on the record the "plain facts" before the delegates, and his words had some impact on the more intelligent among them. Although the majority still supported Barnes's amendment on "class legislation," its terms were so modified — thanks to the intervention of Wickersham and Stimson — that it became merely the expression of a pious wish.

When the convention adjourned it was conceded on all sides that Smith had covered himself with glory. Elihu Root said that he was "the best informed man on the business of the State," while George Wickersham called him "the most useful man at the convention." They had not really known much about Smith before this. Once the sessions began, however, some of the bigwigs who had only thought of him as the representative of a Tammany district, realized that they had a kind of genius of popular politics in their midst, as Frances Perkins wrote.

But while his own contribution to the discussions was outstanding, the convention did much for him too. His acquaintance had been largely limited to local politicians up to 1911, when the Factory Commission had thrown him together with social reformers such as Frances Perkins and

Mary Dreier, as well as public-spirited lawyers like Abram Elkus and Bernard Shientag. But he had never had much contact heretofore with men of large affairs and national reputation. The debates with personages like Root, Stimson, Wickersham, Low, and Schurman offered a challenge to his mind. They discussed general ideas or theories of government in a way that was novel to him; yet he caught on quickly, and stored away a good deal of what he had learned.

His motions were voted down at almost every turn, to be sure, but in the last analysis he proved himself more sagacious than his Republican opponents. At one moment he urged them strongly to submit the proposed constitutional amendments to popular referendum as several separate items, warning that if they were presented in a single package the good and the bad would be rejected together. His advice was ignored, and the amended charter was voted down overwhelmingly by the electorate in November, as he had predicted.

Popular recognition of his public services and acclaim in the press was sweet, but he was still poor, nevertheless, on his $1500 a year and a few real estate fees. Promotion had come to him all too slowly. He had let it be known in party circles that the session of 1915 would be his last in the Legislature, and for a year or more Tom Foley had been prodding Murphy to put Smith in a way to gain higher office. "We can't keep Al Smith in the Assembly any longer," Foley is said to have told Murphy. "His kids are growing up and he is a poor man."

By the standards of the time, Smith was indeed poor, and especially so for a Tammany politician. Despite the temptations and opportunities of years in the political arena, he had never been touched with the breath of scandal, had never been charged with profiting from his position or his information. Franklin Roosevelt once told Frances Perkins that "Murphy always made it a point to keep Al honest. He never let Smith get smeared or tangled up with any of the dirty deals. He took great pains that they should never involve Al in any of these things because he thought he was a capable fellow and could go far." Actually Smith never needed Murphy as his moral preceptor, and Roosevelt's compliment seems backhanded.

On one of the last days of the convention Smith had the floor — he was discussing the Speaker's power to obtain a quorum by directing the Sergeant-at-Arms to bring in, or even "arrest" members who had intentionally absented themselves — when Mark Eisner, a Democratic Assemblyman, asked if he would yield.

> Eisner: The gentleman has been speaking a great deal about the power of the Sergeant-at-Arms to arrest members. I desire to announce . . . that if the gentleman is successful this fall he will be in a position to arrest everybody but the Coroner . . . Word has just been received that Alfred E. Smith is to receive the Democratic nomination for the office of Sheriff in the County of New York.

The office of Sheriff was one of the richest plums within the purview of the party machine, with salary based on fees then amounting to about $60,000 annually for a two-year term. For Smith it meant, at long last, relief from near poverty, as well as the prospect of being able to put something aside for the future. His nomination in New York County, with the blessings of the machine, was, moreover, equivalent to certain election. All that summer, week after week, the metropolitan dailies had carried full accounts of his speeches at the constitutional convention. Never a man to hide his light under a bushel basket, he admitted that the convention had afforded him a great opportunity, adding frankly, "And I never allowed my campaign managers to overlook anything that happened [there]."

His candidacy won broader support than Tammany was accustomed to receiving. The New York *World* commented that Murphy had been driven to call on the party's strongest stump speaker, and an honest man, as well, to help the Democratic slate. An editorial in the (Republican) *Tribune* saluted Smith as the city's most valuable representative in Albany these eleven years, and gave him credit for "tons of brains." To be sure, the writer continued, he was a machine politician who took his orders, but "he has not hesitated to oppose Tammany in conference, and he has never lacked the courage to tell Murphy to his face what other Democrats hesitated to whisper around the corner." And to the astonishment of some of the city's do-gooders, the Citizens' Union, habitually anti-Tammany, also gave the nomination their warm approval. Over the years the Citizens' Union had modified their earlier half-praise, half-censure of his voting record in the Assembly, and they now rated him as a rising politician from whom great things could be expected.

In running for the office of Sheriff Smith campaigned outside of his own bailiwick in the Second Assembly District for the first time in his career. Addressing larger audiences than he had ever faced before, in meeting halls throughout the city, he stumped not only for his own election but in behalf of all the Democratic candidates for city and state offices. The themes of his speeches were the social laws sponsored by the Democrats in the Legislature, home rule, and the proposed constitution, which he urged his listeners to reject, and the air of sincerity with which he addressed himself to these problems made him stand forth as the champion of the great heterogeneous metropolitan population.

Largely as a result of his forceful campaigning, New York City rolled up a huge majority for the Democrats. He was by all odds one of the liveliest campaigners in all the annals of regional politics, reveling in the rough and tumble debates, the excitement, the roaring crowds ("I like it . . . It gets into your blood," he said). However serious and factual he could be on occasion, he never neglected an opportunity to disarm an opponent or turn a question to his own advantage with a quip. When someone happened to ask him whether the Sheriff enjoyed comfortable quarters in the New York County jail, he replied, "They don't punish the Sheriff like that down here. He doesn't have to live in jail. They just feed him to death."

On the Saturday before Election Day he returned home to Oliver Street from an extended speaking tour to be the guest of honor at a neighborhood welcoming party. The street had been swept clean, and the ends of the block were roped off against vehicular traffic; American flags flew from every building, and as night fell lanterns shone at every window, lighting up election posters that carried photographs of Smith's still youthful and handsome face. At 6:30 P.M. the festivities began, when a brass band in a passageway adjacent to Public School Number 1 burst forth, and thousands of people came pouring into the street, some singing, some pairing off into a dance. Even old Tom Foley and Congress-

man Dan Riordan cavorted about. It was Old Home Night
in the Fourth Ward.

Smith's "host of admiring friends" seemed like a gathering
of many nations, including not only a large contingent of
Irish-Americans, but also Italians, Germans, Russians, Greeks,
and Jews, not to speak of Chinese from the nearby Mott
Street area, who appeared in colorful Oriental costumes and
offered Smith lavish gifts from the Far East. Among them
were something like a thousand pretty girls who insisted on
kissing the hero of the occasion. The hero himself bore this
treatment with equanimity, and danced until his face flamed
red, as it often did under exertion, while his stout handsome
Katie looked on good-naturedly. These were his own constituents, and, miraculously, he knew most of them by name.
For eleven years he had looked after them in times of trouble,
playing the part of peacemaker in family disputes, now helping a man win compensation from a neighborhood dentist
because his wife's dentures didn't fit, or getting an applicant
into the steamfitters' union after he had been rejected. The
variety of his unpaid services to the community could scarcely
be reckoned.

At last, still blithe but owning to fatigue, he stationed himself on the stoop of his house, with his wife and sons and
daughters by his side, to watch the children of the neighborhood as they formed a torchlight procession and paraded
around and around Oliver, Henry, and Madison Streets and
back. Someone counted up to three thousand children in the
parade. These immigrants produced large families, one guest
observed. There was Mrs. Lehan with eight, Mrs. McDer-
mott with seven, Mrs. Napoli with nine, and Rabbi and Mrs.
Cohen with fourteen! Didn't Al feel lonesome, one of his

waggish Irish friends asked, to meet "all the local members of the Anti-Race-Suicide Club," and he with only five children? Smith was not too tired for banter. "Don't blame me," he answered. "Remember for twelve years I have been a member of the State Legislature and had to spend my winters in Albany."

CHAPTER IX

The First State Campaign

DURING THE NEXT three years Smith's activities were centered almost entirely in New York City, which came to regard him as one of her first citizens. After the lean years as an Assemblyman he was prosperous, and life was good, for his share of the shrievalty fees, largely from bankruptcies and foreclosures, netted him $105,000 in two years, in addition to his salary. He was earning almost as much per week as he had formerly received per year, a change in fortune that could not but increase his natural bounce and optimism. During this period his hearty laughter and his broad smile were much in evidence at the popular Broadway theaters he regularly attended with his wife and friends, or at political gatherings and banquets where he was in strong demand as a speaker.

The duties of the Sheriff he found not to his taste and quite dull; he was therefore content to have them carried out in routine fashion by his staff, while he "looked for things to do." His boyhood friend, John F. Gilchrist, served as one of his chief deputies. Around that time someone asked him if he did not favor eliminating the large fees of county

sheriffs, and putting them on a straight salary basis, a reform
he himself had once sanctioned. "Have a heart," he said
plaintively, "I have never been a mercenary man." He was
quite willing to have the reform introduced, but only after
he had finished his term, and paid off the debts he had accumulated. Moreover, as Tom Foley warned him, he would
be expected to contribute part of his earnings to help the
party organization and his fellow Democrats, either deserving or needy, unless he chose to show them "the marble
heart" — an unlikely contingency.

Fortune shone upon him, yet he changed in no way, remaining as unaffected, as approachable to all men as before.
Perhaps he was a trifle more dignified, but added poise would
be the natural outcome of his years and his improved situation. Nor did he then dream of leaving the old house on
Oliver Street, now almost engulfed in the slums and shadowed by tall, ugly tenements. But where he had formerly
occupied only the lower floors, he now took over the whole
building and added a much-needed second bathroom.

In frequent appearances during those years, before gatherings of businessmen or meetings of various ethnic groups, he
consciously perfected his technique of public speech. At
one of these affairs, in 1916, he delivered himself of so many
funny cracks and such choice anecdotes that his audience
was convulsed with laughter throughout. A reporter present
recalled that when Smith sat down his listeners rose to their
feet to cheer him. The newspaperman, an old friend, said to
Smith afterward, "That was the most perfect speech. You
were never funnier." Smith astonished him by observing
soberly that he was dissatisfied with his own performance;
he had indulged in too much jesting.

I am in danger of being classed as a humorist [he said]. If I keep on making these funny speeches people will think I can't do anything else. There is nothing more dangerous to the reputation of a public man than that of being consistently humorous.*

The next time Smith appeared in public he would speak in a more serious vein, he promised, and yet make the public listen to him.

About two months later, in February, 1917, he had occasion to address a large audience once more at a banquet in the Hotel Biltmore. The function was a dinner of the third panel of the Sheriff's Jury, attended by 1000 prominent New Yorkers, among them lawyers, businessmen, editors, and college professors, as well as Tammany district leaders and captains. It was customary in those pre-Prohibition days to serve cocktails before, and highballs and wine with the dinner, and by the time Smith rose to give his speech everyone was thoroughly relaxed and cheerful, anticipating the typical Al Smith comedy that was to follow. They were taken by surprise when he rose, assumed a solemn manner, and addressed them on the subject of the international crisis confronting the United States, now on the verge of war with the Central Powers. State and city governments would be seriously affected by the nation's emergency, which called for the gravest kind of deliberation, he told them. His often harsh voice, under beautiful control, was rich and musical as he launched into a discussion of the foreign crisis. Our country would be drawn into the European war on the side of the Allies, he predicted, and eventually we would win.

---

* Adlai Stevenson might have profited by this observation when running for the Presidency many years later.

His listeners were impressed by his approach to national problems, as by the eloquence and breadth of vision of his speech. It is noteworthy that while thousands of his constituents in Manhattan, especially those of Irish and German origin, were strongly opposed to our involvement in the European war, Smith showed no anti-British sentiment, but took what was considered the patriotic line. He could never forget how much he himself owed to our free democratic institutions, he said. This was a new Smith; yet he held his audience spellbound for a whole hour and again received a standing ovation.

There was much gossip in the press at this time about the likelihood of Smith's being nominated for some higher city office. In 1917 the Democrats counted on turning out the Fusionist-Republicans, and many thought Smith's nomination for Mayor would guarantee victory. He remarked afterward that while Mitchel possessed outstanding abilities, he was "a thousand miles away from being a politician," primarily because he did not know how to handle people and had an ungovernable temper.

Frances Perkins was by chance in a position to confirm this judgment, having recently allied herself with one of Mitchel's close associates. In the late summer of 1913 she married Paul Caldwell Wilson, who was appointed budget secretary to the Mayor shortly after the elections of that year. At the time Miss Perkins adhered to no political party, although her work for the National Council on Safety and the Factory Investigating Commission brought her into frequent and close contact with Democratic leaders Smith and Wagner. In the milieu in which she moved, however, there were reformers of every persuasion, and among these Paul Wilson, a Progressive Republican, was rated as a forward-looking economist. The young couple had much in common, despite what Robert Moses has described as a marked difference in temperament. Born in 1876, Wilson was a native of Chicago, and had attended Dartmouth College and the University of Chicago. Coming to New York a few years before the arrival of Miss Perkins, he soon gained the repute of a man of charm, and was known as a gay bachelor with a wide circle of friends.

Miss Perkins came to the married state with some reluctance, she confessed; she had already turned down several flattering offers, including one proposal from Sinclair Lewis, so much did she cherish her independence. Having reached the age of thirty-three, she felt it was only right to retain her own name for professional purposes, on the ground that she had begun to make a place for herself as Frances Perkins, whereas if she were to call herself Mrs. Wilson she would be set back in her career.* Career or not, she had two unsuccessful pregnancies before 1916, when her daughter Susanna was born.

Wilson joined the Mitchel staff through the intercession of his good friend Henry Bruère, head of the Bureau of Municipal Research, an organization for the study of public administration in its various aspects. A whole group of civic re-

---

* Despite malicious stories that gained some circulation, she was not an out-and-out Lucy Stoner. One of these tales describes her as registering at an upstate hotel under her maiden name, even though accompanied by her husband. To the hotel manager, who raised embarrassing questions, the couple explained that they were legally married, and proposed that he call an old friend nearby to confirm it. The old friend is said to have denied any knowledge of the Wilsons at all, by way of a joke, and they had to leave the premises. Frances Perkins said the story was made of whole cloth.

formers were trained there, including Wilson and Robert
Moses, who also became one of Mitchel's aides. Mitchel had
pledged that he would introduce business efficiency into the
city government, and for this purpose he brought Bruère into
his administration as City Chamberlain, relying on the
professor's specialized knowledge to effect a sweeping reorganization of the municipal departments. Bruère went
so far as to recommend the abolition of his own office, which
he characterized as merely ornamental, but his proposals for
draconian reforms in the rest of the city government aroused
horror among the old-line politicians. Even Smith referred
to Bruère as an "outsider" from Chicago.*

The first years of the marriage between Frances Perkins
and Paul Wilson coincided with Mitchel's term of office,
which brought her into close contact with the Mayor and
the group surrounding him. This early opportunity to observe an important officeholder in action was to sharpen her
appreciation of the two other leading politicians with whom
she was to serve, particularly Smith. For although she found
Mitchel "able, effective, sharp," a man capable of engaging
the loyalties of a few associates, he lacked the human touch,
the magnetism to attract the masses of citizens. In the course
of many staff meetings at her home she perceived that he was
a difficult person, temperamental, inclined to be moody. He
was also subject to frequent painful migraines that made him
unfit to work in his office and required that he be protected
from the prying eyes of newspapermen. The reform administration begun with such high hopes quickly ran into strong

---

* Professor Bruère, something of a pioneer, had previously conducted a
course in government administration at the University of Chicago, Paul C.
Wilson having been one of his students.

opposition; as a Fusion group it had no solid backing from either party. Among others Paul Wilson had his troubles with an unfavorable press, a chronic ailment of officeholders, as Miss Perkins was to appreciate when she herself held posts in government later on.

Conditions in New York got out of control soon after Mitchel took office, partly because of the economic dislocations caused by the war in Europe. In 1914, at the start of the war, there was a severe unemployment crisis throughout the industrial areas of the country, and many thousands of the jobless drifted into New York City during the following winter. Some of them were led by the IWW, whose syndicalist doctrines and revolutionary tactics terrified the wealthier burghers, as when one band of Wobblies, under the leadership of young Frank Tannenbaum, occupied a church on the East Side, only to be ejected violently by the police and arrested en masse.

Mayor Mitchel's staff tried to provide some relief for the homeless and hungry, starting some "made work" projects — precursors of the New Deal relief projects during the Depression twenty years later — which earned the Mayor fierce onslaughts in the metropolitan press. Miss Perkins recalled how Henry Bruère and Paul Kennaday induced Mitchel to set up the "Hotel de Gink," in an empty loft building, where meals and lodging were provided for some of the jobless. These timid but well-meaning expedients, however, presently were no longer needed, for as the war dragged on in Europe massive war orders from the Allies reduced unemployment to a point where it ceased to be a problem. And now a fresh municipal crisis appeared as a result of the wartime boom: on the eve of the entrance of the United States

into the conflict in 1917 New York's harbor and transport
system became so congested that the movement of supplies
was seriously delayed. Mitchel lived in a perpetual storm;
the Tammany faction in the Board of Aldermen worked to
frustrate his purposes, and the Hearst newspapers, which had
formerly supported him, now attacked him day after day,
showing a typical reversal of Hearst's attitude toward political friends that was the only constant in the life pattern of
that moneyed Machiavellian. By this time Mitchel wished
heartily to step out of his unhappy office and enlist for war
service, but he was persuaded to run again, although he was
certain to be defeated.

After considerable head scratching the sachems of Tammany Hall, at the conclusion of their summer conference in
1917, announced that the Democratic candidate for Mayor
would be not Alfred E. Smith, but a little-known Brooklyn
magistrate named John F. Hylan. Hylan had the backing of
Boss McCooey of Brooklyn and of Hearst, both of whom
Murphy wished to conciliate. A former streetcar motorman,
Hylan had worked his way through law school at night and
had risen to be a County Judge. He was reputed to be a
bluff and honest fellow, and posed as a friend of the common
people. His mental limitations, which later caused Smith
keen anxiety, were not at first remarked upon.

Smith, meanwhile, was persuaded to stand for President
of the Board of Aldermen, which meant that he would be in
effect Vice-Mayor, and could help direct the legislative work
of the city council. As a seasoned campaigner he played a
leading part in the battle to oust Mitchel and the Fusionists.
Mitchel had formerly had the support not only of progressive
Republicans but also of the independent or Wilson Demo-

crats. But now that the country was at war the New York
City electorate was sharply divided; many who were opposed to American engagement in European quarrels voted
in protest for the Socialist Party candidate, Morris Hillquit,
who ran second to the Democratic nominee, Hylan, while
Mitchel, ardent champion of President Wilson and the war
to save democracy, wound up a poor third. Mitchel, at forty,
at once volunteered for the Army Air Force, and was killed
in practice maneuvers.

That year Smith stumped not only in Manhattan but in all
five counties of New York City. In reminiscences he dictated
long afterward he observed,

> A man gets his first idea of real campaigning when he begins
> to spread out from the locality in which he is known to search
> for votes in a new region. My first nomination taking me out-
> side my immediate neighborhood was for Sheriff of New York
> County . . . I went touring from the Battery to Harlem.

Running for President of the Board of Aldermen, he had to
gauge and respond to local feelings in five different boroughs.
In the Bronx, where his wife had grown up, he found again
the Irish and Jewish people from the lower East Side who
had moved uptown, and calculated that here the sentimental,
emotional approach would be most effective. Brooklyn also
was heavily populated with former East-Siders, but as com-
muters they had special problems; here he focused on the
subject of transportation.

He always had very clearly in mind everything he was
going to say, and by going over it in advance was able to
remember all of it while speaking extemporaneously. A few
brief notes written on the backs of legal-size envelopes were
all he needed to refer to. His talk on the hustings was blunt,

factual, without the rhetoric of the traditional kind, but also without a trace of political hokum; in argument he was close-gripping. Once mounted on the platform he made direct contact with the crowd very quickly, delivering himself with an air of tremendous sincerity.

In the course of the campaign his Fusionist adversary, Robert Adamson, an associate of Mayor Mitchel, was unwary enough to challenge Smith to a debate, and opened by asking the Sheriff to state his special qualifications for the office of President of the Board of Aldermen. Smith's reply fairly blew Mr. Adamson off the platform, as he cited all his legislative and constitutional activities over twelve years, the state budgets he had worked out or helped with, the sums of money, mounting into many millions in appropriations, which he had saved for the state. Without a whit of false modesty he concluded, "If there is any man in the city with as much legislative experience let him speak. I will be glad to surrender my nomination to him and go back to the Fulton Market."

Although in that three-cornered race the Democrats easily won the chief city offices and a majority of the Council, several Socialist aldermen were also elected, and Smith once more showed his liberal spirit by offering them the utmost courtesy when he took over as head of the city's governing council, though it was a time of rising intolerance. He proceeded to arrange for the Socialists to share committee memberships with the Democrats and Republicans, saying,

> The people of the city have placed a grave responsibility upon the majority party . . . But I have a keen understanding of the relationship of the minority and the *minor minority* [Italics added] . . .

Smith presided over the Board of Aldermen and also sat beside Mayor Hylan on the Board of Estimate, which wielded the power of purse in the city government. The business of the Board of Estimate he found to be routine in character, wanting in the broad powers exercised by the state; observing the overlapping of departmental functions, he came to the conclusion that the whole city administration needed drastic overhauling. He remarked to a friend, however, that he would not care to assume the Mayor's post unless he had a free hand to fire a lot of Democratic Party incompetents from office.

One urgent municipal problem that concerned him was the distribution and marketing of goods, especially food, in the port of New York. The movement of freight had become slow and costly in recent years, and the swollen wartime traffic was choking all approaches to the city. Mayor Mitchel had established terminal wholesale markets on city-owned land at the waterfront, appointing the well-known social worker Dr. Henry Moskowitz as his first Commissioner of Markets. Quick to grasp the advantage of this plan, even though suggested by a political opponent, Smith urged an expansion of city-owned terminal markets and dock facilities to speed up the handling of food and lower costs for millions of consumers by reducing the charges of middlemen.

A plan for a vehicular freight tunnel under the Hudson River, which had been advocated for some years by prominent citizens, also promised to relieve congestion. Under the pressure of wartime needs this scheme was broadened to provide for an interstate Port Authority to be chartered as a public corporation, whose control would be shared by the states of New York, New Jersey, and Connecticut, and

by the cities fronting the great harbor. The magnitude of
the plan, its constructive value, captured Smith's imagination. It involved difficult adjustments of national, state, and
city powers, as well as vast engineering and financial problems, which the sponsors of the project had worked out with
much ingenuity. Smith became an enthusiast for the Port
Authority scheme, and made a notable speech favoring its
early establishment at a meeting of the Board of Aldermen,
which Mayor Hylan did not even bother to attend. When
Smith tried to interest Hylan in the Port Authority he met
only with an uninformed opposition.

Why did Hylan use the power of his office to obstruct the
program? Because his mentor, Hearst, rejected the idea of
a tri-state authority, urging instead a corporation controlled
by the City of New York, by its political bosses, and (by implication) by their slippery friend, William Randolph Hearst.
After a brief love affair with Mitchel, Hearst had returned
to the Democratic camp and had given loud support to
Hylan's campaign. As Smith saw it, Hylan dared not move
without the approval of this formidable ally, and subservi-
ently followed his wishes, while at the same time taking
orders from Tammany Hall in the matter of appointments
without demur.

Over and over again Smith tried to present the facts of
life to Hylan, encouraging him to study the problems of the
city administration. But Hylan showed himself incapable
of any such intellectual exercise. He continued nevertheless
to make demagogic speeches about defending the interests
of the people against the trusts, quite in the style of the
Hearst editorials. In the end Smith came to believe that
nothing could be expected of him, and that he was a disgrace

to the City of New York. But before his final rupture with the Mayor, he sometimes exerted himself to protect the man from the consequences of his own stupidity. On one occasion, at a hearing at City Hall on the question of whether to construct a tunnel or a bridge across the Hudson, engineering experts testified on the different estimates of stresses, traffic capacity, and construction costs for the alternate schemes. Hylan listened to the technical explanations, then interposed a question, "This tunnel now — is it your plan to build it by the open cut, or by the bore method?" Newspaper reporters present opened their eyes wide with amazement. Two of them, Smith noticed, quietly slipped out of the room as if with the intention of phoning in a report of the Mayor's latest absurdity to their city desks. Smith shot out after them, caught them in the corridor, and exclaimed, "Say, have a heart. The Mayor wasn't thinking when he pulled that one! A tunnel built under a river by *open cut?* You'd have to hire fish to build it!" He urged them not to let the story get into print, lest Hylan become the laughingstock of the town; out of regard for Smith they passed it over.

He was destined to serve only a year of his four-year term as President of the Board of Aldermen. Shortly after his election to that office his friends launched a movement to bring about his nomination for Governor in 1918. By this time he was regarded as the most popular man in the regular Democratic organization in New York State. (To Murphy's credit it should be noted that there were then several other outstanding men in his stable, such as State Senators Robert Wagner, James A. Foley, and James J. Walker, but none had Smith's voter appeal.) Moreover he had won much acclaim from reform groups and other independents, he was well-known upstate, and promised to be the sort of leader who could unify the different sections of the party.

The Citizens' Union in 1918 warmly endorsed Tammany's nominee Alfred Smith for the Governorship. Whereas he had formerly permitted himself many a pleasantry at the expense of the goo-goos, he now hastened to write the Citizens' Union a letter expressing his deep appreciation of their support and pledging that he would "endeavor to prove himself worthy of the great confidence you have reposed in me."

At an early stage of affairs, however, the immitigable Mr. Hearst moved in to grasp the Democratic gubernatorial nomination for himself. With Mayor Hylan and the New York City administration in his pocket, he was now reaching out for political power in a larger area. Ever since Hearst's newspapers had published fierce attacks on Smith's venerable friend, Tom Foley, during Foley's campaign for the office of Sheriff, Smith had entertained no warm feelings for this intruder. He now announced his candidacy for the nomination, and his many admirers throughout the state worked eagerly to advance his boom. Others also entered the contest with the main purpose of defeating Hearst, among them the esteemed independent Democrat, State Senator William Church Osborn of New York City. Murphy meanwhile let it be known that Fourteenth Street would wait to learn the preference of the upstate Democrats. By the time the Democratic Party conference met at Saratoga to designate its candidate for the primary elections, there were ten names before it, but these were eliminated one by one as impressive support for Smith came in from the cities of central New

York, including Syracuse, Albany, and Troy. Smith proved to be the choice of all the Democratic factions at the party convention in late July, and easily won the primaries. Thus Murphy, who was most anxious for the nomination of Smith, his longtime protégé and co-worker, had the air of yielding gracefully to a consensus of the different sections of the state party, and avoided a break with Hearst.

In truth Alfred Smith had been promoted all too slowly; his intimates knew that for years he had aspired to the Governorship. Murphy had deliberated a long time before risking the nomination of Smith. There was the problem of his being a Roman Catholic in a state that was assumed to be predominantly Protestant. Religious prejudice had worked powerfully, if silently, among the upstate voters. In any case, Smith was going to run in a very close contest, as it would be waged under the troubled conditions of wartime, against the incumbent Governor Whitman, a determined and ambitious man, seeking reelection for a third term.

Smith himself mapped out his first gubernatorial campaign in 1918, as in all subsequent contests. His plan of action had one distinctive feature stemming from his desire to dispel completely the image of himself as a Tammany Hall politician, which his opponents tried to attach to him. To this end he and his friends in New York City organized an Independent Citizens' Committee for Alfred E. Smith made up of anti-Tammany Democrats, former Bull Moose Republicans, and former Fusionist supporters of Mayor Mitchel. Its chairman was Abram I. Elkus, who had become a devoted friend of Smith's while counselor to the Factory Investigating Commission. Elkus was able to bring in liberal businessmen, lawyers, intellectuals, and social workers to lend the campaign the air of a crusade for reform. Among those on the Citizens' Committee were George Gordon Battle, Thomas L. Chadbourne, James W. Gerard, Lamar Hardy, Martin Littleton, Jessie I. Straus, John G. Agar, Frederic R. Coudert, Judge Morgan J. O'Brien, Samuel Untermyer, Augustus Thomas, and Robert Adamson (Smith's Fusionist rival for aldermanic President in 1917). Elkus also brought in his younger partner Joseph M. Proskauer, a leading spirit in the Citizens' Union, and one of America's most successful trial lawyers. Proskauer contributed his sharp wits to the campaign, and soon became one of Smith's most trusted advisers. Bernard Shientag, of the same law office, who had also served on the Factory Commission, was called upon to help prepare the material of Smith's speeches, whose subject and argument he would work out with his advisers, though he always delivered them extemporaneously in his own language. Another new departure was the inclusion, for the first time on such a committee, of a group of distinguished women leaders such as Harriet Stanton Blatch, Elizabeth Marbury, Mary Kingsbury Simkhovitch, and Belle Moskowitz, wife of Dr. Henry Moskowitz, the Commissioner of Markets under Mayor Mitchel.

The leaders of the Irish Catholic communities were rising to dominance in the politics of many of America's large cities. But now, in Smith's campaign organization, a prominent role was assumed by two formerly disadvantaged groups — the Jews and the women — this development in itself reflecting the change gradually taking place in the basis of political power in New York State. Following the lead of eminent Jews like Elkus, Untermyer, and Straus, the large Jewish population of New York City rallied strongly to Smith's banner. It was not only for his winning human qualities that they liked him — as when he asserted that the state was "people" and not just "rivers, forests and green fields" — but because he had long shown himself sincerely tolerant in matters of religion and race. His aides and co-workers included Protestants and Jews, as well as Catholics; for many years Robert Wagner, a Protestant, and Aaron J. Levy, a Jew, both Tammany men, had worked side by side with him at the Capitol. Because of their own experience of discrimination it was a natural impulse for the Jews of New York to support Smith, who like them was subject to the attacks of bigots. Smith had grown up amongst them in the East Side; he knew them well and valued them. Jews were gaining in education and struggling to climb onto the up escalator of society, and like the Irish before them, and the Italians and Slavs afterward, they resented keenly the traditional spirit of prejudice shown by the Old Guard Republicans, who tried to bar them from rising to places of power and influence however accomplished they might be individually.

In 1918, when for the first time women had the right to vote in New York State, their voting patterns were unknown, and no method of enlisting their support had been worked out. Smith himself, although formerly opposed to woman suffrage, had changed his position, and had voted for ratification of the amendment to the Federal Constitution while a member of the Assembly. The record also showed that he had been instrumental in the appointment of a noted woman social worker, Miss Pauline Goldmark, to an important post in the state's labor department, from which she had been dropped when Whitman, in 1915, prodded the Legislature into passing a bill that changed the administrative setup of the department.

It was, however, only late in October that a Women's Division of the Independent Citizens' Committee for Smith was hastily thrown together for the purpose of maintaining contact with numerous women's groups. Smith's old friends of the Factory Commission, Frances Perkins and Mary Dreier, were among its members, but its whole conception was that of Mrs. Belle Moskowitz, who also directed it. Smith was persuaded to try direct canvassing of women voters in their special associations, and agreed to address the Women's University Club at a meeting arranged by Mrs. Moskowitz. She met the candidate for the first time that day when Frances Perkins brought her to Smith's headquarters at the Hotel Biltmore and introduced them to each other. In the course of a brief conversation in the car that brought them to the hotel where the meeting was to be held, Smith outlined the perfunctory speech he intended to give, a talk consisting of a few gallant compliments to the sex and some humorous anecdotes. Mrs. Moskowitz proposed that instead of treating the affair lightly, he speak in all earnestness about the urgent problems of the state in his most informative style, as if addressing a body of lawyers and business executives, for these were women in the professions. By showing a real regard for their capacity as potential citizens, he would make the strongest possible appeal, she urged, and she was warmly seconded by Miss Perkins.

Smith took her advice. He spoke for a solid hour about his work in the Legislature and his qualifications for the Governorship, describing how over the years he had pursued the objective of the humane and responsible state through laws dealing with health, women workers, child labor, fire prevention, and workmen's compensation. He ended up on a characteristic note: "You see, I know what it is to run a great state. You can check up on me, for if I am wrong, it will not be a case of ignorance but of wilful intent." Smith often wound up a campaign speech in this way, saying that he regarded the platform pledges of his party as sacred obligations, and that as head of the state ticket he was ready to be held accountable for efforts to redeem them.

His hearers not only gave him an ovation, but, as they came up to the rostrum to felicitate him, indicated by their comments that nothing he said had been over their heads. He was surprised by their grasp of the problems he had discussed, and pleased by their assurances of support; he also remembered how wise had been the advice of Belle Moskowitz. Mrs. Moskowitz struck him as very knowledgeable in politics; she was not without experience in the game. Formerly allied to the Progressive Republicans, she had helped in the campaigns of Mayor Mitchel and Governor Whitman. She had a broad acquaintance in many fields, and enjoyed using her influence to advance causes she favored. As she confided to Miss Perkins, who had known her for some years, she was bitterly disappointed in Governor Whitman; he had definitely promised her that he would sponsor certain welfare measures — it might have been in the field of public health or housing — and then had put her off, without ceremony or explanation. After reflection she realized that the policies of Smith were more in accord with her own ideas of social justice, and that was why she had volunteered her services.

Born in the Harlem section of New York in 1877, the daughter of a Jewish watchmaker named Lindner, the future Mrs. Moskowitz had attended Horace Mann High School and, for a year, Teachers College. At eighteen, a beautiful dark-haired girl with classical features and fine eyes, she had gone to work in the settlement houses of the East Side at a period when masses of Jewish immigrants from Eastern Europe were flooding New York, bewildered victims of the pogroms of that time, and Belle Lindner, working night and day to bring them help, became something of a heroine among the social workers in the ghetto. In 1903 she was married to Charles H. Israels, of an old Dutch-Jewish family of New York, and one of the architects who had served as adviser to Miss Perkins on the Safety Council. Thereafter, although Mrs. Israels, as she was then, bore three children, she continued part-time social work in the slums, specializing in the supervision of young working girls who were separated from their families. Having uncovered serious abuses in the conduct of dance halls in New York, where unattached girls were frequently victimized, in 1911 she was instrumental in having the first state legislation passed to require the licensing and surveillance of such resorts. Her first husband died at that time, and several years later she married Dr. Henry Moskowitz, also a co-worker in settlement houses. Toward 1912 she served as labor manager for a women's garment manufacturers' association and handled grievances for them; over a span of four years she adjusted more than 1000 labor disputes. Meanwhile she continued to support movements for better housing as well as for playgrounds and recreation centers for city children. In the New York Jewish community she was highly esteemed not only by social workers but also by leaders in business and philanthropy; by her marriage to Dr. Henry Moskowitz, Commissioner of Markets in the Mitchel Administration, she broadened her acquaintance to include city officials.

In 1918 Belle Moskowitz had turned forty; she had grown matronly but had lost none of her power to attract people. What impressed Smith was that this motherly looking person expressed herself with uncommon clarity and logic, and with a calm confidence in her own reasoning. After the meeting at the Women's University Club he sought her counsels and followed them closely, but not unquestioningly, as some thought. "Al Smith makes up his own mind," Mrs. Moskowitz used to say. Their attraction was mutual; in her too there was a strong response to the magnetism of the self-taught, high-spirited man from the East Side. The group of intellectuals who gathered around Smith to advise him on questions of policy came to be called his "board of strategy" in those wartime days; they were the forerunners of the "Brain Trust" of the New Deal. Belle Moskowitz soon became an unobtrusive, reticent, but vital personage in this group. Detached, clearheaded, she fed him ideas, the more useful because she had both education and a keen sense of the game of power. She worked for him unremittingly, and though she was by no means rich, asked nothing for herself in the way of place or official favor. As someone once said, she was "the third woman in his life," after Katie and his mother, though on a wholly respectable and circumscribed plane. What endeared her to him perhaps more than any other quality was that she was full of courage, and proved herself steady and cool in the midst of the rousing political battles Smith was to be engaged in for the next ten years.

✿

While Smith had come to share the views of the liberals
by 1918, he was too experienced a professional to entrust his
political fortunes exclusively to a few college-bred reformers
and female social workers. The State Democratic Committee, headed by Boss Kelly of Syracuse, officially took charge
of his canvassing work; at Fourteenth Street Charles F.
Murphy, Big Tim Sullivan, Tom Foley, and the rest worked
industriously in the purlieus of the great city and helped raise
money. Johnny Gilchrist, Smith's old schoolmate, who had
recently served under him in the Sheriff's office, acted as
liaison officer between the Independent Citizens' Committee
and Tammany Hall. Another political co-worker of Albany
days, George Van Namee, of Watertown, who later became
Smith's private secretary, also maintained contact between
the professional party people and the reformist intellectuals.
Smith raised no objections when William F. McCombs, a dignified financier who had directed President Wilson's 1916
campaign, was drafted by the Independent Citizens' Committee to oversee the financing of the gubernatorial campaign
and enforce a strict accounting of all expenditures.

Repeatedly Smith used to point out to his reformer friends
that he could be more effective in winning the improvements in the "human side of government," which they desired through cooperation with the party stalwarts. The
machine politicians and the reformers made strange bedfel-
lows, but they worked in harmony under him; their alliance
was a distinctive feature of all Smith's campaigns.

As the contest got under way the odds strongly favored
Governor Whitman and the rest of the Republican slate.

Ever since the Civil War the majority of United States citizens had for the most part remained in the Republican camp; it was much the same in New York State, where the Democrats had won the Governorship only twice in the past quarter century.

Soon after the primaries Smith took off for an extensive tour of upstate New York, where he knew he would face the inveterate opponents of the Democrats. An occasionally hilarious account of this first gubernatorial campaign, which had to be fought under special wartime circumstances, is to be found in a memoir he wrote or dictated many years later:

> The first real campaign that introduced me to absolutely virgin territory . . . was my first campaign for the Governorship in 1918 . . . The World War was at its height and the daily lists of casualties among the AEF contained the names of men from all parts of the State . . . Public interest was in the war more than in the campaign.

With each step toward higher office in recent years he had been extending the area of his canvassing, encountering novel conditions and types of people who were not only strange to him, but who sometimes showed strong suspicion of his religion and background. He had journeyed all about the state several years earlier to inspect factory conditions, but never to stump for the votes of its villagers and farmers. Now he put in an appearance at a series of county fairs in the western part of New York, a new experience for this city-bred man. In Delaware County a farmer dressed in new blue overalls and boots, who had won first prize for his herd of cattle, was brought up to be introduced to him. "He stood off about ten feet from me," wrote Smith, "after we shook hands, and remarked: 'Well, you look pretty good, but you can't get no comfort from me!'" Such encounters were not very auspicious. At the fairs in Broome County Smith was regarded mainly as a curiosity; groups of people turned away from the prize exhibits of squash or hogs only to gape at the Democratic candidate, billed as "the Assemblyman from the Bowery."

Yet if his person was unfamiliar in those parts, his name was by then fairly well known and well regarded throughout the state because it had appeared so often in Albany dispatches to the local newspapers. Moving eastward through the rich green Mohawk Valley he reached Albany, where a group of legislators arranged a banquet in his honor. He appeared trimly clad in dinner jacket and black tie, and sat down next to the wife of an upstate Senator. Hearing his name the lady asked him, "Are you the Assemblyman from the Bowery?" "Yes," he replied. "Well," she said, "I thought Al Smith was a big stout man, of two hundred and fifty pounds weight, with a black moustache, a loud checked suit and a diamond in his tie." Though he was always known as "a nifty dresser," he wore no loud suits, but that year, for the first time, he affected a brown derby set on his head at a jaunty angle — as in a spirit of challenge — and it became famous as his battle gear.

A pall of gloom hung over the towns upstate, where little flags with stars for mothers or widows of the war dead hung in many of the windows; the air of gloom was deepened further by the mounting casualties of the Spanish influenza epidemic. As a consequence most of the local meeting halls and school auditoriums where Smith could have addressed the public were closed down. Ostensibly this was done because of the danger of contagion, but actually local mayors were not unwilling to hamstring the Democratic candidate, who tried to arrange for meetings in the open air. Even these were shunned by the wary Yankees. In the larger towns, Buffalo and Albany, where public halls were made available to him, many people appeared wearing handkerchiefs over their mouths and noses. Smith was therefore confined on quite a number of occasions to meeting only with a few local politicians and the newspapermen accompanying him in the sitting rooms of hotels, and it was to them that he delivered some of his campaign speeches. The members of the press respected Smith for his native abilities and loved him well; they were less than enthusiastic about Governor Whitman, a man of many disingenuous compromises. Under the exceptional conditions of that epidemic-ridden campaign the correspondents permitted themselves the liberty of reporting Smith's talks in hotel lobbies as "delivered to overflowing audiences."

Sharing the ardors and rigors of that 1918 tour the newspapermen became attached to Smith in a very special way. On one occasion they put up for the night with the candidate in the only hotel at some jerkwater town in Central New York, a ramshackle building standing right beside the tracks of the New York Central main line. The candidate had retired to his room in the evening together with half a dozen friendly reporters, and relaxing after the day's work they were being convivial after their usual manner, with the aid of a few bottles of whiskey. Suddenly a waiter knocked at the door and came hurrying in to warn them that the Twentieth Century Limited was coming through in a few minutes. All bottles, glasses, and dishes, he said, must be removed from the table and placed on the floor. Ignorant of

what the commotion was all about, but unwilling to risk
spilling their drinks, the guests themselves sat down on the
floor, each man clutching his glass. They were just in time.
The express train arrived seconds later belching fire and
fury, its thunderous vibrations shaking the flimsy old building so violently that it seemed as if the walls would come
tumbling down, while the guests clung for dear life to the
heaving floor. A few moments more and the fierce jugger-
naut was gone; all was still, while Smith and his friends
picked themselves up as best they could, laughing uproar-
iously. Canvassing in the hinterland involved perils they had
not foreseen.

Whitman too was a driving campaigner; in the two preceding elections he had defeated his opponents — including
Judge Samuel Seabury, in 1916 — by a wide margin of more
than 150,000 votes. But of late he had seemed possessed by
his ulterior ambitions; one newspaper article (which Smith
cited) described him as "sitting in the Capitol at Albany with
a telescope trained on the White House in Washington." As
he climbed the political ladder, moreover, he had disappointed many of his supporters, as was the case with Mrs.
Moskowitz. Some of the leading figures in his own party,
who were Progressives, expressed strong dislike of his manip-
ulative methods: after having promised reform of the civil
service, he had placed his henchmen in various bureaus or
commissions for which they were unsuited, so that they
might work for his political advancement. Serious charges
to this effect were made by a Republican rival for the gubernatorial nomination in 1918, Attorney-General Merton Lewis,
who declared that funds of the Food Commission had been

misused, and that members of the Public Service Commission had allowed chaotic conditions to develop in New York City's transit system, while they devoted their time to the Governor's schemes for renomination in 1918 and for winning the Presidency in 1920.

Smith conducted a very aggressive campaign, but tried to keep it on high ground, avoiding personal recriminations, at least in the beginning. "Let us look at the record," he would say, in characteristic fashion: he then proceeded to give in a series of speeches an informed survey of the actual condition of the state government with its more than one hundred and fifty departments — many of them overlapping in function — and made constructive proposals for amalgamating them into fewer units. "The state cries out for reorganization," Smith exclaimed. What had Governor Whitman done during two terms about this? What did he propose now? Smith then went on to recommend economies, and described a whole series of wasteful appropriation bills enacted under the Republican regime. He also recalled that in 1915 the Workmen's Compensation Law had been amended by the Republican majority so that it deprived injured workers of the protection offered in the original measure of 1913. Smith pledged that he would seek to extend the provisions of that law and to safeguard the rights of the injured. He also proposed to establish a state minimum wage for women and children in industry. Finally he promised to reorganize the Public Service Commission, and appoint to it officers who would be "representatives of the people, and not creatures of the corporations they are organized to control." What constructive suggestions did Mr. Whitman have?

The Governor at first tried to answer a part of Smith's bill of complaints by challenging him to name those appropriations which he would not have signed if he were Governor. Smith replied by citing chapter and verse. During the war money appropriations intended to stimulate farm output were "diverted to the wrong hands, and used to build up a Whitman political machine," he said.

Whitman, thereafter, largely avoided argument over public issues and concentrated his fire on Smith's character, which he represented as that of a ward heeler out of the East Side tenements, an habitual flunky of Tammany Hall, who had "never earned any money with his own hands," and therefore knew little or nothing about business or public affairs. He had only survived, Whitman charged, by grace of the Democratic machine, which allowed him to feed at the public trough, and in return he had always made appointments at the bidding of Boss Murphy while serving as Speaker and Sheriff. To elect Smith, he argued, would be to turn all New York State over to the control of Fourteenth Street.

Since Smith's appointment record had won commendation from nonpartisan reformers and even from leading Republican newspapers, these last charges were easily refuted. In a spirited riposte to the allegation that he had never "earned money with his own hands" he cried out, "While Mr. Whitman was a student at Amherst College, I was working from dawn to dark in the Fulton Fish Market." And in this vein he wound up one of his more impassioned speeches:

> In the closing hours of the campaign Mr. Whitman's sole reply seems to be that I am unfit for the office of Governor because I was born in a tenement of the East Side. It is true. In fact it is one of the few things he said which is true. I not only

admit it, but I *glory* in it. That is one of the things which distinguishes America from all other countries under the sun.

This speech was delivered in New York City after his upstate canvas before a crowd of 5000 of his fellow townspeople, who braved the perils of influenza in order to see and hear him. Here the campaign was ending with a powerful drive that promised to balance the advantage enjoyed by the Republicans north of the Bronx County line.

One of Whitman's accusations — that Smith was identified with the liquor interests, as shown by his voting record in the Assembly — was easily parried by his rival, but it also backfired in a way most embarrassing to the Governor, who had ranged himself on the side of the fanatical drys of the Anti-Saloon League. His claims to strict virtue on this issue were sadly impugned when fifty Republican women felt impelled to petition him publicly to pledge that he himself would "refrain from the habitual use of intoxicating beverages."

The campaign turned into a rude imbroglio, and Smith was striking hard blows. Reviewing the record of the Governor who had neither policy nor program, as he claimed, and who would not answer his charges, he introduced drama into his platform orations. He cited the fact that

During the primary campaign [for the gubernatorial nomination] Attorney General Lewis asked the Governor to produce the payroll of the State Food Commission. This the Governor declined to do. I will produce it at this time for the benefit of the people of the State of New York, and as I exhibit it to you, it is fitting that we all ask what the Food Commission did since its organization? . . .

He then cited names and salaries, which were entirely out

of proportion to any services those officers might render —
except to the Governor's political schemes for the future.

In the last days of the campaign there occurred one of
those spectacular disasters to which New York City has long
been prone, a calamity that Smith quickly turned to account
at a time when it was too late for his adversary to undo the
damage. On Friday evening, November 1, four days before
Election Day, at the six o'clock rush hour in the New York
subway system, a train of the Brooklyn Manhattan Transit,
driven by a green motorman, drove full speed past signals;
its leading cars crashed into fragments; about ninety persons
were killed and more than a hundred injured. The worst
transport disaster in the history of Greater New York, it
caused a wave of indignation throughout the city.

Smith was scheduled to speak that very evening at the
Academy of Music in Brooklyn. He had long been aware of
the incompetence of the Public Service Commission, made
up of Whitman's appointees, which was supposed to manage
the city's transportation network. Labor trouble had been
brewing there for many months, while the managers of the
BMT had fired union men and refused to recognize their
organization for bargaining, choosing to run the trains under-
manned, and replacing experienced motormen with inexperienced scabs. In fact the Brotherhood of Locomotive Engineers had called a strike to begin that very morning.

Whatever Smith had planned to say that evening he hastily
altered, substituting a powerful attack on the Governor's
management of the transit system through his Public Service
Commissioners. Whitman, he charged, had made the Commission an instrument of his own political machine, a machine
"to promote the Governor's . . . Presidential aspirations,"

which produced "the most costly fiasco in the history of the state." He went on:

> Does the Governor wish the people to understand that he does not assume any responsibility for it? Does he believe that concern for the health and the lives of the people is all finished when he makes his appointments? Politics controlling the appointments had made itself felt down through the minor employees, and even positions undoubtedly requiring technical knowledge because of their character were filled by Republican district leaders. What has Governor Whitman to say about all this? . . . What does he propose to do for the people of this State?

The Smith campaign committee also hurried out with newspaper advertisements charging the Governor and the Public Service Commissioners with responsibility for the carnage. Under pressure to act quickly, Whitman undertook a hasty investigation, with the help of the Kings County District Attorney, but there was too little time before Election Day for him to recover lost ground.

Smith had counted on a close finish, but the voters of Brooklyn were so much aroused by the subway disaster that instead of giving him a plurality of 50,000, as he had expected, they gave him a margin of 90,000 over Whitman. The big turnout in Greater New York, combined with the poor attendance of upstate voters at the polls because of the influenza epidemic, determined the result. On election night Smith and his aides waited up into the small hours of the morning at their headquarters for the returns to come in by telegraph. The Democratic plurality in the city was so large that the morning papers predicted his victory by a narrow margin. But returns from some small upstate communities were either missing or delayed, so that the Democratic workers began to fear possible fraud. The next morning several of them accompanied Smith on a trip to Syracuse where they could keep in close contact with poll watchers in the central part of the state. The missing ballots were not all counted until two days had passed, showing that Smith led by a scant 7500. Whitman would not concede defeat, and demanded a recount in the New York City districts, which when done only confirmed the earlier result. Moreover the absentee ballots of soldiers in cantonments around the country raised Smith's plurality to nearly 15,000.

In November, 1918, as the war in Europe came to an end, a great swing to the Republicans was to be observed throughout the country. Republican Governors replaced Democrats in most states, and both houses of Congress were lost to Wilson's party. But in New York Alfred Smith had fought against the tide and was triumphant.

On the morning of December 30, 1918, Smith, with his family and his great dog Caesar entrained for Albany to begin his first term as Governor of New York State. Though it was customary for the outgoing Governor to welcome his successor a few days ahead of time and help him adjust to his new office and home, Governor Whitman had been inhospitable and silent, as if embittered by his defeat. Only at the last hour, on New Year's Eve, did he make it possible for Smith to come to the Executive Mansion to take his private oath of office.

The formal assumption of his new duties took place the next day, in the Assembly Chamber at the Capitol, and once more Smith stood surrounded by his wife, his mother, and his five children. And there too to witness his triumph were several score of his old neighbors from the Fourth Ward, Irish, Jewish, and Italian, who had come from New York the night before, in company with two who had furthered his climb to these heights: Henry Campbell and Tom Foley. Murphy also was present. Smith looked at all these old friends with deep affection, for he had a grateful heart and forgot none who were loyal to him, and they too regarded him with a love such as few professional politicians are granted. His party organization had helped him mightily, but it needed more than his party to elect him that year. Men and women of all parties, from all over the state, had voted for him, had recognized his good works, had done him honor. They had put their trust in him, and he told himself he must never let them down. One of those present wrote in the inflated rhetoric then current that he "seemed to glow with an inner nobility of character that reflected his own deep sense of noblesse oblige," adding the special qualification, "the noblesse oblige of poverty." Realizing that he was the first man of his origin to be elected Governor of New York State, as this friend observed, Smith was determined never to shame that origin, but to lend it glory.

CHAPTER X

Governor of New York

FROM THE VERY start Smith's conduct as chief executive of the Empire State surprised and pleased many of his fellow citizens. He was refreshingly different from all governors before him; although his great office had often lent itself to various forms of political venality, he had the air of an honest man despite his political affiliations. His arrival in power signaled a sort of Jacksonian upheaval in the conventions and rituals of the capital, noticeable on his second day in office at the Inaugural Ball, which was attended not only by Albany dowagers such as Mrs. William Bayard Van Rensselaer and Mrs. Hun, but also by Mr. and Mrs. James Colombo, Mr. and Mrs. Sol Bernstein, Dr. and Mrs. Paul Sarrubia, and other neighbors from the Fourth Ward, as listed in the society columns of the newspapers. Now a man of forty-five, Smith had a natural dignity befitting his new role; under all circumstances, including large ceremonial gatherings, he appeared completely at his ease, greeting the hundreds who passed before him, not in the perfunctory style of Governor Odell, but with a special word of greeting for each. His mother, sitting in the box with him and the rest of his family, took pride in showing the visitors an old

picture postcard he had sent her in 1904 when he first came
to the Assembly, on which he had written,

> Dear Mother: This is a picture of the Governor's residence.
> I'm going to work hard and stick to the ideals you taught me
> and some day — maybe, I'll occupy this house.

At the sprawling Executive Mansion on Eagle Street the
Smith family settled down comfortably enough in its spacious
rooms, filled with ponderous Victorian-style furniture and
hung with curtains that darkened the day. The parents
were unqualified, the children as yet too young to be sensitive to the decor, but they knew instinctively what made
a home, and here they conducted themselves much as they
did in Oliver Street, *sans façon,* keeping open house. The
children's playmates had free access to the mansion grounds
and sometimes got lost there or in the rambling old house.
One evening a woman appeared at the door at dinner time
to inquire whether anyone had seen her ten-year-old
daughter; she found the child in the dining room near the
head of the table, seated on the Governor's right hand.

Smith's easy manners and sense of his own worth did not,
however, prevent him from showing a little pique at some
of Albany's social leaders who had administered snubs to
him. The aristocracy of the little capital city considered itself
more exclusive than that of the metropolis, and it was only
after he was inaugurated as Governor that Smith received
an invitation to dine at the home of one of the old families.
He sent his regrets. This led to some gossip in Albany society
circles, so that he felt obliged to explain, "I have been in
Albany some fifteen years. I have met all the members of
that family socially a number of times. This is the first time

they have invited me to their home. Governor Al Smith may be different from Assemblyman Al Smith to them — but not to me." Incidents such as this, however, were rare. Frances Perkins, who was very conscious of social distinctions, commented frequently on the natural grace he showed when meeting with persons of either high or low estate, and she remarked that his affability endeared him to women as well as to men of good breeding.

There was never any question of his appeal to the rank and file. Soon after he became Governor, wishing to illustrate his availability to any citizen, he announced that he would hold periodic receptions in the Governor's Room at the New York City Hall, an elegant salon, furnished with priceless antiques, with which he had become familiar while serving as President of the Board of Aldermen. "He invited all hands to come and see him," wrote Miss Perkins. "The misfortune was that all hands did." They came in great numbers, posing a threat to the rare furnishings and the very structure of the City Hall, until Smith regretfully abandoned a scheme that harked back to the time of a less populous democracy.

Meanwhile, even before he could find his way easily about the many rooms of the Executive Mansion, he went soberly to work in the Executive Chamber of the Capitol on the pressing business of the State of New York. Among his first callers were Charles F. Murphy and William McCooey, whose arrival was widely noted and was presumed to be concerned with the spoils of office. For some years past Murphy had shown a wholesome respect for his protégé, and it was reported that he had promised never to ask Smith to do anything that he felt in all conscience he should not do.

Nevertheless the organization boys were restive; as loyal party workers they expected jobs. The press made much of the Governor's being closeted for a whole day, and the next day as well, with the two powerful Democratic bosses. When the conference was over the Governor's policy was made plain for all to see: as when the Republicans controlled the administration, preference would be shown to Democrats competent to hold jobs not subject to civil service regulations, as for example in such minor offices as janitors of public buildings; but the higher posts, heads of executive departments and members of the Governor's cabinet, were to be filled by men qualified by their intelligence and suitability for the job, rather than by their party affiliation.

In fact during the two months before coming to Albany Smith had spent much time in his New York headquarters interviewing and negotiating with potential appointees, and the choices he made indicated how shrewd were his judgments. The Commissioner of Public Works he named turned out to be a fairly nonpartisan figure known for his experience and good character. The post of Commissioner of Public Highways, a great plum, from whose office contracts for many millions of dollars were distributed, went to Colonel Frederick Stuart Greene, an army engineer of high repute, recently mustered out of the AEF for which he had built military roads during the war. Greene, moreover, was a Republican by affiliation. Just prior to his inauguration Smith had summoned Colonel Greene and offered him the position on the basis of what he had learned of the man's work. Naive in political matters, Greene asked if he was supposed to show preference to friends of the party in power in awarding contracts, a question that made Smith bridle. If he had wanted

a man for political jobbing, he said, he would not have called
on Colonel Greene. On the contrary, he warned Greene to
be wary of grabbers seeking profitable contracts; Greene
was to pick his own assistants, he said, and use his own judgment. "Cut out the peanut politics — build the best roads
you can," he concluded. "If anything goes wrong, I'll hear
about it."

Colonel Greene soon justified the Governor's choice as he
proceeded with the building of a network of new concrete
highways for the motorcar age, but showed a marble heart
to the political wirepullers. When these came wailing to
Smith about the Highway Commissioner's methods, the Governor shrugged his shoulders and said in mock sorrow: "What
can I do?" He's a ————. I speak to him, and he doesn't
even listen to me." The Democratic stalwarts were disappointed not to have access to the rich source of "legitimate
graft" formerly preempted by the Republicans, but Smith,
as one of their own boys, knew how to handle them.

Democratic district leaders were likewise taken aback
when Smith announced the appointment of a woman as one
of the five members of the State Industrial Commission. It
will be remembered that he had protested when Governor
Whitman had reorganized the Department of Labor in such
a way as to eliminate the only woman then serving in a high
post in the administration. Now, partly as a bow to the multitude of women voters, but also because of her intimate
acquaintance with labor problems and labor legislation, he
named Miss Perkins to a similar position. She had an additional claim in that she had worked hard for him in the recent campaign, advising him in matters with which she was
familiar, and speaking forcefully in his behalf before women's

groups. The manufacturers' association protested that she was believed to have radical ideas on labor laws; the Senate threatened nonconfirmation; but the Governor was unmoved. Meanwhile, civic improvement associations and social welfare people in New York City showered the Governor with praise for having chosen as his aide the admirable young woman who had been largely instrumental in securing passage of the Fifty-four-Hour law. Examined by the Senate Finance Committee, the self-possessed Miss Perkins was able to convince them of her special competence, and was confirmed by a large majority. In his autobiography Smith laid down his philosophy in regard to appointments: " . . . the greatest contribution that a man can make to his own success in high elective office is to surround himself with men who know their own business, have intelligence and are interested in the subject but personally disinterested. Instead of trying to fit men into jobs I tried to find the man that fitted the job."

All this was true in principle; he was generally high-minded. But Miss Perkins remembered that in her own case he showed himself unexpectedly fussy about her party affiliation. Soon after her appointment one of the Democratic district leaders had phoned him to report that she was not a registered Democrat, though she had made speeches for him in the recent campaign. Smith called her to his office and spoke to her like a Dutch uncle. He was always very direct, sometimes even blunt. When he put the question to her she answered readily that she was not enrolled in the Democratic Party, and that even though she found the Democrats more sympathetic than the Republicans to the measures she favored, she felt that there were advantages in remaining an independent. Her reply gave Smith the opportunity for a little lecture on practical politics that was a classic of its kind, an exposition of the actual workings of the party system. Independents in politics, he said, ended up nowhere after a short run. He himself was able to do far more to obtain reform legislation than the independents because he always worked within the party organization. Good people ought to be inside the party, not outside looking in, he continued, because inside the party, helping to get out the vote, they had influence. Here Miss Perkins interposed a question: "But suppose you don't have any influence, compared with people who make a big contribution to the party chest?" "You have to wait, you must be patient," he answered. "If you handled yourself properly, you'd make your views felt eventually." And then he added something of great significance: if a candidate knows he has a solid block of voters in his own party, this gives him the freedom to make an appeal to independent voters, or even to disaffected voters of the opposition party. He can figure out what those uncommitted voters want, and satisfy them that he has their interests also at heart. Gravely he urged her to learn these lessons well and go forth and register as a Democrat. And as gravely she said she saw the point and would do as he suggested. Thereupon, "While I was still in the room," she relates, Smith phoned the politician who had complained about her "and told him that he had had a talk with me and that I had said I understood the proposition. He wanted me to hear."

The message the new Governor sent to the Legislature in January was one of the most impressive documents of its kind in the long annals of New York State. It called attention to the difficult problems created by the war just ended, the return of 400,000 soldiers to civilian life, the need to care for many wounded veterans and find employment for the able-bodied. It dealt with the crisis in housing, as indicated by inflated rents and shortages of living space. It proposed a revision of the tax schedule to make its burdens more equitable and compensate for liquor revenues cut off by the Prohibition amendment; the improvement of state hospitals, now badly run down; an expanded conservation and park program; an advanced waterpower policy; the regulation of milk distribution and a reduction in its cost, now so high as to threaten the health of children in low income families; revision of the devitalized Workmen's Compensation Act; and a forty-eight-hour law for women and children. Above all, the message affirmed, the state government needed intelligent planning for the future, and a rational reorganization of its numerous departments. To this end the Governor proposed that a Reconstruction Commission be created, staffed by a group of expert citizens who would make studies and complete a grand plan for overhauling the state's executive branch, which would be submitted to the Legislature.

Just before taking office, Smith had been saying to his advisers, "We need some new ideas. What would have happened to New York State if Governor De Witt Clinton had not thought of building the Big Ditch?" It was his new acquaintance Mrs. Moskowitz who supplied him with the ideas he was looking for. The heart of this whole statesmanlike message was the Reconstruction Commission, the brainchild of Belle Moskowitz, who had dreamed it up soon after the election the preceding November. She had first approached Frances Perkins with the scheme, and, heartened by her encouragement, had conferred with the Governor-Elect and a few other sympathetic persons, showing them a brief draft of the plan. As Smith listened to her and read her notes on the subject he kindled to it. None knew better than he that the government apparatus of New York State had become as complicated as one of those fantasy engines designed by cartoonist Rube Goldberg. Mrs. Moskowitz pointed out that preceding governors, Whitman and the others, had done nothing to correct this state of affairs, and in fact had no policy with regard to it. She wanted Smith as Governor to start off with a bold plan of reorganization of the sprawling executive departments; they must be simplified, consolidated, modernized. A good semanticist, she had hit upon the term "Reconstruction," which she considered nonpartisan and noncontroversial, particularly applicable to the postwar needs of a great commonwealth, as after the Civil War. To be sure the Reconstruction following the Civil War had been carried on planlessly, but during the First World War there had been a real beginning of large-scale planning by the Federal Government, especially for war industries. Thanks to this there were many persons with experience in the field whom the Governor could call on for advice about the economic and social problems now confronting the state. Finally Mrs. Moskowitz had proposed that the reorganization plan should be worked out by a select committee of eminent citizens drawn from both political parties. The use of such select citizens' committees was to be a characteristic feature of Smith's administrations.

Though his imagination was caught by the whole conception, Smith's first reaction was to say, "I want to talk to more people about it." At the time he was still busy during the day in the office of the President of the Board of Aldermen at City Hall, interviewing place seekers; therefore he suggested that Mrs. Moskowitz, and a few others she recommended as possible members of the Commission, meet with him at a downtown restaurant for dinner, then return to his office afterward for discussion. Frances Perkins recalled that when the group assembled a few days later Smith, with his old-fashioned notions of propriety, had brought his wife and mother along, because, as he said, there were to be women present: Ida Blair of the Women's City Club, Miss Perkins, and, of course, Belle Moskowitz. Of the other ten or so persons who attended this meeting Miss Perkins remembered only Bernard Shientag, who had helped Mrs. Moskowitz with her outline. But when Smith authorized Mrs. Moskowitz to give the plan some preliminary publicity, as a kind of trial balloon, she was able to muster an impressive list of prominent citizens who agreed to serve as members of the Commission without pay: Charles H. Sabin, head of the Guaranty Trust; Abram Elkus (who was to be chairman); John C. McCall, insurance company magnate; John G. Agar, a public-spirited lawyer; Bernard Baruch, former chairman of the War Industries Board under President Wilson; George Foster Peabody, the philanthropist; V. Everitt Macy, prominent in Republican circles; Charles P. Steinmetz, the scientific chief of General Electric; Mortimer Schiff, financier; Dr. Henry Dwight Chapin, child welfare expert; Felix Adler, educator; Norman E. Mack, Buffalo newspaper publisher; and among others, Robert Moses, who signed on as research director.

Heartened by this nonpartisan or rather bipartisan support, Smith decided to lay the proposal for a Reconstruction Commission before the Legislature, and appointed Belle Moskowitz as its Executive Secretary. Not only was she the prime mover in this affair, but she had already shown that she could do more than plan; she could get things done. She worked calmly, and seemingly without effort; she handled people well, ever a jump ahead of others in her calculations, yet preserving an air of modesty, even of self-effacement.

A bill providing an appropriation of $75,000 for the expenses of the Commission was introduced before the Legislature, but although the sum was small and funds easily available, the money was denied the Governor in a straight party vote. The Republican machine controlling both houses was determined to pursue an obstructive policy toward all his recommendations. Smith was regarded by them as an "accidental" Governor, elected only as the result of an influenza epidemic, and all signs pointed to a nationwide Republican victory in 1920. Moreover his actions in sacking people from redundant state offices did not endear him to the majority party.

The Reconstruction Commission, nevertheless, launched forth upon its task of investigation and planning with great zeal. Several of its members, men of independent wealth, undertook to raise the money needed for staff expenses as a public service, and the myopia of the legislators became evident when the Commission's preliminary recommendations for tax reform alone, once implemented, saved the state some $3,000,000. Its far-reaching proposals for reorganizing the executive establishment, however, involved more time and study, along the lines laid out by Smith himself in his analysis of the problem at the constitutional convention in 1915.

*

The year 1919, when Smith first took office as Governor, proved to be one of the most turbulent periods in the history of these States, and New York escaped none of the frenzy of the rest of the nation. As the AEF veterans marched off the troopships to the music of jazz bands, they arrived in a homeland filled with unrest, which was reflected in race riots, spreading unemployment, bitter strikes, and strong public protest against inflated prices for commodities and high rents.

The President of the United States, however, was concerned with loftier matters. Although his party had recently lost control of both houses of Congress, he confidently prepared to embark for Europe to draft the peace treaty and the covenant of the League of Nations that he expected to be his monument for all posterity. As he passed through New York to take ship, the notables of the city gave him a reception at the Metropolitan Opera House, which was presided over by Governor Smith with his usual aplomb. Wilson had given his warm endorsement to Smith's nomination in 1918, and Wilson's chief lieutenant and son-in-law, Secretary of the Treasury McAdoo, had also come to the support of Smith in an effusive letter of praise during the campaign, for McAdoo hoped to succeed his father-in-law and courted political friends. Introducing the President on this occasion, Smith in a brief talk not only reflected a regard for his party's leader, but also conveyed the feeling of agonizing hope which many attached to Wilson's mission to Versailles:

> Whatever may be the crossfire of opinion . . . we are all agreed upon one thing, that America will not have completed her part in the great world conflict until she has done everything possible to prevent the recurrence of the death, the misery, the

suffering, and the devastation that has from time immemorial
followed in the wake of war . . . [President Wilson] told the
mothers of our country that they were giving up their sons so
that there would never be another war. To the fulfillment of
that promise he has dedicated himself . . . .

From the start of his first term Smith showed himself
extremely responsive to popular grievances and eager to
attempt corrective action. Early in January he received the
complaints of citizens' groups from New York City about
the high cost of milk (which had risen from eight or ten
cents before the war to eighteen cents a quart) as well as
the scarcity of dairy products. A milk strike was in progress,
30,000 farmers of the Dairymen's League having refused the
terms set by the large wholesalers-distributors, principally
Borden's and Sheffield Farms. Smith promptly called a conference of both sides to the dispute, and after making some
inquiries about the situation, proposed that the State Farm
and Market Commissioner be removed from office for incompetence, and that the Department of Health be empowered
to regulate prices and bring about an increase in the supply
of milk. These measures needed the approval of the legislators, who only two years earlier had curbed the Governor's
authority in this area by making the Farm and Market Commissioner responsible to them, the legislators, presumably
in the interest of upstate dairy farmers! Here again a hostile
Legislature blocked action, withholding approval of Smith's
milk bills.

It will be remembered that Smith had pledged himself in
his campaign to restore the Workmen's Compensation Act in
its original form, as passed in 1913, when he had been instrumental in pushing it through the Legislature. One of his first

acts as Governor was to appoint Jeremiah F. Connor as Moreland Commissioner to investigate the workings of that act
as amended in 1915, under Governor Whitman. In a preliminary report, made in the middle of March, Connor reported that the revised act, by permitting direct settlement
of compensation claims between employer and employee,
instead of adjudication of claims by the Workmen's Compensation Bureau of the Industrial Commission, had worked
many injustices. Not only had Connor found numerous cases
of unfair settlements, but he had also discovered that records
of claims were lost, that a ring of grafters working for the
State Fund extorted money from claimants, that physicians
acting as representatives of the private insurance companies
invariably testified to the disadvantage of the employees, and
that "runners" hunted up injured workers and undertook to
obtain settlements at high cost, thus violating the very intention of the measure. Smith sent this preliminary report to
the Legislature, along with a bill providing that the Workmen's Compensation Bureau approve all settlements of claims
for injury, after proper hearings. In this case the two houses,
otherwise so obstructive, yielded and passed the measure in
the form desired by the Governor. It was a typical instance
of Smith's responsiveness to the public need, of his determination to redeem campaign pledges, and of his resourcefulness
in winning remedial action.

In other areas the tug of war between the Governor and
the Republican machine continued through 1919 and into
the session of 1920. Almost all the bills he sponsored, especially the social welfare measures, were defeated, or shelved
in committee, while for his part the Governor used the veto
power drastically to cut down ripper bills. In fact, to win

support for a measure he advocated — such as one providing
for rent control and tax inducements for low-income dwellings to relieve the housing crisis — he brought out a whole
bag of tricks: his considerable arts of persuasion, the power
of patronage, and the threat to veto bills desired by the majority party. To these he added a new approach: appealing
to the public over the heads of the legislators by releasing
vigorous statements to the press and presenting the issues
clearly whenever he had occasion to address some public
gathering in one of the large cities. Thus at the Jefferson Day
dinner in April in New York City, before a gathering of Democratic leaders both state and national, he inveighed against
the "senseless opposition [of the Republicans] to all progressive legislation in the interests of the health and welfare of
all the people." The rigidly obstructive tactics of the Barnes
Republican machine in Albany, he contended, gave force to
the appeals of radicals

> who seek to shake the very foundations of our government and
> who say to the people: "You can expect nothing from Washing-
> ton and Albany, for the whole government is in the hands of
> the moneyed interest. The only relief you can get is by taking
> the Government into your own hands!"

One group of scholars, combing Smith's record for intima-
tions of his later conservatism, has maintained that he always
had a bent in that direction, but the truth is rather that like
Theodore Roosevelt before him, and the New Dealers afterward, he advocated the "middle way" of moderate social reform as a means of avoiding more extreme alternatives. In
that season of bomb scares and red hunts in the United
States, and of civil war in Germany and Russia, revolution
seemed not too remote a prospect.

The close of the regular legislative session in May found Smith in his office at the Capitol all day and far into the night, conferring patiently with legislative committees and scrutinizing all the fine print in those last-hour bills. He was incensed when he found that the housing relief bill had been allowed to die in committee at adjournment, and used his authority to call the Legislature back in special session to consider it anew. In the last days of June he obtained enough votes from the majority party for the passage of two bills covering this matter, which he was able to sign in good faith, although he would need to call later for broader housing relief.

It was plain that Smith engaged in much horse trading with the standpatter Republicans. If their leaders made him a practical offer, he used to say, he would not hang back. The housing bills he pushed through at the special session were in fact quite modest beginnings; their main purpose was to encourage bank lending at favorable rates for low-income residential construction. Some rumors circulated that the Governor had made secret bargains with the Republican leaders, Speaker Thad Sweet and Senator J. Henry Walters, in order to win his point. He was accused of having promised to allow them to have their way in changing the state primary law back to the old party convention system in return for their support of measures he desired. Smith laughed at these charges and remarked that he could not possibly have lent himself to such a bargain because he believed the proposed repeal of the primary law would surely be voted down by the people.

❋

Industrial conflicts came in a great wave that year, as the now militant workers drove hard to win the eight-hour day, wage increases, and union recognition. The Governor had already distinguished himself as a strong friend of labor, and had spoken as such at the 1918 state convention of the AFL. But when violence broke out at the Bethlehem Steel plants in Lackawanna, Smith promptly dispatched a force of state militia to the scene. Soon afterward, during a strike of copper mill workers at Rome, he tried to act as an honest broker between the warring parties and took the unusual step of sending in Frances Perkins, the woman member of the State Industrial Commission, to mediate the conflict. Her vivid recollections of the affair throw light on Smith's actual role in the contests between capital and labor.

The city of Rome, in upper New York State, a one-industry town manufacturing copper products, was virtually paralyzed toward the end of May when 4000 mill workers walked out. After having enjoyed a wartime boom, the copper mills were feeling the pinch of reduced orders, and had begun to cut wages. At first the strike was conducted in a peaceable manner, but the employers refused to treat with the workers' committee, and imported strikebreakers. Thereupon crowds of idle men and their families gathered at the bridges over the Mohawk and Black Rivers which led to the factories, and tried to picket the scabs, while the town police force of sixty-two stood guard to prevent disorder.

After a fortnight of this partial stoppage, the Rome workers became greatly agitated on learning that striking copper mill hands in Waterbury, Connecticut, had won their fight for an eight-hour day and wage increases. The Rome manufacturers, however, still refused to meet with their men's representatives. Relations between the idle workers and the strikebreakers, meanwhile, became "ugly," as the Mayor of the town judged, and so, in late June, numerous sheriff's deputies were called in to guard the plants. On July 13 John A. Spargo, President of the Spargo Wire Company, tried to drive his car through a crowd of strikers massed before the gates of his plant. The car was stopped, he was roughly handled, and in the melee, it was reported, he took up a gun and fired it off. Some claimed he had shot right into the crowd, and that two men had been killed, a report which, though never verified, swept like wildfire through the town, rousing the population, many of whom were Italian immigrants, to a pitch of excitement.

Mayor H. C. Midlam, who had been trying to mediate the dispute, now telegraphed Governor Smith that the workers were riotous, and that state troopers were needed to preserve order. The attorney for the copper mill association, a former Assemblyman and old acquaintance, also called Smith on the telephone, repeating the Mayor's request. "I told him I was quite ready to do so," Smith wrote afterward in *Up to Now,* "for the preservation of law and order, but that I believed the officials [of the companies] should first be willing to sit around the table with a representative of the Department of Labor and talk terms of settlement." His choice of Frances Perkins for this delicate mission was a token of his confidence in her judgment.

As a matter of fact he also dispatched troops, some two hundred strong, to the scene, a day ahead of Miss Perkins, who arrived to find that quiet was restored on the surface, while underneath the situation was fairly explosive. Not only were the workers arming themselves, some with rocks and some with guns, but a few were reported to have hidden a cache of dynamite somewhere in the working class section of town. Miss Perkins talked with the Mayor, conferred with the union's grievance committee, met with members of the Chamber of Commerce, impressing all those she spoke to with her poise and sweet reasonableness; but underneath, as she related afterward, she was harrowed by fear of what might happen at any moment. Fortunately Patrick J. Downey, of the Industrial Commission's Bureau of Mediation, who accompanied her on this mission, made some discreet inquiries, and with the aid of the more moderate union men, located the explosives, which were carried off in the dead of night to be dumped into the Mohawk River.

Now Miss Perkins could breathe more easily, but in the course of a week, after which the militia were withdrawn, nothing had in reality been settled. The town was paralyzed still, the merchants lamented their losses, and the Governor continued to urge both sides to meet with each other. Before leaving town Miss Perkins made a very sensible proposal which the Chamber of Commerce, speaking for the manufacturers, accepted with some reluctance, namely that a public hearing on the dispute be held before the State Industrial Commission sitting in Rome, with power to subpoena witnesses, take testimony, and examine records and books, though without authority to impose a settlement. The purpose of this procedure, not altogether new in such cases, was to bring everything out into the open and use the power of public opinion to bring about peace.

On August 3, therefore, Miss Perkins returned to Rome, on this occasion in company with three other members of the Industrial Commission, including its chairman, the aged

John Mitchell, famous leader of the coal miners in the early years of the century. The public hearing opened ceremoniously in the main chamber of the Rome Court House before a large crowd. Just before the hearing Mitchell had made a last effort to induce both parties to seek a compromise at a private meeting, but the employers, through their attorneys, continued to reject these proposals, insisting that the commissioners treat with each side separately. Mitchell, hero of the great coal strike of 1903, could not but have been reminded of that earlier struggle, when George Baer, President of the mineowners' association, refused President Theodore Roosevelt's request to sit down with a representative of the striking miners (Mitchell) in a time of national emergency.

At the public hearing workers testified that they had been subjected to speedups and wage cuts, that all their proposals had been rejected, that immediately after they had walked out, strikebreakers had appeared on the scene. One witness described how when a strikers' committee called on Mr. Spargo he had thrown them down the stairs. When afterward the strikers submitted their demands by mail to Spargo, he had replied in a letter studded with obscenities, which being submitted in evidence, Mitchell felt obliged to read aloud, distasteful though it was to him. Indeed the lawyer for the manufacturers was led to declare that his group dissociated itself from Spargo and all his works.

The reading of this obscene letter marked the beginning of a break in the ranks of the employers, and caused their chief attorney to concede that an upward adjustment of wages, in line with those paid by competitors in the Connecticut mills, was just and due. Mayor Midlam was also brought to testify that in his appeals for aid to Governor Smith, he had exaggerated the disorder in the town, and that, in fact, no one had been killed in any street brawls. Within a few days of the close of the hearings direct negotiations between the employers and the workers, undertaken through the offices of the Mayor, brought an end to the strike, with agreements on improved hours and wages, and eventual recognition of the union.

The Governor's Industrial Commissioners received praise on all sides for their good performance, and left town, as Frances Perkins recalled, "in a blaze of glory." On her return to Albany she filled in the Governor on all that had taken place, including some details not mentioned in their telephone communications during the crisis. Smith was both consternated and amused at the episode of the dynamite cache. "You sure had your nerve," he exclaimed. "It was a risky business. But now it's all over and I congratulate you, Commissioner." In his autobiography Smith recalled that while the Rome manufacturers had at first been taken aback when he proposed sending a woman to deal with their labor problems, they sent word afterward: "Do us a favor and ask the Governor where he got that woman."

Some years later, when the Governor asked Miss Perkins for a written statement on whether the state should establish compulsory arbitration of labor disputes, she answered somewhat sententiously, "Such a practice can hardly be followed now, but compulsion should be a moral compulsion brought about by public opinion rather than by statute." That was how the problem had been worked out through the open hearings at Rome.

The year 1919 also signalized itself as the heyday of the superpatriots and the red-hunters. Soldiers and sailors returned from the war formed into mobs in the street, made festivals of hanging the Kaiser in effigy, and also attacked physically processions of Socialists or gatherings of labor unionists — against whom the cry of "Bolsheviks" was raised. Bombs went off before the home of U.S. Attorney-General Mitchell Palmer — who distinguished himself by his pursuit of alleged radicals — and in New York and Seattle. The chain of mysterious bomb episodes, attributed to anarchists, seemed to end with the catastrophic explosion in September, 1920, outside the Morgan bank in Wall Street. Meanwhile a huge expansion of the Federal Bureau of Investigation was carried out, enabling Palmer to send its agents all about the country to arrest Wobblies and radicals of every stripe, and deport those who were alien immigrants. In Massachusetts, in the period of this drag hunt, two anarchists, Sacco and Vanzetti, were indicted on charges of having perpetrated a payroll killing, tried, and sentenced to death.

At the end of the war there had been a spirited uprising of the American labor movement, AFL and IWW alike — provoked by the inflated prices of all goods — and a million workers were out on strike by November, 1919. The great "anti-Bolshevik" crusade of 1919–1920 was promoted by American business and manufacturing interests in reality as a counteraction aimed mainly at organized labor, the like of which, for public hysteria and folly, was not equaled until the era of Joseph McCarthy thirty years later.

Not to be outdone in patriotic fervor, the New York State Legislature set up a joint committee under the chairmanship of Senator Clayton Lusk to investigate "seditious activity" not only in political and labor organizations, but in schools, even as manifested in books and other publications. Lists of persons presumed to hold "dangerous anarchistic sentiments" were compiled and made public, including such names as Jane Addams, Oswald Garrison Villard, and Lillian Wald. Witnesses were subpoenaed and examined before the Lusk Committee in an atmosphere of wartime frenzy.

Governor Smith was one of the few public men who struggled to stem the frantic anti-Red campaign. In April, 1919, at the Jefferson Day dinner, for example, when he took the Republican opposition to task for obstructing the people's legitimate demands for reform, he also argued that "the Committee appointed to investigate Bolshevism may be creating something for it to investigate." But he could not reverse the tide. After the November elections in 1919, when five Socialists were sent up to the Assembly from New York City, the Legislature opened its 1920 session by voting to expel them, and then proceeded to put them on trial on charges of "plotting to overthrow our system of government by force." The Bar Association of New York City issued a strong protest against this highhanded action, which was echoed by Charles Evans Hughes, the 1916 Republican Party presidential candidate and future Chief Justice of the Supreme Court. But the Legislature was unmoved; the trial continued while the three so-called Lusk Bills, which proposed to curb freedom of speech, test the loyalty of teachers, require the registration of private schools, and control their curricula in order to safeguard the minds of the young from dangerous thoughts, were debated.

Bowing to the fashion of the day Governor Smith himself, on at least one occasion, also indulged in a little tirade against the evils of Bolshevism. This was during an address at Cornell University, in the course of which he stated that the universities were suspected of being hotbeds of subversive ideas (then as in later years). The extravagances of the Lusk Committee, however, repelled him. On the day after the five Socialist Assemblymen were expelled from the Legislature he issued a strong statement to the press rebuking the lower house for its drastic action and affirming his belief in the doctrine of freedom of dissent in a democratic society:

> Although I am unalterably opposed to the fundamental principles of the Socialist Party, it is inconceivable that a minority party, duly constituted and legally organized, should be deprived of the right of expression so long as it has honestly, by lawful methods of education and propaganda, succeeded in securing representation . . . It is true that the Assembly had arbitrary power to determine the qualifications of its members, but where arbitrary power exists it should be exercised with care, because from it there is no appeal.

No proof was offered that the Socialist Assemblymen intended to overthrow the government of New York State by violence, he contended, nor were they being tried by orderly processes; hence they should be presumed innocent and allowed to retain their seats. He concluded:

> Our faith in American democracy is confirmed not only by its results, but by its methods and organs of free expression. They are the safeguards against revolution. To discard the methods of representative government leads to misdeeds of the very extremists we denounce and serves to increase the number of enemies of orderly, free government.

This statesmanlike utterance was ignored by the Legislature, which passed Lusk's three anti-sedition bills with the support of many of Smith's fellow Democrats, for the contagion of crowd hysteria about Red sorcery respects no party lines.

Smith decided to veto the Lusk Bills and to make his veto

message a forceful appeal for the defense of the rights of minorities. In preparing this message he leaned on the advice of the group of intellectuals he had attracted to his staff, particularly Mrs. Moskowitz. She called on Joseph Proskauer, who had helped write speeches for Smith during the gubernatorial campaign, to draft the veto statement, which he couched in elegant prose, flavored with apt quotations from classical writers on human liberty such as Jefferson, Franklin, and Tocqueville. Now Smith always insisted on editing his own messages, and after reading Proskauer's draft he turned to Mrs. Moskowitz, and asked her who Tocqueville was. She explained. "Tell Proskauer," he said, "I know who Jefferson is, and I may be supposed to know who Ben Franklin is; but if I quote Tocqueville everybody will say Al Smith never wrote that. He never heard of the man."

In the veto message as finally worked out Smith argued that one of the bills was designed to authorize the prosecution of people for criminal anarchy by establishing a section of secret police in the District Attorney's office. "The traditional abhorrence of a free people for all kinds of spies and secret police," he said, "is . . . justified and calls for the disapproval of this measure." Of the bill providing for loyalty tests for teachers and permitting someone in authority to place the stigma of disloyalty upon teachers without a hearing, he pointed out that

> Every teacher would be at the mercy of his colleagues, his pupils, and their parents . . . The bill unjustly discriminates against teachers as a class. It deprives [them] of their right to freedom of thought, it limits the teaching staff . . . to those only who lack the courage or the mind to exercise their legal

right to just criticism of existing institutions . . . The bill . . . strikes at the foundations of democratic education . . . I might rest upon the saying of Benjamin Franklin that "They that can give up essential liberty to obtain a little temporary safety deserve neither liberty nor safety." But I go further — the safety of this government and its institutions rests upon the reasoned . . . loyalty of its people. It does not need for its defense a system of intellectual tyranny which, in the endeavor to choke error by force, must of necessity crush truth as well.

Neither did Smith forget the five Socialist Assemblymen, whose long trial ended in their conviction. On September 16, 1920, he issued a proclamation calling for a special election in their districts, declaring that he could not in all conscience accept the "undemocratic way of thinking" that would permit five Assembly districts, containing a quarter of a million people, to go unrepresented.

Another manifestation of Smith's attitude toward freedom to express dissent was given a few years later, when several members of the Sinn Fein called on him and besought him to "do justice to Jim Larkin." This daring Irish revolutionary, who, in transferring his activities to the United States, had become a leading figure in the IWW movement, stood convicted of criminal syndicalism during the war for having published a pamphlet entitled "Left-Wing Socialism." Smith knew how to address these impetuous Irish rebels; his blue eyes flashing, he spoke to them sternly, pointing out that the question of justice was not involved in the instance of Larkin, since there had been a proper court trial. There was only the question of "mercy," and since he was then running for the Governorship again, he emphasized that it would be unlawful for him to make any promises, except that if he were reelected he would give careful consideration to Larkin's case. Several months afterward, following his return to Albany, one of his first executive acts was to issue a full pardon to Larkin, on the basis that it was wrong of the state to punish a man for his political beliefs, or for his "public assertion of an erroneous doctrine." Moreover, he held, Larkin had never been accused of "moral turpitude" or of committing any overt insurrectionary act. Smith's decision was based on the dissenting opinion of two eminent judges of the Court of Appeals (which had earlier refused to review Larkin's conviction), one of them being Benjamin Cardozo. Two years later still, when the case of the Communist Benjamin Gitlow, identical with that of Larkin, was finally lost in the United States Supreme Court, Smith granted executive clemency to Gitlow on the ground taken by Justice Holmes, that the condemned man presented no "clear and present danger" to the state.

According to veteran state officials of his era, Smith gave more time and labor to appeals for executive clemency than any governor before him. He worked closely with the Pardons Clerk, often studying the recorded evidence minutely, especially when the death sentence had been imposed, and entertained every last-minute plea by relatives or counsel. On several occasions he confessed that he had been unable to sleep all night while going over testimony in his mind, and he once made a special trip to New York City to study the site of a crime so that he could form his own judgment. It was his habit too to have mothers, wives, and sisters of criminals seeking mitigation of a sentence admitted to him without delay. Judges remarked that in time he became a highly informed criminal lawyer in his own right. The burdens of the pardon system were almost intolerable to him, and he was evidently tormented while waiting for news of the execution of some hardened killer to whom he would not grant reprieve.

At the same time he had a soft spot for rascals or offenders of the more amusing, less deadly kind, who approached him through old political cronies, and he sometimes tried to have their sentences reduced, or their sojourn in prison made more tolerable. Robert Moses recalls the story of a certain Mrs. Knapp, a high Republican state official, and a very attractive woman, who was caught red-handed at fraudulent practices just before the Republicans went out of office. While her trial was going on she came to see the Governor, an old acquaintance, put her hand in his, and murmured, "You haven't lost faith in me, Al?" To strengthen her appeal "she was done up all in pink from head to toe," Smith told Moses, adding, "She looked like a basket of peaches." He interceded discreetly to obtain a suspended sentence, but failing to move a judge with a stern Scotch-Irish conscience, he saw to it that she spent the year of her imprisonment in comparatively comfortable quarters, after which she disappeared forever from public view.

The Governor's most ambitious project, however, in his first as in his later terms, was the reorganization of the state's executive departments, and to achieve this he kept pressing the members of the Reconstruction Commission to come up with definite recommendations that could either be introduced as bills before the Legislature or presented as constitutional amendments. Mrs. Moskowitz and Robert Moses, hard at work with numerous subcommittees, needed no urging. Preliminary reports were issued during 1919, and a fairly complete report covering many areas of the state administration was ready in time to be submitted to the 1920 session of the Legislature.

The chairman of the Commission, Abram Elkus, related that Smith came down to one session of the Commission in the autumn of 1919 to examine a chart representing the many departments and subdivisions of the state government, which they had prepared with great pains. The chart, tacked to a wall, was eighteen feet wide. Smith studied it for a few minutes, then launched into an informal exposition of how most of the bureaus had grown up, recalling in detail the various bills that created them, the time and purpose of each, and how they had been "put over to do work that was already being done by other bureaus." "We had spent six months in finding out what the Governor told us in one hour," Elkus recalled. "We should have had him make his talk in the first place."

The Commission's proposals called for three principal amendments to the state constitution. The first, the "consolidation amendment," would have merged the many scores of bureaus into approximately sixteen executive departments whose directors would be responsible to the Governor and members of his Cabinet; it also provided for a short ballot, by which certain elective offices, such as that of state architect and state engineer, would be made appointive. A second amendment would change the Governor's term of office from two to four years, and a third, perhaps the most important of all, would establish an executive budget system, whereby total annual expenditures could be effectively planned ahead, instead of being left to chance. Other significant passages of this voluminous report set up programs for public works to be initiated during times of depression, low-income housing projects to be sponsored by the state and carried out by limited-dividend corporations, and for sweeping reconstruction of the state's hospitals and mental health institutions.

In order to bring about a climate of opinion favorable to these reforms Smith and Mrs. Moskowitz began an educational campaign as early as October, 1919; they sought to exert pressure on the next session of the Legislature, but more important still, to inform and influence the public. Charles Evans Hughes was persuaded to join with Smith in speaking for the program before the City Club on December 8. On the basis of his own experience as Governor, Hughes warmly endorsed the plan of reorganization. Smith pointed out that there was a general trend toward consolidation of overgrown state bureaucracies throughout the nation, notably in Illinois and Massachusetts. In reference to the Reconstruction Commission's proposals for an executive budget, he explained that although New York's appropriations had doubled in the last five years, exceeding the then enormous sum of $100,000,000, the Governor had no power to plan or control the state's expenditures, as his authority was limited to either accepting or vetoing in toto the estimated appropriations of the numerous bureaus or departments. Smith wished to make the Governor directly responsible for the proper functioning of the state's administration, and accountable to the Legislature and to the people for every penny spent.

Mrs. Moskowitz, a pioneer in public relations work in those days, laid stress on winning the support of businessmen's and civic organizations for the Commission's program,

and succeeded in gaining broad press coverage and widespread editorial approval. It was in fact a nonpartisan and
nonpolitical project, as Smith emphasized. He went so far
as to promise that he would give credit for realization of
most of the program to both parties:

> I am not going to be like the fellow who insists on getting his
> bill the way it is printed . . . If they won't take it all, I will go
> along with [the Republicans] as far as they will, and I will
> promise that at no time will it be referred to as any program
> of mine. The real truth about it is that I could not think that
> all out myself.

The Legislature, however, continuing its obstructionist
tactics, supported the "consolidation amendment" only, and
blocked the executive budget plan and the four-year term for
Governor. Smith, showing himself a stubborn adversary,
continued to bring pressure to bear upon the Republican
majority. He would continue to fight for long years for the
rest of the program until it was completely incorporated in
the state apparatus under the governorship of his successor
and disciple, Franklin Roosevelt. As Robert Wagner said,
reorganization of the state government was to be Smith's
great monument written into law.

Nevertheless he came under sharp attack from opponents
of the reorganization program. A high state official who was
a Republican, debating with him before the Women's City
Club during the election campaign of 1920, contended that
Smith was aiming to concentrate all state power in his own
hands, to make himself a kind of "tsar," or at least a "king."
As he rose in rebuttal, Smith rapidly turned over in his mind
what he might say to undo the impression that he was an
incipient tyrant, then suddenly flashed his broad grin and

said in the most disarming tone, "Well, meet the King, the King of Oliver Street." The absurdity of the title aroused much laughter. But it also prefigured events to come with some accuracy, for as a result of the election that year the seat of Smith's "kingdom" was indeed to be removed for a while from Albany and returned to the old Fourth Ward.

CHAPTER XI

The Duel with Hearst

THE MOST DRAMATIC episode of Smith's first term as Governor of New York State grew out of a vendetta into which, like many other men in public life, he was drawn, almost against his will, with one of the most unpredictable characters in American history. Where he was simple and direct, his opponent was devious; where he was blameless, his adversary was guilt-ridden, but in this encounter Smith turned on his tormenter with a blazing passion that he himself was unaware that he possessed. As a boy he had shown a distaste for brawls; as a young man he had made his way by cultivating the friendly arts of persuasion and conciliation, but he was never without courage, and if, as a rule, he held his emotions under firm control they were none the less powerful. The enemy he now faced was not to be placated, not to be won over by reason. He had to be beaten into the ground.

William Randolph Hearst, lord of the yellow press, was one of the mighty beasts that prowled the political jungles of New York in the days of Smith's rise to state leadership. Having removed from his native California to the wider stage of New York City in 1895, he had used his inherited wealth

— as earlier in San Francisco — to build up two sensa-
tional newspapers, which operated in fierce competition with
Joseph Pulitzer's *World*, then America's most powerful daily.
Indeed Hearst was accumulating a whole chain of news-
papers spreading from Boston and New York to the Pacific
Coast.

The millions of readers he addressed made him a man to
be reckoned with. But can we discern in him any values, any
direction or object in life? Several historians and biographers,
puzzling over his random movements and his erratic career,
have suggested that he was an amoral "superman." Certainly
his defeats, his blunders were on the grand scale, and so were
his losses, which only the mining fortune bequeathed to him
by his father could cover. If there was any recognizable pattern in Hearst's life it was based on his lust for political
power, his ambition to be "king," which in the United States
meant to be President. Failing in that he could at least make
or unmake other "kings," by playing the role of president-
maker.

After combining forces with the lowest element in Tammany Hall (Croker and his gang) Hearst managed to buy
himself a seat in Congress, but this proved boring, and next
he tried in vain in 1904 to win the Democratic nomination
for the Presidency. Nor did he have better success when he
aimed lower, meeting defeat as he ran successively for Mayor
of New York and for the Governorship. For a period thereafter he fell out with the local politicians and with Tammany,
only to return later to an uneasy alliance with Boss Murphy.
A large man with small eyes, a small mouth, and a cold, limp
hand, Hearst was certain that his money could buy anything
he wanted — men, women, position, political power — as

easily as he could buy landed properties, antiques, and art objects; yet few loved him and fewer still trusted him.

In 1917 he did, however, acquire some political capital, when he supported the candidacy of John Hylan; with Hylan's victory he gained a decisive influence in New York City. He next coveted the gubernatorial nomination in 1918, but was easily bested by Smith. Smith even went so far as to make a public statement rejecting Hearst's offer of help in that campaign. Thick-skinned when it suited his book, Hearst tried nonetheless to make overtures to Smith after the election, and thus extend his influence over the new state administration, only to be rebuffed again. The publisher's reawakened ambitions for some high office that would permit him to strike out for the Presidency later were frustrated by Smith's indifference to his requests for official favors, and Hearst determined to cut him down to size.

He had plunged large sums in the hiring of some of the ablest newspaper writers and cartoonists in the country, and when they were instructed to lay down a barrage of mud it was generally so effective that the bespattered victims soon came to terms. Day after day the New York *American* now published venomous attacks on Smith in editorials questioning "the sincerity of [his] professions of progressive principles," charging him with having always been "too close to Tammany, and too close to certain public service corporations." It was claimed that Smith had pledged himself to promote the public ownership of certain public utilities by the cities, but had gone back on his promises. "The people hate a trimmer, a backer and filler . . . a compromiser and temporizer," thundered Hearst's minions.

These first unkindly reflections proved to be only a light

shower compared to the storm of abuse that followed in the summer, when the milk crisis that had threatened the city in the winter months became acute. While ignoring Smith's earlier efforts to obtain a milk-control bill from the Legislature (without which he was powerless to intervene), the New York *American* in August and September published a series of articles accusing the Governor of being principally accountable for the chaotic condition of the food markets, and for the scarce supply of milk and its high cost. Impure, unpasteurized milk was being sold to the poor of the city, Hearst's reporters claimed. "BABIES ARE DYING IN NEW YORK" ran the grim headlines of the *Evening Journal*, whose front-page editorial held that the Governor condoned such evil-doing:

> Governor Smith! You have sold the babies to the Milk Trust, as that other Judas, President Wilson, has sold the world to British tyranny.

Accompanying these fantastic accusations were heart-rending drawings by great cartoonists such as Rollin Kirby or Art Young showing gaunt, ragged mothers clutching their infants to their dry breasts, begging for milk.

The tenderhearted father of five, in whom love of children was very strong, was sorely wounded by these false accusations, and by the vivid cartoons picturing him as a monster, but for the while he made no answer. It is not always wise for a public man to dignify blatant slander by giving it notice. The attacks continued through the fall, when he had occasion to go to Brooklyn to visit his mother, who was seriously ill. It was reported to him that while delirious with fever she had been heard to cry out something to the effect that

"My son did not kill those babies. He was a poor boy. He loves children." Catherine Smith too had seen the Hearst papers.

For the Governor that was the last straw. He was a politic man, disinclined to conflicts, slow to anger, but once driven to fight he could be a savage antagonist. True, his opponent was known to show no quarter in any contest; his private eyes shadowed his victims or their friends and relatives, gathering every scrap of evidence or information that could be put to use in some slanderous way; he held a sword over the Democratic Party in New York City, it was said, and could, at will, cause them to lose an election. Most politicians made it their rule not to "answer" Hearst. Smith understood all this, but under extreme provocation resolved to come to grips with the man, though acknowledging that this was going to be "the dirtiest fight" of his life.

On October 10, 1919, the Governor appeared before the Women's Democratic League in New York City and for the first time in public spoke in reply to Hearst's attacks. He represented the publisher as an unprincipled demagogue who for his own selfish reasons pretended to be devoting himself to the welfare of the masses. Through his newspapers he had made false statements about the milk situation, and about the Governor being in league with the "milk barons." Once and for all he must be called to account for all the falsehoods he had circulated. Then his powerful voice rising, his face flaming, his fist crashing on the lectern, the Governor challenged Hearst to meet him in debate on the issues between them. A citizens' committee had been formed, Smith said, to help clear up this business, and had hired Carnegie Hall for the evening of October 29; let Hearst come there and substantiate his charges.

New York buzzed with excitement over Smith's declaration of war, the politicians prophesying darkly that it would cause an open breach between Hearst and Mayor Hylan on the one side, and Smith and Tammany Hall on the other. No one knew what the consequences of such a split would be, in view of Hearst's immense resources and his press power. Some of Smith's advisers had tried to dissuade him from answering Hearst, but hundreds of citizens, on the other hand, had written letters commending him on his stand. Three days after his first challenge Smith issued another statement reminding Hearst of the invitation to a joint debate, about which the publisher's "filthy sheets" remained strangely silent. His "Irish" was up, Smith said; he was "going to the mat" with Hearst, and not all the publisher's millions nor his widespread newspaper empire could save him from the consequences of an open discussion.

Hearst was known to be in New York at the time, but soon it was reported that he had left for Palm Beach, and from there had proceeded to the California coast, where the man whose heart bled for the starving children of New York was busy overseeing the construction of a fabulous castle at San Simeon. To explain his absence he inserted a statement in his newspapers to the effect that he had no time to waste answering the complaints of "faithless and unreliable public servants" about criticisms of their performance.

On the evening of October 29 Carnegie Hall was packed from pit to gallery as Smith appeared, alone, amid wild cheers, to enact his drama of passion as a monologue. Although he began gravely enough, he soon roared like a lion as he went on, the words spilling from him in a torrent. It was not a speech prepared in advance, or that anybody wrote for him, but it was one of his greatest performances.

I am going to ask for your absolute silence and attention [he said]. I feel I am here upon a mission as important not only to myself but to this city, this state and this country, as I could possibly perform. Of course I am alone. [A voice: "He hasn't got the nerve to face you, Al!"] I felt that I would be alone because I know the man to whom I issued the challenge and I know that he has not got a drop of good, clean, red, pure blood in his whole body. And I know the color of his liver, and it is whiter, if that could be, than the driven snow. In his morning edition he has a picture of me with a laboring man on one side, and a mother and her children on the other. The heading of it is: "Answer these people, Governor Smith." I want to say to this audience that I was anxious to bring him on this platform so that *he* could answer to these people. They need no answer from me. They need it from him.

The Governor reviewed the series of incidents that had led to the breach between Hearst and himself. A jingo during the war with Spain in 1898, Hearst had opposed our entrance into the war with Germany in 1917; he had assailed President Wilson, and later acted as an implacable opponent of the League of Nations program. Yet early in 1919 he asked Smith to put him on the Governor's Reception Committee to welcome New York's Seventy-seventh Division on its return home. Feeling that it would be unseemly for him to appoint the leading opponent of the wartime administration to such a committee, Smith refused. Again Hearst, through an intermediary, asked that a friend of his be appointed to one of the state commissions, but the Governor appointed a woman from western New York to that place. "Ten days after that — and watch the circumstantial case, follow me along with it . . . ten days after that the first editorial appears in the New York *American* . . . one of those editorials of warning," Smith told his attentive audience.

Then in May, he refused to appoint Hearst's own attorney as
a Judge of the Supreme Court, naming instead a man he
considered of superior merit. Now, said Smith, the editorial
warfare began in earnest. First he was charged with having
"conspired" with wealthy men to prevent the building of
homes for the poor, next that he favored the traction corporations, and finally when these attacks proved to be duds, he
was accused of causing starvation among the poor children
of New York because he "refused to reduce the price of milk."
The speech went on:

> Any man that . . . conjures up for you a fancied grievance
> against your government or against the man at the head of it,
> to help himself, is breeding the seeds of anarchy . . . more disas-
> trous . . . than any other teaching . . . because the wildest
> Anarchist, the most extreme Socialist, the wildest radical at
> least may be sincere in his own heart . . . But the man that
> preaches to the poor . . . discontent and dissatisfaction to help
> himself and to destroy, as he said he would, the Governor of
> the State, is a man as low and mean as I can picture him.
> [Hearst] attempted to fix in the minds of the people that there
> existed some place in the statutes power on the part of the
> Governor to fix the price of milk . . . He knows that is not so.
> His lawyers know that it is not so — and he has the best legal
> advice, because he never utters a word until it's scrutinized
> by an array of lawyers to keep him from libel suits. No power
> exists in my hands or in the hands of any other agency of the
> State to fix the price of anything in this state, whether it is milk,
> shoes or houses.

He listed other lies published in the Hearst press, and
added that this policy of deception was not to be wondered
at, for Hearst constantly tried to spread the belief that "no
one ever elected to office has not been tainted in some way,"

that no man in office had enough Christian principle or respect for himself to do the right thing.

> What kind of a seed does that breed in your mind? [Smith
> exclaimed] . . . What difference does it make how much mis-
> representation there is, if there is a Governor that has got to
> be destroyed because he is not amenable to orders? . . . No-
> body that ever went up to the Governor's office went there
> with a graver sense of responsibility than I did. What could
> there possibly be about me that I should be assailed in this
> reckless manner by this man? I have more reason, probably,
> than any man I will meet here tonight to have a strong love
> and a strong devotion for this country, for this State and for this
> city. Look what I have received at its hands; I left school and
> went to work when I was fifteen; I worked hard night and day;
> I worked honestly and conscientiously at every job I was ever
> put at, until I went to the Governor's chair at Albany. What
> can it be? It has got to be jealousy . . . envy, it has got to be
> hatred, or something that nobody understands, that forces me
> to come down here into the city of New York before this audi-
> ence and urge them to stay the danger that comes from these
> papers . . . to the end that we may be rid of this pestilence that
> walks in the dark.

It was not a statesmanlike oration; its sentences were
bludgeons; nor did the Governor present a pretty picture as
he thundered on, perspiring freely, his face livid, his impassioned gestures carrying him sometimes to the very edge
of the platform. But his audience was with him to a man,
and the people of the city always remembered that the mil-
lionaire publisher had been too craven to answer the Governor's charges. Al Smith made politics in New York State
dramatic. Hearst's big rivals, the *World* and the *Times,* were
only too happy to print the full text of Smith's explosive
speech, which was ignored, naturally, by the *American* and

Al Smith at the age of 4
at Coney Island, 1877

Al Smith's father (right) and friend
on the South Street docks

Al Smith (first row, second from left), wearing medal he won
for elocution, St. James School, Second Class, 1885

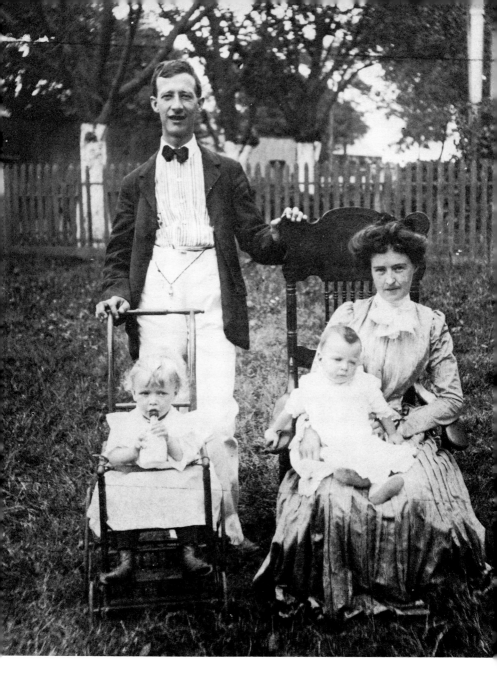

Al Smith at the age of 27 with his wife and children

Frances Perkins, Executive Secretary of the Consumers' League, c. 1911

Katie and Al Smith, Speaker of the Assembly, 1911

Al Smith with his wife and two younger sons,
during the 1918 campaign for Governor

Al Smith taking oath of office as Governor, 1922

Governor Smith's mother
(picture taken by the Governor
in her Brooklyn backyard), 1924

Governor Alfred E. Smith and
his family at Albany, 1923

Al Smith and Theodore Roosevelt, Jr. "You can't teach him much, Governor"—
Rollin Kirby cartoon during the 1924 gubernatorial campaign

Belle Moskowitz

Al Smith campaigning for the Presidency from train, 1928

Al Smith in Indianapolis, 1928

Al Smith with Governor Roosevelt in Albany, 1929

Al Smith, c. 1930

Colonel Edwin Halsey, secretary of the U.S. Senate; Nancy Cook (center), of Hyde Park, N.Y., and Secretary of Labor Frances Perkins, snapped at the evening session of the Democratic National Convention in Philadelphia, June 23, 1936

Mayor La Guardia, Smith, Katie, and Robert Moses at the dedication
of the Belt Parkway, Brooklyn, June 29, 1940

the *Journal;* after that it came to be generally accepted that one could put no faith in anything Hearst or his papers said, and men feared him less. Hearst's technique of the "big lie" (perfected later by Nazi propaganda chief Joseph Goebbels) was frustrated by Smith's indignant outburst that night at Carnegie Hall, and thereafter, although they continued to sneer at the Governor, the Hearst papers refrained from publishing outright lies about him.

Indeed the beginning of Hearst's decline in influence dated from that night in October, 1919. Ten years later, looking back on that episode, Smith expressed satisfaction with what he had done: ". . . I taught Mr. Hearst and his cohorts a lesson. It was the first chime in the death knell of Hearst's political power in the eastern part of this country." He seldom spoke of Hearst again in public, and he resumed his usually cool manner toward political opponents or critics. But Hearst did not yet acknowledge himself beaten in his drive toward national power in the Democratic Party; he would return several years later for a second, and final, round in his struggle with the redoubtable Smith.

Smith, meanwhile, had gained stature in the contest, appearing as a man jealous of his independence as of his reputation, looming above his chickenhearted fellows from Tammany Hall — who tried to compose their differences with Hearst — and now emerged as the strongest figure in the state's Democratic Party. And, incredible as it may seem, in 1920 the Hearst newspapers veered about again to support Smith for reelection to the Governorship.

The violence of his conflict with Hearst did not blind Smith to the continuing crisis in the milk situation. A month after his speech at Carnegie Hall he told a consumers' group in New York City that "the first and most sacred duty of every government is the preservation of the life and health of its people. If you take this view of it, the state, with its sovereign power, has to say what the price of milk is going to be." He empowered a Moreland Act Commission to investigate the milk problem, and later set up a Fair Price for Milk Committee under former Governor Martin Glynn. Mrs. Moskowitz, too, got into the act by issuing a report on behalf of the Reconstruction Commission urging that the distribution of milk be regulated as a public utility, like gas, electricity, and traction. Foreseeing the opposition to any regulatory measure by the Republican-dominated Legislature, Smith made numerous appearances in New York and other cities in an effort to gain public support. On one occasion he said that the need for milk was "not Democratic, not Republican and not Socialist." Why then should the big distributing corporations be free to shut down their creameries to reduce supply?

> There's no use having committees to discover the reason for Bolshevism, or criminal anarchy . . . or to expel Socialist members from the Assembly, when four men can sit around a table and say that the biggest city in the United States shall do without milk for three days.

He urged his hearers, many of them women, to write to their representatives in Albany, and their response to his appeal sometimes struck fear into the hearts of organization Republicans. This was probably Smith's greatest role: the teacher, educating the public on the state's problems and the state's business with his plain talk.

Still on April 14, 1920, the State Senate, submitting to the powerful lobby of the Dairymen's League (a giant milk combination) killed a measure sponsored by Smith that would have authorized a state commission to fix milk prices. In the closing days of the legislative session of 1920 the Governor kept a nightly vigil — up to midnight on the last Sunday — while he pressed the lawmakers to pass various social welfare bills; in vain, for they were all "put to sleep" with adjournment. The Barnes machine would yield nothing to the Democratic Governor, whom they confidently expected to be unseated in the fall elections. Disconsolate and angry as he left the Capitol that last night, Smith issued a statement berating the lawmakers. "The great forum for public discussion," he said, "was darkened, and the decision on humanity's needs left to be made in a side room behind closed doors."

As he faced the campaign for reelection in 1920, Smith said that it seemed "crazy" to limit the term of Governor to two years. He had thought he knew a great deal about the Governor's duties before he took office, but found that it needed two years merely to learn all the details of the job. The Legislature, as expected, had refused to support a recommendation for a constitutional amendment to extend the Governor's term to four years, among other proposals of the Reconstruction Commission. Nevertheless, as Smith modestly expressed it, he felt he had been "gradually making an impression upon the voters of the state." Indeed he had shown himself the most popular and colorful Governor New York could boast of since Theodore Roosevelt, whom he clearly surpassed in knowledge of the state's business. His renomination by the Democratic Convention in September, 1920, was to be made by acclamation, without opposition, for despite his leanings toward a "meritocracy" in the civil service, he had kept on good terms with the regular party workers, and they were proud of him.

Before running in the gubernatorial race, however, he was to have the honor, purely formal, of being nominated for President of the United States as New York's Favorite Son. The movement to put his name before the national convention had begun in February, 1920, when he was elected chairman of the state Democratic delegation to San Francisco, but Smith refused to regard it seriously, knowing that his nomination by the Tammany organization on the first ballot would be nothing more than a move in the horse trading that was to follow. The New York State group then had only slight leverage in the Democratic National Convention, mainly because its delegates were "Wets," pledged to modify the Volstead Act, while the bulk of the party, especially the Southern and Western faction, led by Bryan, was made up of Prohibitionists. In any case there were few who really wanted the hollow distinction of becoming the Democratic Party candidate for President in 1920, the first postwar election, which the Republicans were expected to win in a sweep.

As a Democratic Party "insider" Smith had served as a delegate to national conventions since 1904, on one occasion traveling as far from Manhattan Island as Denver, Colorado; now as Governor of the Empire State, head of the state delegation, and a Favorite Son to boot, he made the trip to San Francisco with Charles F. Murphy and his retinue in a private train equipped with enough stimulating beverages to make the long journey cheerful for the passengers.

On June 30 in San Francisco, after the opening ceremonies, Bourke Cockran, a veteran of Tammany Hall, widely known for his eloquence, rose to offer Smith's name to the convention in a curious and incoherent speech whose appeal could only have resided in the musical voice of the aging Congressman. "I came here to nominate a candidate who in his own life and career constitutes the most perfect platform for a political party," he began, and then represented Smith as a composite of an Abe Lincoln of the big city and a Horatio Alger hero, risen "from the peddler's wagon to the Governor's chair." He wound up:

> As Republican Senator James Wadsworth has said: "If there is a man in public life who deserves the love and respect of his fellows, that man is the Governor of New York." We offer him reluctantly to the Nation. The rest is up to the Convention. If you do not take him, New York will claim the privilege of taking back this favorite son of hers, and by making him candidate for Governor assure the success of the Democratic Party in our State.

What followed was the only spontaneous ovation and parade of that rather drab convention. The boys from Tammany seized banners and yelled and stomped about the auditorium; the band played Irish tunes, and also came up with a catchy air that henceforth became associated with Smith's name, "The Sidewalks of New York," the crowd joining in the chorus with great good will. When the commotion subsided Smith's nomination was seconded by Franklin D. Roosevelt, then Assistant Secretary of the Navy, who referred to the candidate as "our beloved Governor." "I love him as a friend," said Roosevelt, "look up to him as a man. If you could come to the Empire State and learn to know him you would nominate him." Smith received the ninety votes of the New York delegation, as well as a few from the Wets among the Illinois group. Then the convention settled down to the real contest.

The two leading candidates were Secretary of the Treasury William G. McAdoo, considered the heir apparent of President Wilson, and Governor James M. Cox of Ohio. McAdoo, the choice of the California delegation, had a slight edge on Cox when the convention opened, but he had antagonized the New Yorkers by coming out strongly as a Dry. Murphy moreover wanted the party to forget "Wilsonism," that is, foreign war, taxes, government controls. On the sixth ballot the deadlock between McAdoo and Cox was broken when Smith, with Murphy's approval, swung the New York delegation to Cox. For second place on the ticket Murphy, Boss Brennan of Illinois, and Cox's supporters turned to Franklin Roosevelt. It was Smith who now rose to second the nomination of Roosevelt, declaring that the Democrats espoused liberal doctrines, "and no one typifies such principles more than young Roosevelt . . . a leader in local legislative reform who, during the present administration, has held a position of great power and importance." There was much courtesy, if only moderate warmth, in this exchange of compliments between the two men, whose esteem for each other had been less marked when they had first met eight years earlier, in the Legislature at Albany. Now they were both moving on to a larger stage. Roosevelt, however, was in worse case than Smith in 1920; Smith had not expected to gain the Presidential nomination, but Roosevelt had really been maneuvering to get the nomination for the United States Senate, a seat he could not have won in any case in the Republican landslide of that year.

Smith remembered the 1920 campaign in New York as one in which national issues completely overshadowed local or state problems. Public opinion was moved by the backlash against the world war experience, against wartime controls, as well as by disillusionment with the peace. The Republicans had been building up powerful sentiment against Wilsonism, the treaty, and the League of Nations, representing the Democrats as instruments of British imperialism. Smith himself, who supported the League of Nations, was also tarred with this brush. As he wrote afterward, the Republicans stirred up the Irish in the big cities, blaming Wilson's party for not setting Ireland free, while promising that they would recognize the Irish republic; they also led the German-Americans to believe that the election of a Republican President would help soften the harsh terms of the Treaty of Versailles, and they gave the Italian-Americans reason to hope that they would manage to have Fiume turned over to Italy. The electorate was further disaffected with the Democrats when a severe postwar depression hit the country. Skillful though he was on the hustings, Smith found it very difficult to focus the attention of the public upon the state's business as he campaigned for reelection.

As Judge Abram Elkus of the Court of Appeals was unable to serve again as his campaign manager, the candidate invited Elkus's able law partner, Joseph Proskauer, to serve in his place. The tall red-haired Proskauer was the offspring of a German-Jewish family that had migrated before the Civil War to Mobile, Alabama, where he was born in 1877.

He had been sent north to study at Columbia College, in New York, where at first he showed strongly literary interests, later taking a law degree. Although he had already helped Smith in drafting speeches in the last campaign, Proskauer pointed out to Smith that he knew nothing about handling the Democratic organization workers. To this Smith replied, "Oh, you don't have to worry about that. I'm the organization. Anyway, all the political work will be taken care of," he explained, that is to say, by Murphy, Foley, Johnny Gilchrist, Van Namee, and Jimmy Walker. "What I want you to do," he went on, "is just to line up those college people." And so the eminent lawyer again set in motion the Independent Citizens' Committee for Smith, with the help of a group of intellectuals including Belle and Dr. Henry Moskowitz, Robert Moses, Frances Perkins, William Church Osborn, Samuel Seabury, and others of their stripe. Proskauer also helped raise money for the party's war chest among the Jewish capitalists and philanthropists with whom he was associated, such as the Lehmans and the Strauses.

Showing a wholesome respect for Smith's fighting power, the Republicans chose as their gubernatorial candidate one of their ablest and most intelligent adherents, Judge Nathan L. Miller of Syracuse. A crusty but reputable lawyer of strongly conservative views, he had formerly been associated with large utility corporations, and served, for a time, as general counsel to the United States Steel Company. Miller was a keen debater, highly conversant with complex financial questions, and this knowledge gave him some authority when he challenged the Democrats' financial management of the state, holding that Smith's had been the costliest administration in New York history. Smith could argue that it was the

Republican Legislature that had made the cost of government so high, and that he had actually lopped off $5,000,000 from their appropriations; Miller countered that Smith was a follower of Wilson, and favored a League of Nations. Democrats, Miller implied, were the next thing to being Reds. One tends to suspect that the usually pugnacious Smith avoided coming to grips with Judge Miller on the subject of finance; still he held his own in his speeches on other state issues: the gouging tactics of the traction and public utility corporations, the milk trust, social welfare legislation — matters in which his opponent showed little interest. The contest was on the whole rather dull, however, since both Smith and Miller avoided personal recrimination and kept the tone of debate on a level of reason and moderation. Once more Smith toured the state, drawing large and friendly crowds, and evoking cheers and laughter wherever he went.

But the outcome was never in doubt. The national vote for the relatively unknown Republican candidates, Warren G. Harding and Calvin Coolidge, assumed the proportions of a tidal wave, and the wave lapped over all states and cities, so that even Murphy's own Gashouse District in Manhattan's East Side was lost to the Democrats, Harding carrying sixty-one out of sixty-two Assembly districts in New York City! An astonishing aspect of the Democratic disaster was that while the Republican national ticket in New York State ran 1,200,000 ahead of the Democrats, Smith ran 1,090,000 ahead of his own national ticket, being defeated by the narrow margin of some 75,000 votes.

It was a glorious defeat by any standards, and one that gave the New York Republicans an abiding fear of Smith's electoral prowess. Belle Moskowitz, who had worked night

and day during the campaign and had repeatedly demonstrated her remarkable abilities, looked at the record of
Smith's popularity and confidently predicted that he would
easily be reelected Governor in 1922, and that it would not
be long before he became the candidate of the Democratic
Party for the Presidency. It was conceded everywhere that
his defeat in 1920 was far more brilliant than his lucky victory in 1918.

Smith spent most of his last days in office signing orders
relating to appeals for executive clemency; he commuted
eleven death sentences, "so as not to be unfair and leave
those heartaches to my successor," as he put it. "If ever a
man had reason to be grateful to his fellow-men and al-
mighty God I am that person," he exclaimed, as messages of
good will kept pouring in from members of both parties. He
made the transfer of power on New Year's Eve a cheerful
occasion, showing Miller many courtesies, and providing him
with much useful information about the management of the
Governor's office, for which the new chief executive was duly
appreciative. In a final public message Smith called on the
Democrats in the Legislature to cooperate in a nonpartisan
spirit with Miller on measures of economy and reorganization such as the new Governor had espoused.

Some of his good cheer was due no doubt to his awareness
that the Democratic Party, and Tammany too, would have
need of him soon. The Smith family returned to Oliver Street
— "right where we started from," he jested — and although
the whole house had been renovated, it was rather confining
after the spacious Executive Mansion, even with the two
daughters, Emily and Catherine, attending boarding school

at Riverdale. On the morning of the second of January, Smith walked to his new office as chairman of the Board of Directors of the United States Trucking Corporation, whose headquarters were then at the corner of Canal and Thompson Streets. He could not afford to be idle, for all the money he had saved from his Sheriff's fees in 1916–17 had been spent in Albany.

Soon after his defeat the preceding fall he had received many handsome offers to serve as a director of large banks and insurance companies, but he would not accept them. The invitation to head the United States Trucking Corporation was more to his taste. "Here," he said, "I know I can be useful." He referred to himself as a "trucking boss," content to work at a business with which he had been familiar when his father was alive, run by the sort of men he knew well. Indeed he had known several of the executives and directors of the firm since his boyhood, men who had risen in the world as the city grew until they now represented big business. James J. Riordan, President of the concern, who had persuaded Smith to become chairman of the board, was a West Side Irishman who had long idolized him, and had made liberal contributions to his campaign funds. He had, some years earlier, inherited a trucking business from his father, but had dropped out as manager to go into banking. During the war boom he had made some successful financial speculations, and lately he had brought about the amalgamation of twenty-eight trucking firms (including his own) into one big company.

The United States Trucking Corporation owned some 2500 horses, 2000 horse-drawn trucks, and 500 motor trucks, and employed about 2500 drivers, handling about eighty per cent of the city's truck business. Its prospects were good, but 1920 was a year of depression, and the new company started out by losing money. Its financial condition at this time was really quite shaky; it was overextended, and its principal officers and directors, formerly small truckmen themselves, were not yet a harmonious team. They hoped Alfred E. Smith would help build up their organization. He had been called a born administrator while in public office, one who knew men and knew how to handle them. Now he was interested in testing his abilities in big business, whose rewards could be enormous compared with those of a political officeholder, and he went at his new job with characteristic zeal.

Smith looked over the stables, the horses, and vehicles, ordered the trucks freshly painted, and then went out to get new business. An anecdote has been preserved of one of his efforts at salesmanship: calling on Frank Munsey, owner of the *Sun,* the *Herald,* and the *Telegram* (then separate newspapers), he was prepared with exact figures to show how his firm could save the publisher money on newsprint trucking. Munsey, who was universally known as a Tory Republican and a cold fish, waved all that aside. "Let's talk politics," he said. Smith gladly plunged into a subject much closer to his heart than the trucking business for an hour or more. Munsey was enthralled, and when the conversation ended he ordered his large trucking contracts turned over to Smith's concern. He also became the Governor's firm friend and supporter — in private, not during election seasons. At his death in 1926 Smith declared that after their first meeting Munsey had repeatedly used his influence with leading Republicans in support of Smith's legislative programs.

The former Governor was reputed to be earning close to $50,000 a year, including fees as a member of the board of two or three other corporations. He worked as well as he could to bring about some improvement in the United States Trucking Corporation's affairs. On some occasions he represented the New York truckmen's association as a whole in opposing legislation that would have added to its special tax burdens, inequitably, in the view of truck owners. Outwardly he gave the impression of enjoying his business job. Nevertheless, when the problem of choosing a Democratic candidate for Mayor of New York came up in the summer of 1921, Mayor Hylan, and all Tammany, were apprehensive, until Smith gave assurances that he would not run for that office under any circumstances. With considerable reluctance he supported Hylan's renomination in 1921; it was well known that he had a low opinion of the Mayor's abilities. "The good Lord gave Red Mike very little brains," he used to say to his intimates, but he was blessed with "luck." He never went so far as to explain why, if the Lord was so sparing in His endowments, Tammany Hall was so bent on using them.

For all that the breezy Smith of former years had grown closemouthed, his friends, and especially the intellectuals of his old Kitchen Cabinet, were well aware that he counted on returning to the Governor's chair at Albany within two years. The truth was that business and money-making interested him very little in comparison with the job as head of America's most important state. Around this period young Robert Moses, who had done good work on the Reconstruction Commission and was one of his "literary advisers," used to see Smith almost every day; he would meet the former

Governor at Oliver Street in the morning and walk with him
to his office on Canal Street (later at 280 Broadway), while
Smith discoursed on politics, nothing but politics. He "looked
back and ahead to plan his return to Albany," wrote Moses.
"Most of what little I know of practical politics I learned
from this remarkable Gamaliel. Without him I would have
been just another academic researcher." One of the subjects
they discussed with great animation was the interstate Port
Authority project, for early in 1921 Smith had been appointed by Governor Miller as one of its three members
from New York State.

During this interlude as private citizen Smith made a number of public appearances both at the Capitol in Albany and
before the Board of Estimate in New York City, at which he
described with clarity and enthusiasm the great advantages
that would accrue both to New York and to New Jersey*
from the development of the Port of New York Authority.
The natural barriers girdling Manhattan, he explained, would
be overcome by bridges, tunnels, strategic warehouses, and
special freight belt lines; Staten Island would be linked with
New Jersey, the Hudson spanned to join the two states more
closely. And the beauty of it all, he argued, was that tax
exempt securities issued by the Authority as a public corporation, at low rates, would finance the vast project; tolls would
assure maintenance costs, and there would be little burden
on the taxpayers.

One of Smith's speeches on the Port Authority question,
originally written in collaboration with Mrs. Moskowitz and
Robert Moses, was a famous instance of how he took off from

* The original plan to include the State of Connecticut in the project had
by this time been revised.

a prepared statement to make a subject vivid and lend it his own special flavor. Addressing a joint legislative session in 1921, according to Moses, he

> described the artificial interstate barrier in New York harbor not in terms of statistics but as the arduous journey of Mr. Potato from a farm in Ohio by freight car to the Jersey waterfront. There Mr. Potato languished for ten days, dirty, starved, thirsty, listless and pathetic, waiting to be ferried across the Hudson to Manhattan. There was hardly a dry eye in the Assembly Chamber. Smith lifted the port plan from dull economics to human drama.

When he spoke before the Board of Estimate, Mr. Potato became a barrel of cabbages coming from Rockland County, directly across the Hudson River, which took days on end to reach the New York City markets as it was moved from train to ferry and again to truck, with countless delays and starts and shifts. Then Smith took that same barrel of cabbages and put it on the transport network of the future Port Authority, whisked it under the Hudson into an underground freight line and waterfront warehouse and down to market, within a matter of a few hours! "It costs as much at present to bring freight two to seven miles [from] outside of New York City as to bring it 1000 miles over the railroads out West," he concluded.

Smith's support of the Port Authority scheme did not win over Mayor Hylan or the Tammany boys, who had other views as to the management of such an enterprise. Editorials in the Hearst newspapers charged that "British money was behind the plan" which Smith advocated. Prodded by Hearst, Hylan asserted that the Port Authority development should be run by the New York City bureaucrats, and in an attempt to win Smith over, offered the Governor the job of heading the Hearst-Hylan scheme — to Smith's disgust.

This was one reason why at a meeting at Tammany Hall in support of the Democratic city ticket Smith all but forgot to mention Hylan, whom he had endorsed as Mayor with evident misgivings, feeling it was one of his own grossest political compromises. After paying the usual compliments to the Tammany slate, he finally mentioned the Mayor by name, apologizing for any blunders Hylan might have made in the past four years. "Whatever mistakes he has made were made with the best impulse," said Smith. "He will try with all his soul to do his best." There were no cheers.

Nothing could have kept Smith from setting off on the road back to Albany in 1922, but when he learned early in the year that Hearst was maneuvering to preempt the gubernatorial nomination for himself, the former Governor was possessed by a savage determination. His public chastisement of the press lord in 1919 had silenced the man so that he no longer dared make an open assault on Smith, but in the intervening years Hearst had burrowed in and around Tammany Hall and the New York State Democratic Party; he had trained Mayor Hylan to submit to his wishes, he had succeeded in having some of his agents appointed to well-paid city offices, and he had come to believe that his old aspirations toward the Governorship and the Presidency were not unattainable.

It was reported to Smith that Hearst's agents in upstate New York were working to build up a skeleton political machine which might threaten to become a third party, a device that Hearst had played with years before in New York City politics; but more serious still, Smith heard rumors, in the spring of 1922, that nearly two hundred delegates to the forthcoming state convention were lined up to nominate Hearst for Governor. Careful investigation by Smith's political aides, however, indicated that Hearst might win the nomination only if the former Governor remained inactive, but could not win the election running against Governor Miller.

Smith's associates at U.S. Trucking knew that they could not hold him if he chose to run for office, but for the moment he remained silent about his intentions. As the time for the nominating convention approached, however, leading independent Democrats began to issue Macedonian calls to Smith to save the party from Hearst. Judge Samuel Seabury, the Democratic candidate for Governor in 1916, who had supported Smith in 1918, addressed an open letter to him warning that "an alleged demand for Hearst was being drummed up" through liberal use of his money. Tammany feared it would lose New York City again if it opposed him, wrote Seabury, yet the man had no claim on their party loyalty. His newspapers had attacked Governor Smith throughout his term; he had supported Harding in the last presidential election. "It is to be hoped," Seabury concluded, "that former Governor Smith, who has so unequivocally condemned Hearst, will assume the leadership of the party . . . If he will but do this he will deserve the support of all the independent voters. If not, no one else can resist Hearst."

Franklin Roosevelt, stricken with infantile paralysis, and confined to his bed, also made public, on August 13, an open letter appealing to Smith to take the helm:

The Democratic Party [he urged] must put its best foot forward. Many candidates for office are strong by virtue of what
they promise they will do. You are strong by virtue of what
you have done. People everywhere know that in 1920 while
you lost by a narrow margin in a landslide, you received a million more votes in this state than the presidential ticket . . .
Your support came not only from Democrats but from hundreds of thousands of Republicans.

   Frankly I don't want to see things go by default . . . I am
taking it upon myself to appeal to you in the name of countless
citizens of upstate New York . . .

   You represent the type of citizen the voters of this state want
to vote for for Governor, and you can be elected. The decision
must be made now . . .

In his reply to Roosevelt, which was quickly publicized,
Smith reflected his willingness to be drafted. He had said
earlier that he must stay in private business for a period for
his family's sake. Now he wrote:

Dear Frank,
   I have your letter of August 13 . . . I appreciate your kindly
sentiments, and they compel me to talk to you from my heart.
I would not be entirely frank with you if I did not admit that
evidence has been presented to me that would indicate a desire
on the part of the Democratic rank and file that I again take
the post of leadership. It has been and still is my desire to
remain in business life — but during the past twenty years I
have been so honored by my party that even the members of
my family would be dissatisfied if I did not answer the call.
   Therefore, considering the facts . . . I feel myself that I would
be ungrateful if I were to say that I would be unwilling to assume the leadership. The state convention will be composed
of elected representatives . . . If a majority of them desire me
to accept the nomination for Governor and lead the party to
what seems to me to be a certain victory, I am entirely willing

to accept this honor from their hands and to battle for them
with all the energy and vigor that I possess.

With kind regards to your mother and Mrs. Roosevelt and
all the children, I am

Sincerely yours,
Al

There now seemed to be little chance that anyone could
take the nomination away from him, though Hearst continued his opposition. In his devious manner, however, the
publisher indicated that he would be satisfied to accept the
nomination for United States Senator from New York in lieu
of the governorship, and would be favorably disposed to run
on the same slate with Smith! He would run with the man
whom he had denounced not long before as a crooked politician, who robbed babies of their milk, the man who in turn
had called him a white-livered scoundrel! To achieve his
ends he now made friendly overtures to Smith, offering him
the support of his newspapers, and sending as emissaries (as
from one potentate to another) leading Democrats who
seemed to have been won over by his impressive bankroll.
These old party stalwarts pleaded with Smith to do what
many successful politicians had done before: to compromise
with his principles, swallow his feelings of revulsion, and
work with Hearst for the sake of party harmony and victory
at the polls. They stressed the value of having the Hearst
newspaper chain on Smith's side, and intimated that if there
was to be a struggle between Smith and Hearst, Hylan might
turn many Tammany men out of their jobs, at Hearst's command, and control of the city as well as of the state might
be lost to the party.

While every conceivable form of pressure was being put

on Smith to yield, late in the summer he fell sick with what was diagnosed as neuritis, and could not walk without great pain. He was engaged in a struggle with his own conscience as well as with most of his party comrades. It was only with difficulty that he managed to make the journey to Syracuse several days before the state nominating convention was to open, and once there he holed up in a suite of rooms on the eighth floor of the Onondaga Hotel, unable to move.

Insincerity and the arts of compromise are in the nature of the American professional politician, as well as those of other countries. But Smith could not bring himself to consent to an alliance with a man he abominated more than anyone else in the world. Boss McCooey of Brooklyn came to him, and after him Norman Mack, the Buffalo leader, and others too. One after another they pleaded with him to forget and forgive for the sake of party unity. "Help us out," they begged. In the pinch he had always proved a party regular. But now, his eyes steely and cold with anger, he cried "No!" to all his petitioners, and "No" again. He reminded them of how the Hearst papers had "nearly murdered" his mother with lies about how he had deprived babies of milk — "Me, a man with five children of me own!" He said he would not be able to live with himself if he accepted Hearst. Should he agree to run with Hearst on his slate, whether for Senator or Governor, the Republicans would have a field day repeating what the one had said publicly of the character of the other.

The party leaders in their perplexity conferred uneasily for several days as the work preliminary to the convention got under way, while Smith remained secluded in his hotel suite. They did not like to throw out Hearst, and they could

not win without Smith. Murphy, of course, was in Syracuse too, but for some days he had neither intervened nor
approached Smith directly, although it was reported that he
leaned toward an accommodation with Hearst. Finally,
Murphy played his last card; he sent Bourke Cockran, the
old Irish tenor of Tammany Hall, up to the eighth floor suite
to make a last appeal. Smith loved Cockran, whose speeches
he used to memorize in the 1890's, when he was only an
aspiring clubhouse politician. This time Smith was unmoved.
"Think of it," he exclaimed afterward, "they even sent Bourke
Cockran after me!"

A few old friends of the former Governor stood by him
throughout these days of trial. Tom Foley, an old-time victim of the yellow press, put his head in the doorway of
Smith's room at one moment and whispered, "Stick!" Belle
Moskowitz steadfastly counseled him to reject all appeals for
this unholy alliance. Down in the ornate lobby of the Onondaga, where the delegates and their wives congregated, she
carried herself with her usual aplomb. To the newspapermen
who waylaid her she said calmly, "Alfred E. Smith will never
consent to join with Mr. Hearst; but he will be nominated
just the same, and he will be elected," adding that the statement should not be attributed to her, nor must her name be
mentioned.

On the day before the convention was to open one of
Tammany Hall's fuglemen, an old friend of Smith's, turned
up at his hotel suite with a report from the field that the
Hearst movement was rapidly gaining strength among the
delegates. Was this really another nudge from the party
leaders to get Smith to move over? "If the party is going for
Hearst," he replied gravely, "then I'm through." When this

statement was reported over the press wires, indicating that he might retire from the contest, newspapermen burst through his door to seek confirmation of the rumor. "Me quit?" he roared. "Never! Hearst'll quit." Was the report that he had dropped out to be denied as an error? he was asked. "I'll have something to say about that! They don't vote until tomorrow night," he replied quickly.

Now, according to an account given by one of Smith's newspaper friends, Charles S. Hand, the veteran Albany correspondent of the *World,* an alarming rumor swept through the crowd of waiting delegates: Smith would appear in person before the convention and "talk." What would he say? Would he repeat the performance at Carnegie Hall, pour fire and brimstone on Hearst once more, open a great breach with Hylan and even denounce Tammany Hall for its betrayal? It was a fearsome prospect for the politicians: Smith's strength was so great that he might like Samson pull down the whole structure of the Democratic Party in the state.

Panic spread among the party leaders. Whatever tide had been running for Hearst now turned swiftly about as the frightened district leaders suddenly realized that without Smith they would all come to grief. In New York City Hearst received a telegram from his agents describing the altered picture, and by telegraph he sent word to his personal representative, William A. De Ford, that his name was to be withdrawn. Faced with a knockdown, drag-out fight, he threw in the towel. In his message of capitulation he showed himself once more a poor loser. "I certainly would not go on any ticket," he wrote to De Ford, "which, being reactionary, would stultify my record and . . . principles, and . . . would be a betrayal of genuine Democracy." As a contender for high political office, he had received the coup de grâce from Alfred Smith; never again did he seek to enter any electoral contest, although he tried still, through the power of his newspapers, to play the role of kingmaker.

The morning after Hearst's withdrawal Smith's health miraculously improved. He came down the elevator to the hotel lobby wearing his broadest smile, with Murphy by his side, as silent as ever. In the end Murphy had to come around, indicating to Hearst that he could do nothing for him. Smith had been proof against Murphy's strongest and wiliest efforts; he was stronger than Tammany. The unofficial count of the delegates showed that he would win overwhelmingly, by as much as four to one, and his supporters now took command of the convention. State Senator James J. Walker, one of Smith's protégés, made the opening address as temporary chairman, after which Herbert Claiborne Pell, another Smith adherent, took over as permanent chairman. The platform was a Smith platform, and he was nominated for Governor by acclamation. As a consolation prize to the Mayor of New York, Dr. Royal S. Copeland, his Health Commissioner, was nominated for United States Senator.

In a dispatch to the *World* Charles S. Hand drew a vivid picture of the battle scene and its outcome:

Syracuse, Sept. 29: — Alfred E. Smith not only is the Democratic nominee for Governor but is undisputed leader of his party. He made his fight on a principle from which he never swerved. Even his foes, who saw him struggle single-handed against Hearst, Hylan, Murphy and McCooey also admit his supremacy.

The whole anti-Smith combine collapsed this afternoon. First, Hearst quit cold . . . Second Hylan packed up his duds

and beat it to New York. Third the whole Hearst outfit evacuated the town in the wake of Mayor Hylan, leaving Smith the
boss of the works.

Three hours before the first nominating speech there was
not a Hearst boomer left in Syracuse. The Hearst bubble burst
like a child's balloon that had been touched by a lighted cigarette. Mr. Hearst himself wrote the final chapter of his
defeat . . .

During his term as Governor Judge Miller had comported
himself like an honest conservative, but this virtuous conduct
had aroused little enthusiasm among the voters or the politicians of his own party. To the claims of labor for higher
wages and improved working conditions he remained cold,
while keeping a kindly eye out for the welfare of the public
utility corporations. In principle he shared Smith's views on
the need for consolidating the too numerous state agencies,
but in practice he avoided calling for a constitutional amendment to effect such changes. Again he earnestly favored
economies in the budget, but, rejecting Smith's executive
budget scheme, he was able to save the state a little money
only by such measures as crippling the Labor Department
and allowing the state hospitals and mental institutions to
run down. Vocally he was for civil service reform, but actually he dismissed Colonel Greene, Smith's able Commissioner
of Highways, though Greene was a Republican, and replaced
him with an upstate district boss of no special qualifications.
He had also alienated the liberal sector of the electorate by
signing the Lusk Bills to combat the alleged spread of Bolshevism in the schools, which Smith had vetoed, but which
had been repassed as soon as Smith went out of office.

Smith had his own ideas of how to oppose the alleged

threats of political extremists, and these were incorporated
in the 1922 party platform, whose planks constituted a bold
program for the advancement of human welfare in New York
State. It called for the forty-eight-hour week and a minimum wage for women and children, housing relief in the
metropolitan areas, more home rule for large cities such as
New York, the conservation of state lands and hydroelectric
power sites, as well as the establishment of a state power
authority. And finally, to appease the laboring classes, it proposed that New York State petition Congress to modify the
Volstead Act in order to permit the sale of beer and light
wines.

A party platform, according to old-time politicians, was
only a net to catch flies, made up of pious wishes not to be
taken seriously. But Smith said his party's platform was a
"promissory note" that had to be paid, and he was so firm
in propounding it that people were led to believe he meant
business. He would fight to carry out his party's pledges, he
said, or he himself would be carried out. In this season of disillusionment and reaction, the heyday of Harding and the
corrupt Washington gang, Smith of New York State stood
forth as one of the nation's most outspoken progressives, as
the peer of Senators La Follette and Norris and a few others.

Al Smith led that campaign with all the panache that people were coming to expect from him. Proskauer brought
forth his reformers and "college people"; the Women's Division again played an active role in the campaign, sending
able and well-spoken women like Frances Perkins and Eleanor Roosevelt into all fifty-two counties of the state to or-
ganize and enlighten the newly enfranchised voters of their
sex. Early in the autumn of 1922 Smith set off on his stump-

ing tour in a mood of high optimism, under conditions vastly different from those of his first gubernatorial campaign. The actor in him, the performer now with the stellar role, loved the cheering crowds, the brass bands, and torchlight processions, even the hecklers. He was acclaimed as a David who had slain the Goliath of party corruption, as exemplified by Hearst, and indeed the aura of a David clung to the brown derby he wore so jauntily, as a campaign symbol, not unlike the helmet on the sculpture of David by Donatello. His baritone voice, grown huskier with the years, still retained an East Side accent and yet what he had to say was so forceful, so much to the point, that his hearers were barely conscious of the intonation. Frances Perkins said that to his friends and admirers his intonation was not only not offensive but actually appealing. Patiently, day after day, facing great crowds, he labored to educate the public on important state and regional problems.

On his return to New York City late in October he issued a challenge to Governor Miller to meet him in joint debate at Carnegie Hall; unlike Hearst, Miller accepted the invitation. Miller was an experienced lawyer, a fluent speaker, and he was eager to display his knowledge of the state's affairs and finances. With the help of his Kitchen Cabinet, Smith prepared himself thoroughly to take Miller on. The incumbent made a stout defense of his administration, at the same time, as in the 1920 campaign, charging his rival with habitual extravagance; Smith replied with good effect that the modest economies claimed by Miller were ill-advised in a state with a growing population and rising tax revenues, and had been achieved at the cost of worsening health and housing problems. And what had Miller done to prevent increases in telephone and other utility rates? Nothing.

But the two candidates really came to grips on the subject of conserving the state's power resources. Miller held that turning over power sites to private companies would result in their businesslike development, while public operation would be wasteful and socialistic. Smith countered by citing the words of one of his Republican predecessors as Governor, Theodore Roosevelt, who maintained that the waterpower sites along the St. Lawrence and upper Hudson Rivers were "the precious heritage of the people of New York," and should never be allowed to fall into the hands of the "power barons." There was a potential of some 4,000,000 horsepower in those rivers, equivalent to all the coal consumed in the state, he continued, more than enough to light all of New York City, and he favored the development of this energy by a public corporation, like the Port Authority, which could sell the power to private utilities and also use part of it for economical lighting and heating of many state buildings and institutions. Even under Governor Miller recently it had been found practical to set up some small publicly owned power stations along the Erie Canal. "The State should use its assets reasonably. The State should not be prohibited by law from using ordinary human intelligence," he concluded.

The press commented favorably on the high level at which the debate had been carried on by both contestants at the Carnegie Hall meeting, praising them for the avoidance of mudslinging and for their efforts to educate the public. But Smith had the greater appeal; he addressed himself to questions that concerned the voters in the most immediate sense: the creeping rise in gas rates, the congestion of transport, low income housing. In a state with more than half a million trade union members he spoke for the rights of labor. Echoing the cry of the unions that "human labor is not a commod-

ity," he pledged that his party would enact legislation to curb
the use of the injunction in strikes, would strengthen the
Labor Department which had been "wrecked" under Governor Miller, and would clean up the Workmen's Compensation Bureau. In a speech he gave on the eve of Election Day
he pounded away at this subject:

> The whole record is as clear as the noonday sun. To the build-
> ing up of our labor code I gave during all my legislative career
> the best that was in me. I helped to stop the exploitation of
> children in the canneries. I helped prevent women from being
> employed in foundries. I helped to enact the One Day of Rest
> in Seven Act. I helped to secure the Workmen's Compensation
> Act and felt a great satisfaction when I heard those laws re-
> ferred to throughout the country as the most enlightened fac-
> tory code in the United States . . . Not only did I do this, but
> I devoted the later years of legislative activity to protecting
> those laws, and that fight to attempt to destroy them would
> make a very interesting chapter in the history of Albany.

Thus he won the ranks of labor, as he had won the masses
of rent payers in the cities by championing low-cost housing,
as well as many thousands of school teachers outraged by the
Lusk Bills, which he vowed to have repealed. The voter in
that off-year election, no longer distracted, as in 1920, by
the national issues of war and Wilsonism, gave him a plurality of 400,000, the largest ever won up to then by any Governor of New York. Despite the inequitable apportionment
of election districts in the cities, the Smith "wave" swept in
a majority in the State Senate, sent numerous Democratic
Congressmen to Washington, and elected Copeland to the
United States Senate. The Assembly, to be sure, remained
Republican, but only by a narrow margin. Besides winning
the downstate urban voters in overwhelming numbers, Smith

ran nearly on even terms with the Republican candidate in the upstate counties, and captured the large cities of Buffalo, Rochester, Albany, and Syracuse, the last being Miller's hometown. Smith's vote-getting power inspired feelings of awe in the opposition. Observing the results, Murphy permitted himself to say, in one of his rare press interviews, that this signal victory was "owing to the great body of independent voters . . . and also to many public-spirited Republicans." At all events, Smith could now return to Albany with a free hand, owing nothing to the bosses of the Democratic state machine.

CHAPTER XII

The Fighting Governor

FEW LEADERS in all the annals of our regional politics were ever returned to high office with such an overwhelming popular mandate as Governor Smith of New York enjoyed at the beginning of his second term in 1923. To be sure, he was confronted by the Republican majority in the Assembly, a disciplined group that knew how to conduct a stubborn opposition under Barnes and other upstate bosses. Moreover the stakes were very high in the Empire State, and behind the scenes there lurked always those powerful interests of finance and industry, as Thorstein Veblen described them, who manipulated the machine politicians to their own profitable ends: the rising electric utilities, the railroad and traction groups, the heavy industries, the real estate crowd, the great investment banks of New York — interests counseled by canny old corporation lawyers like Senator Elihu Root and by aggressive and sharp-witted lobbyists. Fully aware of the strength of his adversaries, the Governor from the start of his new term took the offensive in favor of his reform measures and carried on the fight with unflagging spirit. He entered into these battles with zest, and the people came to know him as the "fighting Governor."

Schooled during many years in local politics, expert in legislative affairs, Alfred Smith knew also how to bring the most powerful pressure — public opinion — to bear on the opposition party. He had his vision, his grand design for the reconstruction of the state bureaucracy, and kept that constantly before the eyes of the voters. Far more than the other reform politicians of recent times, Theodore Roosevelt and Charles E. Hughes, Smith communicated to the great public an understanding of their own immediate interest in the political decisions being made by the state's legislative and executive departments.

That he was able to go as far as he did in the realization of his program — despite the parliamentary resistance he faced during all his four terms in office — was due in no small part, as he himself admitted, to the opposition party and its obstinate leadership. On more than one occasion, as also in private talk with Belle and Henry Moskowitz, he said, "If the Republicans had not used obstructive tactics against me, I should have been back in private life long ago."

Only a fortnight after the 1922 elections an incident occurred that explains the secret of his great hold over the citizenry. The Democratic platform had promised conservation of the state's waterpower resources, and he held himself accountable — as for payment of a promissory note, he used to say — to redeem the pledges of his party. On November 22 he learned that the State Waterpower Commission was to meet the next day and act on licenses permitting private corporations to develop electrical energy from the waters of the Niagara River below the falls. One large holding company in particular, the so-called Frontier Corporation, was expected to get the most remunerative rights, but behind

that company stood a combine of America's industrial giants:
Aluminum Corporation, Du Pont, and General Electric, all
interested in obtaining quantities of cheap electric power.
It seemed likely that as a first step some 1,500,000 horsepower would be signed away to this combine for little or
nothing. The "lame-duck" members of the Waterpower Commission in these last days of Governor Miller's term were
Speaker of the Assembly Machold, President of the Senate
Lusk, and also the State Engineer, the Conservation Commissioner, and the Attorney-General, Republicans all, and
all apparently ready to lend themselves to this brazen power
site grab just before they were to be replaced by Democrats
in January.

The Governor-elect was not to be vested with the power
of his office for another six weeks; he had, as yet, no legal
right to intervene, and many a shrewd politician in his place
might have reasoned that it was wiser to let things be, to
use the old tactic of planned inactivity. No one could possibly reproach him for the sins of the Republicans. Alfred
Smith thought otherwise: he went into action at once, sending a telegram to Attorney-General Charles D. Newton to
the effect that he had read about the impending meeting of
the Waterpower Commission in his morning paper, and pointing out that in the late election contest he had taken a strong
stand against the handout of such state-owned resources to
private companies. The telegram concluded:

> I would therefore ask you, in view of the decision of the people
> at the polls following the campaign, in which this subject was
> a distinct issue, not to grant any licenses or permits to private
> corporations . . . for waterpower resources that belong to the
> state and permit that subject to be dealt with by the incoming
> administration in accordance with explicit promises made dur-
> ing the campaign.

By sounding the alarm — and Smith made certain he had
full coverage in the newspapers — he frightened off the commissioners, who decided to grant no licenses at the moment.
The great corporations found it best to bide their time, but
they could be very patient and stubborn; they would return
to the attack later, when their political friends once more
held a clear majority in both houses of the Legislature. This
only gave Smith another opportunity to make a burning
issue of public waterpower in 1926 and 1927. Slow to learn,
the Republicans continued to contribute to the Governor's
political capital and to his popularity with the masses of
voters.

Toward the end of December Smith rode back to Albany
with his old-time staff: George Van Namee, formerly his private secretary (who was to become Commissioner of Licenses), George Graves, his new private secretary, Bobby
Fitzmaurice, assisting Graves, and various members of his
Kitchen Cabinet which included a complement of women
who had served under him earlier, notably Belle Moskowitz
and Frances Perkins. The parade scheduled for Inauguration
Day had to be called off because of a drenching rain, but all
of Albany and many well-wishers from other parts of the
state crowded into the Capitol for the ceremony of induction,
and here the ovations to the new Governor were so loud, so
prolonged, that Governor Miller remarked to Smith with
good grace, "They seem to prefer your politics to mine."

In his short inaugural address Smith said, "I am mindful
of the heavy responsibilities I must assume. I know what it
means. I have been through it before." He then touched
on the momentous changes he hoped to introduce into the
state government. To carry out his plan of administrative

reorganization, he said, "I expect the full cooperation of the members of my party," and then added with a grin, "and also of the other party."

In the Assembly, where they commanded a slight majority, the Republicans reelected Smith's old adversary Machold as Speaker, making clear their determination to hold the thin red line against all attacks. But in the Senate, controlled by the Democrats, Jimmy Walker, a skilled parliamentarian, was chosen President. It was going to be harder than before to block the Governor's program, for he could be formidable when he went over the heads of the legislators with his appeals to the people. Ably assisted by Belle Moskowitz, his public relations expert, he used the press with powerful effect to get his message across, and began to reach out for an even larger audience when his husky baritone was heard for the first time over radio on Inauguration Day.

Just as in 1919, Boss Murphy was in Albany as the new term began in 1923, operating as discreetly as ever in regard to appointments. But on this occasion, *The New York Times* reported, his main function was to soothe the wounded feelings of disappointed officeseekers. The spoilsmen were rebuffed as never before. Filled with a new self-confidence, and the sense of his commanding position in the New York State Democracy, Smith insisted on choosing men and women of outstanding merit for the higher state offices. The crusty Colonel Greene was brought back to the key post of Highways Commissioner; Bernard L. Shientag, the liberal New York lawyer, was named Industrial Commissioner; Frances Perkins returned to serve as a member of the Labor Board. Some Republicans of ability were retained in office; in other cases, where, for example, the heads of state hospitals or prisons had quit or retired, their experienced lieutenants were chosen to replace them.

Proskauer tells a story to illustrate how Smith could be firm, yet courteous, in dealing with Murphy about appointments. In the spring of 1923 the Governor appointed Proskauer to fill out a term as judge of the New York Supreme Court (after which Proskauer won election to the full term). This was not particularly pleasing to Tammany Hall, for as an active member of the Citizens' Union Proskauer during long years had assailed the Tammany machine. What was more offensive, Proskauer proposed to name his own clerk, a key position in the courts, which was usually filled by some Tammany stalwart. Smith agreed to let him have his way in this, but added, "It would be nice if you went in to see Murphy," implying that he wished to preserve the amenities. Proskauer called on Murphy to thank the old boss for having been friendly about his appointment. "I understand you've been a great help to the Governor," Murphy said. Then Proskauer went on briskly to tell him the name of the man he wanted for his clerk. "Governor Smith has approved of him," he added quickly. At this Murphy's face turned purple. "He looked as if I'd kicked him in the teeth," Proskauer recalled; "I got out of there as fast as I could."

After 1923 the Tammany people used to weep in their beer over Smith's apostasy, that is, his addiction to reform, and his inclination to choose descendants of Kings of Israel, rather than of Kings of Erin, as his counselors. They even devised a sad little ditty, the burden of which was:

And now the brains of Tammany Hall
Are Moskie and Proskie and Mo-o-o-ses.

Smith's drive to establish a "meritocracy" in the state government won him the plaudits of the press; in fact between
1923 and 1928 he made the longest strides toward an honest
and efficient public service since the dawn of civil service
reform under the Governorship of Grover Cleveland in 1883.
It was his contention that the day of the party hack in office
was ending. On several occasions he remarked that the party
machine workers could be useful in getting out the vote in a
close election, but that new ideas and policies were more
important in winning over the growing number of independent voters. Frances Perkins describes the changeover from
the old spoils system as a gradual process, and specially slow
in effect on the minor jobs. She remembers Smith saying
patiently to some Tammany follower (sent him by a district
boss) who had asked for promotion, "How many times have
I told you that while you don't need to pass a Civil Service
test to be an elevator operator, you do need to pass a test
to become an elevator starter."

It was his ambition to be not only a political leader but
also a successful executive and administrator, roles of the
greatest importance now that the state's expanding activities
involved the disbursement of some $200,000,000 annually.
By reorganizing the administrative apparatus he hoped to
make it operate as efficiently as a big business corporation,
and to this end he endeavored to make a shrewd choice of
assistants. "In politics," he said, "you must know people,
and know how to work with them." Once he brought people
into his service he supported and trusted them. He knew
how to delegate authority to his aides, but virtually all of
them were given to understand that they must keep him
informed about their work and their problems. He always

wanted concrete information, facts above all. "Let us look at the facts" was his constant refrain. Commissioner Greene was called on to supply the Governor with an exact report of what the Republican county bosses had been doing with regard to the state roads during the interregnum. Miss Perkins was told to assemble data on how the factory safety codes had been administered since 1920, how many manufacturers complied with the rule about enclosed staircases, and how many were delinquent. He seemed to remember everything, and when he touched on these questions in conferences with the legislators, or in public interviews, he used precise figures to support his conclusions. The administrative personnel were always on their mettle, and the closer they worked with the Governor the more intense was their loyalty to him. At the same time leaders in business and finance who became acquainted with Smith often expressed surprise at his native ability in handling large affairs, as well as the imagination that led him quickly to the heart of a complex problem.

At the opening of the 1923 legislative session Smith delivered his annual message in person in the Chamber, a message bristling with what the press described as proposals for "radical new laws." Boss Barnes flatly defined them as "socialistic." These cries of alarm ignored the fact that the program of legislation set forth by the Governor corresponded precisely to the Democratic Party platform in the recent campaign, which had won overwhelming support from the voters. He called for extended home rule for cities such as Greater New York, permitting them ownership of utilities and traction systems; shorter hours and a minimum wage for

women and minors, as well as an anti-injunction bill; the
extension of rent control and the promotion of low-cost housing; and finally a resolution petitioning Congress to modify
the Prohibition enforcement act in favor of light wines and
beer. He also urged action leading to an interstate treaty
with the government of New Jersey to speed the development of the Port Authority of New York.

These plans amounted in fact to a fairly moderate program
in comparison with the sweeping social laws adopted well
before this time by the capitalist nations of Western Europe,
or Australia and New Zealand. If adopted they would bring
New York into line with progressive states farther west, like
Wisconsin, under La Follette's leadership, or Washington,
which had enacted into law a humane code for women workers long before this.

Smith, as well as his labor adviser, Miss Perkins, always
argued that these measures of social welfare were not only
humane, but could easily be afforded by capital. Indeed
capital in the great State of New York was never frightened
away by Alfred Smith, who was friendly to sound businessmen, and wanted only to regulate industries where human
suffering was prevalent — for he was also governed by his
innate sympathies for the underdog. Even while he was
Governor, as one of his intimates, Raymond Ingersoll, observed, "He did not believe in undue interference with business." Meanwhile he had the political support of consumers
as well as of labor, and of the leaders of New York's light
industries, important in that region. The rich dry goods merchants of New York City, for example, such as Michael
Friedsam, of Altman's, and Jesse and Nathan Straus, of
Macy's, had been generous donors to his campaigns. It is

noteworthy, moreover, that Smith's program was an attempt to satisfy the growing demands of the urban masses, the most recent immigrant groups centered in the large cities — Catholic Irish, Italians, Jews, and Poles — for improvement in working and living conditions. It gave recognition to the changing composition of America from an agricultural to a predominantly urban society, a change that had been accelerated by the great war. The state government, however, had continued to be ruled by representatives of the farmers and small townspeople, who tried to resist the pressure of the city masses through unequal apportionment of voting districts. These upstate Republicans were also in alliance with the Anti-Saloon League and the WCTU, Southern whites, and leading industrialists like Elbert Gary of U.S. Steel and Henry Ford, in their resolve to deny the urban workers beer with which to slake their thirst after nine or ten hours of labor, thus bearing out the contention of Oscar Handlin that the Prohibition movement was in essence a manifestation of racial and religious prejudice.*

In response to the Governor's program Speaker Machold affirmed that the Assembly would defend the conservative position against all such subversive schemes. Smith on the other hand protested that the whole party system itself would be endangered if the opposition continued its narrowly obstructive tactics. A skilled strategist of these parliamentary wars, Machold maneuvered warily against the Governor, and each continually studied the other's moves as in a chess

---

* It is interesting to note that in the North, industrialists favored Prohibition because workers returned to the assembly lines on Monday morning in more sober condition than formerly, although their employers had no difficulty obtaining as much liquor as they wished; while in the South the dry laws were intended to keep alcoholic beverages from the Negroes, not their masters.

game. The Republicans tried to avoid an uncalculated opposition that would injure their own party and play into Smith's hands, knowing that his great popularity made it dangerous to refuse him everything. If they made moves toward adjournment without acting on bills the Governor sponsored, he would threaten to call them back into special session, which they found irksome. He did in fact call a special session in 1923, holding the legislators through May and into June before he would let them go.

Meanwhile they wrangled over bills for the eight-hour day for women and for housing relief, the former inspiring a memorable struggle in the Assembly. Miss Perkins evidently was deputed to defend the bill at a committee hearing, which was attended by a number of women union leaders and social workers. In her presentation she charged that the textile manufacturers had set up a powerful lobby made up of various ad hoc associations who claimed to represent a "National Women's Party" demanding "equal rights" for women — notably the right to work eleven hours a day. There were now a million women workers in the state, yet only a third of them would be covered by the measure in question. But for fear of losing their jobs, she contended, thousands would have come to Albany to plead for this protective law, instead of the handful present. Twelve years earlier, she said, the manufacturers had fought bitterly against the Fifty-four-Hour Law, holding that it would ruin them.

> They told us they would never be able to operate . . . but statistics show that in the factories production has increased under that law and there is no reason to believe that it will not do the same under the 48-hour law. Industries have gone forward, and their workers have been giving better results under the shorter hours.

Her arguments fell on deaf ears. In the late hours of the
1923 session, while a large delegation of women kept the
death watch in the gallery, the Assembly voted the measure
down. Rose Schneiderman, leader of the shirtwaist workers
at the time of the Triangle Company fire in 1911, was one of
those on hand. Along with other women she rushed downstairs to the Governor's office to report the defeat, and, as
she recalls, burst into tears. The Governor was no less disappointed than she, but he chose to conceal his emotions
under a gruff manner, and chided the women leaders, "What's
the matter with you girls? Are you getting tired?" And he
allowed that he intended to return to the attack, the next
year and the year after, and the year after that, if necessary,
and expected their help as before.

Other bills sponsored by the Governor dragged their way
through the Senate and the Assembly while the opposition
fought a stubborn rear guard action. Often Smith attended
conferences late at night with committee members of both
parties, and by threatening to veto all appropriation bills introduced by the Republicans, he was able to win passage in
his second term for at least a few more of his measures. Thus
emergency rent laws were extended and an act providing
for public housing corporations was voted. Others, like the
Forty-eight-Hour Bill, were not passed until two, three, or
even four years later.

The Republicans' maneuvers to embarrass the Governor
went on without respite. Frances Perkins, who had long
observed the strategems of the legislators, noticed that when
the Forty-eight-Hour Bill came up for a roll call vote a surprising number of Assemblymen, including some who had
promised to support it, wandered off and were reported ab-

sent. Yet five minutes later they were all back in their seats ready to vote for the repeal of the Mullan-Gage Act. This was a measure repealing the state law authorizing local enforcement of the Federal Volstead Act and was to be the Republicans' Trojan Horse.

When Smith learned that at two o'clock in the morning of May 9, 1923, the Legislature had voted the repeal bill, he was staggered. "They have me down and out!" he is reported to have exclaimed to one of his advisers. Whether he signed or vetoed the bill he was in for trouble. In the recent election contest he and Miller both had largely evaded the Prohibition issue. In past years he had voted with the Tammany men as a Wet; he liked his glass of an evening, and believed it was wrong for the government to interfere with an individual's liberty, or with his private pleasures, as long as indulgence in them worked no harm. On the other hand he was not a fanatical Wet, having become convinced that the day of the old-time saloon was over.

In 1921 Governor Miller had signed the Mullan-Gage Act, which duplicated the Federal Volstead Act in permitting search and seizure by local authorities. Smith held that it was a redundant law, since the United States Constitution and the Volstead Act had to be enforced in all states. Mullan-Gage had merely added state police and deputy sheriffs in New York to the army of Federal agents, and would involve many of them in the bribery and corruption that accompanied dry law enforcement everywhere. Now the Republicans, who under Governor Miller had voted for such added enforcement as the Mullan-Gage Act authorized, turned around and voted to repeal the law, presenting Governor Smith with a very unpleasant dilemma. If he signed the repeal bill the

Drys and the Anti-Saloon League, who directed a powerful propaganda organization, would rage against him as a tool of the liquor interests, a Governor who fostered resistance to national law. If he vetoed the repeal bill he would antagonize the Wets in his own party, with whom he tended to sympathize. At that period, and indeed ever since 1918, the Anti-Saloon League, under its implacable Superintendent William H. Anderson, flooded the state with vitriolic pamphlets denouncing Smith; that he had spoken in favor of legalizing wine and beer, the Drys argued, meant that he carried on a conspiracy of "aliens" — that is, in behalf of Tammany and the Catholic Church — to wreck Prohibition. Even beer was characterized by them as "the monster vice . . . it killed people twenty-five times faster than whisky."

The Ku Klux Klan also made its appearance in New York State at this time and joined in the campaign of the country people against the town; its hooded agitators in the upstate villages tried to inspire a love of water among Protestants and hatred of liquor, Smith, Tammany, and the Catholics. Fortunately for the Governor the Anti-Saloon League's Anderson came to grief in 1924, when he was indicted and sentenced to a term in Sing Sing for extortion, forgery, and grand larceny of some of the Anti-Saloon League's own funds.

The Governor, meanwhile, had permitted himself an indiscretion. One day a reporter called his attention to the fact that Senator Edge of New Jersey, a Republican, had come out for three per cent beer, thus stealing Smith's thunder. Smith laughed and answered, "He can have all my thunder that he wants. I will be glad to go down to help him, if that will get us somewhere where we can put a foot on the rail and blow off the froth." He was talking off the cuff, with the understanding that he was not to be quoted, but the reporter betrayed his confidence, and his unguarded remark appeared in *The New York Times*. Thereafter Smith was represented everywhere by the Drys as an Irish brute who wallowed in beer.

Smith's board of strategy appears to have been dubious about the propriety of his signing the repeal bill. If he vetoed it, some argued, he could do so on high moral ground, as a moderate Wet who, nevertheless, recognized his duty to support the Federal Constitution and Congressional law in New York State. This might add to his prestige nationally. At this time Franklin Roosevelt wrote him, "I am mighty sorry for the extremely difficult position in which you have been placed over this darned old liquor question." Roosevelt favored straddling the whole issue. Like others who offered Smith their advice, he pointed out that by signing the repeal bill the Governor might well destroy his chances for nomination to the Presidency. To this Smith is reported to have answered that he would never, as long as he lived, make his acts as Governor subserve his ambition for higher office, and that he knew no other way than "to be exactly as I am."

He had thirty days in which to make up his mind. The eyes of the country were on him. For the first time Al Smith, who usually arrived at decisions quickly, acted as if he were in a quandary. On one day he gave hints that the Wets might feel disappointed with him; on the next day, however, he went to consult "Mister" Murphy, whose views were not to be disregarded in such a matter. Edward J. Flynn, the young boss and Sheriff of Bronx County, was present at their meeting at Murphy's estate on Long Island. As a rule Murphy deferred to Smith's wishes, according to Flynn, but on this

occasion the habitually stolid boss held his ground, insisting
that Smith sign the repeal bill. Flynn remembered Murphy
exclaiming, "Al, you will either sign this bill, or I will not
support you for Governor, or President, or anything else."
Smith made no reply in Flynn's hearing.

A few days later, on May 31, the Governor held a hearing
in the Assembly Chamber, attended by a large audience, to
give advocates of both sides of the question a chance to present their arguments. Wayne B. Wheeler, general counsel
for the Anti-Saloon League, delivered an impassioned plea
for a veto; he was seconded by the United States District
Attorney for Southern New York, who said he needed the
help of all state law officers. The case for the other side was
urged by representatives of the American Federation of Labor, whose membership pined for the return of beer.

The next day Smith signed the bill repealing state enforcement, and issued a statement giving the grounds for his action. Using the doctrine of state rights, he argued that a state
was not required to duplicate a Federal law — in this case
the Volstead Act — which in any event would continue to
be enforced by Federal agents and courts. And he would
still cooperate with them. "I yield to no man in respect for
the Constitution," the statement read. Both parties had voted
for the repeal bill in the Legislature, he pointed out, adding
that he favored it also because it would end complaints of
double jeopardy and of divided authority. "Much has been
said with respect to the effect my action on this bill may have
upon my own political future. I have no political future that
I am willing to obtain by the sacrifice of any principles or
any convictions." There was in truth a good deal of juristic
quibbling in this state paper, the writing of which was at-

tributed to Judge Proskauer. Prohibition had brought in an age in which underworld crime and official hypocrisy flourished together. President Harding, who was a Dry only in public, expressed deep shock at Governor Smith's action, while William Jennings Bryan, who in old age led a holy crusade to save his people from both the demon rum and the godless doctrine of evolution, uttered great cries of indignation.

In the day-to-day administration of his office there was no department in which Governor Smith took greater pride than the Labor Department. Its principal functions were to see that safety standards in factories were maintained, and to adjudicate the compensation claims of many of the 400,000 workers in the state who suffered industrial injuries each year. In a spirited account of the operation of the Industrial Board, its problems, its achievements, the attacks it suffered, Miss Perkins has provided an invaluable record of the relations between the Governor and his administrative officers in an area where they were breaking new ground.

In Smith's first term, as under his predecessors, the Labor Department had consisted of an Industrial Commission of five members and a staff of referees, inspectors, and clerks. Under this arrangement the members of the Industrial Commission had administrative, quasi-legislative, and judicial powers. A reorganization of the department under Governor Miller divided up these functions by creating a single Industrial Commissioner, who was to be the administrative officer, and an Industrial Board of three members with the quasi-legislative, quasi-judicial functions of the old Commission. Like Smith, Miss Perkins had opposed this scheme vigorously when it was debated in the Legislature, but after he appointed her to the Industrial Board in 1923, she found that it worked better than the old arrangement. Bernard Shientag, Smith's old friend from the Factory Investigating Commission days, was now Industrial Commissioner, and Miss Perkins soon became the dominant figure on the Board.

The field was still relatively uncharted, and many of the Board's decisions were challenged in the courts, especially in workmen's compensation cases. In all but one of these, according to the recollection of Miss Perkins's secretary, the Appellate Division of the Court of Appeals upheld the decision of the Board. With the concurrence of the Governor, Miss Perkins extended the compensation coverage beyond what had been previously allowed, as in the case of a man who broke a leg on the steps of the building where he was employed, although he had not yet reached the machine at which he worked, or in the matter of giving death benefits to common-law wives, if the relationship with the victim had been steady and responsible. Judge Benjamin Cardozo, who sat on a court that upheld one of her rulings, once said that Miss Perkins had made new law with certain of her rulings on the Industrial Board.

In the area of safety codes for factories the Industrial Board had to use great vigilance in seeing that statutory rules were observed; it also needed to keep a sharp eye on its own inspectors, some of whom became so cozy with the employers that they failed to report violations. Because of changing industrial conditions and new processes constantly being introduced, some of the codes could be modified to the advantage of the employers without endangering the lives of the workers; but at the same time the new processes often

gave rise to new health hazards not covered by the workmen's compensation law. Where new legislation was necessary Miss Perkins always found the Governor ready to help
in obtaining it, and where some staff inspector was found
guilty of incompetence, or venality, Smith could always be
relied on to back her up in having the man fired — even
though he might be a most "deserving Democrat."

Confident therefore that the Labor Department was in
good hands, Smith was greatly vexed when on January 13,
1924, he received a letter from Associated Industries, the
New York State affiliate of the National Manufacturers' Association, charging that the Industrial Board was riddled with
politics, the State Insurance Fund was being squandered, the
Compensation Bureau's services had broken down, and the
Industrial Commissioners had exceeded their authority under
the law. The letter to the Governor was given the widest
notice in the press, thanks to the manufacturers' lobby, whose
chief agent, one Mark Daly, a paid spokesman for business
groups, was an inveterate opponent of all welfare legislation.

"I guess the labor laws are being enforced too strictly to
suit these people and the shoe is beginning to pinch," Smith
told the newspaper reporters. He announced that he was
ordering a full investigation of the charges under the Moreland Act, and that he himself would serve as Moreland Act
Commissioner. "If anything is the matter with the Department of Labor no man wants to find it out quicker than I do,"
he said. Within two days of receipt of the letter he issued
subpoenas for all the directors of Associated Industries to
appear before him in the Executive Chamber at Albany on
January 22. Wealthy industrialists all, they were said to be
"put out" by the Governor's brusque action; nevertheless

they turned up on the appointed day, somewhat apprehensive, flanked by their eminent counsel, former Appeals Court Judge Robert Sutherland.

Smith conducted the hearings in an informal but hard-nosed fashion, prodding the manufacturers and their secretary relentlessly for the facts behind their trumped-up complaints, and making them look exceedingly foolish when he exposed their ignorance. One by one the Associated Industries directors were forced to admit that they knew nothing but what Daly, their lobbyist, had told them; their president, Alfred Swan, confessed that he had no personal knowledge of mismanagement of the State Insurance Fund, and pointed out that charges to that effect had already been withdrawn in Sutherland's preliminary statement. But did he know why those charges had been withdrawn? Smith queried sternly. Because they were "incorrectly stated," Swan answered. "No, not that," roared the Governor, "but upon the ground that the allegations were false!"

Daly was the Governor's prime target at the hearing. Questioned as to the source of his information that the Department was "dominated by politics," he declared that it was confidential, and took refuge in his right as a journalist to protect his informants. "Do you feel you ought to protect a man who makes a false statement?" Smith asked, and under the Governor's hammering Daly withdrew the statement as an "unfortunate phrase." The increased budget of the Department (criticized by Daly) had been passed by both houses of the Legislature, one of them with a majority of Republicans, Smith pointed out. "Could there be any politics in that?" "Of course I do not know much about politics, Governor," replied Daly smugly. Smith fairly snorted in de-

rision, "Oh no, you don't!" Daly maintained that the charges
had been made "without any intention of embarrassing you,
without any ulterior motives, of politics or otherwise." Smith's
rejoinder to this bit of hypocrisy reflected his great aplomb:
"If the man is big enough for the job he is not embarrassed.
This doesn't embarrass me at all. I am perfectly at home
here." It was in fact his opponents who felt embarrassed.
The confrontation had become so farcical that Sutherland
said the directors of Associated Industries wished to disso-
ciate themselves from the "overzealousness" of their Executive Secretary.

When Smith called on his people in the Labor Department
to testify, the evidence of their efficient and conscientious
administration was overwhelming. Shientag was able to
prove that the charges of high-cost ratios for the State Insurance Fund were false, and that there were no unreasonable
delays in the payment of compensation awards. It was also
shown that politics did not govern the choice of appointees:
of eight officials handling compensation cases, seven had
passed civil service tests.

Miss Perkins had been accused by Daly of having exceeded
her lawful authority by extending the factory code to cover
smaller plants of only two stories, supposedly exempt from
its regulations. As her two fellow Board members were more
or less inactive, she and Industrial Commissioner Shientag
actually ran the Department. When the Board's chairman
seemed unequal to drawing up a budget, for example, she
undertook to do it, and also saw to it that the Governor was
kept informed about developments. "It has been said that
I have a domineering character," Miss Perkins observed on
one occasion, and there was some truth in that inference.

The complaints against her, however, she refuted easily, when she demonstrated that the smaller plants that fell under her regulation were only two stories high on one side, but three or more on the other, and therefore required enclosed staircases to protect workers in case of fire. When on the witness stand, she was not easily daunted by opposing counsel. The memorandum to Governor Smith, which she read in testimony, constituted a spirited reply to charges of arbitrary behavior on her part:

> Members of the Industrial Board had knowledge . . . in reports from inspectors that buildings of this class were unsafe under the provisions of Rule 2. With such knowledge before them, the failure to meet the inadequacy of that rule to protect human life would have constituted a neglect of duty so serious that your Excellency would have been justified in removing us.

The hearings ended on a note of peace and conciliation. Sutherland complimented the Governor on the fairness of the proceedings, and the Governor thanked him for his kind remarks, adding, "In the last analysis everything is for the best. In the two days' session we have had here we have been able to demonstrate that we have an infinitely better Labor Department in this State than I thought we had." An editorial in *The New York Times* the next morning expressed the general sentiment with regard to the members of Associated Industries: "It seems a wonder," it read, "that persons so gullible as they are now shown to be should be able to keep their money."

After Smith's "victorious defeat" in 1920 Mrs. Moskowitz had predicted that he would be reelected to the Governorship in 1922, and after that prediction came true she con-

fidently predicted that he would be nominated for the Presidency in 1924. "Who is Mrs. Belle Moskowitz? How does
she come to have so much power?" many persons asked about
this time. The political writers described her variously as the
minister-without-portfolio in Smith's cabinet, his Colonel
House, a "mystery woman." Why the mystery? Because
most of those who went into politics did it either for place
or money, but Mrs. Moskowitz had refused the highest offices
the Governor could have given her, contenting herself with
the post of publicity director of the Democratic State Committee at $4000 a year. She had a self-effacing air, but if you
wanted to reach the ear of Governor Smith, it was best to see
Mrs. Moskowitz first. One of Smith's intimate friends among
the newspaper correspondents at Albany wrote in 1923 that
he and his colleagues had long been aware that

> before arriving at a decision on questions of prime importance
> Governor Smith almost invariably has taken counsel of Mrs.
> Moskowitz. But a sense of delicacy has prevailed against fre-
> quent use of Mrs. Moskowitz's name in despatches from the
> Capitol. Hence the public has no conception of the important
> part she has played in heightening Governor Smith's political
> stature to an altitude of Presidential proportions.

Other well-informed observers also credited Mrs. Moskowitz with the growth of the Smith presidential boom, which,
at the beginning of 1924, was assuming considerable strength,
at least among Eastern Democrats. Highly realistic and
tough-minded on the one hand, she seemed obsessed by a
dream on the other, a dream in which she saw Alfred E.
Smith, a Wet, a Roman Catholic, brown derby, cigar, and all,
as Chief Executive of a dry, Protestant nation. One writer
described the stout Jewish matron as having a "Madonna-

like face," and being imbued with "all the idealism, the passion for progress of her race. To her Al Smith was the Savior of Tolerance." The rise of the East-Sider to the Governorship of New York had been the pride and joy of the city masses in the North who were children of recent immigrants and belonged to minority religious groups. His elevation to the Presidency, in her view, would remove the stigma, the sense of inferiority from all minority groups suffering from social disabilities because of race or religion. She had unbounded faith in her own gifts of prevision, based on what she referred to as "certain powers of sensory reaction . . . that men lack. The intuitive sense of women is the biggest thing they bring to politics." To be sure, hers was not the only sex that at times, rightly or wrongly, proceeded by intuition. At all events, she seems to have been fairly romantic about her Great Commoner from the East Side. Her first great love had been for her talented first husband, who died young. Now, in middle age, ambition and sublimated love were both centered in Alfred Smith.

Her idealism, her romanticism, did not, however, blind her to the necessity for a lot of hard work, if the end was to be gained. She telephoned constantly to Smith at Albany about the campaign's preliminary moves from her office on Madison Avenue, near the Biltmore, and rode to the Capitol once a week on the night train to see him. Her judicious management of publicity in his behalf, her skillful approaches to many people she thought could advance his candidacy, her unobtrusive surveillance of policy decisions that might enhance his image all combined to make him regard her intelligence and foresight almost with awe. When the idea of his running for the Presidency was broached to Smith by his friends he tended at first to make sport of it. He was passionately absorbed in the task of reorganizing the state government, and did not intend to neglect his duties — like Governor Whitman — for the sake of such a will-o'-the-wisp. He knew his name would be presented at the convention as New York's Favorite Son, as in 1920. "Nothing will come of it," he said to Frances Perkins. "But it's a very great honor. I'm very grateful."

Belle Moskowitz, however, was in deadly earnest. Smith was also urged to seek the nomination by Tammany Hall, as well as by the Democrats of Massachusetts, Rhode Island, New Jersey, and Illinois, populous areas where the Democratic Party had been steadily growing in power. The death of Harding in August, 1923, the accession of his colorless Vice-President, Coolidge, the scandals connected with the Veterans' Bureau, and the even greater scandal of Teapot Dome gave the Democrats high expectations in 1924. Not surprisingly, therefore, Smith came to entertain his presidential aspirations seriously. Once the Governorship of New York seemed the highest rank an East Side Irish boy could ever reach. But he had demonstrated great fighting power; he had known how to set the public on fire in populous New York. Was it not possible that he might go further still?

In mid-April, a few days after the Legislature adjourned, the Democratic State Convention met in Albany and pledged the New York delegates to the national convention to the nomination of Smith. The Governor appeared before the meeting to thank them for the honor they had conferred on him. He had heard about the boom, he said, but he had done nothing about it, because he had been busy night and day reading the mass of bills the Legislature had just passed.

The man who used one office and neglected it in order to climb to a higher office was not deserving of the one he held, he told them. On the other hand, "The man who would not have an ambition for that office [of President] would have a dead heart." Whatever came of it, he assured the delegates that they would have no cause to regret the confidence they had reposed in him.

Early forecasts indicated that there would be as many as fifteen candidates in the field, with William G. McAdoo having an initial lead of some three hundred pledged delegates to Smith's two hundred, while the rest were Favorite Sons. Compared with the Republicans, who embraced the Protestant Anglo-Saxon middle classes, Midwestern farmers, and skilled laborers, the Democrats were a divided party, a loose coalition of city people, principally in the Northeast, with the conservative whites of the South. Since 1856 they had won only four presidential elections, of which the 1912 victory was attributable to a split in the opposition. And in this minority party the Democrats of the urban Northeast, despite their numbers, had actually played a minor role. New York State figured large in Republican national affairs, but New York Democrats felt neglected in their national organization. The Irish and other Catholic racial groups, as well as the Jews, who together formed the backbone of the local Democracy, were then effectively excluded from their proportionate share of Federal offices. For example, out of two hundred Federal judges appointed during the decade of the 1920's, only eight were Roman Catholics and eight were Jews.

In regional party affairs, to be sure, the Irish, and the other immigrant masses in the cities for whom the Irish acted as

political intermediaries, were gaining more and more authority. As in New York, so in Massachusetts and northern Illinois, the birth rate favored the Irish-led machines supported
by the urban groups. Meanwhile no one knew better than
Charles F. Murphy how much patient subsoil work had to be
done before a presidential boom could be fairly launched,
and so early in 1924 he sent out his associates — Ed Flynn
of the Bronx and Norman Mack of Buffalo — to form alliances
in those other Democratic areas for a show of strength at the
convention. The results were encouraging, Curley and Fitz-
gerald of Boston, along with George Brennan of Chicago,
rallying strongly to the Smith candidacy. In another move
to help Smith Murphy also joined with important business
groups in New York City to contract for the use of Madison
Square Garden as the convention hall, hoping that the
crowds demonstrating for the Governor in his hometown
would exert a favoring psychological effect on the visiting
delegates. These arrangements proved to be too clever by
half, but Murphy did not live to see the error of his move,
for he died in late April, two months before the convention
was to open.

All the faithful Democrats of New York and other states,
Irish, Protestant, and Jewish, attended en masse the imposing
funeral of the great regional boss at St. Patrick's Cathedral.
But afterward, someone recalled Mrs. Moskowitz having said
in private that the passing of Murphy was "the best thing
that could have happened for the Governor." The de facto
leadership of the Democratic state machine was now completely in his hands. Ever since 1922, to be sure, when Smith
had defied Murphy to reject Hearst, the Governor had been
the dominant leader of the state's Democratic Party. Still

the old ties of sentiment and trust were strong between the two men; Murphy treated Smith generally with great consideration, and at times Smith deferred to Murphy's wishes, out of respect for the boss's long experience.

President-making is truly a complex game in the United States, and with Murphy gone, a certain lack of professionalism showed itself among the Smith backers. Very sketchy preparations were made in the interim before the convention began. A Citizens' Committee for Smith was hastily thrown together in April, but Proskauer, who had directed the last gubernatorial campaign, was now a New York Supreme Court Judge, and could not act as its chairman. Looking about for some nationally known Democrat from New York to head the new committee and deliver the nominating speech, Smith's War Board fixed on Franklin Roosevelt. Although he had not lost hope that he would someday recover the use of his legs, Roosevelt was still immobilized, and obviously could not be expected to take an active part in the campaign, as he pointed out. He agreed to serve when Proskauer, who called on him with Mrs. Moskowitz, promised that they "would do the work" if he would accept the post of official chairman. Another recruit to the Smith bandwagon at this time was Eleanor Roosevelt, who was active in the Women's Division of the New York State Democratic Committee directed by Caroline O'Day, Nancy Cook, and Marian Dickerson.

This must have been a period of considerable emotional strain for Alfred Smith, for a few weeks after the death of the man who had fathered his political career, his mother died. He took what comfort he could in the knowledge that these two had always shown complete confidence in his ability to reach the highest post in the land. He now dropped the pose of modesty and began to speak as if he expected to win the nomination. On the eve of the convention he said to an interviewer, "My real strength is that the real people of this country want to see me nominated . . . The people want a winner."

It was a fact that liberals and working people all over America were beginning to regard Alfred Smith with strong sympathy. He now ranked as the outstanding progressive in the Democratic party. In 1924 the midwestern farmers and the organized labor movement seethed with anger at the Harding-Coolidge Administration. Senator La Follette actually waited to learn if Smith would be nominated at the New York convention before proceeding with his own plan to launch the Progressive Party as a third party. For if Smith had been a candidate he would certainly have carried with him the votes of several million members of the AFL, who ended by supporting La Follette.

As the delegates streamed into the metropolis from the provinces and cities further west, leading New York Democrats tried to put them at their ease with hospitable attentions, particularly the women. A hospitality committee made up of women prominent in social and political life found lodgings for the women delegates and entertained them at luncheons and receptions. Frances Perkins addressed a large group of women delegates and the wives of delegates at a breakfast in the old Waldorf-Astoria Hotel, telling them what the Governor of New York had accomplished for the women in his state, and indicating tactfully that he was in no way an uncouth fellow, as many of them had been led to believe. But no social graces or courtesies could allay the fears of the

Bryan contingent, who came to the great city from the South and the Midwest as to enemy country; for them it was the new Babylon, whose sinful inhabitants defied the Prohibition amendment, and which also contained the concentrated power of the banking and stock exchange community that robbed the American farmer of his hard-won earnings.

The arrival of the Bryan forces, as potential backers of the candidacy of McAdoo, prefigured the great split that was to develop in the convention. On the one side, behind Senator McAdoo, whose boom had originated in California, were the Drys, the Ku Klux Klan, the farmers, and small-town nativists. The Wets rallied behind Smith, leading the strong push of the urban Democrats toward a position of power within the party. Curiously enough, when debate on the party platform began on the opening day of the convention, June 29, the question of Prohibition was bypassed, as if neither side wished the battle to be joined on that issue. Almost immediately afterward, however, the polarization of the delegates became apparent when the issue of the Ku Klux Klan was brought up.

A majority of the Platform Committee had voted to include a plank directly censuring the Ku Klux Klan, which in recent years had grown to a membership of 4,000,000 in the southern and border states. A secret society, hostile to Negroes, Catholics, and Jews, the Klan exerted its influence through the threat and the use of terror, over many state legislatures and officials, including some governors. Even intelligent and progressive young men, like Hugo Black of Alabama, later Senator and Justice of the United States Supreme Court, were obliged to join the Klan if they hoped for any political preferment in the South.

At that period the Klansmen seemed less concerned about the Negroes, then so thoroughly intimidated as to be quiescent, than about the "international Catholic" conspiracy, which their spokesmen made the principal target of an irrational propaganda of fear. After the "alien" Catholics, the "international Jews" were the favored subject of the rurals' songs of hate. In short they rejected a whole multitudinous community, the world in which Al Smith had grown up.

Presentation of the anti-Klan plank to the 1098 delegates provoked a great brawl, in which Bryan took a leading part. McAdoo had avoided any comment that might lose him the support of the powerful secret society, but Smith, questioned before the convention opened, had freely expressed his loathing of the racial-religious bigots. He said in frank terms, such as those he had used on other occasions, that the Klan was abhorrent to thinking Americans of all denominations.* Though he did not take the floor, he figured as the leader of the fight against the Klan. Bryan, that mighty champion of unenlightenment, led the opposing forces, arguing against direct condemnation of the society in a labored and long-winded speech; it had its virtuous aspects, he contended, and good reasons for being. To the 14,000 New Yorkers packing the galleries this was inflammatory; they hooted and whistled and tried to shout him down like so many Dodger fans baiting an unpopular umpire. Indeed Bryan's Fundamentalist tirade stirred the locals to such a pitch of anger that bloodshed might have resulted had there not been an augmented force of city police on hand to protect the visitors. Many of the inland and southern delegates firmly believed that Tam-

---

* In 1928 he said of the Klan, "It must in time fall to the ground of its own weight. The Catholics of the country can stand it. The Jews can stand it. But the United States cannot stand it."

many had filled the galleries with toughs and hoodlums in order to intimidate them into voting for Smith, and this only made them more obdurate in their opposition to the Governor. As one historian put it, "Here rural nativism and urban rowdyism clashed in head-on collision," a contingency not foreseen by Murphy when he chose New York as the site of the convention. In the end the anti-Klan plank was voted down by the narrow margin of five hundred and forty-six to five hundred and forty-two, reflecting a cleavage that augured ill for Smith's chances.

The proceedings became more orderly when time came to place the names of candidates before the convention on July 1. It must be remembered that at this period the unit rule still operated; each state voted as a bloc, and a two-thirds majority was required for the winning candidate. In alphabetical order the states were called on; Alabama presented its perennial aspirant, Senator Oscar Underwood; in due course California offered McAdoo; and when its turn came, New York named Smith. The nominating speech for Smith by Franklin Roosevelt was the high point of this dissentious convention. Borne to the platform by two strong men, he clung to the lectern gamely, his face betraying none of his pain and fatigue, his rich, warm voice ringing through the great hall.

In those years Roosevelt's attitude toward Smith was that of an admiring young disciple, yet not untinged by envy. He had been held for some years under the huge shadow cast by the Governor within the New York Democratic organization. Late in 1923 he had written to a friend, "If I did not still have these crutches I should throw my own hat in the ring." At all events, after having been forgotten by the public during his illness — the name of an unsuccessful can-

didate for the Vice-Presidency is rarely remembered — he
was eager to leave his seclusion and appear before the convention on behalf of Smith. The Smith faction considered
that they had done well to assign the nominating speech to
an upstate, anti-Tammany Democrat, a Protestant moreover,
with a name that had great resonance in political circles.

Roosevelt had tried his hand at writing the speech himself,
but Smith's friends Proskauer and Herbert Bayard Swope
had judged his version inadequate; Proskauer was mainly
responsible for the final draft. At the convention Roosevelt
barely had time to get the name Alfred E. Smith past his
lips when pandemonium broke loose, pro-Smith delegates
and the audience in the galleries joining in a demonstration
that alarmed many out-of-state visitors once more. When
order was at last restored Roosevelt began his eulogy:

> On our candidate for twenty years the white light of publicity
> has pitilessly beaten, and revealed only spotless integrity. Here
> in this state through the leadership of this Governor, govern-
> mental efficiency has so increased that the executives of other
> states have done us the honor of copying our model. He has
> been elected to office seventeen times. Chosen Governor first
> in 1918, he suffered the only defeat of his long career in 1920.
> But it was a defeat more glorious than a victory. When our
> national ticket went down to defeat in New York State under a
> plurality of 1,100,000, he lost by only 74,000. He got a million
> more votes than I did, and I take my hat off to him . . . And in
> 1922 [he had] the largest plurality ever given any candidate
> for Governor . . . Ask your Republican friends whom they
> would least like to see nominated.

And he ended with the well-known lines from Wordsworth,
which, at first, he had been reluctant to quote, thinking they
were too literary for an audience of district politicians:

This is the happy Warrior: this is he
That every man in arms should wish to be.

"The Happy Warrior" was Judge Proskauer's literary contribution, a phrase made memorable by Roosevelt, and forever afterward attached to the name of Alfred Smith. Smith himself wrote in 1929 that Roosevelt was "the most impressive figure in that convention." He had not hesitated to use Roosevelt for his own ends, but in doing so he had brought the man forth from the political oblivion to which he had been consigned by his illness. Roosevelt's fine bearing and ringing speech gave more than one person in that assemblage the idea that if he could walk again he might one day serve to unify the Democratic Party, now so ridden by faction.

A deadlock had been expected in the contest between McAdoo and Smith; in the meantime balloting for Favorite Sons persisted for a long period. In the first three days McAdoo's vote held at about four hundred and Smith's at the figure of three hundred, more or less. The unit rule binding the state delegations seemed to favor McAdoo, but he was far from achieving the required two-thirds majority without a break in the Smith ranks, and as these held firm it became apparent at length that unless both leaders agreed to withdraw, no other candidate could gain the nomination. Neither would give way, and each stubbornly blocked the other. At the thirtieth ballot Bryan tried to lead a stampede for McAdoo, netting him about one hundred more delegates, but it proved to be insufficient, and in subsequent ballots McAdoo began to lose ground, while Smith's position improved slightly, although not enough to win.

For nearly a fortnight the deadlock continued, until the

delegates were not only worn out but flat. At long last, on July 9, after the one hundred and third ballot, McAdoo and Smith conferred on the proposal that they both retire and leave the field to John W. Davis of New York. It was so agreed, and Davis was nominated on the next ballot. A native of Virginia, who had served for a time as Ambassador to England, Davis was a man of intelligence and great personal charm, but he was almost unknown to the public. As a leading corporation lawyer his political views were on the conservative side, and he aroused little interest in the electorate. To complete the ticket, which one historian has characterized as schizoid, the delegates chose Charles W. Bryan, Governor of Nebraska, brother of William Jennings Bryan, and a close follower of his brother's views.

By resolution of the delegates Smith was invited to deliver the closing address to the convention. It was one of his less happy efforts. Worn out after the many late night sessions, he made a feeble effort to be jocose in his opening statement:

> If you have been annoyed in any way by the various people with whom you have come into contact, in their zeal to explain to you why I am the greatest man in the world, overlook it.

Then he rambled along about the achievements of New York State under his Governorship, boasting of what had been done for the welfare of factory workers, women, children, the sick, the veterans, even the farmers. Tactlessly he claimed to have enforced Prohibition more effectively than the hypocritical Drys in other states, some of whose governors were in his audience. He concluded with a pledge that he would work for the success and the unity of the party.

The out-of-state delegates were not pleased with their
direct exposure to Smith in this, for him, unusually lame
performance. What had happened to this ever buoyant man?
Was he so deeply grieved by the display of religious bigotry
throughout the sessions that he had lost his spirit? Was he
conscious of the hostility of large numbers of his hearers, he
who responded with so much sensitivity to the good will of
an audience? Or was it possible that, inured to success, he
had forgotten how to accept defeat?

All his life he had shown an unreserved tolerance toward
the different races and sects with whom he had happily lived
and worked in the Melting Pot of New York, a tolerance that
grew out of his simple faith, his own concept of what was
true Americanism. It meant that the giant symbol of liberty
in New York Harbor held out her arms to the oppressed of
all lands hospitably offering them refuge. It meant that
whatever his origins a man was a man. In his annual talks
before the Newsboys' Club in New York he used to cite his
own career as proof that our system of democratic equality
offered an open road to talent without regard to race, creed,
or color.

It was not quite as simple as all that: America also had
its Ku Klux Klan whose friends at the 1924 convention may
have put Al Smith momentarily into a state of despondency.
To some who listened to him that night he seemed a poor
loser; in fact one delegate from North Carolina who had
long admired his record concluded that he was not yet ready
for the Presidency. His counselors had no recourse but to
await another opportunity four years later. The Governor
was only fifty, a man in his prime. "Those people just
weren't educated up to it," Belle Moskowitz used to say

calmly after such a reverse; the next time his team would do
more extensive preparatory work.

He had promised to help the party in the national campaign; this he could do best, Mr. Davis told him, by running for Governor of New York once again. In September
he received the nomination by acclamation, and returned to
the hustings. Later many people found it hard to remember
the name of his Republican opponent in the state election of
1924, although the name itself was one to conjure with.
Lieutenant Colonel Theodore Roosevelt, the eldest son of
the Rough Rider, had served with credit in the First World
War, and, following in his father's footsteps, had been elected
to the Assembly; then he had been appointed Assistant Secretary of the Navy. The younger Roosevelt, short like his
father, was an amiable man in private life, but without any
talent for politics. The local party bosses had not really
wanted him as a candidate, but they hoped he might be
elected in a presidential year, in which the Republicans usually held the advantage. The GOP was also to profit by the
breakaway of the Progressive Party, led by La Follette,
which drew 4,800,000 votes, mainly from the Democrats.

Smith waged his fourth campaign for the Governorship
like the old pro that he was, against an inexperienced opponent who committed a series of blunders, ranging from
incorrect statements about Smith's conduct as Governor to
minor errors of fact. Alerted by his sharp-witted War Board,
Smith quickly capitalized on these foolish slips. At a meeting
in a small town Roosevelt congratulated the local townspeople on the recent triumph of their home football team,
only to learn from the indignant audience that it was the
opposing team that had won the game. The candidate apologized, then turned to the group of aides accompanying him

and said, "I wonder who told me that?" Smith relates that
he took up this incident immediately and used it with great
effect in a speech in which he corrected twelve misstate-
ments by his opponent about the state government. After he
listed each item he wound up with the question: "And who
told him that?" "Repeating this phrase as I went along,"
Smith said, "the audience soon caught the idea, and when I
asked the question again, it chorused with me repeatedly:
'Who told him that?'" In the heat of battle he became again
the Happy Warrior.

The year 1924 was significant for the political fortunes of
the two branches of the Roosevelt family. Smith had drawn
Franklin out of his Hyde Park retirement and put him in line
for advancement, but if the Governor had not quashed the
aspirations of the Roosevelt from Oyster Bay, the future
prospects of the Roosevelt from Hyde Park would not have
been very good. Coolidge, in that prosperous year, won the
election in a tidal wave, carrying New York State by 700,000
votes. Smith, however, breasted the powerful Republican
tide, winning reelection by 140,000 votes. This meant that
hundreds of thousands of Republican voters went to the
trouble of splitting their ticket in his favor. He was the only
Democrat on his slate to be elected.

In his inaugural address, on January 1, 1925, Smith noted,
in a spirit of gratitude, that he had the honor of being the
first Governor to be elected to that office for a third term
since De Witt Clinton a century earlier. "My party was
beaten," he said, "and I seem to stand almost alone amid the
wreckage and the disasters that overtook it." More than
ever, he concluded, he would need nonpartisan support so
that by its constructive legislation New York might be kept
"in the forefront of the commonwealths of the Union."

CHAPTER XIII

Harvest: 1925-27

IT WAS JUST as well for Smith that he did not receive the Democratic Party nomination for the Presidency in 1924. Thus he was able to return to Albany for two more terms, during which he managed to realize his grand plan for the reorganization of the government of New York State, the outstanding achievement of his public career upon which his present-day renown is based.

On the death of Murphy his command of the state party was unchallenged even by Tammany Hall. A successor to the old boss was not elected until the presidential convention was over, when Smith could give his attention to the matter. The first choice of Smith and the district leaders was Murphy's son-in-law, Surrogate Judge James A. Foley, a man of proven ability who had hitherto submitted to the machine's orders without protest. But Foley refused the office flatly, saying that he was unequal to the task of dealing with rival factions within the organization and settling their conflicts. His father-in-law had endured fierce pressures without breaking under the strain, but Foley was a scholarly fellow; he liked his present job, and he wanted peace of mind above all. When he was offered the Mayoralty of New York on a platter a year later, he refused that also.

Smith then fell back on his second choice, George W. Olvany, who was elected chairman of Tammany Hall in July, 1924. Known as "Smith's man," Olvany had been chosen as counsel to the Sheriff of New York County in 1915 when the Governor held that office, and had proved to be an honest public servant both in this post and later, when he became a judge of the city court, remaining for some years a loyal ally of the man to whom he owed his advancement. Later Olvany would draw away from Smith and walk on his own feet.

The old order of Tammany Hall was changing as the aging sachems passed away. Early in January, 1925, Smith's loyal political patron and counselor, Tom Foley, died of a heart attack. Observers commented that when the Governor visited the old district leader in his last days, he seemed much more affected than he had been by the death of Murphy. "My personal and political welfare," he said to a reporter, "were to Tom Foley a matter of concern as though I were his own son. The old neighborhood that was the cradle of New York will miss him as it would no other man." Generous with his money as with his friendships, Foley died in modest circumstances.

As the dominant figure in the Democratic organization Smith was now obliged to make decisions not only in state affairs but also in matters affecting New York City, for the new men at Tammany Hall lacked Murphy's authority. Of these problems the first in order of importance was the selection of a candidate for the office of Mayor, for by 1925 Hylan's colossal incompetence could no longer be endured. The city was as ill-governed as at any time in its history. Once more the police were charged with protection graft, now more widespread than ever because of the liquor smuggling, speak-easies, and racketeering fostered by Prohibition. The city's transit system again came under attack; in the winter of 1924–25 Smith ordered an impartial investigation of subway service in New York City, an inquiry whose findings laid the blame for delayed construction of lines and insufficient passenger trains directly at the Mayor's door. As indicated earlier, Smith and Hylan also clashed bitterly over the work of the Port Authority. To all charges of obstruction or incompetence Hylan's response was to echo the slogans regularly published in the Hearst newspapers to the effect that Smith was bent on "serving the Wall Street interests."

At a meeting at the wigwam in April, 1925, Smith warned his colleagues that he would actively oppose the renomination of Hylan. Olvany and Flynn supported this decision, but other party professionals did not relish the internecine struggle that loomed ahead, for several score of district workers had been placed on the city's payroll, and they might be expected to battle for Hylan in the primaries. If the Governor lost the "Hylan-Smith War," as the press called it, he would lose face, and what was more significant, presidential availability.

Hylan was not to be beaten with a feather duster. Smith went after him hammer and tongs; Hylan retorted with vituperation, in the interim before the primary elections. Meanwhile Smith, seeking a suitable candidate for Mayor, tried in vain to interest Judge Foley and Robert Wagner in running. On their failure to accept, he turned to State Senator James J. Walker, a native son of Greenwich Village, who had served the Governor and the party in the Legislature for sixteen years with considerable parliamentary skill. Although Walker was well-spoken and popular in New York, he was regarded with some disfavor by several of the Governor's advisers. Judge Proskauer and Robert Moses warned Smith that Walker was a man of light character, who rarely took the trouble to read reports on the bills he sponsored in the State Senate. The Citizens' Union also stigmatized Walker as one inclined to make "cynical deals," who, if he were elected Mayor, would "tolerate vice . . . and leave the city wide open." At the time, however, Smith was obsessed with the idea that he must beat Hylan somehow, and that even Walker would be a good instrument for the purpose.

As might have been expected, Smith prevailed over Tammany; after tense negotiations between the Governor, Olvany, and McCooey of Brooklyn, who had been the original sponsor of Hylan, it was announced that the city's Democratic organization would support Walker. Defeated in the primaries, Hylan threatened to head a third party ticket, but in the end declared that he would retire to private life. "Private life?" remarked Smith, somewhat unfeelingly, "Well, I don't see how he can be kept out of that!"

Jimmy Walker was then in his forties, still a youthful figure in his natty clothes, with a ready wit and enough Irish charm for half a dozen mayors. He seemed made to be an ornament of public life, but the Governor knew that his protégé was pleasure-loving, a romantic playboy, that he had a taste for champagne and nightclubs and pretty girls. It was in fact no secret to newspapermen and politicians that Walker was neglecting his wife for one girl in particular. When Tammany at length settled on his candidacy, which was equivalent to election, the Governor took Walker for a long ride around and around Central Park in his limousine, in the course of which Smith chided the younger man for his behavior and exacted a solemn promise that he would mend his ways. Smith's argument ran along the lines of a talk he had given before the Friendly Sons of St. Patrick, and bore on the need for keeping Irish names, now so prominent in public life, beyond the breath of scandal. A great future now opened before the candidate, Smith maintained, and the Governor would help him all the way, if only he would be good. Walker presumably agreed; he would shun speakeasies and patch up relations with his wife. Part of the unwritten agreement between the two men called for the transfer of George V. McLaughlin, one of Smith's most trusted aides, to the office of Police Commissioner of New York City, in order to clean up the department. Hopefully, Walker's was to be a reform administration.

Judge Proskauer was of the opinion that Smith "trusted overmuch the integrity of some of the men who served under him." In the case of Walker, Smith certainly misjudged the man's weakness of character — which he hoped he could control. Walker began to cheat on his promises at the very first opportunity: he spent the night of his election not with his wife but with his mistress.

The triumph over Hylan, following that over Hearst, had won for Smith a growing national fame. In September of 1925 he was invited to go to Chicago and address a great open-air festival of the Cook County Democrats, attended by 100,000 of the faithful. This affair, arranged by Boss Brennan of Illinois, marked a stage in Smith's renewed presidential boom. Disassociating himself from the old corrupt

Tammany machine, he spoke out for progressivism in government and impressed his hearers as a practical reformer of uncommon powers. He was quite guarded, to be sure, on the subject of Prohibition, which was of keen interest to his Chicago audience, but the rest of his speech caught the attention of thoughtful men all over the country. A comment made at the time by Senator Borah, the Progressive Republican from Idaho, was widely quoted in the national press: "We have a Democratic candidate for President in Governor Smith."

The year 1925 was marked by furious activity on his part to speed the reorganization of the state's administrative machinery and effect the other reforms to which he was pledged. It will be remembered that in his first term he had authorized the Reconstruction Commission to draw up a whole series of constitutional amendments embodying this program, but a constitutional amendment required the approval of two successive Legislatures before it could be submitted to the electorate, and there had been no time for Smith to obtain this before he was superseded by Governor Miller. After Smith returned as chief executive in 1923 he renewed his pressure for consolidation and other amendments upon the Republican-dominated Legislature with rare tenacity, also presenting proposals for various bond issues to finance important public works. Should the reorganization plan and the bond issues win through the Legislature, they would still be subject to a popular referendum. The Republicans clung to the old system of overlapping bureaus, in preference to consolidation, because this was a

rich source of patronage. They were also opposed to the
issuance of bonds for public improvements, espousing instead the pay-as-you-go method advocated by Governor Miller, by which the needed facilities would be built at a very
slow rate.

Over the years Smith had perfected three methods of gaining his ends: he could trade or bargain with the Republican
opposition in the Legislature itself, he could go over their
heads in a direct appeal to the people, asking them to put
pressure on their representatives, and he could put his program to the test of the referendum. The referendum reflected the will of the electorate directly, overcoming the
limits of the rotten borough system that obtained in the
Legislature, whereby unequal apportionment of the seats
gave the upstate rural voters an immense advantage over the
city dwellers.

The Republicans dared not refuse the Governor everything
he asked for, and were often obliged to pursue their purposes
by indirection. For example, in 1924 an increase in the
state's revenues, caused by the growth in population and
wealth, had led to the enactment of a twenty-five per cent
reduction in the state income tax. In 1925, since there was
again a surplus of several million in the treasury, Smith
proposed a similar reduction. In the last hours of the session
the Republicans decided to block a tax reduction that would
redound to the Governor's credit, and proceeded to draft
various special appropriation bills to sponge up whatever
surplus funds were available. It was alleged that these would
cover future claims against the state for condemnation proceedings that had not even been judged in court, and that
Smith described as imaginary.

The Governor decided to get the story to the people quickly, and arranged for a radio hookup from the Executive Chamber. In his memoirs he describes what was then a novel approach to the public:

> I prepared a statement of the whole financial situation of the state and reduced it to simple, everyday language. At that time I had little experience in talking through a microphone; but I spoke over the radio for an hour and a half on Saturday night, April 11, 1925.

Who but Alfred Smith could talk to several million people for an hour and a half on prime time about financial questions and hold their interest! He made the statistics come alive. In closing he appealed to his listeners to write or telegraph their representatives in Albany. The following Monday he could look out of his office window and watch the great bales of letters and telegrams being carried into the Capitol. Reluctantly the legislators reversed themselves to approve his tax reduction. The success of this ploy was so immediate that during the middle twenties one of the familiar sights in New York City was a knot of people gathered around a loudspeaker connected to some restaurant or drugstore, all listening intently to that husky voice explaining the business of the state government in simple, common-sensible terms. It was always a good show, as good as Amos and Andy.

In trying to educate the public he did not neglect his former method of appearing in person to explain his program. In January, 1923, there had been a disastrous fire in an overcrowded state hospital — a building of frame construction dating back to 1853 — in which twenty-five persons had lost their lives and many more had been injured.

> I seized upon [this fire] as an opportunity to awaken the public
> mind to the obligation of the state to get rid of these dilapi-
> dated old fire traps as well as to provide new construction to
> meet [the needs] of the growing population in the hospitals.

The state's prisons were in the same condition. By the old
methods of financing improvements piecemeal, it would take
seventeen years to bring about the needed changes. Touring
the state from one end to the other Smith aired his proposal
for big bond issues to be offered at the rate of $10,000,000
a year for ten years to cover new hospital and prison construction. He did the same for a bond issue of $15,000,000
to develop a state park system, and argued forcefully in favor
of still another bond issue to provide for railway grade crossing elimination, totaling in the end all of $300,000,000. Bond
issues, he observed shrewdly, were favored by the city
dwellers who regularly gave him his large majorities in a
referendum, because they paid rent, whereas individual
property owners, rurals or farmers, feared the borrowing
method for improvements because it might lead to higher
taxes.

The Republicans acceded to the proposals for amendments
not only because they could not appear to be obstructive,
but also because many of the projected changes in the state
constitution, particularly those dealing with reorganization
of the executive, had long been championed by their own
leaders, such as Hughes, Stimson, and Root. Furthermore
they hoped that the amendments would be defeated at the
polls. "Beat all the amendments" was the word passed along
to Republican Party workers. But in a referendum Smith
could always depend on the popular vote to uphold his side.
In November, 1925, four constitutional amendments were
submitted to the voters and passed: one to consolidate the

executive, including a short ballot,* one to reorganize the judiciary, and two for bond issues.

Anticipating that the consolidation amendment might pass, the forehanded Republican leaders thought to win the battle with a rear guard action. They forestalled the Governor by setting up an informal committee to draw up enabling legislation that would, they hoped, render the amendment ineffectual, or mere window dressing. To make sure of the desired result the legislative leaders planned to invite Machold, former Speaker of the Assembly, but now President of the Niagara-Mohawk Paper Company, to serve as chairman of the commission. Machold was Smith's old adversary, who had long fought the Governor's plans for reorganization. Moreover any change in the laws eliminating state commissions useful to the private utilities or other corporate interests was a matter of importance to Mr. Machold. He would be as a wolf sent to guard the sheep.

Smith moved in secret to scotch these well-laid plans. He could rely on the Democratic minority named to the committee to support his views, but he desired above all that the spirit of the group be nonpartisan. There is a tradition that the finesse of Mrs. Moskowitz came into play at this juncture. Charles Evans Hughes, having resigned as Secretary of State in Coolidge's Cabinet, was vacationing at Lake George in the early autumn of 1925. In secret, Smith went to call on Hughes and urged him to serve as chairman of the Reorganization Committee. Hughes indicated that he

---

* The voters in those days were given a long ballot, with some fourteen state executives and commissioners to vote for, including the state engineer and state architect as well as local candidates. The Governor would address the citizens over the radio with crushing logic: "Why should we go on voting for a State Treasurer who hasn't a cent, or a State Secretary who is nothing but a clerk?"

would be available if called upon. Smith said nothing, at
the time, of his visit to Hughes, but soon afterward certain
liberal Republicans in the Legislature proposed that the
former Governor be named in place of Machold. Smith made
public his satisfaction at this suggestion, and stated that he
would give full support to the recommendations of a commission headed by Hughes. It now seemed impolitic for the
Republican organization to select an old party hack in preference to so distinguished a man, and the move to name
Machold collapsed.

Once the consolidation amendment was approved, the
Hughes committee lost no time in getting to work. Eminent
men of both parties served together with Hughes: among
others, Stimson, Wickersham, and Whitman representing the
Republicans; John W. Davis and William Church Osborn the
Democrats. They devised a statesmanlike plan to consolidate
the multifarious state agencies, reducing them from more
than one hundred and fifty to eighteen departments, and
eliminating numerous state offices as well as certain commissioners responsible only to the Legislature. To the indignation of the Republican machine leaders the old Waterpower
Commission was to be abolished, its powers being transferred
to the office of the Conservation Commissioner, responsible
to the Governor. Other proposed changes left New York
City's traction lines under the control of the State Transit
Commission, and provided for a four-year term for Governor,
the elections to take place at the same time as the presidential
elections. Neither of these changes was acceptable to Smith,
the first because it violated his principles with regard to
Home Rule, and the second because, as the Governor said,
"No second-rate man . . . should be given the opportunity
to steal a ride into the Executive Chamber on the back of the

national bandwagon." He had, however, promised that he would abide by the results of the Hughes Committee report, and refrain from vetoing even those proposed amendments, or parts of them, of which he disapproved.

The completed report, further refined by an official commission of the Legislature, was ready for the lawmakers in April, 1926. It called for a statute implementing the consolidation amendment, which provided for a gubernatorial Cabinet responsible to the Governor; this was passed before the close of the session. It also outlined fifteen more amendments to the constitution to carry out the rest of Smith's reorganization plan, as well as several bond issues. These too were grudgingly passed, in the sessions of 1926 and 1927, and in the fall of 1927 were submitted to the electorate in a referendum. Smith made powerful propaganda to secure their acceptance — all save the amendment concerning a four-year term for Governor. In accordance with his promise he had not vetoed this measure when it passed the Legislature, but he felt free to oppose it when it went before the people. As before, the Republicans agitated to beat all the amendments, while Smith urged the people to "Vote No on Amendment Number 6" (the four-year term) and "Vote Yes on All the Rest of the Amendments." These were complicated instructions, or would have been for an uneducated electorate, but the people of New York State had been to school to one of the great teachers of government, and they did exactly as he told them. Amendment Number 6 was defeated; all the others passed by a comfortable margin.

Making the executive branch of the government more compact and more responsible was only one of Smith's great innovations. Another was to make the government take an

active part in clearing the slums of the great cities by foster-
ing low-cost housing. This seemed to him "good Christian
principle," but good Christian principle often ran counter
to widely held notions of good business. In 1923 the Legislature had adopted his proposal to establish a Commission on
Housing and Regional Planning in the State Architect's office,
and the Governor had appointed the pioneering city planner
Clarence Stein as its first director. (One of Stein's assistants
was young Lewis Mumford, who was assigned to report on
conditions in the tenements of New York's Lower East Side.)
In 1926, Stein's successor as head of the bureau drew up a
plan for low rent urban housing development through limited dividend corporations. These corporations would have
powers of condemnation, they would enjoy reduced real
estate taxes, and their securities would be exempt from state
corporation taxes; the apartments they built would be subject to limited rentals fixed by the state. To finance the
project a state housing bank able to borrow large funds at
low interest rates was also planned, and the whole program
was to be under the supervision of the New York Board of
Housing.

Smith fought earnestly for the bill embodying these proposals, but the Republicans shied away from the idea of a
housing bank as "paternalistic" and "socialistic." "Keep the
government out of business" was their cry. The great banks
were frightened, and United States Senator Wadsworth was
reported to have told the state legislators "never to give in
to Smith on the housing bank." Smith himself could never
understand why the charge of socialism was directed at relief
for city tenement dwellers, but not at an institution like the
Federal Farm Loan Bank, which aided needy farmers. As

the housing measure was very popular with large numbers
of voters, however, a modified bill was wrung from the Legislature, and in a memorandum approving it Smith said:

> We must make a beginning in the attack on the entrenched
> system of constructing housing for speculative purposes only
> . . . . This legislation is not perfect, nor . . . the last word on
> the subject . . . In approving this bill I do so with the sincere
> hope that it may prove the beginning of a lasting movement to
> wipe out of our state those blots upon civilization, the old
> dilapidated, dark, unsanitary, unsafe tenement houses that long
> since became unfit for human habitation and certainly are no
> place for future citizens of New York to grow in.

Under the provisions of the act one excellent housing project
— still in many ways a model — was completed by the Amal-
gamated Clothing Workers Union in the Bronx. Another
group of low-cost apartments in Manhattan's Lower East
Side was initiated by philanthropic capitalists friendly to
Smith, among them Herbert Lehman and Aaron Rabinowitz,
a member of the State Housing Board. Little real progress
was made in this field, however, until the country came to
the changed economic climate of the 1930's. Still to Smith
and his advisers credit is due for the actual start of state-
aided low-cost housing, which later assumed enormous proportions. He took great pride in this, and much satisfaction
in the fact that his housing plan involved cooperation between the state government and public-spirited capitalists,
for his program was essentially pragmatic and moderate,
rather than radical.

Another area in which the Governor started the state on a
progressive program was education. It has been noted earlier

how in his first term he fought the Lusk Bills that were designed to limit freedom of thought by teachers, but it should be added that at the same time he had sponsored and signed bills raising teachers' pay through state funds, in 1919, by the sum of $5,300,000, and the next year by $20,-500,000. No one understood better than he, as he used to say to the Assembly in 1911, the importance of good schools and good teachers. School buildings, after the war, proved to be woefully inadequate, partly because there had been no new construction for some years, and partly because of the growing birth rate. Neither in the country nor in the cities were there enough seats for all the children. Smith gave strong support to bills for consolidating and improving the old one-room rural schoolhouses, a program that called for the expenditure of some $40,000,000. In 1925 he appointed one of his philanthropic admirers, Michael Friedsam, of B. Altman's department store in New York City, as head of a special commission to prepare a program for expanding state school aid. The commission in 1926 set the figure for this assistance at $89,000,000 a year for three years. By 1928 Smith could boast that he had done more to advance public education in New York State than any Governor before his time.

Much of Smith's legacy to the people of New York State is confined to intangibles, such as the reorganization of the executive branch of the government, or the shift in political power from the rural population to the city masses, but in more than one field his contribution is visible and enduring. It was in his second term as Governor that he initiated the Council of Parks for the purpose of coordinating and expanding the historic, recreational, and natural beauty areas of the state for the benefit of the public.

Smith was ably assisted in his ambitious plan for the new park system by Robert Moses, who largely provided the inspiration for it, and who not only lobbied actively for the scheme, but also drafted much of the enabling legislation for the great network of state parks that would extend from Niagara Falls to Montauk Point. Moses, who headed the Council, proved to be one of the most capable administrators Smith had in his stable, dedicated, resourceful, even ruthless at times in the execution of any project to which he was assigned. But even Moses could not have achieved what he did without an occasional assist from the Governor.

One of Smith's most cherished projects was an oceanfront park area accessible to New York City which should offer the people of the metropolis all the amenities of a seaside resort without the garish tinsel, clamor, and litter of a Coney Island. Toward this end the State Council of Parks contracted to purchase at low cost a large acreage on the south shore of Long Island in Suffolk County. Horrified at the prospective invasion of hoi polloi, the wealthy residents of the area sought to have the contract canceled so that they might buy the land themselves, for "protection," as it is now called. "Where are we millionaires going to find a place to live, with all this rabble coming in?" a member of the old Havemeyer (sugar baron) family is said to have wailed to the Governor. "What *rabble?*" Smith exclaimed. "I'm the rabble."

Temporarily low in funds appropriated for parks, the state had delayed its down payment for the land, and some of the rich Suffolk County residents tried to block the purchase by claiming a technical violation. In the emergency Smith called on philanthropist August Hecksher and asked him to deposit $260,000 temporarily to cover the down payment. Hecksher acted promptly, and in fact donated the funds requested to the state park system. And so Jones Beach came into being, an abiding monument to the vision of Alfred Smith and Robert Moses.

"In 1926 I was beginning to reap a part of the harvest of the work of preceding years," Smith wrote in *Up to Now.* Most of the constructive undertakings launched in 1919 were being brought to completion, and the others were being written into the statutes, despite the dogged obstructionists in the two chambers. That summer Smith made a feint at retiring from the governorship. Some of his advisers thought it might be good for his national image for him to retire from state politics for a year or so. The state Democratic Party however could not do without him. When the convention met at Syracuse in September he was nominated for the fifth time, again by acclamation. After his name was put up the chairman of the convention, Jimmy Walker, asked with tongue in cheek, "Are there any other nominations?" There was a roar of laughter, and, when Smith appeared, great cheers for "the next President of the United States." Smith waited for the delegates to be silent, then quipped, "One nomination at a time, please!"

The party platform, in accordance with the Governor's wishes, was a strongly progressive document embracing proposals for advanced labor legislation, public housing projects in cities, state ownership and development of waterpower sites, and increased expenditures for public improvements. It also included a moderately wet plank, and a resolution in favor of the World Court. This last, a reflection of Wilsonian ideals, indicated Smith's growing interest in questions of national and international policy, the proper province of a man who would be President.

At this same convention New York Supreme Court Judge Robert Wagner, with Smith's strong backing, was nominated for the United States Senatorship, and undertook to run against the popular incumbent, Senator James Wadsworth, no easy task. As Speaker of the State Assembly Wadsworth had befriended Smith, to be sure, but politics was politics, and Smith worked hard to help win the seat for Wagner. During his two terms in the Senate Wadsworth had become a leading figure in the national councils of his party and the real head of the New York State Republicans. "I have a great deal of respect for Senator Wadsworth," Smith said at the time, "but he does not fairly represent the progressive thought of this State." Reelection for a fourth term as Governor would add to Smith's glory, and the defeat of the Republican Senator would show his power reaching into the national scene.

For their part the New York Republicans found considerable difficulty in persuading one of their number to run for Governor, that is, to qualify for membership in what Will Rogers called the "club of Al Smith's victims." At last one of their younger Congressmen, Ogden L. Mills, was brought forth, though Mills would have much preferred to stand for Congress again in his silk-stocking district in Manhattan. Born in Newport, Rhode Island, the grandson of the mineowner and financier Darius O. Mills, he had been educated at Harvard and passed for an intelligent conservative. He was therefore expected to conduct his campaign on a high level. On the contrary, he quickly resorted to crude sensationalism, charging the Governor with being the "tool" of Tammany (although, if anything, the reverse was true), with having given the state "six years of unprecedented extravagance," and with planning to introduce "socialistic" policies. In proof of this last indictment Mills said Smith hoped to put the state into the business of producing electric power, which he would turn over to Tammany's "political oligarchy" to be milked for what it was worth.

Taken aback by the violence of Mills's onslaught, Smith's campaign aides urged him to go into action quickly. But Smith was on holiday at Saranac Lake with his family, and refused to be hurried. It was not until the second week in October that he took off on a speaking tour of the state that would reach from Niagara Falls to Long Island. The Republican candidate had claimed that if he were elected Governor he would not be at cross-purposes with the Legislature; he would get along with its majority "like a cooing dove." Smith's reply to this was characteristic:

> It is known to everybody in the State of New York . . . that I am no cooing dove, and what is more I never will be. The people want clear-headed, strong-minded fighting men at the head of the government, and not doves. Let the doves roost in the eaves of the Capitol, and not in the Executive Chamber.

In a long speech before a huge audience in New York City toward the end of the contest the Governor reviewed the claims of his opponent one by one and struck them off. "I shall call my talk this evening 'Looking for Issues,'" he began. His adversaries, he held, were lacking in good ideas. They had caused accountants to search his whole record, all his expense accounts, and had found no evidence of wrong-doing. Mills claimed the virtue of economy for the Republicans, but the truth was, said the Governor, that he had vetoed $20,000,000 in appropriations passed by the Republican-controlled Legislature, and had also forced an income tax reduction. Mills had also assailed Smith's waterpower policies as socialistic, but there were Republican precedents for what he was attempting to do, at Boulder Dam, for example. Perhaps the difference over the waterpower issue, Smith argued with some asperity, arose from the fact that the Mills family and other leading Republicans held stock in companies seeking valuable power franchises. Finally Mills had fallen back on the old canard about adulterated or inferior milk sold in New York City, a charge still circulated by the Hearst press, which was supporting Mills's candidacy. Smith disposed of this groundless accusation by declaring simply that Hearst had "tied a can of milk" around Mills's neck.

Mills countered this blast by declaring that Smith himself had no bright ideas, but had to depend mainly on the advice of Judge Proskauer and Mrs. Moskowitz for answers to the questions raised by the Republicans. Affecting to hold those advisers in high regard, Mills nevertheless accused them of not checking the record with sufficient care to explain away the Governor's untruthful claims. Descending now to personal abuse, Mills exclaimed at one point in a speech, "There is no truth in him, and men who cannot tell the truth are not to be trusted either in public or private life."

By this time Smith had reached the Bronx in his tour; he was on his home grounds. Mills's speech gave him the opportunity to cry shame, indulge in some vituperation, and defend his personal character in a mighty theatrical outburst. His advisers, he said, had brains, and Mills needed their kind of advice; in fact he needed some of their brains. They had tracked down the Republican "scientists" engaged to test New York's milk and had forced them to admit that the quality of the city's milk supply was equal to that being sold in other parts of the state. The Republicans and the Hearst papers had merely distorted the results of their tests. It was a false issue, and besides, the Republicans had insulted the state's dairy farmers.

Having disposed of these minor matters, Smith now worked himself up to a grand climax in defense of his private character. Holding up the Hearst newspaper in which Mills's defamatory charge had been headlined on the front page, he demanded a retraction, failing which he would take legal steps against him. Everyone knew, he said, that his private family life had always been beyond reproach (whereas Mills had been divorced, though it was not mentioned here), and he added:

> I have been obliged to put great pressure on the men and women of my organization to keep them from speaking about the private life of Ogden Livingston Mills. If he has anything against my public or private life, I defy him to produce it.

Then he tore on about how twenty-seven years ago he had knelt before the altar of God, and while the white light of Heaven beat down from the Great White throne, had promised to care for, honor, and protect the woman of his choice. And he had kept that promise. "Let the Congressman lay his own private life beside my own."

Knowingly or not, the Governor had misread the passage in which Mills seemed to cast a slur on his character, and used the opportunity for some corny, but as usual, effective histrionics. Mrs. Smith, like many others in the audience, was in tears as he wound up. The next day Mills apologized publicly, saying that he had not the slightest intention of assailing the Governor's private character, as would have been evident if the offending remark had not been taken out of context. Yet some newspapers commented that his criticisms of Smith were not only exaggerated, but were largely false, and that he was responsible for bringing the whole tone of the campaign down to the level of a vulgar brawl.

A week before Election Day Charles E. Hughes, ever a staunch Republican, came out in support of Mills, warning that Smith was still identified with Tammany Hall. Newspaper articles also appeared citing the signal services of Hughes and other leading Republicans on the reorganization committee. Smith countered this easily by issuing a statement revealing the plot of the Republican machine to have Machold named as chairman of the committee, and his own sly maneuver to bring about the selection of Hughes.

Smith won by a goodly margin of a quarter of a million votes over Mills, who had proved a stronger opponent than had been expected. The Governor also carried the whole slate with him except for the office of Attorney-General, which the Democrats lost to Albert Ottinger (who had the support of the Jewish voters of New York City), and he contributed in good measure to Wagner's victory over Wadsworth. Another cause of Wadsworth's defeat, however, was the fact that he had had the moral courage to stand as a Wet, a position shared by a strong majority of New Yorkers, as shown in a recent referendum. In order to punish him the Prohibition Party entered a third ticket candidate only for the Senate seat, and split enough votes upstate to get Wagner in.

Following the November elections, the Republican state machine made a last attempt to put over the Niagara Falls waterpower grab in which they had been frustrated in 1922. The Waterpower Commission, which they dominated, was to go out of existence within six weeks, as a result of the referendum on the reorganization amendments, and they had no time to lose. No sooner had the Commission announced hearings on leases of state-owned sites to various private companies than Smith and his aides went into action. The Governor spoke at a large public dinner arranged by Mrs. Moskowitz under the auspices of the Survey Associates, repeating his earlier arguments about the importance of having the state retain ownership of the water power sites. Although this talk was well publicized, a more significant step was the naming of Samuel Untermyer as special counsel to the Governor, in order to study the legality of the proposed leases to the holding companies. Untermyer, a formidable investigator of corporate affairs, had directed the Congressional inquiry into the Money Trust in 1913. His appearance on the scene frightened the lame duck Waterpower Commissioners to such a degree that they annulled the applications already granted. Smith remarked at the time that while he had not definitely made up his mind what ought to be done about the Niagara power sites, his defense of them proved to be a very popular action. Judge Proskauer suspected that Smith was vague on the subject because he had not thought through the problem of waterpower development by the state. It was not until the advent of Franklin Roosevelt as Governor that a workable program was advanced.

Early in 1927 Smith named the first gubernatorial cabinet, as provided for in the reorganization amendments recently passed, and summoned its members to meet with him in the Executive Chamber of the Capitol. The members of the cabinet included, among others, the Superintendent of Public Works, the Commissioner of Taxation and Finance, the Commissioner of Education, the Commissioner of Agriculture and Markets, the Commissioner of Mental Hygiene, the President of the Civil Service Commission, the State Architect, the Director of the Executive Budget, the Director of State Charities, the Secretary of State, and the Assistant to the Governor, together with the Assistant Secretary to the Governor.

At their first meeting, on February 9, Smith said, "This is probably what might be termed a meeting of the directors of the big institution, of the big business of New York State." He proposed to leave to each man all the details of his department, he went on to explain; he would talk to them in turn at the fortnightly meetings to learn what he needed to know of their problems. Each department head would be asked to present his plans for the year ahead, along with his budget estimates, which the Governor would combine with those of the other departments for presentation to the Legislature. Thus he would have clearly in mind what his program was and just what it was supposed to cost; his Cabinet would be responsible to him, to the Assembly and the Senate, and to the people of New York. Out of the labyrinthine confusion in which New York State's administration had been floundering for well over a hundred years Smith had made an ordered structure.

✦

Although Frances Perkins was not a member of the Governor's Cabinet, she continued as one of his close administrative assistants throughout his incumbency. In 1926, when John Higgins retired, Smith appointed her Chairman of the Industrial Board, and as the Industrial Commissioner who had succeeded Shientag, James A. Hamilton, was a political hack with little interest in the department, Miss Perkins was frequently called upon to inform the Governor about departmental matters in his stead. The latitude he gave her in working out her problems, the encouragement she got from him in trying new solutions must have been typical of his relations with other members of his staff. Under the demands of her job Miss Perkins had been growing year by year in mastery of the subject of labor law, to the point where she had few rivals anywhere in the country. One particular case, the Mahti Latti case, illustrates how she kept moving out into new paths.

Mahti Latti was a Finnish-born carpenter engaged in repairing a dock on New York's waterfront. In order to get at the rotten wood underneath the dock Latti and another man rigged up a raft, tied by a rope to one of the piles, on which they could stand and keep their tools. While working on the raft Latti was seriously injured, and made a claim under workmen's compensation against the contractor who had employed him. The insurance company representing the contractor refused the claim on the ground that Latti had been on an object afloat in the water, and therefore was subject to maritime law, under which their client was not liable. Referees for the Workmen's Compensation Division sustained the insurance company, but Miss Perkins overruled them. The insurance company appealed to the courts, and fought the case all the way up to the United States Supreme Court, where the final decision upheld Miss Perkins.

Her rulings tended to extend the coverage of workmen's compensation to any disabilities incurred in the course of employment, and this led inevitably to more protection against occupational diseases. Certain of these were covered by law, such as lead poisoning from the manufacture of paint, or "the bends" resulting from work deep underground, and others, like silicosis, could be dealt with gradually as the origin of the diseases was traced directly to manufacturing processes. In the end Miss Perkins came to the conclusion that a general coverage of occupational diseases would be more equitable, leaving it to the Industrial Board to decide whether the disability claimed was in fact a result of that particular type of employment. To implement this policy the existing law had to be amended, and Miss Perkins would occasionally ask the Governor to give a speech on the subject, or make some reference to it in a message or statement, and this he did gladly, for he had always been concerned about Workmen's Compensation.

He was moreover very sensitive to criticism of the Division's operation, as was seen in his reaction to the charges made by Associated Industries in 1923. Again in 1928 the Labor Department came under attack, and once more Smith appointed a Moreland Act Commissioner to make an investigation. Professor Lindsay Rogers of Columbia was named to the post, and it is interesting to note that while some abuses still persisted in the operation of Workmen's Compensation, such as ambulance chasers who tried to act as intermediaries between injured workmen and the division's referees, or insurance company physicians who habitually cleared the employers of blame for continuing disability, the instances of outright fraud by Labor Department officials were found by Rogers to be limited to minor bureaucrats, only four or five in all, out of many hundreds working in the department, and involved comparatively small sums of money.

Frequently when Frances Perkins worked late in Albany with the Governor on budget or other legislative matters, the Smiths would ask her to spend the night at the Executive Mansion, since she was then living in New York City. The picture she has drawn of the Governor's home life is as warm and cozy as a Norman Rockwell painting. At about eleven or twelve o'clock in the evening the Governor would put an end to the business meeting in his Capitol office and say to his associates, "Well, that's enough for tonight. Let's go over to the house." And they would all troop over to the Executive Mansion, where Mrs. Smith would invariably be waiting up in the little sitting room on the first floor, "pretty as a pin and prettily dressed," as Miss Perkins recalls.

The Smiths had made but few changes in the décor of the house on Eagle Street, which has been so aptly described by a writer for *The New Yorker* as "Hudson River helter-skelter." A decorator from Altman's department store had been engaged to do over the drawing room which the lively Smith children on first view had found so forbidding. The room was stripped of all its clutter; the walls were paneled and painted white; straight hanging draperies were substituted for the old ball and fringe dust catchers; the Axminster carpet gave way to solid color broadloom; and reproduction Jacobean and Sheraton furniture was arranged in uncrowded groups to give an air of dignity and comfort. In a contemparary photograph the room suggests a rich man's club or the lobby of an expensive hotel of the time, but it was at any rate more cheerful than the faded elegance it replaced.

After greeting his wife, Smith on these occasions would call for refreshments — sandwiches and beer or ginger ale. Then, as Miss Perkins recalled, "The Governor would heave a deep sigh, put his arm around Katie and say, 'What about a little music?' " and without any further coaxing Katie would sit down at the piano and accompany him as he sang the old songs of their courting days. They were obviously having a good time, said Miss Perkins, and their guests shared their simple pleasures. The singing seemed to relax the Governor after the strain of the long day's work.

This picture of domestic felicity showed the Governor and the wife he loved in an informal setting that only a few of his intimates were privileged to see. But he was, after all, a public figure, chief executive of the richest state in the Union, and a man whose hopes were now being directed toward even higher station. The public figure, some newspapermen remarked, changed perceptibly in manner in the mid-twenties. He was more dignified; his lips were often buttoned as he resorted to what experts of politics used to call the art of voluble silence. He had always dressed with a certain elegance, if a bit on the dapper side; now he was more inclined to wear a cutaway and top hat, the uniform of the successful politico, saving the brown derby that had become his heraldic emblem for election campaigns.

During his second term in office the Governor and his family had at last moved from 25 Oliver Street to a comfortable suite of rooms at the Hotel Biltmore for their visits to the city; here Smith also had offices after 1923. Some thought he should never have left the Lower East Side where his forebears had lived for nearly a century past. But his growing children had no sentimental attachment for the old neighborhood. When they were obliged to leave the spacious Executive Mansion in Albany after the election of 1920, the family felt frightfully cramped in the Oliver Street house. Moreover the neighborhood had deteriorated rapidly after the First World War; Irish families of long residence had moved to the Bronx or Brooklyn or the suburbs; Germans and Jews, as their incomes increased, had moved uptown in Manhattan, or to the other boroughs, to find "better air for the children," as they used to say. Oliver Street was an island of respectability in the dreary slums surrounding it, but hardly the right milieu for the Smiths' gently bred daughters.

Emily and her sister Catherine had been sent to a Catholic finishing school in Riverdale, and the boys too had been away much of the time in recent years at boardingschool, but still in Emily's affectionate memoir of her father, *The Happy Warrior*, there is an undertone of complaint at their long residence in the drab Lower East Side. The girls had grown up to be attractive young ladies and were approaching the marriageable age. Emily, the eldest daughter, was clearly the favorite of her father, whom she resembled. Vivacious, gregarious, with a lively intelligence and considerable grace, she enjoyed some social success in Albany in her own right, besides showing a keen interest in her father's political problems. As she grew to maturity Smith enjoyed talking politics with her, although he would tease her or play practical jokes when she became too inquisitive or disputatious. Emily's development was the more gratifying to the Governor in that his sons were disappointing. Alfred Smith Junior, the eldest, made an unfortunate marriage at an early age, followed by a divorce, and neither he nor his brothers followed careers in which their father could take any pride or satisfaction.

In Albany the Smiths had a busy social calendar, the round of official receptions and teas being managed smoothly by Emily, acting as her mother's social secretary. They also dined out with many of the old families, who had been won over by the charm of the Governor. Among the eligible bachelors attached to this small but select circle, a new face appeared late in 1923, when the Superintendent of State Police resigned and Captain John A. Warner was appointed in his place. Warner had been Deputy Superintendent for some years, but the Governor did not remember ever having seen him. A graduate of Harvard, a war veteran, scion of a well-to-do Rochester family, Warner came very highly recommended, and Smith promptly promoted him, although the young man had Republican affiliations.

After a while it was noticed that the Superintendent of Police was present in the Executive Mansion much more frequently than was necessary to guard the Governor's person. No one, therefore, was surprised when Major Warner, as he was titled in 1926, asked for Emily's hand. He was a Protestant, and that would have been an insuperable barrier to the marriage for the Smiths, but Warner undertook to be converted to the Catholic faith, and so the way was smoothed for the most sumptuous wedding ever held in the state capital. The date was set for June 5, 1926.

Frances Perkins thought that the idea for so splendid a ceremony might have come from Smith himself: he wanted to show the world, like many a devoted Irish father, that there was nothing too good for his daughter, of whom he was so proud, and he wanted to prove that the Smiths could carry off such an occasion with all the proper style and splash. Fifteen hundred guests were invited, including state officials, dignitaries of the Catholic Church and other denominations, old friends from the East Side, and social leaders from upstate and downstate, as well as Tammany braves and members of the Legislature. The matter of precedence was so delicate that as Miss Perkins recalls a protocol officer from the State Department at Washington was called in for advice. Cardinal Hayes himself came from New York City to officiate at the rites in the Cathedral of the Immaculate Conception in Albany. In the crowded Cathedral, filled with flowers and lit by innumerable candles, the services were delayed until a papal messenger arrived bearing the papal blessing in a great scroll to be delivered at the altar at the close of the ceremony. (The poor man had missed a train connection, and came panting up almost an hour late.)

The reception at the Executive Mansion afterward was no less elaborate. In the June sunlight the women in all their finery and jewels, the men in cutaways and top hats, the Governor's military aides and the State Police in dress parade uniforms flashing with gold braid, a cardinal or two in red biretta and cloak all made a splendid show of fashion, beauty and rank. Champagne flowed, and a rich collation was served up by a New York caterer, including caviar, pâtés, chicken Gallatin, and Lobster Newburg. The Governor stood in the receiving line for hours, but when at last he was free to circulate, he put on no solemn airs, but was as easy and jovial as ever, if at moments a bit flustered. When someone exclaimed that it was a lovely party he answered, "Do you like it? Elizabeth Marbury helped us out." Miss Marbury was not only a Democratic National Committeewoman, personally devoted to Smith, but also a famous *arbiter elegantiarum*, who earned her living by arranging lavish parties for people of means who did not know how to manage such affairs for themselves. Since she was determined to make the Smith-Warner wedding a posh social event, and as a rule spared no expense for her clients, a number of the guests speculated on the possibility that the Governor, who was often short of funds, might have to go into debt to pay for it.

Looking about her at the animated scene on the lawn of the Executive Mansion Frances Perkins reflected on how far her host had come from the little house on Oliver Street where she had first seen him at home. There were many guests at the Executive Mansion in Albany that lovely June afternoon who were confident that the wedding of Smith's second daughter, Catherine, would be held at the White House, in Washington. Catherine, however, decided not to hinge her happiness on that eventuality, and two years later, just before the Democratic Convention nominated her father for the Presidency, was married to Francis J. Quillinan in the same setting as her sister.

CHAPTER XIV

The 1928 Campaign

WITHIN TWO YEARS after the explosive scenes of internal strife that had rent the Democrats at Madison Square Garden in 1924, the senior politicians of the party, even those from the South, moved to bring about harmony with the populous urban section whose unchallenged leader was Alfred Smith. The schism had produced a fearful electoral disaster. Now the Drys strove to compose their quarrel with the Wets and the Catholics. They were forced to recognize that their party was a loose coalition of the northeastern city voters and the Solid South, but it could never hope to win the country without the block of northeastern states, New York, Massachusetts, and New Jersey, where Smith and his followers were so strong. Bryan had died in 1925, and Senator McAdoo's star was fading. After Smith's great feat of winning reelection for a fourth term as Governor in November, 1926, the more intelligent Southern leaders, such as Cordell Hull of Tennessee and Josephus Daniels of North Carolina, acknowledged that he could not be denied the nomination for the Presidency in 1928.

Smith stayed close to his job at Albany and took the line of ignoring his revived presidential boom, but all through

1927 his allies and advance agents were busy in the field. Boss Olvany made a number of trips to the South to confer with state leaders there, Mayor Frank Hague of Jersey City worked for the cause during a winter visit to Florida, and Norman Mack of Buffalo, Ed Flynn, and Thomas Chadbourne, a corporation lawyer long associated with Tammany, made pilgrimages to the provinces to seek alliance with the regional politicos.

"Let the demand for your election come from elsewhere in America [than New York]," Joseph P. Tumulty, Woodrow Wilson's former private secretary, wrote to Smith in 1927 from somewhere in the interior. That year the experienced Tumulty performed great services as an advance agent for Smith and kept in close touch with Van Namee in Albany. Soon favorable reports began pouring in from all quarters: Smith-for-President clubs sprang up in South Dakota, Montana, and Wisconsin; in Nebraska the maverick Republican Senator George Norris declared for Smith, adding, "I'd rather trust an honest Wet who is progressive in his make-up and courageous . . . than the politicians who profess to be dry but make prohibition ineffective. And I do not believe Smith would sell out the country's natural power resources to monopolies and trusts as they have been in the past." At about the same time Mayor Rolph of San Francisco predicted that Smith would capture California, and a conference of leaders from twelve Mountain and Pacific Coast States hailed the Governor as the party's logical choice for President.

By the beginning of 1928 Smith clearly ranked as the nationwide favorite among regular Democrats. Grooming himself for the more exalted role, Smith tried to improve his image as a statesman concerned with national affairs. His

annual message to the Legislature on January 4, 1928, not
only reviewed the improvements that had been wrought in
the state government over the past ten years but also touched
on broader issues, including proposals for a modification by
Congress of the Volstead Act, relief for farmers, and the
creation of state-owned power authorities. Smith's fame as
a progressive statesman throughout the country had been
augmented by his battles with the electric power combine
in New York State. Consumers then stood in great fear of
the power trust, and in the country districts there was a growing movement for rural electrification by cooperatives under
local or federal authority, which made it a live issue for the
Governor.

As Governor, Smith had carried on his social welfare program with great zeal. His instincts, his feelings about questions like widows' pensions, workmen's compensation, or
shorter working hours for women and children were humane
and sincere, but he was not unaware that his brand of progressivism brought him political fortune. Even Boss Murphy
once admitted to Miss Perkins with some astonishment that
the welfare and labor laws really brought in a lot of votes.
The cost of gas and light too was of great moment to large
numbers of plain citizens, and in fighting to keep the rates
low Smith only increased his popularity. But for the rest he
was in no sense a radical system builder. He believed with
all his heart in the equalitarian free-for-all of American society, through which he had scrambled in his youth, and
often cited his own success story as proof of the essential
rightness of our private enterprise society.

Franklin Roosevelt, always a close student of Smith's strategy, wrote in 1928 that in his judgment "it was the policy

of Governor Smith to let business look after business matters."
Walter Lippmann had pointed out even earlier that Smith
was essentially "a perfectly conservative man about property,
American political institutions and . . . the established order
. . . who never promised the city people a new heaven and a
new earth." While in his years of power he showed strong
sympathy for the underdog, it should be remarked that the
reforms Smith espoused were designed to reconcile class and
ethnic divisions, not to set them against one another. He
used to warn his narrowly conservative opponents in the Republican Party, as we have noted, that unless a greater measure of social justice were extended to the underprivileged
the masses would one day turn to socialistic or revolutionary
goals, whereas the changes he urged would help stabilize
society. Theodore Roosevelt and Woodrow Wilson had used
the same arguments, but Smith surpassed them in his skill
at playing according to the rules of the political game.

In the later stages of his career Alfred Smith's political
friendships shifted perceptibly. Formerly he had relied for
a flow of ideas on his Kitchen Cabinet, which included such
party workers as John F. Gilchrist, Commissioner Van Namee,
and his secretary, George Graves, as well as the group of
intellectuals and ghost writers made up of Mrs. Moskowitz,
Moses, and Proskauer. But toward 1925 and 1926 a different
breed of men began to figure prominently in his inner circle,
those Ed Flynn called his "golfing cabinet." Among these
were a new-rich group of native New Yorkers, such as the
construction magnate William F. Kenny, whom Smith had
known since his boyhood; James Hoey, who had returned to

New York after striking it rich in the West; George Getz, who had established himself in Chicago, but remained an intimate friend of Smith's; and James Riordan, formerly of the United States Trucking Corporation, but now heading the County Trust Company. All these joined in making generous contributions to Smith's campaigns. A new and impressive figure appeared in the Governor's golfing cabinet around 1926: John J. Raskob, vice-president of General Motors Corporation, business associate of the Du Ponts, and one of the financial wizards of the postwar stock market boom.

Kenny, with his lavish hospitality, provided a discreet meeting place for these associates of the Governor's. Kenny's father had served in the New York City Fire Department, and the son had maintained close relations with Tammany insiders all his life. Of late he had specialized in the construction of power stations for Consolidated Edison, a company that was on the friendliest terms with the Democratic machine, and, according to rumor, provided an important source of "legitimate graft." Having accumulated a fortune reckoned at $30,000,000, Kenny lived in ostentatious style, often traveling about the country in his own railway palace car, with guests such as Charles F. Murphy and Alfred Smith and their families. He had settled the problem of Prohibition for himself by maintaining what was in effect his private club in a penthouse at the top of a high office building he owned on Fourth Avenue at Twenty-third Street. It was known as the "Tiger Room," because Kenny had decorated it with stuffed tigers, bronze tigers, tiger rugs, and photographs of old Tammany Hall leaders. At one end of the great barnlike space there was a bar and grill, and at the other, behind a partition, shower baths, and a barber shop. Robert Moses, who visited there occasionally, described it as an informal, predominantly Irish-American men's club, where Kenny and his friends relaxed after business hours "like a bunch of boys," with "drinks, playing poker, singing songs, swapping yarns, and talking politics." Ed Flynn, however, rated the last as its most important function; he called it a "clearing house" for the city's Democratic leaders, and the scene of many important political conferences. The local politicians enjoyed Kenny's hospitality as well as his openhanded donations to their campaign funds, and none more than Smith, whom Kenny admired unreservedly.

Smith made no secret of these and similar donations. In May, 1928, as the drive for his nomination warmed up, he was subjected to a formal examination by a United States Senate Committee inquiring into the source of his campaign funds. He testified frankly that his friend Kenny and others had already contributed as much as $70,000 to his campaign treasury voluntarily, and without any quid pro quo. The others who had given sums of over $10,000 included James Hoey, James Riordan, Herbert Lehman, and William H. Todd, the shipbuilding magnate. When Todd was called before the committee and asked if he intended to make further contributions to Smith's campaign, he said, "You'll have to speak louder, I got a bum ear." On the question being repeated he replied, "Sure I'll give him anything he needs as long as I got anything to give." Todd happened to be a Republican except when Al Smith ran for office. It was customary at that period to try to conceal sizable contributions to campaign funds, but Smith's friends spoke with refreshing candor. Smith too, when questioned particularly about Kenny's large donations, said simply, "There is nothing in the world Bill Kenny wouldn't do for me — he'd take his shirt off for me."

In the days when he ruled as the unchallenged political leader of New York City, as well as New York State, Smith was a frequent visitor at Kenny's Tiger Room, and it was here that he met Raskob for the first time, perhaps as early as 1925. Ed Flynn has related that it was he who brought about the momentous introduction of Raskob into Smith's circle. Having met Raskob at the Du Pont works in Wilmington, Delaware, Flynn introduced him to Kenny, who, at Flynn's suggestion, invited him to dinner at the Tiger Room, Flynn calculating, no doubt, that Raskob might give money to the common cause, and might even obtain more funds from the Du Ponts. Raskob, a Republican in politics, then ranked as one of the leading Catholic laymen in America, having donated more than a million dollars to the Church, and having been named by Pope Pius XI a Knight of the Order of St. Gregory the Great.

At their earlier encounter Raskob had told Flynn that he had no acquaintances among politicians; he confessed however to some interest in the New York City subway system, for General Motors was an important producer of electric locomotives. Flynn replied that Smith was a man who knew a great deal about the subways — the Governor had recently been making speeches on the subject — and Raskob indicated a desire to meet him. The introduction at Kenny's place was casual, but after dinner Smith and Raskob went off to a corner of the big room for intimate talk.

The financier was greatly taken with the politician, and Smith, for his part, was impressed by Raskob, a self-made man like himself. The two men had in common not only their religion — Raskob was half-Irish, half-Alsatian — but their common experience of poverty in boyhood. Born in Lockport, New York, Raskob, like Smith, had gone to work at an early age to support his widowed mother and his younger siblings, starting as a typist and clerk at five dollars a week. Eventually he found employment with the Du Pont Chemical Company, where he rose to be secretary to Pierre S. Du Pont, and finally vice-president of that company as well as of General Motors, which he helped to reorganize. By the late twenties he had garnered a fortune reckoned at about $100,000,000, thanks to the spectacular rise in General Motors stock. In those carefree days, whenever Raskob permitted himself to make a few optimistic remarks about the market, Wall Street fairly boiled over with bullish enthusiasm. He was to be known to fame also as coauthor of an article in a mass magazine entitled, "Everybody Ought to Be Rich," that was published on the eve of the great crash of 1929. But Raskob might well have envied in Smith the inspirational qualities which he himself lacked. His was one of those colorless visages you might pass in the street and never remember. The two men became close friends, though Raskob, like other big tycoons, kept himself in the background in the earlier phase of their friendship. But he quickly resolved to help Smith win the presidential nomination and election, and to this end donated large sums of money to the campaign chest. John J. Raskob too was going to be a president-maker.

New York's Governor had drawn quite a flock of wealthy patrons to his cause, but nowadays many millions would be needed, for presidential politics in the Age of Plenty was becoming a war of the moneybags. This fact worked a subtle change in the spirit of Alfred Smith, now a veteran of fifty-five, engaged in the most important battle of his life.

The foundations for a presidential boom were being laid, and the money to swing it seemed to be forthcoming, when a formidable obstacle to Smith's hopes made its appearance. In the spring of 1927 the question of whether it was proper for a Roman Catholic to become President of the United States was raised in a serious way by a New York lawyer named Charles C. Marshall. A member of the Episcopal Church and an expert on canon law, Marshall set forth his doubts in "An Open Letter to the Honorable Alfred E. Smith," which was published in the April issue of *The Atlantic Monthly*. In the event that Smith attained the highest office, Marshall asked, what influence would the authority of the Roman Church have on his judgment of temporal matters? How would his administration of a government three-fourths of whose citizens were Protestants be affected? Marshall cited numerous encyclicals of Popes going back to medieval times in which the temporal as well as the spiritual authority of the Church over its communicants was strongly affirmed. On the domestic plane he posed the question of a Roman Catholic's attitude toward the relationship of government and church-directed schools, and on the foreign plane that of possible military intervention against countries where Catholic church properties were confiscated and parochial schools suppressed. At that very moment in Mexico a revolutionary government was engaged in just such activities.

Ellery Sedgwick, editor of *The Atlantic Monthly*, forwarded advance galley proofs of this polemical tract to Gov-

ernor Smith, and offered him space in which to reply, suggesting that this would be an opportunity to clarify the mind
of the public and prevent the controversy from smoldering
in secret. From what Smith could make of Marshall's open
letter, it revived once more old fears that a loyal Roman
Catholic might not be able to reconcile the doctrines of his
church with the provisions of the Constitution and the rulings of the Supreme Court regarding civil and religious liberty and separation of church and state. Now he had served
his state for many years without ever being aware of any
conflict between the religious principles he had been taught
and his public duties. In fact he thought so little in terms
of theology or church doctrine that he was strongly minded
to consign Marshall's letter to the wastebasket, rather than
trouble to answer it. *The Atlantic Monthly* was of relatively
modest circulation, and perhaps it would be best to let sleep-
ing dogs lie. When he had first run for the Governorship in
1918 a good many people had raised the old cry of "Rum,
Romanism, and Rebellion" — the theme song of the Cleve-
land-Blaine campaign in 1884 — and yet the upstate Yankees
had come around, and now voted for him by the hundred
thousands. Frances Perkins was of the opinion that his first
instinct — to ignore the issue — was the correct one.

Mrs. Moskowitz, however, did not agree that the article
should go unchallenged. She advised the Governor to consult Judge Proskauer, who, as Miss Perkins recalls, came at
once when Smith called him. Like Mrs. Moskowitz, Proskauer held that the letter required a full and clear reply, and
that it was far better to deal with the religious issue in advance of the election contest. Smith protested, "But I know
nothing whatsoever about papal bulls and encyclicals!" (One

of the professors on his staff at the time, Lindsay Rogers, remembers that he pronounced the word "enclickycals.")

Franklin Roosevelt too contributed his advice at this juncture. Since his speech at the 1924 convention Roosevelt had
stood forth as one of Smith's most fervent supporters; because of his well-known interest in Smith's presidential boom,
Ellery Sedgwick, his old Harvard friend, had sent him advance proofs of the Marshall article for *The Atlantic*. Roosevelt promptly wrote the Governor a letter urging him to act
quickly. (At this period Roosevelt pursued Smith with his
attentions in a fairly voluminous correspondence.) The religious issue was dangerous, in his view: "You do not know
the Bible Belt," he wrote, an area with which he, Roosevelt,
had become familiar while stumping the country in 1920,
implying that Smith knew only his own home region. Roosevelt proposed three alternative courses in dealing with the
questions raised by Marshall: 1) ignore the whole business,
2) arrange to have some well-known Protestant answer the
Open Letter (he suggested himself), or 3) have Smith answer it himself, after having sought competent legal and
canonical advice. At the same time Roosevelt dashed off a
note to Sedgwick arguing that Marshall's letter was a lot of
legal and theological nonsense that would create ill feeling
and misunderstanding; it should simply be suppressed.

Smith's reply to Roosevelt was reserved and brief; he would
answer Marshall in his own way, he said, and Roosevelt
would soon be able to read his reply. Smith's attitude toward
the younger man, formerly one of tolerance, had grown very
kindly since Roosevelt had become paralyzed, and specially
so after the Happy Warrior Speech of 1924. He had recently
appointed Roosevelt to two state commissions of the honorific

sort. Roosevelt's attitude toward the Governor, on the other hand, was quite starry-eyed; if he was ever to play a role in state and national politics, he seemed to feel, that would depend largely on what happened to Alfred Smith.

The alternatives suggested by Roosevelt, however, had been examined independently by Smith's close advisers. In the end Smith decided to get up an article rebutting Marshall, to appear in the May issue of *The Atlantic*. This was drafted with the help of Proskauer and Judge Irving Lehman, who was strong on constitutional law; the famous wartime chaplain Father Francis P. Duffy contributed a good deal to the theological passages of the article, which was then submitted to Cardinal Hayes for his approval with regard to its presentation of modern Catholic doctrine.

What, in truth, were Smith's religious convictions? Proskauer said once, "He was the most fervently religious man I ever met," but what this meant was that he held simply by the faith received from his parents and teachers all the more strongly because of the persecution to which his Irish forebears had been subjected by the English on the score of their religion. As an American of the third generation, however, he accepted unreservedly the principle that state and church were absolutely separate in his country, and he had conducted himself in such a way that no charge of bias in favor of his coreligionists was ever seriously lodged against him. On the other hand, he refused to be circumspect, as some Catholics were, in displaying his attachment to his church; he kept a picture of the Pope hanging in his office at the Capitol, and, as a prominent layman, thought it his duty to attend the Eucharistic Congress in Chicago in 1926. He had also taken part in a reception to welcome the visiting cardinals at the New York City Hall, and had knelt and kissed the ring of the papal legate. Miss Perkins thought such a public display of piety might appear distasteful to stiff-necked Protestants, but Smith was stubborn about it, saying, "I'll be myself, come what may!" He could no more disclaim his religion than he could disavow his old friends in the Tammany organization.*

The redoubtable Florence Kelley had once charged him with taking the position of the Catholic Church in the matter of a child labor law, but Smith and Frances Perkins denied the allegation. According to Miss Perkins, Mrs. Kelley came storming into the Governor's chamber one day in 1925 breathing fire and fury because, she claimed, he had not put enough pressure on the Legislature to obtain passage of her long-cherished measure, and had denounced him for submitting to the orders of the Church. The truth was quite the contrary, Miss Perkins recalled: he had resisted the argu-ment of one church dignitary, an emissary from Cardinal O'Connell of Boston, who urged him to oppose the child labor law on the ground that it interfered unduly with paren-tal authority and the sanctity of the family. On that occa-sion Smith summoned Frances Perkins to witness his reply to the priest, in which he asserted that he was a good and loyal Catholic, that he would obey the instructions of his Church in all matters of faith and morals, but that he would not accept clerical advice, as such, on economic, social, or politi-cal issues. Miss Perkins supposed at the time that Smith

---

* These men would probably have understood that it might be undiplo-matic for him to associate himself publicly with them when he was ob-viously a candidate for the Presidency. Yet early in 1928, when the Tam-many Society celebrated its centennial, he came down from Albany to lend his presence to the occasion and speak at the ceremony.

wished to go on record as having stood up to the Cardinal. But Mrs. Kelley long thought otherwise, because although he endorsed the idea of limiting child labor, he recommended that it be embodied in an amendment to the constitution, which he knew would not be approved by the Legislature.

Certainly the Catholic Church played a part in politics in Boston and New York and elsewhere, but it commanded no more influence than the Baptists in the South, or the Methodists in other areas, those same Methodists that Lincoln used to refer to as the "third House." The Federal Constitution forbade religious tests for all candidates for public office, but this did not prevent repeated manifestations of intolerance in earlier times directed particularly against Catholics by the Know-Nothings and the American Protective Association, and more recently, by the Ku Klux Klan. After 1926, when the likelihood of Smith's being nominated for the Presidency was widely conceded, there were loud protests from spokesmen for the Klan in the South. "Keep Al Smith in New York," was their slogan. In the Senate the Klansman's firebrand, Tom Heflin, ranted violently against the Governor of New York. After a tour of Virginia, Arthur Krock, the Washington correspondent of *The New York Times*, reported on May 23, 1927, that the sentiment of the voters was against Smith on the Prohibition issue, but added, "the religious issue is also a handicap here." Leading Southern Democrats, even those who later supported his candidacy, such as Senator Joseph T. Robinson of Arkansas, Senator Pat Harrison of Mississippi, and Josephus Daniels of North Carolina, hinted that Smith would be unpopular in their sections as much because of his religion as because he was a Wet. Thus there were reasons enough, as Smith's advisers urged, for him to answer fully those who questioned his loyalty to the American system of government in a statement that could be used as campaign literature in the ensuing presidential contest. The article rebutting Marshall's letter was sent off to *The Atlantic Monthly* in mid-April, and was released to the press in advance of publication.

To Marshall's essential argument that there was "a conflict between his religious loyalty to the Catholic faith and his patriotic loyalty," the reply was that no such conflict existed:

> I have taken an oath of office nineteen times. Each time I swore to defend and maintain the Constitution of the United States . . . I have never known any conflict between my official duties and my religious beliefs.

He added that it was well known that he had been a battler for extensive social and political reforms, and these had caused no such conflict to show itself. Moreover he had never asked any man whom he appointed to public office what his religious belief was; in his present Cabinet ten were Protestants, three were Catholics, and one was Jewish. George B. Graves, Assistant-to-the-Governor, and an intimate aide for twenty years, was a Protestant and a 32nd-Degree Mason.

In his "Open Letter" Marshall had raised the question of who was to decide whether some issue fell under the civil jurisdiction or under the authority of the church. Who was to judge what was to be rendered unto Caesar and what unto God? Smith's reply was that in cases of seemingly conflicting authority — should they actually arise — only a man's individual conscience could be the ultimate judge, not the Pope. Perhaps, he declared, there might be some nearly unimaginable crisis in which political duty and religious duty clashed, as when

some law were to be passed which violated the common moral-
ity of all God-fearing men. And if you can conjure up such a
conflict, how would a Protestant resolve it? Obviously by the
dictates of his *conscience*. That is exactly what a Catholic
would do. There is no ecclesiastical tribunal which would have
the slightest claim upon the obedience of Catholic communicants in the resolution of such a conflict.

In making this profession Smith cited the recent declarations
of Cardinal Gibbons and Archbishop Ireland to the effect
that "both Americanism and Catholicism bow to the sway
of personal conscience." As Walter Lippmann commented
at the time, modern Catholics, having moved far from their
medieval notions of religious authority, fully embraced the
essential post-Reformation doctrine of the right of private
judgment in all matters where secular interest was involved.
Religious authority in secular life was thus held closely compartmented in the modern state, and this view of things,
asserted by Alfred Smith (as by John F. Kennedy after him),
was given with the full approval of the prelates of the Roman
Catholic Church in America.

To dispose of the imputation that a Catholic President
might possibly involve the country in a foreign war on religious grounds, he said:

My personal attitude, wholly consistent with that of my church,
is that I believe in peace on earth, good will to men, and that
no country has the right to interfere in the internal affairs of
any other country. I recognize the right of no church to ask
armed intervention . . . merely for the defense of the rights of
a church . . . I believe in the worship of God according to the
faith and practice of the Roman Catholic Church. I recognize
no power in . . . my Church to interfere with the operations of
the Constitution of the United States for the enforcement of

the law of the land. I believe in absolute freedom of conscience and equality of all churches, all sects, all beliefs before the law . . . I believe in the absolute separation of Church and State . . . I believe that no tribunal of any church has any power to make any decree of any force in the law of the land, other than to establish the status of its own communicants within its own church. I believe in the support of the public school as one of the cornerstones of American liberty . . . in the right of every parent to choose whether his child shall be educated in the public school or in a religious school supported by those of his own faith . . . And I believe in the common brotherhood of man under the common fatherhood of God.

In this spirit I join with fellow Americans in a fervent prayer that never again will any public servant be challenged because of his faith . . .

Smith's reply to Marshall's letter received widespread and favorable notice in the newspapers, and the editor of *The Atlantic* ventured the hope that publication of Smith's profession of faith would "end all whisperings and innuendos." But that was not to be. Although Smith knew a good deal about the persistence of religious prejudice in his own state, he had no conception of how rife was the spirit of intolerance among the nativists of the hinterland. It would need another third of a century for light to penetrate those dark jungles of the provincial American mind.

Meanwhile the Republicans too were preparing for the contest. In August, 1927, President Coolidge had made known his refusal to stand again for the Presidency in his classic statement, "I do not choose to run." Herbert Hoover, Secretary of Commerce, then became the leading Republican contender; his impressive record of public service under three administrations, including Wilson's in wartime, gave promise of a respectable performance as his party's standard-bearer.

Among the Democrats the Smith drive gathered irresistible momentum in the early months of 1928: the April primaries in Wisconsin and Michigan were easily won by his supporters; the large northeastern states then came into his camp and several western states followed. Some of the elder statesmen in the South confessed that they would have liked some other northern personality to head the ticket, but at the Jackson Day dinner in Washington in January, 1928, they showed a conciliatory spirit. At all costs, they now wished to avoid the dissensions that had led them to ruinous defeat in 1924; as one of their spokesmen said, "It would be less embarrassing to accept Al Smith and risk loss of the election than to turn him down and alienate four million Roman Catholics in New York, Illinois, New Jersey and Massachusetts."

As a gesture of courtesy to the Southerners the northern faction agreed to hold the convention in Houston, Texas, and the large Smith delegation closed in on the steaming city in mid-June, full of confidence. Officially the delegation was headed by Franklin Roosevelt (as "window dressing," he suspected), since he was again to put Smith's name in nomination, but the actual management was entrusted to Van Namee and Olvany, who let it be known that more than five hundred delegates from twenty-seven states were already pledged to their candidate, and that the two-thirds majority needed would be won quickly. The Smith forces also gave the impression of strong financial backing: on the sidings near the tentlike convention hall were gathered the private palace cars of Raskob, Nicholas Brady, and Kenny, whose party included Mrs. Smith and her sons. Smith remained in Albany

with his daughter Emily, but he wished his wife to be seen
by everyone at the convention, his good, simple, handsome
Katie, for there had already been whispers that she was a
dowdy, vulgar woman, and a heavy drinker, unfit to be the
First Lady. These rumors continued to spread throughout
the campaign, despite the efforts of distinguished women
like Eleanor Roosevelt, Ida Tarbell, and Frances Perkins to
represent her as she really was, a delightful homebody, of a
retiring disposition, with unaffected good manners. Receiving groups of Texas ladies in Houston, Mrs. Smith conducted
herself with natural dignity, as Smith knew she would, and
when she confronted the reporters, she was simple and correct: "I am not a politician," she said. "I have devoted my
whole life to my home and family. I am unable to discuss
the political situation."

The convention opened with a keynote speech by Claude
Bowers, who delivered a violent philippic against the Republicans, branding them as men given over to corruption and
bribery, as illustrated by the Teapot Dome scandal. The
platform, however, turned out to be an amorphous affair,
neither conservative nor liberal. It promised aid to farmers
and the development of public power resources, but in defer-
ence to the Southerners it took no firm stand on the issue of
Prohibition. Before the convention ended Smith in a telegram
declared that he would make his own views on Prohibition
clear during the campaign.

With the platform out of the way, the time had come to
choose the presidential candidate. The names of several
Favorite Sons were proposed, and then Franklin Roosevelt
was brought out to repeat his "Happy Warrior" speech of
1924, with a few variations, stressing Smith's magnificent

record and his "habit of victory"; this evoked a tremendous ovation from the Smith adherents. Back in Albany Alfred Smith heard both the speech and the ovation, because for the first time the proceedings at a political convention were broadcast over a nationwide radio network. He felt some momentary alarm, however, when during the customary parade of his supporters about the hall he heard sounds of scuffling on the floor, caused by the refusal of the Alabama delegation to join the march. There were, to be sure, invocations to party harmony by some southern leaders, but more than one observer, like Lewis Gannett, noted at the time that the crowd concealed with difficulty their prejudice against the Irish Catholics and the big city people from the East. Although Smith was nominated on the first ballot, the choice was not unanimous. In an effort to balance the ticket regionally, in the time-honored way, Senator Robinson of Arkansas, a well-liked figure in Congress as in the South, was named as his running mate.

Smith had won the nomination of his party easily, but the auguries for winning the election were less than favorable to all but his perfervid partisans. Franklin Roosevelt, a shrewd watcher of the political skies, observed in a letter to a friend at the time that Smith had left the safe anchorage of Albany to give battle to the well-fortified Republicans in the national arena, and added that he was pessimistic about his party's chances in that year of "Republican" prosperity.

The next important decision Smith faced was the selection of a man to be the new chairman of the Democratic National Committee, the man who would manage his election campaign. The politicians around him, and his Kitchen Cabinet as well, favored Senator Peter Goelet Gerry of Rhode Island, a wealthy supporter of Smith's, a man of pleasing personality, with some experience of politics, and a Protestant of old Dutch-Yankee lineage. But Smith hinted to his friends that he was inclined to name Raskob. Roosevelt, quick to perceive the Governor's errors, observed in private that by adding a moneyed Roman Catholic to the party leadership, when the candidate himself was a Catholic, the antagonism to Smith in the South and the West would only be increased. And an independent Republican who was friendly to Smith remarked to Frances Perkins that the choice of Raskob was "a terrible mistake." The Democratic Party, he said, didn't need any more Roman Catholics to head it.

As Miss Perkins recalled, Belle Moskowitz also was definitely opposed to the naming of Raskob. The Democratic National Committee was to meet in New York City on July 12 to "elect" a chairman, actually to accept the choice of the candidate, according to tradition. The night before, Judge Proskauer, a house guest at the Executive Mansion, added his own pleas to those of Mrs. Moskowitz that the Governor take Gerry rather than Raskob. Smith listened, but would not give a final answer. Early the next morning Proskauer arose to hear the Governor singing lustily in the bathroom while he shaved, and waylaid him when he came out. "I've made up my mind," said Smith; "it's Raskob." And later he said to Belle Moskowitz, "It's the only thing Raskob has ever asked of me, and I've got to give it to him."

In those days the rich financiers or industrialists, such as the Du Ponts, or Samuel Insull or Thomas W. Lamont, preferred to work behind the scenes in politics, but Raskob plainly wanted a big public role. Just prior to the Houston convention he had stated in a widely reported interview that business did not fear the election of Alfred Smith. Smith, he said, was a man who "would not disturb honest business . . . and could be depended upon to hold even the balance between capital and labor." This concurred with a statement of the Governor's that in choosing Raskob as chairman of the Democratic National Committee he wished "to let the businessmen of this country know that one of the great industrial leaders of modern times had confidence in the Democratic Party and its platform."

As one of Smith's younger aides of that time once said, "If you mix with financial people you absorb their prejudices." It would not be true to say that Smith had *turned* conservative, at least not yet. He had never been opposed to business; he had never been a socialist; his progressivism had been limited to administrative reforms, social welfare legislation, and the increasing regulation of public power resources, ameliorative measures on the whole, hardly calculated to endanger the capitalist system. Nevertheless there is perceptible at this time a shift in emphasis that was to become more marked as time went on. In 1928 he was apparently obsessed with the idea that the Democratic Party could not win the election unless it could call on big business for support and for huge sums of money to pay for literature, speakers, advertisements, and also radio time.

It was reported that Raskob sought to raise $4,000,000; he actually spent at least $5,300,000, and some estimates ran to $7,000,000. Rumors about the selection of Raskob to manage the Smith campaign may have inspired the political journalist Frank R. Kent to publish his timely essay on Fat Cats in politics that summer.

A Fat Cat [he wrote] is a man of large means and no political
experience who having reached middle age, and success in
business, and finding no further thrill . . . or satisfaction in the
mere piling up of more millions, develops a yearning for some
sort of public honor and is willing to pay for it. The machine
has what he seeks, public honor, and he has the money the
machine needs.

Raskob's first step was to install the Democratic National
Headquarters in the General Motors Building at Broadway
and Fifty-Seventh Street, thus creating the impression that
he proposed to use General Motors' advertising and publicity
experts to sell Governor Smith to the voters in much the
same way as Chevrolets were sold. At the very start of the
canvassing season it was said that the feelings of regular
Tammany workers were ruffled because they were not assigned to salaried jobs for which they thought they were
qualified. They felt that Raskob was "high-hatting" them.
Miss Perkins heard that some disgruntled New York politicians were saying that "Raskob thought he'd bought the
Democratic Party, and he was going to run it in his own
way, like a branch of General Motors." He showed his inex-
perience when after raising large funds he spent them un-
wisely, as in Pennsylvania, a rock-ribbed Republican state.
Another Fat Cat, the banker Herbert Lehman, was head of
the finance committee, and fairly matched Raskob's efforts
at money-raising, but Lehman showed far more understanding of the political game.

Smith's next problem was to find a strong candidate for
Governor of New York to succeed himself, and one who
would help carry the state for the Democrats. There was

some talk of inviting Judge Townsend Scudder of the Court of Appeals to run; the name of Owen D. Young, chairman of General Electric, was also mentioned, but Scudder aroused no enthusiasm and Young was not interested. Smith and his aides then turned to Franklin Roosevelt as the best choice.

In his syndicated newspaper column Will Rogers said at the time that Roosevelt "could have gone far in the Democratic Party himself . . . but he has devoted his life to nominating Al Smith." Few then thought of Roosevelt as anything but a disciple of New York's maestro of popular politics. Two years earlier he had refused the opportunity to stand for the United States Senatorship, and in the summer of 1928, after his fine performance at Houston, he had gone back to continue his cure at Warm Springs, Georgia, for he still hoped that two years more of treatment would restore the partial use of his legs. Yet even without his legs he had made several impressive public appearances at national and state party conventions, and he had plainly enjoyed the opportunities Smith gave him to come into the limelight again. Now in early middle age, handsomer and more robust than ever, save for his crippled legs, he gave the impression of having grown mentally during the long years of his illness. To Frances Perkins, who had known him ever since he came to Albany as a green young State Senator, he no longer seemed supercilious or shallow.

The story has often been told of how Roosevelt's strategist, Louis Howe, planned for him to wait until 1932 or 1936 before striking out for the big prize, and strongly urged him to refuse the nomination for Governor. Late in September Smith interrupted his strenuous continental speaking tour to come East in preparation for the state convention at Rochester. Roosevelt had been alerted about the project to nominate him and on October 1 he sent Smith a wire stating emphatically that he would not run. But Smith would not be denied, and with the aid of Eleanor Roosevelt was finally able to reach Franklin by telephone at Warm Springs, appealing to him, for the sake of the party, statewise and nationally, to accept his proposal. To Roosevelt's objections that he must continue his cure at all costs, Smith and his aides replied that the duties of Governor would not keep him from spending several months a year at Warm Springs; they also pointed out that his running mate would be the able Herbert Lehman, who would serve as his "stand-in" when necessary. Roosevelt spoke of his anxiety for the future of the Warm Springs Foundation, in which he had invested part of his personal fortune; the Democratic leaders then put their moneybags, Raskob, on the telephone, and Raskob promised to help finance the foundation. Lehman also spoke encouraging words and promised his aid. Noting that Roosevelt's resistance was weakening, Smith, in another turn at the telephone, used his utmost efforts at persuasion, then asked if he would not run even if the party convention drafted him. The hesitant silence at the other end of the line gave Smith the answer he wanted.

"Never has a candidate for Governor been subjected to so much pressure to run as Roosevelt," a well-informed newspaperman reported. In the end it was the lure of high office that led Roosevelt to yield, as well as the opportunity to escape from the seclusion and boredom of full-time therapy for who knew how many more years. Roosevelt's nomination was entirely the work of Alfred Smith, and marked a turning point in the career of the younger politician, who had his own reserves of courage and his vaulting ambition. Smith's action, on the other hand, was not quite selfless, for with two Roman Catholics at the head of the national party, the Democrats badly needed an Anglo-Saxon Protestant of distinguished name for the gubernatorial race in the Empire State.

Roosevelt was nominated by acclamation at Rochester, along with Herbert Lehman for the second place. The Republicans chose as their candidate Attorney-General Albert Ottinger, the only Republican elected to a state office in 1926. Ottinger was a conservative type and a strong opponent of Smith's policies on state-owned power resources, which Roosevelt, however, embraced. During the campaign Republican newspapers played up the idea that Franklin Roosevelt was severely handicapped, and that his health was being endangered in the sacrifice play for Smith in New York State. To which Smith replied with one of his apt improvisations, "We don't elect a Governor for his ability to do a double backflip or a handspring. The work of the Governorship is brainwork." Roosevelt himself disposed of the legend of his ill health by tearing about the state in his open car, giving as many as seven speeches a day in seven different towns.*

The Republican platform in 1928 might have been summed up in the one word: prosperity. The GOP claimed a monop-

* Smith, and Ed Flynn as well, had the impression that Eleanor Roosevelt, who had been in Rochester during the convention, wanted her husband to come out for the Governorship, and that she doubted whether continued physical therapy would restore the use of his legs. Although it was she who made it possible for Smith to talk to Roosevelt on the telephone at Warm Springs that fateful evening, she herself followed her practice of not seeking to advise her husband in the case of such a critical decision.

oly in the management of upward business cycles and attributed depressions to the ways of Democrats. In time the economic cycle actually showed indifference to party lines. Moreover the Republican administration under Coolidge and Secretary of the Treasury Andrew Mellon had little to do with the wave of prosperity in the twenties save by supporting a policy of easy money. This generated a dangerous amount of speculation in securities, which made 1928 a year of soaring markets, and 1929 more airborne still. Though certain Cassandras pointed out that the prosperity of which the Republicans boasted was unevenly distributed, Hoover claimed that his party had put "a chicken in every pot and an automobile in the yard." The Republicans, meanwhile, played down the issue of Prohibition, because in several populous northern states it had recently been demonstrated that a majority longed for modification of the dry laws.

In national elections the Republicans in those days enjoyed a large advantage; they were dominant in the farm states, and also in the industrial centers, including the twelve most populous cities. (In 1924, although Smith won the Governorship, New York City had given a large plurality to President Coolidge.) There were signs, however, that the party ratios were changing, for since 1924 the Democrats had been showing rising strength in the Northeastern states and in the cities, while at least several of the Western farm states that had turned to La Follette had reason to be disenchanted with the Republicans. Smith, however, would have his hands full; he needed to win not only in those sections where he was favored, but also in parts of the West, and above all in the South — an incongruous combination of states, whose voters held conflicting views on questions such as repealing the

Eighteenth Amendment or obtaining federal help for farmers. Smith's forthright statement in favor of revising the Volstead Act to allow state option on light wine and beer, but banning saloons, made public after the Houston convention, did him no good south of the Mason-Dixon line. Senator Robinson urged that a regional center be set up in the Deep South as soon as possible in order to educate the voters there, but several weeks passed before Raskob got around to it. It was assumed that the South would hold fast in the Democratic column.

Plans to woo the corn-hog farmers of Nebraska and Iowa, and the wheat growers of Kansas were, on the other hand, drawn up many weeks before the nomination by the Governor's staff. A survey of the farm situation, financed by Kenny and others, had been undertaken by George N. Peek, assisted by General Hugh S. Johnson, one of Bernard Baruch's employees, and (for a while) by Professor Rexford Tugwell of Columbia University. Peek had been associated with Baruch in a farm implement company in the Middle West, a business that gave him familiarity with the more urgent farmers' problems, namely surplus crops and falling prices. For several years Peek had lobbied for the McNary-Haugen Bill, which proposed to equalize the market for surplus crops through a form of export subsidy by the Federal Government. The bill, which had long languished in congressional committees, was opposed by both Coolidge and Hoover as unsound. Peek's group prepared a comprehensive scheme for the relief of farmers based on McNary-Haugen, which Smith used in his tour of the Western states.

Other intellectuals were called on to help with the Smith campaign: Professors Lindsay Rogers and Philip C. Jessup, both of Columbia University, helped draft speeches on national and foreign problems; journalists, diplomats, authorities in various fields were recruited for special writing jobs; a Women's Division was once more set up to woo the women voters. Tons of literature were printed, and arrangements made for the use of radio on a large scale. The itinerary for Smith's barnstorming tour as finally mapped out covered a large part of the country, including the Midwest, the Mountain States, and the border South. So many calls for speeches came in that Smith felt obliged to limit himself to no more than three a week, over a period of six weeks.

The opening broadside was of course the ritualistic acceptance speech, which the Governor gave at the State Capitol in August, reading his long, written address into the "pieplate," as the radio microphone was then called. His friends listened to this speech with some apprehension; he was a genius of state administration, admittedly, always at his best when he knew his ground well, but would he sound like himself when talking of broad national questions? Would this Great Commoner from the East Side project his personality to people in widely scattered areas of the country as he had in his own state? Would he be effective when discussing the problems of sheep raisers in Montana or Colorado? He was in truth no orator, but rather a speaker who was able to dramatize his feelings and ideas, while using his own racy language, especially when able to move about the platform and gesture freely, a habit that made for poor recording. (Smith said later he found the radio a cold affair; it did not respond to him, or laugh or stimulate him, as did the live crowd.) Some finicky persons found themselves disconcerted by his New York accent, not to speak of his mispronunciation of words like "radio" and "hospital" ("raddio" and "horsepital" were an affectation on his part, for he knew better, and pronounced them correctly in private conversation) in an aspirant to the Presidency of the United States. Others, no less cultivated, like Henry Wallace, remarked that they never noticed his mannerisms, but reacted only to the kindly common sense of his speech. "I was delighted with . . . his sincere and wholesome personality," Wallace wrote Miss Perkins afterward. To his admirers the mannerisms were endearing; to his opponents they were gross and alien.

Smith himself was brimming with optimism as he set off from Albany in mid-September for his continental tour, the corps of journalists at the Capitol remembered later. "I'm going to beat the pants off Hoover," he told them. For after all he had long been a miracle worker in electioneering, having lost only one election in a political career stretching over a quarter of a century, while Hoover in his view was a dry sort of man, who had never taken to the hustings or won a popular following. Smith's strategy and that of his managers was to maintain the debate at a lively tempo, without acrimony, if the Republicans were willing to go along with them.

In an eleven-car special train Smith and his party made directly for Omaha, Nebraska, the heart of the corn-hog country, where he was to open his tour with a speech on the farm question. Accompanying him were his wife, his daughters Emily and Catherine, his son Alfred, his nephew John Glynn, William F. Kenny, General William Haskell of the New York National Guard, Norman H. Davis, former adviser to President Wilson, Mrs. Caroline O'Day of the Women's Division, Judge Proskauer, Judge Shientag, and Mrs. Charles Dana Gibson, as well as forty-six newspaper correspondents, and a number of stenographers and mimeograph clerks; there were also four tons of campaign pamphlets on board. During the journey the train stopped from time to time to take on various Democratic notables and drop them off further along the route.

The large audience in Omaha seemed friendly and respectful. Smith was committed to the McNary-Haugen scheme, and this was the program he offered the Nebraska farmers, although he expressed reservations about the methods proposed for executing it, noting that the right tools would still have to be perfected. Since Hoover opposed McNary-Haugen on the ground that it would lead to even more burdensome farm surpluses, Smith stigmatized his opponent as the "foe" of the farmers, echoing the charge of Republican Senator Borah a few years earlier. There was some hope that the Granger States would be induced to break away from the Republican column because of Smith's concern for their problems and his offer of relief. (Raskob, however, did not focus the party's effort on the issues of interest to that section, but concentrated instead on Prohibition!)

The Smith caravan steamed on all the next day through Kansas to Oklahoma City, stopping frequently for water or fuel at way stations where there was always a knot of supporters gathered to catch a glimpse of the candidate. "Come out, Al, we want to have a look at you!" someone would shout, and he would appear on the rear platform to deliver some wisecracks.

As the train slowed down on the approach to Oklahoma City, night had fallen. Suddenly in the fields along the railroad tracks Smith and his party saw a line of flaming crosses: the barbarous salute of the Ku Klux Klan. The Governor was somewhat shaken by this spectacular demonstration; then he noticed on descending from the train that although a huge throng had come to the station to meet him, they were strangely quiet, suggesting a hostility he had rarely encountered in all his experience. Some of his aides sensed an ominous note in the crowd's cool reception, which might presage some violence later. Judge Proskauer remembered that the guards accompanying the Governor closed around him, and everyone in the party breathed a sigh of relief when he reached his hotel without incident.

The burning crosses outside of Oklahoma City were but the outward manifestation of the Klan's violent opposition to Smith; they were the visible symbols of a campaign begun in 1924, and renewed with even greater passion when his candidacy on the Democratic ticket gained momentum again after 1926. For two years now spokesmen for the Klan had been girding at him, and some of their leaders had even come north to rant against him in upstate New York and Long Island. More sinister still, the Klan inspired a whispering campaign that circulated slanderous accusations against Smith and his wife. During the summer and autumn of 1928 Republican campaign literature was obliquely slanted to play upon religious prejudice, but this was mild in comparison with a vast quantity of clandestine printed propaganda, filthy libels that passed from hand to hand. In these Smith was pictured as a man who profited from "the business of New York brothels," and drove recklessly about the streets of New York under the influence of liquor. (The readers of these effusions could not know that Smith never drove a car.) "Bootleggers and harlots would dance on the White House lawn" if he were elected, it was prophesied. Smith's aides,

George Graves and Robert Moses, burned up whole trunk-loads of such "literature" for fear that the Governor might see it and be carried away by indignation. The metropolitan press of New York reported briefly on the slander campaign, but in general played it down, possibly on the assumption that wider coverage would only worsen the situation. It was charged at the time that a certain Republican Senator and some agents of the Republican National Committee had knowledge of the circulation of these scurrilous pamphlets in New England, as well as in the South, but did nothing to stop it.

Without stooping quite so low as the Klansmen, certain knowledgeable Republicans were not averse to playing on the fears of the ignorant and bigoted among their fellow citizens. William Allen White, the famous editor of the Emporia, Kansas, *Gazette*, pictured Smith as the representative of the saloon and gambling interests, a man who was ready, if elected, to nullify the Eighteenth Amendment by some legal trick. And in Ohio, Mrs. Mabel Walker Willebrandt, Assistant Attorney-General of the United States, addressing a convention of Methodist ministers, urged them to enlist the 600,000 members of their church in Ohio in the war against Smith, the Roman Catholic. Their votes alone, she said, would be "enough to swing the election."

Inevitably Smith learned about the whispering campaign and the poison pen pamphlets. Although his advisers held that he should ignore the fanatics and the bigots, he came to the conclusion that he could not go on pretending that they did not exist. The flaming crosses of the Klan outside of Oklahoma City and the curiously silent crowd at the terminal there had their traumatic effect, and when he read in the local paper that former Senator Robert Owens of Oklahoma was bolting the Democratic Party because of his nomination, Smith resolved to speak out on the religious issue whatever the consequences. The Catholics among his counselors argued that that sort of thing just wasn't done, and perhaps it is unwise for politicians, under any circumstances, to give way to just passion. In the heat of the moment, at any rate, Smith swiftly dictated a revision of the speech he had planned to give in Oklahoma City. Charles Michelson, veteran reporter for the *World,* and practiced ghost-writer for presidential candidates, worked with him, and recalled afterward how agitated the Governor was at the time. On the one hand Smith told Michelson and others that he would feel like a coward, unfit for any public office, if he were to permit all those scurrilous attacks to go unchallenged. And yet at dinner the next evening, before going off to the meeting, he said to Michelson, "I'm scared, Charlie. I'm wondering how it will go. I don't know those people out there. I don't speak their language." Michelson suggested that he could speak the King's English as well as the best of them, and might use this occasion to moderate his habitual accent and turns of speech. But Smith would have none of that. "No, I'm going to campaign as I am," he replied. "I wouldn't change now even to get into the White House."

The Oklahoma City Auditorium was one of those vast halls often used for cattle fairs and great revival meetings, the proper theater for an iron-lunged orator like William Jennings Bryan. When Smith came to speak there on September 20, 1928, some 30,000 were on hand, by his recollection, and they made a continual murmur, so that he needed to stretch his voice to the full to be heard. "All day long there has been an undercurrent of hostility perceptible," one observer reported. To the Fundamentalists and nativists of Oklahoma the New York contingent seemed foreign and wicked, while to the New Yorkers present the audience seemed made up of weather-beaten, wooden-faced rustics (like those in the painting by Grant Wood: "American Gothic").

The Governor began his speech coolly, "with as little sign of emotion as if delivering a routine budget message to the New York State Legislature," as the correspondent for the New York *World* described the occasion. The *Daily Oklahoman* on the other hand, said that at times he showed anger, although this impression may have been caused by the fact that he had to shout in the great hall. In New York he usually was artful enough to contrive a dialogue with his public; he knew how to seize them by the throat, but here, on these strange hustings, facing a sea of stony faces, he was not at his best. Listening to the speech on the radio that evening Herbert Lehman thought it did not come up to the talk originally planned for Oklahoma City by Smith, who had rehearsed a quite different version in Albany a week earlier. "Smith, more than most political leaders," said Lehman, "responded quickly to the mood of an audience. If it was cordial he let himself go; if hostile he felt frozen."

His opening dealt with the accusation spread by his enemies that he was a corrupt machine politician, and outlined his record over the past quarter of a century, the laws passed in New York State under his aegis, the commendations he had received from leaders of both political parties. Then he boldly launched into the subject of the religious intolerance to which he was exposed: "I know what lies behind the pretense of Senator Owens and his kind," he said, "and I shall take that up."

> I have been told that politically it might be expedient for me to remain silent upon this subject, but as far as I am concerned no political expediency will keep me from speaking out . . . I attack those who seek to undermine [our institutions] not only because I am a good Christian, but because I am a good American and a product of American institutions. Everything I am, and everything I hope to be, I owe to those institutions.

Citing Jefferson and the Constitution, he said it was sad that no amount of education had served thus far to check the attacks on American principles, the negation of our whole history, which had been fostered by the Klansmen. They were not good citizens, he continued, when, like the Grand Dragon of the Realm of Arkansas, they urged his defeat because he was a Catholic:

> The world knows no greater mockery than the use of the blazing cross, the cross upon which Christ died — as a symbol to instill in the hearts of men a hatred for their brethren, while Christ preached and died for the love and brotherhood of man.

But Smith's appeal for religious tolerance, his attempt to answer baseless slanders with a catalogue of his achievements in public life, were so many words whistled down the wind. The next evening 30,000 people again filled the Oklahoma City Auditorium to listen to a previously scheduled address by the popular evangelist Dr. John Roach Straton on the theme of "Al Smith and the Forces of Hell."

Back in New York Smith's friends were fearful for his safety; an unusual amount of static on the radio led them to believe that a riot had broken out during the proceedings. On returning to his hotel after the meeting the Governor called Mrs. Moskowitz. "Where are you?" she asked in a panic. "Back at the hotel," he replied. "Thank God for that!" she exclaimed with fervor.

With spirits somewhat restored, after having faced down the inimical Oklahomans, he rode on to Denver, and thence to Montana, and back to the friendlier Middle West cities such as St. Paul and Milwaukee, where the people were keen for the restoration of beer and wine. In his more thoroughly prepared speeches he carried on a thoughtful discussion of national affairs, and many who reflected on what he said commended him. His opposition to Prohibition was expressed in reasonable terms, on the ground that it had not done away with liquor, which was available everywhere, but had promoted crime and the corruption of local and federal officers. On the farm question he spoke with marked concern, in Wisconsin, for example, recalling what had been done in New York to help the dairy farmers. In the Rocky Mountain region he urged the development of public power sites along the Colorado River, and charged Hoover and his associates with having long been the allies of the private electric power interests. And yet for the most part he did not seem able to exert his usual magnetism in the course of this long speaking tour beyond the Alleghenies. As Miss Perkins observed later, "He did not sound like a man who knew pigs and chickens." And Congressman Sam Rayburn of Texas said afterward, "I never thought the brown derby helped."

To the rural provincials the man who wore the brown derby was an "outlander," one of the newer breed of immigrants who had been crowding into the country to supplant the descendants of the earlier arrivals. Their ignorance of

events in the eastern part of the country was total; they knew
nothing about how Smith had become one of the greatest
of American governors. Months before the campaign began,
Herbert Croly, a perceptive political philosopher of that era,
had predicted that Smith might come to grief once he moved
outside his home grounds as a presidential candidate. In an
article in *The New Republic* Croly conceded that Smith had
functioned greatly in New York State, that he had taught the
people of the state to know and love him, and that he had
generated excitement over important issues. Yet he was
plainly unfamiliar with world questions, said Croly, and he
"did not know the West and the South of the United States."

As the tour continued he lost some of his resilience, and
seemed not to be extending himself to woo the western and
southern provincials. On the ride through Montana there
were flaming crosses once more beyond the railroad tracks.
When told that the train was approaching Butte, he said
irritably, "Never heard of it." The Irish copper miners there
were disappointed when he indicated in a speech that he
knew nothing of their colorful town, which had made world
history with its fabulous mineral wealth. He also insisted on
pronouncing the name of their state capital as "He-*lee*-na,"
and when told that it should have been "*He*-le-na," replied,
"Well, He-*lee*-na is good enough for me." By mid-October,
when he had completed his swing around the continent, he
was willing to admit in private that the campaign had turned
into a hard uphill struggle.

A difficult contest was inevitable, and yet the outlook
was not wholly unpromising, for in two great cities beyond
the Alleghenies Smith met with a welcome vouchsafed to

few Americans up to that time. In the course of a second, less extended tour (undertaken after the Rochester convention), the Governor visited St. Louis, where vast crowds, as Miss Perkins recalled, laughing, shouting, and weeping, pressed through police lines to try to touch him. Did this mean victory, or was it simply that the population of St. Louis was predominantly Catholic? In Chicago too, later in this trip, as Smith's daughter Emily reported, she was separated from her father at the station and could not rejoin his party for two hours, so dense was the cheering throng.

Miss Perkins has left a sometimes hilarious and sometimes grim memoir of what it meant to campaign for Smith in 1928. The Women's Division of the Democratic National Committee had cooked up a plan to send some Protestant-Anglo-Saxon ladies into the South in order to dispel fears about Smith's character, which had been so falsely portrayed in underground campaign literature. Miss Perkins was at first paired with Mrs. Charles Dana Gibson, who, as one of the Langhorne sisters of Virginia, was looked to as being able to rally the "best people" to Smith's standard. In Baltimore they were entertained at the home of Senator and Mrs. William Cabell Bruce, where, whenever she tried to put in a word about Smith's brilliant record as Governor, Miss Perkins was brought up short by mention of Robert E. Lee, that great Christian gentleman, the greatest of all Americans. Senator Bruce warned her that it was going to be hard to sell a man like Smith to Southern Democrats, and that without the South he would lose. "The people will always compare him with Robert E. Lee," put in one of the guests.

At women's luncheons Mrs. Gibson tried to reassure her hearers as to the social qualifications of the Smiths, and particularly of Mrs. Smith. One of the most vicious slanders persistently circulated by the Governor's opponents represented Katie Smith not only as a coarse and ignorant woman, but also as a confirmed alcoholic. "People would tell you," said Miss Perkins, "that they had personally seen her drunk in a night club," although during an acquaintance of many years Miss Perkins had never seen Mrs. Smith take a drink even in her own home. To counter the whispering campaign, Mrs. Gibson told her Southern audiences what she had observed of Smith's home life in Oliver Street, of Katie's poise and self-possession when dining with the Gibsons, of how conscientiously she brought up her children. "Anyhow," she would end up in a burst of homely sentiment, "I tell you he loves her!"

This always drew applause and nods of approval, but still Miss Perkins detected an abiding mistrust of Smith among the Southerners that she attributed to their persistent anti-Catholic bigotry. On a trip down the East Shore of Maryland — a Ku Klux Klan stronghold — she was told as a fact that a luxurious waterfront estate had already been bought for the Pope, who would move there to take over Washington as soon as Smith was elected! In her talks to Democratic groups she therefore took pains to represent her candidate not only as a practical reformer, but also as a man whose religion constituted no threat to American institutions. Not only did he believe in the absolute separation of church and state, but he was a man of high moral standards with a simple, fervent belief in God, a man who said the prayers his mother had taught him every day of his life. And she too would wind up with an appeal to the devout respectables: "I would rather have a man in the White House who says his prayers than one who doesn't pay attention to religion!" a statement that always got a big hand, even in Methodist and Baptist circles.

Continuing their tour of the South, Miss Perkins and Mrs. Gibson stopped off at Danville, Virginia, where they were met by a brass band, a committee of local Democrats, and the Mayor of the town, a bald man with a bushy beard who presumed on his distant kinship with Mrs. Gibson to kiss the ladies on both cheeks. This was a novel experience, Miss Perkins recalled, "something to go through for Al Smith!" A round of receptions and rallies followed; there were sumptuous meals, at which she was frequently invited to have a shot of corn liquor. Prohibition was needed, she was told, not for white folks, but to keep the Negroes from getting out of hand. After dinner there would be a "speaking," attended by the whole town. Here in the rural South she realized that the voters were not interested in Al Smith's social legislation, and the only safe note to strike was loyalty to the Democratic Party. But in Danville, as in Raleigh, North Carolina, Atlanta, Georgia, and towns in Alabama, she found a bigotry impenetrable to argument. In the Deep South the prejudice was not covert; it was open and vocal, and Miss Perkins was made uncomfortably aware of this when at several meetings groups began chanting "Yah-yah-yah" to drown out the speakers' voices.

Miss Perkins then returned to the North to speak in several industrial centers, where her account of the Governor's social legislation met with a warmer response, a welcome antidote to the fiasco of the southern trip. Then she was called on to go to St. Louis, Kansas City, and a few other towns in Missouri, on this occasion in company with Aileen Webb, the daughter of William Church Osborn. In St. Louis the ex-

traordinary enthusiasm shown for Smith by the whole city
raised her spirits, and thus she was not apprehensive when
Senator Harry Hawes, who had sponsored her appearances
elsewhere, warned her that the town of Independence, where
she was due to speak, might be "a little rough." The people
there, he said, were very narrow-minded and wrought-up
about the idea of having a Catholic in the White House, and
he insisted on accompanying her.

When they arrived in Independence, the streets were so
crowded that the progress of their car was impeded, and a
sign in front of the hall announcing the meeting was torn
down as they approached. Senator Hawes hustled her out
of the car and into the hall by the back door. The meeting
was to begin at eight o'clock, but time passed and only a
handful of people took their seats, for a band of rough men
were barring the entry of the public. Eventually the hall
was filled, but it seemed that the proceedings could not be
opened until some man of the cloth offered up a prayer, and
no such man could be found in Independence that night.
At length a Mormon elder consented to ask the blessing, the
efficacy of which was sadly compromised when a tomato
thrown from the back of the hall struck the lectern. Miss
Perkins remained composed, but hoped that if something
was aimed at her she would not duck, as that would be
undignified.

Senator Hawes then rose to speak in the rolling periods of
the conventional political orator, and "gave the audience hell
for being doubtful about Al Smith," as Miss Perkins put it.
He had not been long on his feet when bedlam broke loose;
there were shouts of "He's a damned Catholic," and a volley
of eggs and tomatoes were aimed at the platform. Hawes did

not budge, even when one of the missiles struck his starched shirt front; he pleaded with the crowd to show some courtesy to the visiting speaker, a lady, and hear her out.

Thanks to this appeal Miss Perkins was able to begin her little talk, picturing Smith as a God-fearing man, a good son, husband, and father. There was a scattering of applause at this, but it proved to be only the signal for rowdies in back of the hall to renew their bombardment. A tomato hit Miss Perkins's skirt; another landed on a table nearby; a third landed on her shoe. Like the Senator she did not flinch, but went on to finish what she had to say before she sat down, closing with a good-humored compliment to the strength and good aim of the men of Independence. The meeting ended in a brawl, despite the efforts of some of the saner citizens of the town, among whom was one Harry Truman, to quell the troublemakers.

One further experience of Miss Perkins's in the course of the campaign had some significance in view of the ultimate result. "Piped into" a Methodist convocation in one of Ohio's southern counties, she reduced an audience of some six hundred persons to tears with her account of Smith's early struggles as a poor fatherless boy who had gone to work at the age of thirteen to support his mother and sister. When she was done the applause was so warm and so sustained that she, and her local Democratic sponsors too, were convinced that the people of that region had been won over to Smith's banner. After the elections, she made a point of looking up the results for that area, formerly a Democratic stronghold, and discovered that it had gone solidly for Hoover!

In the twenties the United States was still "compartmented," as André Siegfried noted at the time, with fairly clear demarcations between North, South, Middle West, Far West, and border areas, each characterized by its peculiar history, geography, and ethnic character and the attitudes springing therefrom. Few men were able to judge how much ancient fears, prejudices, and superstitions worked upon the minds of different groups and sections. Later on, in the thirties, the common experience of the Depression, in which Christians and Jews, Protestants and Catholics, whites and blacks suffered together, served to polarize popular feeling more along the lines of class and economic, rather than racial and religious issues. The shared experience of World War II also brought people of diverse religious denominations closer together, while the saturation of the mass media, particularly television, helped further to blur sectional boundaries, so that the most crucial domestic problem Americans face today — the uprising of the disadvantaged blacks — transcends all local divisions.

Nearly a third of a century after Smith's race against Hoover, when Senator John F. Kennedy ran for the Presidency, his political advisers also urged him to be wary of the religious issue in canvassing the people of the South and the West. He chose rather to face up to the sectarian fears of a Roman Catholic in the White House, and deliberately prepared to deal with the whole ethnic-religious problem. Both in his speeches during the West Virginia primary contest and in his later confrontation with the Greater Ministerial Association in Houston, Texas, he worked with skill and patience to dispel mistrust of his candidacy on the ground of his religion. He invited questioning by critics and answered them on the spot, fully and frankly. The arguments he used were much the same as those advanced by Smith in his reply to Marshall in *The Atlantic Monthly:* his loyalty to the Constitution and to the principle of the separation of church and state. Compared with Smith, his attainments in the field of government were negligible, and on the record he deserved far less from his countrymen, but his personality, now projected through the nationwide television network, was winning, his voice bore no trace of slum origins, and his birth and education gave promise that he could fill the office of President with dignity and grace. By 1960, it is true, the whole climate of opinion had changed along with the shifting ratios in the population; the attitude of the press was more enlightened; the level of public education had been substantially raised even in the provinces. But Kennedy's chances for success would have been diminished had not Smith broken ground for him in 1928.*

As far as possible Hoover avoided argument with his dangerous foe, but made his bid for the Presidency by harping on the Golden Calf of Prosperity. As the eastern newspapers of both parties had spoken out in condemnation of the scurrilous anti-Smith literature that was being circulated, Hoover somewhat tardily issued a public rebuke to those who spread falsehoods about his opponent, or decried his religious faith. The Republican candidate read his speeches meticulously into the microphone, speeches in which he professed himself a liberal and a friend of labor, and claimed that the Republi-

---

* As Frances Perkins said in recollection of that earlier contest; "We who campaigned for Smith in 1928, and also the candidate himself, were not prepared to deal with the degree of prejudice we encountered . . . and were surprised and shocked by the way in which our opponents appealed to the basest passions and the lowest motives of the people."

cans had virtually eliminated unemployment. Although as a rule he shunned controversy, he did on one occasion go so far as to charge that Smith's schemes for government control of farm export surpluses and for the creation of public power authorities would foster state socialism. Smith easily refuted this accusation by citing the record of his Republican predecessors in New York State, Theodore Roosevelt and Miller, who had also favored the conservation of power resources for the public; he went on to say that almost all the great reform measures enacted into law by state and nation had been denounced by the American moneyed and corporate interests as "socialistic."

Aside from these differences, in accordance with the long established American political rule that presidential platforms and candidates should offer the people the same line of goods, there was really little to choose between the verbalized claims of the two men, barring the religious matter and the question of Prohibition. Hoover was both Dry and Wet; Smith was openly Wet. If Hoover chanted of the triumph of American Republican capitalism, Smith, as the ally of men like Raskob, the Du Ponts, and Owen D. Young, promised to be as friendly to business interests as anybody in the other party.

Crossing the Appalachians again toward the end of his second campaign tour, Smith seemed to breathe more freely as he returned to the smoky industrial cities of the East Coast; surrounded by his partisans he became his old exuberant self. The Irish and the Catholics were beside themselves with excitement wherever he appeared. In Chicago 200,000 had turned out to greet him, but in Boston, a city with a far smaller population, a monster throng of 250,000 lined his route. Similar mass demonstrations occurred in Newark, Philadelphia, and finally in New York City, where 500,000 crowded into the streets, adding up to the "greatest crowds on record," as the newspapers reported. None of the idolized party leaders before him, not even Bryan or Teddy Roosevelt, had inspired such public homage. He rode for days through the streets of the great cities in a state of euphoria, his brown derby happily tilted on his head, his cigar cocked sidewise, wearing his widest grin, and exchanging quips with all and sundry. Here in the East, when he faced his urban audience, he was at his best, an inspired actor. "His voice quavered, his eyes flashed, his face crimsoned, passion shook him," as one observer accompanying him wrote. In winding up the campaign he gave a superb performance, and the common people showed how much they loved him and believed in him. While he raised no burning issues that season — as the liberals had hoped he might — he still presented the image of the fighting progressive, the friend of man. The city masses, many of immigrant origin, only half-franchised, looked upon him as one of themselves, a man who had risen from the slums to one of the highest places in the land through his brains and courage. American history was full of the romance of poor boys of the older American stock, born in a log cabin, whose sterling qualities had led them to the White House, but never before had a poor city worker who stemmed from the later ethnic groups taken that path. The workaday people of the cities "identified" with Al Smith more than with any presidential candidate of recent times; they looked on him as one who incarnated all their own hopes and dreams.

Although big crowds do not always mean votes, they did this time signify a change in the composition of the political parties. The huge crowds also affected men's judgments. The Republicans were alarmed as the betting odds favoring Hoover narrowed, while Smith and his friends were deluded by the hope that he could not fail to win through. Once again, might he not work a miracle?

The Democrats counted on some two hundred electoral votes of several northern states, as well as the solid South and some support in the West. One good augury for their side was the fact that registration that year made a spectacular rise, and the turnout of voters was tremendous. In the northeastern tier of states, Massachusetts, New York, and New Jersey, between twenty-five and forty per cent more women voted than in 1927, many of them Catholics and immigrants going to the polls for the first time. Smith's vigorous campaigning had brought out a quantity of new Democrats in addition to the Catholic women, among them the Negroes of Harlem. In fact Smith won the largest vote ever given to any Democrat, almost 15,000,000, which was twice as many as the total for Davis in 1924. But the ranting and the undercover work of the religious bigots excited many more to vote against him. About 21,500,000 cast their ballots for Hoover, and the electoral college results were even more calamitous because of Smith's near miss in several populous states.

Early in the evening of November 6 Smith and his family, along with many of his friends and advisers, went to the 69th Regiment Armory in New York City to await the news of the nationwide balloting. Franklin Roosevelt, his wife, and his mother were also on hand. Roosevelt had completed a strenuous state campaign; one of his strongest speeches, in a town in western New York, was a denunciation of those who had introduced religious prejudice into the national elections. Both Smith and Roosevelt turned glum when Herbert Bayard Swope of the New York *World* reported by telephone that Virginia, North Carolina, and Florida were going Republican. But an even more stunning disappointment came when they learned that New York State seemed lost to the Democrats by a very close vote. Roosevelt's lieutenants, Ed Flynn and James A. Farley, sent off wires instructing party workers to watch late returns from upstate closely. As the evening wore on, however, the truth was borne in upon Smith; his face turned gray as his confidence ebbed. It was one thing to lose, to lose honorably against overwhelming odds, but to be repudiated by his own party in the South, and in his own state, was bitter indeed. He was reported to have said grimly, "Well the time hasn't come yet when a man can say his beads in the White House."

Franklin Roosevelt went to bed that night believing that he too had lost, while his mother and Frances Perkins sat on in the Armory to read the last returns. In the morning he was awakened to be told that he had been elected Governor by the slim margin of about 24,500 out of 4,200,000 votes cast in New York. In Erie County, at the western corner of the state, a Republican boss had knifed Albert Ottinger, with whom he had a personal vendetta, and swung some 20,000 Republican votes over to the Democratic candidate. Thus, by a combination of luck and accident, the man who had campaigned on the strength of Smith's record, and as his disciple, survived the wreck of his party leader's fortunes.

Many perplexing crosscurrents were revealed in this election contest, as well as some significant new trends that foreshadowed the future. In New York State, for example, about 100,000 independents who voted for Roosevelt split their tickets to vote for Hoover for President. There was a flurry of anti-Catholic voting upstate, and also some manifestation of anti-Semitism against Ottinger, while Herbert Lehman won Jewish votes for the Democratic ticket in New York City. Over against this confusion, in industrial Massachusetts the Irish, Italians, and French-Canadians carried the state for the Democrats in a national election for the first time since the Civil War; the same was true in Rhode Island. In populous Pennsylvania and Illinois, as in Wisconsin, Smith lost, but ran more strongly than other Democrats of recent times, narrowing the margin between the parties. Several farming states also showed a bulge toward Smith, while in the solid South five states broke from the Democratic column in an unprecedented upset.

The most significant trend was to be seen in the big cities in the North; for the first time the Democratic Party, under Smith's leadership, showed a net plurality over the Republicans in the nation's twelve largest urban centers, from Boston to San Francisco. In a three-party contest Wilson had held together a coalition of the old South with several key northern states. Smith's campaign witnessed a shrinkage of the southern wing of the party to a minor role, while its supporters in the northern industrial section became more numerous. As the leader of the urban voters Smith hastened this new alignment, which led to a historic change in the relationship between the two parties. The children of the immigrants, many of them Catholics, with a higher birth rate than that of Protestant American rurals, were now coming of age, and, as Samuel Lubell has demonstrated, they were destined to play an even greater role in leading the Democratic Party to victory in 1932 and 1936.*

But the political fortunes of Alfred Smith himself had taken a disastrous turn. The morning after the election he appeared at his New York City headquarters briefly, his cigar clamped between his teeth, his air as jaunty as ever. The statement he gave out, however, revealed how deeply he was hurt, how much his fighting spirit was quenched:

> I have no regrets. I certainly do not expect ever to run for public office again. I have had all I can stand of it. I've given a quarter century of the best years of my life to it. I will never lose my interest in public affairs, that's a sure thing; but as far as running for public office is concerned — that's finished.

Meanwhile it was widely noted in the eastern press that a new star had risen on the political horizon of New York State: Franklin Roosevelt, the country squire, a politician in his own right, but one who for many years had lived in the shadow of his great preceptor.

---

* In 1932 Roosevelt was to inherit all of Smith's city following. Lubell concludes his discussion of the 1928 contest: "Al Smith may be today's Forgotten Warrior, but the line he drew across the map of America's politics has never been erased."

CHAPTER XV

The Unhappy Warrior

THE SCENE at the Executive Mansion on the afternoon of December 31, 1928, was one of distressing confusion: the ground floor and corridors were a clutter of trunks and suitcases, those of the Roosevelts moving in and those of the long-resident Smiths moving out. The remains of a cathedral-sized cake ordered in celebration of the retiring Governor's fifty-fifth birthday the day before were still on the dining room table; the servants, who over the years had become deeply attached to the Smiths, and who, in Frances Perkins's view, had grown a bit slack in the process, were excited and tearful; Katie Smith was weeping openly. Nevertheless the outgoing chief executive and his wife received the new arrivals with hospitable warmth, and prepared the stage for the preliminary swearing-in of the new Governor later that evening, a function that was to be repeated formally the next day at the Capitol.

There was no outward sign of any disagreement between the two men when they stood together on the dais of the Assembly Chamber for the inauguration, although in his introductory address Smith sounded a note of regret and nostalgia. First he gave heartfelt thanks to his old Albany associates, then, addressing himself to Roosevelt, he said:

> I am turning over the government to you — not perfect — no
> human instrumentality reaches perfection — but good as it can
> be made . . . While I feel happy and eager to lay down the
> heavy duties of the Governorship which I have carried for so
> long a period, the only dark cloud . . . is the fact that I have
> to go away from Albany. But I will be back.

A long ovation greeted these parting words, but Smith ended
on a more personal note:

> Frank, I congratulate you. I hope you will be able to devote
> that intelligent mind of yours to the problems of this state.

Roosevelt followed with a generous tribute to his predecessor, speaking of himself once more as Smith's disciple,
promising to continue the welfare program initiated by
Smith, and to go even further in advancing the state development of waterpower resources.

Smith rode down to New York City in the private car of
Bill Kenny, accompanied by his family and numerous associates, to be greeted at the Grand Central Terminal by the
Sixty-ninth Regiment band playing "The Sidewalks of New
York." In February he left for a winter vacation in Florida,
and on his return busied himself with helping his political
friends collect funds to pay off the deficit of $1,400,000 in-
curred by the Democratic National Committee in the lost
battle of 1928.

There is little doubt that Smith could scarcely bring himself to believe that he was actually leaving Albany, the scene
of so many struggles and triumphs, or quitting the office with
which his life had been bound up these many years. Under
the surface, too, the relations between the incoming and out-

going governors were not as easy as they had been formerly. According to Smith's intimates, and in Miss Perkins's recollection as well, some strain had shown itself shortly after the elections in November.

"Smith was never the same after November 6, 1928," Robert Moses remarked later; "that day was his Gethsemane." The cruel circumstances attending his defeat caused the memory of it to rankle in him for a long time. He could have endured defeat itself, but he had no defenses against the ugly passions aroused by that contest, the bigotry, the hatred that showed its face among the people of the hinterland. Like everyone else, he wanted to be loved, but unlike most of us, he was accustomed to being loved. Before the election he had had a certain innocence that made him refuse to admit to himself that intolerance was so deeply rooted, or that a democracy could still have its hordes of hypocrites and beetle-browed halfwits. He had believed with all his heart in Emma Lazarus's sonnet, "The New Colossus," engraved on the pedestal of the Statue of Liberty, which proclaimed his country the refuge of the oppressed of all lands.*

In the midst of the drama of the campaign, moreover, he had had no moment in which to reflect on what would become of him if he lost, if he were to hold no public office for the first time in twenty-five years, barring the short period

---

* ". . . Here at our sea-washed, sunset gates shall stand
A mighty woman with a torch whose flame
Is the imprisoned lightning, and her name
Mother of Exiles. From her beacon-hand
Glows world-wide welcome . . .
Give me your tired, your poor,
Your huddled masses yearning to breathe free . . .
Send these, the homeless, tempest-tossed, to me:
I lift my lamp beside the golden door.

of 1921 to 1923. For a decade he had been patiently reorganizing the state's entire administrative system, and now
at last his plan for an executive budget was to go into effect
in January of 1929. He had put much thought and all his
experience into this project, which could easily be misman-
aged by a successor lacking his own expert knowledge. Alfred Smith had greatly loved three women: his mother, his
wife, and, in a different way, Belle Moskowitz, but as Frances
Perkins remarked, "his real true love was the Empire State."
New York State was to him as the Grande Armée to Napoleon. Now the Happy Warrior was a general without an
army. Could Franklin Roosevelt really replace him? It
seemed incredible.

The whole situation, in fact, bristled with possibilities of
misunderstanding between the two politicians, each of whom
could honestly contend that the other owed him something.
As the leader of the New York Democracy Smith had made
Roosevelt Governor by pressing the nomination on him.
Roosevelt, however, could claim that he had made sacrifices
to enter the campaign for the Governorship, which he had
undertaken with reluctance, and had discharged his debt by
winning out in New York State while the party went down
to defeat in the national elections. The circumstances of his
victory were such that they immediately gave him a key
position in the party, and people were talking about him as
one who might unify the Democrats as a contender for the
presidential nomination in 1932. Indeed some of the younger
professionals on Smith's team hastened to kneel to the rising
sun, thus giving evidence of a shift in power that must have
been galling to the old leader.

Smith's Kitchen Cabinet had consistently underrated

Franklin Roosevelt, holding him to be an amateur in politics and a vacillating character. "After all, Franklin isn't very bright," the sharp-tongued Moses used to say, none too privately. The very speeches Roosevelt read when nominating Smith for the Presidency had been largely dictated by Judge Proskauer and Mrs. Moskowitz. On the other hand, the Dutchess County squire had his adherents, notably Louis Howe, who saw a great potential in him. Howe was intensely suspicious of Smith's advisers and particularly hostile to Robert Moses. In 1925 Smith had appointed Roosevelt Commissioner of the Taconic State Park, an unsalaried office in which Roosevelt took some pride. Some time later Roosevelt asked Moses, head of the State Park Council, to appoint Louis Howe as secretary to the Taconic Park Commissioner at a salary of $5000 a year. Howe at that period was devoting all his time to Roosevelt, having given up all other employment when his friend was stricken with infantile paralysis; in an interview with Moses he explained that he would continue to do so, if he received the appointment as secretary. This was one of those political favors that an easygoing public official might have granted without pangs of conscience, for after all Roosevelt was a useful party man, and Howe was financially dependent upon him. But Moses was made of sterner stuff. With an asperity that was becoming characteristic, he refused to give Roosevelt's Man Friday a sinecure at the expense of the State Treasury, and he did this so bluntly that Roosevelt neither forgave nor forgot.

Repeatedly Roosevelt had declared himself a disciple of Smith's, and he had run for the Governorship pledged to carry out Smith's policies. It was nonetheless far from gratifying to him to read in the newspapers, after the election, that Smith, and Smith's men, including Lieutenant-Governor Lehman, intended to help him run the state government, and that most of the former Governor's experienced officials were expected to remain in office. The implication was that the older man's knowledge of the state's administrative and legislative operations, in contrast with Roosevelt's ignorance in these areas, coupled with his physical disability, made such a continuance inevitable.

Roosevelt, however, intended to be nobody's prince regent. He was becoming something of an artist in Democratic politics on his own. This handicapped man, who put up such a brave show, had caught the eye of the public. Frances Perkins noted that in the excitement of the gubernatorial campaign he seemed to grow stronger than he had been for many years. In earlier times, she had heard from Roosevelt's secretary, Miss Le Hand, when he passed so much of the year on his houseboat, several hours of the morning would pass before he could rally his spirits against black despair over his condition, and pull himself together enough to appear before visitors at noon with a bright smile and a cheerful line of talk. This animation led some people to believe that he made light of his terrible disabilities, but in reality there was a stubbornness, an iron core of will in the man, that had kept him restlessly scheming, even during his years of retreat, to win his way to high office someday. And because he had been for so long incapacitated, obliged to depend on others literally at every step, he was now all the more determined to be his own man, to show that he could walk by himself.

At first Roosevelt was outwardly as cordial to Smith as ever. For some years past he had made many personal approaches to the Governor, often pressing him to spend the weekend at Hyde Park, but Smith had accepted only rarely. And on November 17, after the 1928 elections, he again wrote Smith extending an invitation to come and use Hyde Park as "a restful retreat." But the old Governor felt that he had to wind up his work at Albany, and declined.

Formerly Roosevelt had pursued Smith with his attentions, with his advice on national policy, and sometimes with requests for little political favors, such as jobs for deserving Dutchess County Democrats. Now, apart from the social amenities, he suddenly became rather evasive with Smith, who, for his part, soon began to pursue Roosevelt with advice on state policy and appointments. The tables were indeed turned. Unaware of the changed climate, Smith offered Roosevelt the full benefit of his experience soon after the election. "I'll come to Albany any time you want me; I'll talk to anyone you want me to talk with, negotiate with anyone," he is reported to have said. At a meeting on December 14, attended also by Lehman, at Roosevelt's East Sixty-Fifth Street house, Smith spent four hours urging the Governor-elect to retain some of his experienced assistants, Moses, for example. As an administrator Moses was dynamite, he said; he knew all about the executive budget, the great park program, the new hospital construction over which Smith had labored for so long. But at the suggestion that he reappoint Moses as Secretary of State, Roosevelt pulled down his long upper lip and said at once that he "would not have Moses around him"; they rubbed each other the wrong way. In addition to resenting the Howe incident of a few years back, Roosevelt may have got wind of some of Moses's unfriendly gibes. It was a pity that these two men who in their different ways were so talented for the public service disliked each other on sight.

Next Smith urged Roosevelt earnestly to appoint Belle Moskowitz as Private Secretary to the Governor, the office formerly held by George Graves. Mrs. Moskowitz, he argued, knew all the machinery; she knew and could reach everybody in the party and in the state government, and was accustomed to working with him, Smith. She might even help write the inaugural address for Roosevelt, Smith suggested. Roosevelt seemed dubious about her as Secretary to the Governor; for this post, he said in an offhand way, he was considering a certain friend, a tall, strong man on whose arm he could lean when he walked into a room. Smith, who considered the man a nonentity, then proposed that Mrs. Moskowitz be placed in some other office, possibly the Public Service Commission, where she would be close enough to the Governor to advise him. Roosevelt replied, "I'll think about it." Which meant in effect that he would do nothing, as Frances Perkins understood it, for Roosevelt's ways were not as frank and direct as Smith's. But Smith had so high an opinion of Belle's capabilities that he would speak in her behalf once again.

Roosevelt had decided, however, to retain a number of Smith's able assistants, among them Frances Perkins, whom he appointed Industrial Commissioner, a step up from the post of chairman of the Industrial Board, which she had occupied recently. Smith knew that Hamilton, the man she replaced as head of the Labor Department, was an empty valise, but when Roosevelt mentioned his plans for Miss Perkins the old Governor remarked that though she was a very able woman it might not be wise to place her in an executive office where she would be giving orders to a lot of men. Roosevelt later repeated this to Miss Perkins, adding that he had a "more liberal" attitude toward women in public life than Smith. Miss Perkins reminded him that Smith had been bolder still in appointing her to high office at a time when few women were thus chosen.

Samuel I. Rosenman was another protégé of Smith's whom Roosevelt retained on his staff to help him draft speeches and public messages. A lawyer and former Assemblyman, Rosenman had been trained in the school of Tammany; he was one of the educated and honest men the local bosses found useful. And on December 7, as if trying to mollify Smith, Roosevelt wrote him that he was keeping Bobbie Fitzmaurice, one of the old Governor's favorite aides, on his executive staff as his appointments secretary. Smith expressed himself as "very gratified," but this was, after all, no great plum. At their December meeting, Smith had also asked Roosevelt to retain the then Conservation Commissioner in office for a while longer. This official was a Republican who had served the state honorably for most of his life and needed only a year more to qualify for a full retirement pension. Roosevelt agreed, but either forgot his promise or changed his mind, for soon after his inauguration he appointed his Hyde Park neighbor, Henry Morgenthau, Jr., to the place. Whatever Morgenthau's qualifications, he did not need the job as much as his precedessor.

As this December conference broke up Roosevelt told the newspapermen waiting outside that Governor Smith would join him for another conference in a few days at Hyde Park, as if to indicate that their relations were very friendly. But it was not until mid-January that they returned to the sub-

ject of Mrs. Moskowitz and other appointees, at a meeting
in Albany. Smith had gone to the capital for the weekend,
hoping for long consultations with the Governor, but, as he
told Miss Perkins later, "I only had an hour with Frank all
the time I was there. So I decided I wouldn't go to Albany
unless I was asked. I don't think he's going to do anything
about Belle." When Smith made a final plea in behalf of his
old assistant Roosevelt answered, "Let it ride a while," and
Smith put this down to the Governor's inability to make up
his mind. In addition to his loss of power Smith suffered
from the uncertainty known to many who did business with
Roosevelt; he did not realize that he was getting the brush-
off. Mrs. Moskowitz was left dangling for months, thinking
that she was being seriously considered for some office, and
holding herself in readiness to give loyal service to the new
Governor. "I know I could be very useful," she said hopefully to Miss Perkins, but months passed and nothing happened, another source of bitterness for her and for Smith.

Ever since the day when Franklin Roosevelt had consented
to run for the Governorship, Smith had sensed that Eleanor
Roosevelt exercised a subtle influence over her husband's
decisions, and he was not far wrong. He himself admired
Eleanor for her grace and her intelligence, and appreciated
her work in the Women's Division of the party, as well as
her stumping of the state in his own earlier campaigns. That
formidable old battle-ax, Sara Delano Roosevelt, was another
kind of woman altogether. Once during the 1928 campaign
when Mrs. Moskowitz arrived at Hyde Park to confer with
Roosevelt Eleanor pleaded with her mother-in-law to invite
Belle to stay for lunch. The older woman refused, saying she
wouldn't have "that fat Jewess" at her table. Then word came
from Franklin that Mrs. Moskowitz was to be their guest,

and his mother gave way, putting herself out, in fact, to be affable to Belle and her small son. Later on, when Smith visited at Hyde Park with his wife and his daughter Emily, his womenfolk also had the impression that Sara Roosevelt "looked down on them," as Frances Perkins learned. But there was no trace of snobbery or anti-Semitism in either Franklin or Eleanor Roosevelt. Eleanor's opposition to Mrs. Moskowitz was based rather on her acute understanding of her husband's character.

Having worked closely with Belle Moskowitz for many years, Eleanor Roosevelt knew her to be capable, farsighted, and on the square. If she said she would be loyal to Franklin Roosevelt, that she would be. Frances Perkins, however, gathered that Eleanor also presented the other side of the question to her husband, suggesting that if Mrs. Moskowitz were his secretary she would run the show, subtly, to be sure, in such a way that he would naturally accept her decisions as if he had arrived at them himself. Vincent Sheean has expressed the view that Eleanor Roosevelt heartily disliked Mrs. Moskowitz, who could on occasion be sharp to those she considered to be dilettantes in politics. The implication that Smith had deferred to Mrs. Moskowitz in all matters of importance, however, was unjust — he was not a man to be ridden — as one can judge from his insistence on choosing Raskob as his campaign manager over her objections; but still Franklin Roosevelt did not relish the idea of having a person of such strong character in his immediate entourage. He would make his own decisions.

In this he was fervently seconded by Louis Howe, who was opposed to having Mrs. Moskowitz serve in any capacity close to the Governor, contending that the suggestion was "a

piece of effrontery." Dedicated to the cause of making Franklin Roosevelt President of the United States, Howe resented
the idea of having another president-maker around Albany,
and he fed Roosevelt's suspicions of the Smith group. Years
later, in recalling the tension that arose between the two men,
Eleanor Roosevelt reflected plainly what she and her husband
felt in 1929:

> I was not greatly surprised when after [Smith's] defeat it be-
> came evident that he thought he was going to retain a behind-
> the-scenes leadership in the state. It would not work; and he
> soon discovered that it would not work, and he left Albany for
> New York City.

Smith is said to have kept a room at the De Witt Clinton
Hotel for a fortnight or two in January, awaiting a summons
from the Governor, before closing up his affairs at the capital.
Roosevelt must have known that in refusing the appointments requested he would be giving offense to a man who
had not only been Governor for many years but had also
been the real leader of the state party organization since
Murphy's death in 1924. It was remarked long ago by some
British commentator on the political arts that nothing is more
tiresome than a retired Prime Minister hanging about the
Cabinet of his successor, offering advice, and also serving as
the vessel for the complaints of grumblers and talebearers.
Smith fell into just such a situation at the very start of the
Roosevelt regime in Albany: his old assistants and members
of his own family fed his growing resentment at what seemed
a striking display of man's ingratitude.

As for Belle Moskowitz, sometime architect of his career,
she was to disappear from the political theater with the declining fortunes of her chosen hero. For her the tragedy

would be almost as poignant as his. She had given ten years of her life to the service of Alfred Smith and to the grand design of installing him in the White House; she had gained extraordinary political prestige by controlling the channels that ran to the great Governor, and her only recompense was to enjoy a secret fame in high quarters and among newspapermen who respected her strong and shaping influence. The crushing defeat her idol had suffered in a national campaign featured by widespread calumny had been a great emotional shock to her. "The people just weren't educated up to it," she told Miss Perkins again. And after Smith, and she too, had been rejected by Roosevelt, she said to Miss Perkins, "How shortsighted a man *your* Governor is." But she was also a woman of a philosophical temper, able to reconcile herself to the loss of hidden power and glory of the past. "I am a contented sort of person," she told her friends. "Whatever life brings I can live with it," and she went back to her private business as a public relations counselor.

During the late winter and spring of 1929 Smith dictated his memoirs, which had been intended for publication during the campaign of 1928, but could not be prepared in time. An editor helped turn his oral expression into passable prose, though less colorful than his speech, and the book was published serially in *The Saturday Evening Post* early in the autumn before its appearance in hard covers. In *Up to Now* there are vivid reminiscences of Smith's boyhood and youth on the Lower East Side, as well as amusing episodes of his early career in Albany. His observations on the day-to-day work of the politician were not only shrewd; they were highly informative; as was also his analysis of the administrative changes he had achieved in the state government. The account of the heartbreaking presidential campaign however was put down with extreme reserve, suggesting how deep were the wounds it had left.

Frances Perkins, working at the State Labor Department center in New York City, managed to see her old political mentor from time to time and found him restless and nervous. "Al Smith badly needed a job, if only to distract his mind," she noted. His daughter Emily also remarked that for several months he really did not know what he was going to do. It was not until late in August that the problem of Smith's enforced leisure seemed to be solved, when it was announced that he had been named president of a corporation formed to build the world's tallest skyscraper. Fittingly named the Empire State Building, this mammoth office structure of one hundred and two stories, more than 1200 feet high, and costing some $46,000,000, was to be located on the site of the old Waldorf-Astoria Hotel at Fifth Avenue and Thirty-Fourth Street. The controlling directors of the enterprise were John J. Raskob, Pierre S. Du Pont, and Louis G. Kaufman, the big realtor, who had invited their old friend Smith to head the corporation at a salary of $50,000 a year. It was a job, at any rate, and $50,000 a year was not to be sneezed at even in those heady times. After he had been there a while Miss Perkins received the impression, however, that his duties were devoid of interest for him. It was a phony job, she surmised, and "his office was only a place to hang his hat."

The stock-market boom roared on all through the spring and summer of 1929, as for several years past, and since money gained from speculative profits was being spent freely, it seemed a propitious season for Alfred Smith to be launched in private business. In September he let contracts for dismantling the Waldorf-Astoria and for the erection of the huge new office tower. Besides heading the Empire State Building Corporation, he accepted invitations to serve as director of an insurance company, a commercial bank, and a savings bank, all of which brought him small additional fees.

Now that all their children were married, the Smiths moved from their suite at the Biltmore Hotel to a modern apartment at 51 Fifth Avenue, in the vicinity of Washington Square, where they remained only a year or so before taking more spacious quarters farther uptown, at 820 Fifth Avenue. Here among his neighbors were the grandees of finance, the Du Ponts, the Whitneys, and some of the Rockefellers. An added attraction in the new location was the fact that the apartment house faced the Central Park Zoo, which he visited regularly with a small boy's delight. Around that time Lillian Wald, founder and director of the Henry Street Settlement, urged Smith to settle down at Corlear's Hook, an area of the East Side near his birthplace which was being razed for a housing development. It would be symbolically fitting, she maintained, for him to return to the old neighborhood where low-cost housing developments such as Knickerbocker Village were under construction — projects that owed their existence, in great measure, to his labors as Governor to rebuild the city slums. But, as his old political friends remarked at that period, Al Smith had really "gone Fifth Avenue." In 1933 he admitted before a Senate investigating committee that "after having lived in a mansion for six years, I couldn't see First Avenue very well, so I went over on Fifth Avenue. I signed a lease for $10,000 a year."

Outwardly he faced the world with his old wide grin. In
those later years he enjoyed an unofficial rank as New York's
First Citizen, a beloved, familiar figure at whose call taxis
stopped at once, while trains waited for him at the terminals
if he were late. His daughter Emily tells a story of how once,
when he was caught in the rain and could not find a cab, he
took a bus uptown from his office; the driver, observing that
the downpour continued, ignored the regular bus stop and
halted directly in front of the marquee at Number 820, where
his distinguished rider was met by a uniformed doorman. He
was in constant demand, moreover, not only for political
meetings but also as an after-dinner speaker at fund-raising
banquets of philanthropic and religious societies, anything
from the Boy Scouts, or the American Jewish Committee, to
the Catholic Charities. At college commencements, where
year by year he reaped a harvest of honorary degrees, he was
also a favored speaker. On one of these honorific occasions,
in the spring of 1929, he appeared before a group of the
Harvard University faculty, forty of whom had signed a public letter signifying their support for his candidacy in 1928.
The introductory talk by philosopher Alfred North White-
head, noted for his charm as for his profundity, as well as the
intellectual endowments of his audience, at first made Smith
feel something akin to stage fright. But he overcame his
initial shyness and plunged into an informal lecture on state
government in his characteristic style, giving a performance
described by one of those present as equivalent to "the most
brilliant and informative text book on civics" ever written.

His social horizons were widening in other directions too.
His daughter Emily, after her marriage to John A. Warner,
had begun to move in fashionable Long Island society, and

toward 1929 had taken a summer cottage at Southampton. On frequent visits there Smith too became a familiar figure at the seaside resort. In the course of his political career he had made the acquaintance of many prominent socialites, but he had never before consorted with them on such intimate terms. They belonged to the caste against which so much of his fire had been directed, those whom in his earlier days he had thought of as "grinding the faces of the poor", or, more recently, as the sort of people who would try to block the formation of a state park, or the development of public waterpower resources. Now, meeting them socially, he found that as individuals and in their leisure activities, they had considerable personal charm. The fact that he was employed by men of the same economic station also lowered his defenses against these new friends. They, for their part, like so many before them, found him irresistible, with his bubbling good humor, his superb storytelling and his quick wit.

Among these newfound friends was one of the grand panjandrums of intellectual conservatism, Nicholas Murray Butler, President of Columbia University, and a perennial aspirant for the Presidency on the Republican ticket. Butler and Smith were the leading lights of an informal dinner group at Southampton called "The Occasional Thinkers," at whose functions they vied with each other in an amiable exchange of witticisms. A younger member of the Long Island set, Cornelius Vanderbilt Whitney, also became devoted to Smith at this period, and in 1929 he induced the Governor to contribute a weekly article on the political situation to *The Outlook*,* which Whitney subsidized. (In the days of his enforced retirement Theodore Roosevelt had also written a col-

* Later renamed *The New Outlook*.

umn for that magazine.) The society notes of the time list
Smith as a guest at a Rockefeller wedding, where he was
photographed in formal attire, top hat and all.

Lindsay Rogers tells an anecdote that points up the swift
change in Smith's view of men of wealth after 1928. During
the campaign he accompanied the Governor on an overnight
visit to Senator Gerry's residence, then in the fabulous mansion at Asheville, North Carolina, built by the Vanderbilts in
imitation of a royal palace. After dinner and highballs Smith
and Rogers wandered off together through splendid corridors
and galleries to find the bathroom, which proved to be a
spacious chamber lined with marble and furnished with gold
fixtures. Smith was awed. "Jesus," he exclaimed, "anybody
who has the money to spend on this kind of a place just ought
not to have that kind of money!"

The President of the Empire State Building Corporation
would not have reacted in the same way to this example of
conspicuous waste. But Smith was a man whose ideas were
formed when he was in action; they took color from the work
in hand, the immediate problem, the people around him.
When he solicited the votes of the masses, and relied on
humble party workers and social reformers, he appeared as
an ardent progressive; in the company of corporation directors he adapted himself to a new set of values, their values.
In a newspaper interview published soon after he had assumed his new responsibilities he declared that he found
private business easier than public administration and political action. It was laborious and time-consuming to manage
the affairs of a great state, he said, not to speak of winning
the consent of several million partners to what had to be
done. Dealing with his fellow directors was comparatively

simple. "The difference is that I will not have to go out every week and talk into a 'pie plate' to explain to them why I want to do certain things," he told the journalist. Evidently he could not bring himself to confess that he really preferred the more difficult job.

There was a further contributing cause to Smith's altered attitudes, a very human factor. Throughout his long political career, save for the brief interval as Sheriff, he had never known any financial security. Even as Governor he received a salary of only $10,000 a year and perquisites — an income which he had to supplement with his own or borrowed capital. Now, gaining five times as much, he and Katie were safe from want, and a phase of private life cast along pleasant lines seemed to stretch out before them — a reward only due him after almost a lifetime of ill-paid public service.

The bull market of the twenties came to its sudden, calamitous end at the very time when Smith and his associates had committed themselves to finance the construction of the Empire State Building. Many who had got rich overnight, and who had then pyramided their credit in new market speculations, saw all their paper wealth disappear within several weeks of catastrophic decline. Even men of enormous resources like Raskob — one of the leaders of the bull party in Wall Street — were rudely shaken. But things were much worse for some of Smith's friends, and members of his family as well, who had joined in the national sport of plunging in stocks on the basis of "inside information." James J. Riordan, head of the recently formed County Trust Company, was one of those who were brought to ruin, carrying down with him a whole circle of his business and political friends.

Riordan was a perennial boomer imbued with the most generous intentions. The year before, when the Smith campaign fund was short a million dollars, Riordan had advanced the needed money to the Democratic National Committee by means of personal bank loans, for which a dozen or more of Smith's friends had signed notes individually. Moreover the banker had assured those involved that they would never have to pay up because he would apply their credits to stock "investments" such as he had been managing with success during the market boom. With a similar sales talk he had encouraged Smith's two elder sons and his nephew John Glynn to take flyers in the market. Now in deep trouble, they were being pressed to pay their indebtedness to County Trust, along with the donors of campaign funds, one of whom refused to honor his note (for $100,000) and threatened suit against the bank's President.

On Friday, November 8, 1929, believing his bank about to go under and himself personally ruined, Riordan committed suicide. The news was kept out of the newspapers until after the close of business the next day to give Riordan's friends the weekend in which to come to the rescue of the bank, which opened on the following Monday prepared to meet the demands of its depositors. To confirm its solvency it was hurriedly announced that Alfred Smith would become acting president of the County Trust and that John J. Raskob would join the board of directors. In that time of panic Smith's sons and nephew called on him to help them meet their notes, and he assumed their debts, which he undertook to pay off over a term of years. Thus he saw his own hopes of untroubled affluence quickly dimmed.

Smith had got into business life, and big business, only a

few weeks before the start of a financial panic that was followed by the worst and most prolonged economic depression in American history. No sooner had construction on the skyscraper begun than he and his associates heartily wished that they had never conceived of such an undertaking. When the Empire State Building was at length opened for business on May 1, 1931, in an imposing public ceremony, office space was going begging in the city; Smith put on a cheerful face for the occasion, but no one was deceived. During a long period the building remained about eighty per cent unoccupied, and as the business cycle sank to ever lower depths New Yorkers used to point to the great white tower as one of the Follies of 1929.

Had he devoted twenty-five years of his life to the pursuit of the dollar rather than to public service Alfred Smith might possibly have become a successful businessman. He had chosen politics, however, and had become a great expert in the art; he did not have the temperament for business. Now he was entitled to question the sagacity of those financial leaders with whom his lot was cast: Raskob, the Du Ponts, even the Rockefellers, whose Radio City project, more extensive even than the Empire State Building, involved losses that could only be supported by earnings from their huge industrial empires. But Smith had no time to raise such questions; he was too busy trying to fight off bankruptcy for his corporation. His job was to use his personal influence to sell office space in hard times; his fate was to preside over the "empty Empire State Building," as it was called.

One of his tenants was Belle Moskowitz, who moved her little public relations outfit to a room one floor below Smith's office, which was on the thirty-second story. For two or three

years she continued to be his devoted counselor, never doubt-
ing that he would make a new bid for the Presidency, and
extending herself to keep his name before newspaper readers
and the radio audience. "You'll see, he'll make a great come-
back," she used to say to Frances Perkins, "and the next time
he'll be elected."

The truth is that Alfred Smith never quit politics; political
power and influence slowly ebbed from him. Though he still
ranked in the nation as the Democratic Party's titular leader,
he no longer enjoyed the godlike prerogatives of high office.
A typical newspaper article on his weakened political role at
this period was headlined: SMITH'S POWER WANING, and many
newspaper stories recounted the details of how Roosevelt
was building up his personal machine in the state with the
help of professionals like Farley and Flynn, while holding the
ex-Governor at arm's length.

Through 1929 and 1930 the differences between Roosevelt
and Smith were papered over. The new Governor wanted to
keep their relations friendly on the surface, but tended to
make them ambiguous in reality. They exchanged solicitous
notes about the health of members of each other's families;
on only a few rare occasions did Roosevelt consult Smith on
the telephone. He would write as on February 7, 1929:
"There are many things I would like to talk to you about.
Do be sure to let me know when you expect to come back
to New York." Yet he would happen to be away in Warm
Springs, Georgia, when Smith came to Albany to see his
daughter Emily. Emily's husband Colonel Warner still
guarded the Executive Mansion, which their infant daughter
sometimes visited when children's parties were held there.

The Governor in February, 1930, wrote Smith (who was then in Florida) about the new waterpower bill and about meeting his granddaughter at the Mansion, adding, banteringly, "She soon was calling me 'Ganpa!' I felt highly honored, and have certainly cut you out." Whereupon Smith replied, "I will be glad to see you and will take that little girl away." A while later Smith wrote that he would like to make suggestions for appointments to the New York Port Authority, but it does not appear that his advice in this matter was followed.

In New York City too the authority of Smith was flouted. There the playboy mayor, Jimmy Walker, though he owed his original advancement to Smith, who had also supported him for reelection in 1929, began to oust Smith men from his staff and replace them with Tammany regulars. Mention has been made of Smith's insistence that Walker appoint George V. McLaughlin, known for his integrity and ability, as Police Commissioner, but McLaughlin had soon felt obliged to resign in protest against the Mayor's covert opposition to his housecleaning in the Police Department. Tammany Hall had a new leader, John F. Curry, an old antagonist of Smith's, and the worst element in the machine was now virtually running the city. By 1930 the situation had become so shameful that Charles H. Tuttle, the Republican Attorney-General, began assembling evidence of widespread graft for presentation to a Grand Jury, and succeeded in getting indictments against several prominent personages close to the Mayor. Quick to see that it was open season on Walker, the Republican-dominated Legislature then passed a bill authorizing the Governor to investigate the Mayor's conduct of the city administration. This measure was plainly intended to embroil Roosevelt in conflict with Tammany Hall and Curry, to whom the Governor at that period was making friendly overtures for his own good reasons. He vetoed the bill on constitutional grounds, recommending instead that the Legislature set up its own investigating commission. Of course there was an immediate outcry that Roosevelt was merely straddling the issue in order to further his ambitions.

In most areas, however, Roosevelt's performance as Governor was praiseworthy — an excellent imitation of Smith's program and methods. On the one hand he strove for harmonious working relations with the Democratic machine; on the other, like Smith, he gathered around him a kitchen cabinet of university scholars and social workers — the nucleus of the future "Brain Trust" — and pressed hard for legislation to provide state aid to farmers, an ambitious power authority bill, and the forty-eight-hour week for women workers.* Faced with the opposition of the Republican majority in both houses again, like Smith, he went to the people, using the radio in his first "fireside chats." In place of Belle Moskowitz he had Louis Howe as his Privy Councilor; the university-trained Ed Flynn sat in place of Moses as Secretary of State, while Professor Raymond Moley and Sam Rosenman, the Governor's Legal Counselor, helped draft his speeches.

The Republicans in the Legislature made prodigious efforts to block the implementation of the executive budget system for which Smith had fought so long, but the resourceful

---

* An earlier Forty-eight-Hour bill had been passed in Smith's last administration, but it contained a provision enabling employers to grant women workers overtime adding up to a fifty-four-hour week. The new bill was designed to close this loophole.

Roosevelt prevailed. After a two-year struggle he also won passage of the Forty-eight-Hour Bill. Though there was some feeling of stalemate in Albany during his first term, Smith's disciple had made a good if not a spectacular record, as James MacGregor Burns has concluded, and he campaigned skillfully for reelection in the autumn of 1930. Smith, in fact, asked for the privilege of renominating his protégé at the New York State convention, where he played the part of the good soldier, using terms of lavish praise that gave no hint of the underlying friction between the two men:

> No man has accomplished more in the office he occupied than Franklin D. Roosevelt. He has a clear brain and a big heart. For his humanity, the love and devotion he has shown the poor, the sick and the afflicted, Almighty God has showered down on his head the choicest graces and his choicest blessings.

A great campaigner by disposition, eloquent and magnetic on the platform and over the radio, Roosevelt defeated his able Republican opponent, Attorney-General Tuttle, by a plurality of 1,700,000 to less than a million in 1930, also carrying most of the upstate counties, an unprecedented feat for a Democrat. (A Prohibition Party ticket in the field that year to punish Tuttle, who had declared himself a Wet, helped the Democrats, as in 1926.) In his smashing victory Roosevelt had exceeded even Smith's huge pluralities. James Farley, his field general, had done much to build up the state party, and to Farley and Flynn Roosevelt remarked that the road to the presidential nomination was now open.

The rift between Smith and his successor became a matter of public knowledge only in the latter part of 1931, when

the question of who was to be named as the next Democratic
standard-bearer began to be widely discussed. Ill feeling
between Roosevelt's entourage and the pro-Smith "fanatics,"
as Louis Howe called them, was steadily nourished by one
or the other side. Robert Moses certainly did nothing to improve the relations between the two factions. He had, as he
has confessed, a number of "unfortunate bouts" with Governor Roosevelt, while completing some unfinished business
for Smith. According to Miss Perkins, Moses had adopted
the style of the roaring boy in conferences on affairs of state.
Having learned that patient reasoning with people often got
him nowhere, he had taken to pounding the table and shouting his opponents down, a method that seemed to produce
results. His conferees would be terrified into giving way,
while he would laugh in private over the outrages he had
committed. Though he was fond of his old friend Frances
Perkins, he sometimes yelled at her too, as when she urged
that he use union labor in public works such as Jones Beach
or the Triborough Bridge. If union labor threatened to hold
up the completion of one of his projects, he made what
arrangements he could elsewhere. Miss Perkins at any rate
was used to his displays of temperament and continued to
be amused by him all her life.

Having been promoted by Roosevelt to the office of State
Industrial Commissioner she found her job both challenging
and absorbing; moreover she needed it badly, for she was
now almost entirely responsible for the support of her family,
as her husband, Paul Wilson, had become a chronic invalid.
From 1918 on, as she said in her notes of reminiscence, her
husband knew only "short periods of reasonably comfortable
accommodation to life." At intervals he would be hospital-

ized. Early in 1929 he stopped working on the executive staff of the Equitable Life Assurance Society of New York, where he had been employed for a good many years. Meanwhile his wife was becoming one of the most visible of America's career women. When she earned promotion to some new appointment she would come to her husband and ask for his counsel; he would express pleasure at her success, and she would listen to him, then do what she thought was in their best interests, which was to go on with her chosen work. Because her home situation had its unhappy aspects she seemed to throw herself into her government duties with all the greater zeal.

Frances Perkins got on very well with the new Governor, different though he was from Al Smith: less quick of mind, less direct in speech, but also more sophisticated and more artful, she thought. Whereas Smith would call for all the facts, then would move promptly to a decision, Roosevelt appeared more calculating and more ambiguous in his responses. "When I talked things over with Smith," she related, "I told him what I had to say once only, and he understood me; but with Roosevelt I always had to tell him things three times." If Roosevelt made some decision or ruling for her guidance she would also repeat that three times before leaving his office, so that there was no possibility of misunderstanding on his part. On the whole, however, Roosevelt, like Smith, "let her alone," as she said, never interfering in her department.

In another discerning comment she observed that Roosevelt at times set different people to work on the same tasks, which led to rivalry and friction among his aides; Smith always tried to avoid conflicts in his official family. Miss Perkins in fact would frequently talk with Roosevelt about Smith's modus operandi, and the Governor would listen to her attentively. She also urged him to maintain friendly contacts with Smith and in some instances seek his advice. This Roosevelt was loath to do. On the other hand, when she sometimes encountered Smith and spoke to him about how well the new Governor was doing, Smith gave the impression that he did not want to hear about it. Miss Perkins was lodged between the two factions; she always loved Smith, but she also saw that Roosevelt had great attractions as a public man and was growing in stature. She would have liked to mediate between them, and was one of the few persons who tried to do that, but she realized that she was not a member of Roosevelt's inner circle. "I did not advise in negotiations, I was not a wangler like Howe and Farley. I was regarded as an administrator, a social worker, a do-gooder . . . while they were doing their plotting." Long afterward she said regretfully, "The breach between them could have been healed in the first year, it wasn't so wide — but for Louis Howe and, on the other side, Belle, Bob Moses and Raskob."

In the autumn of 1931 there occurred the first open clash between the two New York leaders, when an amendment to the state constitution allotting $20,000,000 for a reforestation program was submitted to a referendum. This measure, which had originally been sponsored by Governor Roosevelt, was also favored by conservationists of both parties, but Smith attacked it with great vigor, calling on the public to vote it down. His objections, as given at a political meeting in New York City, seemed at the time technical and legalistic; one provision of the amendment, he argued, would "put the government in the lumber business," by way of helping upstate farmers to extend their woodlots. This represented a curious reversal of attitude on the part of a man who scarcely two years before had favored putting the government into the electric power business. Smith was showing himself much more sensitive than formerly to the prerogatives of private enterprise. There were some other well-founded objections he raised, which had to be dealt with in later revisions of the law. Nevertheless the public voted overwhelmingly in favor of Roosevelt's project, reflecting his mounting popularity as well as Smith's waning influence in New York State.

A few days after the referendum victory in November — widely commented on in the press as a trial of strength — Roosevelt addressed a friendly personal note to Smith touching another sector of the state's business and inviting the ex-Governor's counsel:

Executive Mansion
Albany

November 11, 1931

Dear Al,

The first trial balance of the budget will be sent down Monday the 16th and I'm coming to N.Y. that night. Don't you want to run in any time on Tuesday or Wednesday the 17th or 18th and talk with me about it. Come to lunch at 49 East 65th St. or else later in the afternoon.

I go to Warm Springs Wednesday evening at 6.

Love to the family and my best to you.

As ever,
Franklin D. Roosevelt

By this time the two men were preparing to enter the race against each other for their party's presidential nomination. They met at lunch on November 17 and were photographed together — for the last time. Roosevelt's emissaries had already been going to Smith privately to ask him what his intentions were with regard to the 1932 campaign without learning anything definite. But it is doubtful that at this November meeting there was any discussion of national politics; they evidently confined themselves to the state's business. Smith grinned as he left and said no more to the reporters than, "It was a good lunch." There was nothing there to encourage the aspirations of his host, but Roosevelt had by then learned to be a shrewd tactician. At a time when the strain between them had become known to the public, he executed a characteristic maneuver by having Smith appear and be photographed with him for the newspapers. (He would try to repeat the same tactic later in 1932 and in 1936, when there were open hostilities between them.)

After that luncheon in November their meetings were rare; their correspondence virtually ceased, or was merely perfunctory; they moved apart. Roosevelt knew where he was going. To get there he would need to bypass or eliminate his predecessor, and no doubt in awareness of that grim necessity he shrank from facing Smith, for the future President never enjoyed confrontations with those he was going to hurt.

The depression cycle continued relentlessly, soup lines grew longer, veterans sold apples on Fifth Avenue. In all the big cities charity drives were being launched, and Al Smith was called on repeatedly to lend his voice to appeals for private funds at public meetings and over the radio.

In January, 1930, President Hoover had tried to sound a note of good cheer, announcing that employment had begun to rise again — only to be flatly contradicted by New York's

Industrial Commissioner Miss Perkins, whose challenging
statement made the front pages of the nation's press: the
statistics assembled by the President's own Departments of
Labor and of Commerce, she declared, as well as those of
New York State, proved the contrary of what Mr. Hoover
was saying.

The elections of November, 1930, swept the Democrats into
power in most states as well as giving them control of Congress. Throughout 1931 Roosevelt's advance agents, headed
by Farley, journeyed to the South, the Middle West, and the
Pacific Coast to gather support for his presidential candidacy,
while Smith made no overt move. Before committing himself to his new chief, Ed Flynn, who had long been associated
with the Smith faction, called on the old Governor to ask if
he had any political plans for 1932. Smith gestured toward a
heap of papers on his desk. "All debts," he said. Ever since
the crash of 1929, and Riordan's suicide, he had been struggling under the weight of obligations he had undertaken for
the sake of members of his family. He would not be a candidate for any office in 1932, he told Flynn, and to Herbert
Lehman and James J. Hoey, who also consulted his wishes
before turning to support Roosevelt, he said the same thing.
To his daughter Emily he explained that a fight for the nomination would require a sizable organization and a great deal
of money, neither of which were available to him then. He
had tried for the Presidency twice, he said, and did not care
to become "the Bryan of the Democratic Party." Farley too
on February 1, 1932, came to sound him out about his intentions, but Smith for some reason thought he was disingenuous, and later charged him with disloyalty in promoting the
Roosevelt candidacy. He recalled that he had "made Farley

politically" years earlier when he had appointed him State
Boxing Commissioner, and he prophesied that Farley would
one day turn against Roosevelt also. This prediction was
borne out in 1940.

In the interim between the elections of 1928 and 1932 John
J. Raskob held the most powerful position in the party, as
chairman of the Democratic National Committee. Having
bought his way in, he thought himself qualified to shape its
policies, and also to reorganize the whole administrative setup. For this purpose he called on the services of a conservative Kansas lawyer named Jouett Shouse, a prominent party
man unsympathetic to Roosevelt. Raskob fully intended to
control the 1932 convention in Chicago through the Arrangements Committee, which was headed by Shouse; he also
planned to play a strong role in writing the platform; and,
as far as possible, in helping to select the nominee.

Raskob was cool to Roosevelt, essentially because the
Governor's candidacy was a serious threat to the renomination of Smith, but also because Roosevelt's views on the big
issues of 1932 were quite at variance with his own, and those
of Smith also. Although he favored repeal of the Eighteenth
Amendment, Roosevelt wanted to play down this question
for the while in order to avoid the internal party strife that
had arisen in 1928. Raskob hoped to move the party toward
a strong stand against Prohibition, but at the meeting of the
Democratic National Committee in March, 1931, Roosevelt's
supporters, in alliance with the southern bloc, were easily
able to defeat the proposals of the Raskob-Smith faction on
the issue. Roosevelt, like some other Democratic leaders,

wanted to stress economic issues in this time of growing depression; Raskob wished these issues to be muted.

While evading the troubling question of corruption in the New York City government, Roosevelt was in fact trying to move the state toward energetic action in the economic crisis, offering proposals for the relief of dairy farmers, for the relief of the unemployed, and for the development of waterpower resources, that went beyond programs previously formulated by Smith. A genuine compassion for the victims of the depression showed itself in the "kid glove politician" from Dutchess County, impelling him toward the left, while Alfred Smith, the man of the people, was drifting toward right of center, under the influence of his new associates.

Late in August, 1931, Roosevelt called the New York State Legislature into special session to ask for an appropriation of $20,000,000 — a huge sum for those days — to deal with the crisis of unemployment by a great expansion of "made work" as well as direct relief. He had arrived at this plan only after long heart-searching discussions with his advisers. Frances Perkins recalled that the word "dole" was offensive to him. "Remember, Frances," he would say again and again, "we don't want the dole." And yet the message accompanying his call asked for the same thing under another name. "What is the State?" the message began, echoing Smith's own language in a speech of 1915, and, like Smith, he continued:

> an organized society of human beings for their mutual protection and well-being . . . One of these duties of the State is that of caring for those of the citizens who find themselves the victims of such adverse circumstances as make them unable to obtain even the necessities of mere existence . . . While it is

true that we have hitherto principally considered those who, through accident or old age, were permanently incapacitated, the same responsibility of the State undoubtedly applies when widespread economic conditions render large numbers . . . incapable of supporting either themselves or their families, because of circumstances beyond their control . . . To those unfortunate citizens aid must be extended by Government, not as a matter of charity, but as a matter of social duty.

This proposal to distribute food and provide shelter on a large scale to starving citizens, which stood in striking contrast to the timid moves of President Hoover, caught the eye of people all over the country. It is also historically significant that Roosevelt clearly related his program to Smith's earlier legislation, arguing that if in the past the state found itself obliged to help widows and orphans, and the sick and the injured, now in this national emergency it must commit itself to go beyond that and aid the victims of mass unemployment. Although this was but the application on an extended scale of the teachings of Alfred Smith, Smith himself now formed the conviction that his successor was going too far.

Unemployed demonstrations, led by radicals or rank and file leaders, were taking place in New York, Chicago, and nearly all the great cities in the country. The farmers in the West were more insurrectionary still. In December, 1931, Hoover belatedly attempted to stem the downward trend by offering aid to banks, insurance companies, and railroads in distress through the Reconstruction Finance Corporation, but he moved tardily to apply federal funds to the relief of people. The citizens were ready to vote "against the depression," and it was plain to see that virtually any Democrat,

even a Roman Catholic, could be elected President in 1932 in
a contest with Hoover.

As this was borne in on him, Alfred Smith underwent a
change of heart about entering the race. He was still, after
all, in the prime of life at fifty-eight. But he was a general
without an army; his Elba the office on a high floor of the
Empire State Building. Why shouldn't he come out of exile
and strike again for the leadership of the Democrats? Belle
Moskowitz kept telling him that he was entitled to the nomination. "It was his right to run again," she told Miss Perkins,
and Judge Proskauer and members of the Smith family seconded her promptings. Raskob was also persuasive. Smith
had felt ill-used in 1928, and now he felt balked by the rising
leader who stood in his path. By December of 1931 he began
to air his resentment at the Governor to visitors. "Do you
know, by God, that he has never consulted me about a damn
thing since he has been Governor. He has taken bad advice
from sources not friendly to me. He has ignored me!" he
said at this time to Clark Howell, publisher of the Atlanta
Constitution. Moreover Roosevelt was trimming on important issues like Prohibition, Smith charged. Howell reported
this conversation to the Governor, and suggested that if
Roosevelt were actually running for the Presidency he ought
to discuss the matter frankly with Smith and try to effect a
reconciliation. Roosevelt listened, but took no steps in that
direction.

His eager-beaver lieutenants were still in the dark about
Smith's real intentions up to the end of 1931, despite his dis-
claimers. On December 28, a front-page story in *The New
York Times* gave substance to their fears, revealing the be-
hind-the-scenes maneuvers of Smith's friends in a Stop-

Roosevelt movement, and predicting that Smith would again seek the nomination. Smith himself made no comment for the moment. Several weeks passed; in late January Roosevelt declared publicly that he would run. This announcement was followed two weeks later by Smith's confirmation of the rumors that he too was available. He owed it to his friends and the public, he said on February 8, 1932, to make it clear that "if the Democratic Convention should decide it wants me to lead, I will make the fight; but I will not make a pre-convention campaign to secure . . . delegates." And then he added that as he was still the titular leader of his party, he would "neither support nor oppose the candidacy of any other aspirant for the nomination." He had thrown his brown derby into the ring, lending excitement to the pre-convention race in which Roosevelt, up to then, appeared to be moving toward victory with irresistible force.

On the eve of Smith's declaration of his candidacy, Roosevelt, as if knowing what was afoot, had sent him another invitation to come to Hyde Park. Smith's brief answer was that he was "sorry," but had other engagements. Much has been written about Roosevelt's coldly calculated strategy, the compromises by which he was able to combine widely scattered and even incongruous elements of the Democratic Party in support of his candidacy. He had brought into his camp the Southern Drys, who were adamant in their refusal to accept Smith again, as well as regional leaders in the West, and a large portion of the urban Democrats in the Northeast who were liberal and wet. In the meantime, for fear of losing his own state, he postponed the day of reckoning with Mayor Walker and Tammany until after the convention, while treating on friendly terms with the notorious boss Curley of Boston, in the hope of winning the Massachusetts delegation. Small wonder that he was called "a master of evasion" at this period. Nonetheless he was exhibiting major talent as a national politician, whose first aim at such a stage is to nail down the party nomination.

However devious his political commitments, Roosevelt did not pussyfoot in addressing himself to the masses of hungry voters. In several pre-convention speeches on national issues he attacked those who had generated unbridled stock speculation during the twenties, urging sweeping reforms in banking and securities market practices. He characterized Hoover's efforts to halt the depression by budget economies, limited public works, and loans to banks and railroads as "stopgap measures." Early in January, 1932, he broadcast a radio address in which he declared that it was "our sacred duty to aid those millions who now starve," and assailed the class that represented "concentrated wealth and power" for their extravagant speculation, for their want of intelligence and sense of justice or humanity. Again in April, in another memorable radio speech, he advocated government spending on a large scale for unemployment relief, as well as "bold, persistent experimentation" aimed at bringing about economic recovery, through projects "that build from the bottom up and not from the top down, that put their faith in the Forgotten Man at the bottom of the economic pyramid." All this was anathema to Raskob, who might well have felt that the Governor was striking at him and his financial crowd, and playing the demagogue.

In a recent public statement Smith too had addressed himself to the problem of the economic depression, likening it to a state of war, and proposing that the Federal Govern-

ment, while it must still work to achieve economies on the
one hand, should on the other borrow money to help cities
and states overburdened with relief costs, and start public
works "to keep the wolf of hunger away from the doormat
of millions." But Roosevelt's "Forgotten Man" speech appeared to be aimed at Smith's more moderate proposals, no
less than at Hoover's, and to Smith's mind called for a strong
retort.

This he delivered at the Jefferson Day dinner in Washington on April 14 when national Democratic leaders came together, regardless of factional differences. Smith used the
occasion to attack his former disciple in his most truculent
style:

> This is no time for *demagogues* . . . When millions of men
> and women and children are starving throughout the land,
> there is always the temptation to some men to stir up class
> prejudice, to stir up the bitterness of the rich against the poor,
> and the poor against the rich. Against that effort I set myself
> uncompromisingly.
>
> I protest against the endeavor to delude the poor people to
> their ruin by trying to make them believe they can get employ-
> ment before the people who . . . employ them ordinarily are
> also restored to conditions of normal prosperity.

A "prominent Democrat," he went on, appeared to favor the
dole; this would be degrading to Americans. As official party
leader he had hitherto refrained from either helping or opposing any presidential candidate, but now he was driven
to speak out:

> I will take off my coat and vest and fight to the end against any
> candidate who persists in any demagogic appeal to lead the
> masses of the working people of this country to destroy them-
> selves by setting class against class.

Raskob presided over this dinner and warmly applauded Smith's tirade against Roosevelt. Raskob's own proposals for combating the depression were scarcely different from Hoover's, save that he wished to restore the legality of beer and liquor, which led one political commentator, Ray Tucker, to liken the financier to Marie Antoinette: "to the millions who ask for food Raskob would give drink." (One of Roosevelt's slogans was "Food not Booze.")

Among the wealthier classes with whom Smith had recently allied himself there was much fearsome talk in 1932 of an imminent revolution inspired by Socialists, Communists, or other radicals. In reality the unemployed were apathetic and the working people were generally quiescent, as they usually are in a period of deep depression; apart from the farmers, the lower classes in America offered no visible threat to society. Yet Alfred Smith, cut off from his earlier contacts with people of small means, kept prodding Governor Roosevelt in his articles in *The New Outlook* to "forget about the Forgotten Man."

The pre-convention work on behalf of Roosevelt had been so thoroughly organized that when his forces came to Chicago they had a commanding lead, a majority of six hundred and sixty delegates against two hundred for Smith and ninety for John Garner of Texas, who was backed by Hearst and Senator McAdoo of California. Yet they were far from confident; Roosevelt needed about one hundred more votes because of the two-thirds majority then required by the rules. Moreover Smith had announced that he would attend the convention as a delegate and take the floor to speak for repeal of the Eighteenth Amendment. The Roosevelt faction feared that a speech by Smith might upset all their plans and create a deadlock. In 1912 Champ Clark had held a clear majority, but lost to Wilson in the end; and in 1924, though McAdoo was well ahead, Smith alone had blocked his nomination. Would Smith now stampede the convention into nominating some Dark Horse if he himself could not win?

As the hour of decision approached the New York Governor made a move that showed how completely he had mastered the game of politics, a game in which he now used brass knuckles rather than kid gloves. Jouett Shouse, Raskob's man, at the head of the party's executive for two years, had made a good record, and expected to be named permanent chairman of the convention. Indeed Raskob thought he had an understanding with Roosevelt's lieutenants to this effect. At the eleventh hour, however, the Roosevelt men broke what seems to have been a gentleman's agreement, and called for a floor vote to select the permanent chairman. As they were in the majority, they had no difficulty electing their man, Senator Thomas J. Walsh of Montana, the hero of the Teapot Dome investigation, rather than Shouse, who was known to favor Smith. Raskob, Shouse, and Smith had been completely overreached; they made loud complaint at Roosevelt's faithlessness in this affair, then and long afterward, for it was not Farley or Howe but Roosevelt himself who had made the ruthless decision to liquidate Shouse.

With Senator Walsh in the chair Roosevelt's aides maneuvered for victory on the first ballot, but were stopped short of the two-thirds majority. It now became "a fight to the death," as Ed Flynn said. Smith's speech for repeal inspired a frenzied, hour-long demonstration by his supporters, who repeated the performance with the same enthusiasm when he was formally nominated by Governor Joseph Ely of

Massachusetts. But his managers made one mistake after another, and Smith himself committed the unpardonable blunder of putting trust in Hearst's promise to stand with him to the end in opposition to Roosevelt.

The second and third ballots dragged through a whole night, and the Southerners in the Roosevelt column began to waver. The Governor's sharp traders offered the Vice-Presidential nomination to almost everyone in sight in return for their votes, finally centering their attention on the Speaker of the House, Garner. Belle Moskowitz desperately tried to reach Garner in behalf of Smith, but the cool Texan refused to come to the telephone to speak to her. In the end McAdoo, with the assent of Hearst, announced that the California delegation would switch their votes from Garner to Roosevelt, thus breaking the deadlock on the fourth ballot. Clearing the barrier of the two-thirds rule by a hair's breadth, Roosevelt gladly paid the price exacted by the Western wing of the party to accept Garner as his running mate.

Smith left Chicago without a word to anyone, just before Roosevelt arrived by plane to deliver his acceptance speech in person. "The Smith movement never had a chance," Moses said afterward. "It started very late, and really had no organization to speak of." One is forced to assume that its main function then was not really to win the nomination for Smith but to serve as a blocking action to stop Roosevelt, and in the hope that some Dark Horse, such as Newton Baker or Governor Ritchie, might win out. Smith was bitter. When he reached New York reporters asked him if he would support Roosevelt in the campaign. "Don't you know what Senator David B. Hill said after Cleveland won the nomination?" he asked by way of reply. "I'm a Democrat still." The rest of that quotation from Hill, which some of the reporters may not have remembered, was *"Very still."*

Yet Alfred Smith was not a vindictive man. At the beginning of September he attended the Democratic State Convention and joined forces with Roosevelt against Tammany, to bring about the nomination of the excellent Herbert Lehman for Governor. This led to a head-on collision with Boss Curry of Tammany, to whom Smith said challengingly that if Lehman were not nominated he himself would run for Mayor of New York in 1933 and smash the Tammany machine. Curry asked, "On what ticket would you run?" Smith replied, "On a Chinese laundry ticket."

The state convention at Albany was the occasion for a famous scene of "reconciliation" between the new and the old party leaders, a bit of playacting in which both men performed artistically. After the Governor had been carried up to the platform of the Albany Armory Smith responded to calls that he go up and join him. As the two men shook hands Smith said, "Hello Frank, I'm glad to see you," and Roosevelt replied, "Hello Al, I'm glad to see you too — and that's from the heart." A journalist present reported Smith's greeting as "Hello, you old potato!" an affectionate phrase, very much in character, which was, however, the reporter's invention. Nevertheless it went out over all the Associated Press wires, and in Farley's view, helped Roosevelt's prospects a great deal, especially among disgruntled Irish Catholics in the Northeast. That autumn Smith took the stump in New York for Herbert Lehman, a bumbling speaker who became one of the ablest and best loved of the state's governors. In the closing weeks of the national campaign Smith also spoke for Roosevelt in cities in New England, New York, and New Jersey. But in a speech at Newark, New Jersey, he digressed to recall the anti-Catholic manifestations of 1928 in words of such bitterness that Roosevelt and his staff were fearful that he might reopen old wounds in the Democratic Party.*

At the polls the voters reversed the Republican landslide of 1928, making this election contest the most decisive Democratic victory since the era before the Civil War. Though Roosevelt was always a great campaigner, in 1932 he did not generate the high enthusiasm that Smith, losing, inspired in his followers; moreover his campaign speeches for the most part promised only moderate changes. Many observed that the public was serious in mood and somewhat subdued; they voted not so much for a man or for principles as against the party in power. On the night of the election Smith turned up at Democratic headquarters in the Biltmore to hear the early returns, and was among the first to congratulate Roosevelt.

In that bleak winter of 1933 the economic crisis assumed a catastrophic character; during the four months' interregnum between incoming and outgoing Presidents no measures were taken to stem the growing money panic. In private conferences with his advisers the President-elect hastily prepared the emergency action of March, 1933. Rumors of these confabulations at Albany and Hyde Park reached Alfred Smith and, as he confided to his daughter, he would dearly have wished to serve his country in some capacity during the crisis.

---

* Smith declared that he had learned on good authority that Mrs. Willebrandt's anti-Catholic tirades in 1928 were continued, despite many protests, with the approval of leading figures in the Republican National Committee, including Colonel William J. Donovan — then running for Governor of New York against Lehman.

Roosevelt, however, never for a moment thought of calling on his old Democratic Party chief, although he did bring Frances Perkins down to Washington with him as Secretary of Labor. In an article in *The New Outlook* for February, 1933, Smith now urged Roosevelt to take dictatorial measures in dealing with the wave of bank runs and bank failures, as in a time of war, and a month later he wrote in warm approval of Roosevelt's first bold steps in the crisis.

On January 2, 1933, he went up to Albany to attend the inauguration of Governor Lehman, and while he was at the Capitol news was brought to him that Belle Moskowitz had died of a coronary thrombosis, following a fall a few days earlier on the steps outside her house. Smith looked and spoke his deep emotion at the loss of this woman who had idolized him, and who had long served as his most loyal and most self-effacing counselor.

Belle Moskowitz was only fifty-five when she died, leaving behind her the reputation of having enjoyed a greater personal influence on statecraft than any other woman in America up to her time, though holding no public office. But much as he admired her and respected her judgment, Smith had begun to lean toward other advisers in recent years. To at least one observer who knew them both well, Gerard Swope, President of the General Electric Company, "It was Belle Moskowitz who kept Smith on the liberal side until 1928, after which . . . Mrs. Moskowitz lost her influence with him." Smith said of her, "She had the greatest brain of anyone I ever knew."

CHAPTER XVI

A Lost Leader

THE WINTER and spring of 1933 were seasons memorable for high political drama: in March, at the height of the bank panic, Roosevelt was inaugurated as President of "a nation without money"; there followed the "hundred days" of law-making for the crisis state, while the Congress signed emergency bills virtually without reading them. From his lofty tower in New York Alfred Smith looked upon the work of his former pupil and, at first glance, pronounced it good. In one of the articles he contributed regularly to *The New Outlook* he avowed that the new Democratic administration had come "to the crossroads of history and taken the right turn on the path back to economic health." Everyone in the country, whatever his party or affiliation, he held, "should support the President loyally and patriotically."

Within a matter of a few months, however, the former Governor began to air his doubts about Roosevelt's experiments in reform and economic control. At first his objections were set down in a tone of good-humored skepticism; he was serving as a watchdog in the public interest. The New Deal, Smith argued, directed by Roosevelt's professorial advisers, tried to cover too much ground and contrived a bewildering variety of programs and federal agencies; the NRA, which sought to control both industrial production and hours and wages of labor, he predicted, would be judged unconstitutional by the Supreme Court. By the beginning of 1934, Smith's criticisms became more caustic: the Gay Reformer (so Smith's friends called Roosevelt) appeared to be reaching out for ever broader powers, he wrote, causing the government to intervene in private business and in private life; moreover masses of the unemployed, through their dependence on federal relief, were tied to the Federal Government, while an army of newly appointed officeholders was being raised to support the New Deal regime. The Democratic administration, he urged, should return to the doctrines of Thomas Jefferson, who held that "the least government is the best."

To Alfred Smith's credit, it should be remarked that he introduced into the debate of that time some of his own humorous and pungent phrases: all those novel regulatory agencies — AAA, NRA, FHA, PWA, and FERA — indicated to him that the "New Deal professors had . . . played anagrams with an 'alphabet soup'"; the "cold, clammy hand of Bureaucracy" was reaching out everywhere, and, early in 1934, as Roosevelt began to buy quantities of gold and lower the value of United States currency, Smith coined the phrase "baloney dollar." Nevertheless he was but echoing the conventional notions about the New Deal then widely held by resentful corporation leaders, bankers, stockbrokers, and also by the owners of empty office buildings.

Had Al Smith, the Great Commoner of New York's East Side, the perennial friend of the underdog, actually turned into a *conservative?* For many of his admirers it was not only a surprising about-face, it tore their hearts. During more than twenty years he had been in many ways the most *effective* reform leader in American politics of his era, for he had directed a remarkable coalition of machine politicians and social reformers carrying on a program that was at once humane, progressive, and paternalistic. He had taken the ramshackle state government of New York, reorganized it, and made it more efficient and more just; he had sponsored measures by which the state intervened more and more widely in different areas of private enterprise, regulating the business of railroads, electric and gas utilities, and traction companies. The owners of factories could no longer maintain fire traps for their workers; nor did they any longer, after Smith's time, enjoy the sacred liberty to work women and children twelve hours a day. And as Smith's welfare laws were copied by many of the forty-eight states they had a tremendous impact on the social life of the whole nation. Now the same Al Smith who had been the idol of the working classes in the industrial cities pronounced himself a "Jeffersonian Democrat" opposed to statism as practiced by Franklin Roosevelt. The name of Jefferson was all too freely invoked in those days by the grandees of Wall Street and Detroit, who belatedly placed the sage of Monticello on their calendar of saints, even though his counsels were addressed to the rural America of 1800.

Franklin Roosevelt had been the continuator of the Smith welfare and regulatory program during four years at Albany; then, as President, faced with the worldwide economic crisis, he had gone further, adapting the New York welfare program, together with the wartime planning ideas of 1917, on the expanded national scale. Can it be said that Smith was a "Jeffersonian"? It is doubtful that he could have been placed in such neat theoretical categories as "Jeffersonian"

or "Hamiltonian." No more than Roosevelt was he much concerned with theories. He was an intuitive thinker, a prag-
matist, a "doer," and at the same time a man of the people
whose nature was imbued with the Christian ethic, so that he
was led toward a humane, if moderate statism in politics.
He had been, in fact, a splendid exemplar of the progressivism of the earlier Roosevelt, Wilson, and Justice Brandeis,
who preached that the state must intervene paternally in the
naked marketplace only to right the balance of force against
the poor and the weak. And Al Smith had helped mightily
to introduce such paternal reforms in the nation's leading
state. The movement of reform, it should not be forgotten,
also won for him armies of voters — which is the *capital* of
the politician. But the idea that Al Smith in the mid-thirties
should have turned into an outright conservative seemed to
his old followers a complete paradox.

He had changed, and he was by no means the only political leader who in his later years turned away from the lights
of progressivism or liberalism to what we call conservatism.
Washington and John Adams had once taken up arms against
legitimate authority; Napoleon I had been a revolutionary in
youth; Theodore Roosevelt had been forward-looking in
politics before turning reactionary in his last years; Ramsay
MacDonald had been a faithful Socialist before he betrayed
the Labor Party in 1931. Bernard Shaw has written somewhere that if a man did not feel like becoming a socialist
at twenty "he had no heart," and if he did not turn into a
conservative at forty he had "no mind." Smith had become
a progressive somewhat later than other men, when he was
thirty-five; now at sixty he had come around full circle to be
a champion of economic orthodoxy.

Political conservativism is actually a vague syndrome, best distinguished by its pessimistic attitude toward the demos, in contrast with liberalism's trust in the long-run good sense and justice of the commoners.* The set of beliefs associated with a Louis XIV or an Edmund Burke are clearly recognizable, but conservatives in the business society of the United States have always been inconsistent in their principles. For example they are seldom opposed to statism in the form of subsidies or a protective tariff favoring their own interests, or pork-barrel legislation for their home districts, or vast expenditures for national defense, though armies of bureaucrats, civilian or military, may be required to administer such measures. To sum up Alfred Smith's case, we may assume that his turn to conservatism betokened a psychological change deriving from the shock of 1928, a change further affected by the complete alteration of his environment. Up in his Empire State tower, he was no longer trying to win over masses of voters; he was removed from the centers of action, as if exiled. Had he been in the thick of the battle — where he always used to function at his best — dealing with the Great Slump, he might have been no more orthodox than Franklin Roosevelt.

These days his resentments and disappointments tended to focus upon the figure of Roosevelt. Smith would not have been human if he had not felt twinges of envy because such great political fortune had fallen to his former disciple. The younger man had displayed magnificent leadership qualities

* The conservative idealogues said they wanted to go back to the Good Old Days of Jefferson and company, and also take along with them, one supposes, the General Motors Corporation and the Empire State Building. But Jefferson hated the world of the big cities with "the people piled one upon another," as well as the dark satanic mills of the industrialists.

in the time of crisis; but he also had his frailties, and sometimes showed unpleasing, even vindictive traits toward some
of his opponents, and specially toward former associates who
stood in opposition to him.

Late in 1933 the President was certainly guilty of a piece
of crude political wire-pulling aimed against Smith and his
group. Running on the Republican-Fusion ticket, the irrepressible Fiorello La Guardia, who had just gained a smashing
victory over Tammany in the New York mayoralty election,
announced the appointment of Robert Moses, State Park
Commissioner, as Commissioner of the new Triborough
Bridge Authority. This project was to be supported by federal funds, through the PWA, headed by Secretary Harold
Ickes. It would be enormously useful and would employ
thousands of idle construction workers. At Roosevelt's order,
Ickes rang up La Guardia and bluntly asked him to drop
Moses, because he was a "bitter enemy of the President,"
and also "a close friend of Smith." La Guardia, as wily as
anyone in politics, played for time and avoided a showdown.
Soon afterward, in the spring of 1934, it became known that
Moses was to be nominated as the Republican candidate for
Governor of New York. To avoid charges of playing politics,
Roosevelt and Ickes suspended hostilities during the election
campaign. But after it was over, and Governor Lehman
safely reelected, Ickes returned to the attack, serving notice
on La Guardia that the PWA would honor no more requisi-
tions for construction projects in New York City unless Moses
were sacked. This drastic order Ickes pretended to justify on
some technical legal ground, although in his *Secret Diary* he
confessed that it was an indefensible action, taken only "at
the instance of President Roosevelt."

Though Roosevelt could sometimes be magnanimous, he

plainly enjoyed being vindictive toward Robert Moses. The irrepressible Park Commissioner, meanwhile, fairly reveled in the fight, and managed to provoke an uproar in the metropolitan press against Secretary Ickes and his chief. The New Deal, it was charged, was playing politics with public works intended for the relief of unemployment. Ickes, who served as the President's "whipping post," lied to the newspapers by denying that he had acted under the President's orders. Smith then joined in the battle with a mighty blast at the Secretary of the Interior's conduct in this affair of "personal politics," which Ickes admitted to himself was well-deserved. Smith's intervention took immediate effect, for the President and Ickes conferred privately and concluded that "a retreat on our part was necessary."

A comic sequel followed these events, about a year later, on July 11, 1936, when the great Triborough Bridge had its triumphal opening ceremony. While Moses, who had completed the huge job with his usual speed (even when funds were delayed), gaily presided over the ribbon-cutting festival, Roosevelt and Ickes were also in attendance on the speakers' platform, since the President, in that election year, wanted to claim credit for the project. But Moses, maliciously enough, managed to do most of the talking, heaping coals of fire on Mr. Ickes's head by saying a few kind words about him. When it came time for Roosevelt to speak, in the few minutes allotted him, he was in his stubborn mood and flatly refused to allow Moses to introduce him. It was Robert Moses who had most of the fun that day.

✸

Smith had turned to private business in his ripe age, as stated earlier, in the hope that he would enjoy a little affluence after so many years of self-denial while in the public service. The real estate trade, however, remained in the doldrums; for years the Empire State Building Corporation was engaged in a struggle to stave off bankruptcy. Its first mortgage interest on $27,500,000 was not even half covered by rents during a decade or more, and it was general knowledge in New York that the Du Ponts and Raskob paid the mortgagor.

Though he scarcely rated as a financial wizard, Smith managed to perform some signal service for his corporation. Just before the unpleasant imbroglio over the Triborough Bridge flared up (worsening his relations with Roosevelt), Raskob had appealed to him to go to Washington and ask the President to have some of the new federal commissions rent office space in the Empire State Building. Smith had previously aired his criticisms of those agencies in *The New Outlook*. He hated the idea of going hat in hand to Franklin Roosevelt; it was humiliating, it was quite a toad to swallow. To Robert Moses he said sadly, "What shall I do?" Raskob insisted that he go, since he felt no shame about whatever they did to cut losses. In the end (it was November 18, 1933), Smith arranged for an appointment at the White House; the President received him with great good humor and graciously agreed to have some of the new federal agencies placed in the Empire State tower. "Roosevelt was absolutely charming to me," Smith said on his return. According to Jesse Jones, Chairman of the RFC, Roosevelt at one moment entertained the fantastic idea of having the Federal Government take over the Empire State Building, though Jones firmly counseled against this.

In 1934 Smith appeared for his corporation as a petitioner for relief before the New York City Tax Review Board and won a substantial reduction of taxes. The great building was then running at a loss of more than a million dollars a year. Several years later, in 1940, an investigation of its affairs by a Senate committee revealed that its second mortgage debentures of $13,500,000 had been purchased in 1930 by the affiliate of a large New York bank whose president was then a director of Empire State; eventually the second mortgage claims had been subordinated at a loss of about three fourths of the value of the original investment. Al Smith helped negotiate the exchange of securities involved at the time, 1937; it was he also who on December 30, 1937, negotiated with President Frederick Ecker of the Metropolitan Life Insurance Company, owner of the first mortgage of $27,500,-000, for a drastic reduction of interest charges, from six per cent to two and a half per cent! In reality there was bankruptcy in all but name. The favoritism shown by the giant insurance company and the bankers toward the Empire State Corporation and its eminent sponsors, the Du Pont group, was considered strange and unwise by the Senate's Temporary National Economic Committee, and could only be attributed to the tremendous influence enjoyed by Raskob and his associates in the world of finance.

Smith had been promised some shares of stock in the corporation, in accordance with the prevailing custom of paying incentive bonuses to executive officers. As the stock, however, became nearly worthless, nothing was done about it. But when toward the end of World War II commercial real estate began to revive strongly, Smith's friends, among them Moses, asked him if he still owned his small portion of stock in the Empire State. Still naive in business affairs, Smith indicated that he had never given the matter any thought. At the suggestion of these friends, he applied for the stock promised him by Raskob and finally had it transferred to his name. It was not until after his death, however, that those shares rose to a high market value.

When Smith from 1934 on delivered himself of scathing criticisms of the policies of Roosevelt and the New Deal administration, the admirers of the President answered him with considerable heat; one of the pro-Roosevelt journalists even stigmatized Governor Smith as an "embittered man" and "an envious man, who did not want his oldest political friend to have that which he could not have himself."

Smith's daughter, Mrs. Emily Warner, on the other hand, has been at pains to represent him, in her affectionate memoir of her father, as a happy being who wanted for nothing and envied no man in his later years. She pictures him growing old, always full of fun, always able to arouse laughter with his telling comments on the ways of men and politicians — in short, the most entertaining of men to the end of his days.

It was with a cheerful countenance that he faced the world as a rule; only occasionally did he reveal the bitterness and rue within. And there were, humanly speaking, sufficient grounds for indulging in such emotions, which were shared by many among the Irish-American and Roman Catholic citizens who had followed him, seeing him as their champion. He had risen from poverty up into the world of power as so many children of recent immigrants longed to do; he had made his bids for the highest office in the land; he had challenged the historic claim that America held careers open to

all talents without discrimination. And yet his challenge had
not been fairly met; he had been "disqualified," together with
some 20,000,000 others.* How could he easily put out of
mind the bitter memory of those events?

Felix Frankfurter, adviser to Roosevelt, and future Supreme Court Justice, paid a friendly visit to Smith at this
period, and judged him — like the activist Theodore Roosevelt when out of office — "a most tragic case of unemployment." Oscar Handlin in his *Al Smith and His America*
(1957), while writing briefly of his later career, has pictured him as a lost leader who sensed that he was just that.
During the fifteen years that followed 1928, he really lost his
way; at the same time his natural genius for public service,
for forensic work, for leading multitudes of men toward positive goals was lost for his country. This had happened to
more than one presidential candidate before him who, upon
losing the race, was brusquely retired from public life.

Smith, several years before, had met Winston Churchill
in New York, when the defeated British Minister had sought
him out through their mutual friend Bernard Baruch. In late
1933, again encountering Churchill, who was then earning
his living by lecturing in the United States, Smith remarked
to him that our party leaders, unlike those in England, suffered from "the lack of continuity" in American political life.
Churchill, at least, could return to play a role in Parliament.
Smith also observed at the time that it might be a good thing

* Recent commentators have held that the reactionary spirit shown by
Irish-Americans and German-Americans in the late forties and fifties, as in
the Christian Front, and the anti-Red campaigns of Senator Joseph Mc-
Carthy, derived from feelings of alienation dating back to the 1928 elections.
The Catholic "problem" in America remained unresolved until the election
of John F. Kennedy in 1960.

to have the runner-up presidential candidate appointed Senator-at-Large.

His friends the magnates, meanwhile, were under heavy attack by the New Dealers; their past errors were being cruelly exposed day by day in Congress or at legislative committee hearings in Washington. Always a loyal soul, Smith leaped to the defense of the men of capital who had given him succor in the time of his defeat. It seemed to him that Roosevelt's Brain Trusters were developing programs imitating the state socialism of Europe, or even of communism! He called on the President to rid himself of the "fanatics, Populists, demagogues, mountebanks and crackpots" in his entourage, and end their "clownish and irresponsible ravings against millionaires and big business . . ." His articles in *The New Outlook* bore titles such as "Where are we Going?" "Is the Constitution Still There?" "Does the Star-Spangled Banner Still Wave?"

In August, 1934, the discontented men of business announced the formation of a nonpartisan political body named the American Liberty League, whose object it was "to combat radicalism, to teach the necessity of respect for the rights of persons and property, and generally to foster free private enterprise." Its initiators were Jouett Shouse, John J. Raskob, Irénée Du Pont, William S. Knudsen, J. Howard Pew, and others of their school. At their head and front stood two defeated Democratic candidates for President, Alfred Smith and John W. Davis, but it was as class-conscious a group as ever functioned in the political field. For the congressional and state elections that year the Liberty League began to distribute printed literature and send out lecturers around

the country to denounce the socialistic "heresies" of the
Roosevelt Administration, and called for a return to the doctrines of laissez-faire economy they attributed to Jefferson.
Their propaganda had but scant effect on the electorate of
1934, which awarded Roosevelt an enormous majority in
both houses of Congress.

Its sponsors, however, continued their propaganda campaign in preparation for the 1936 national party conventions,
with the purpose of opposing Roosevelt's reelection. Early
in January of that year the Liberty League announced
with great fanfare a forthcoming banquet for 2000 of its
members to be held at the Mayflower Hotel in Washington;
it was to be addressed by a number of distinguished political
leaders of whom the principal speaker was to be former
Governor Smith, for the League counted a great deal upon
his powerful voice. As the League's "grandiose banquet"
was widely heralded in the nation's press, the affair created
some anxiety in the White House.

Miss Perkins recalled that Roosevelt, who always worried
about what might happen in an election year, said to her
concerning Smith:

> I just can't understand it. All the things we have done in the
> Federal Government are like the things Al Smith did as Gov-
> ernor of New York. They're the things he would have done
> as President . . . What in the world is the matter?

At this climactic phase of the New Deal the newspapers
bristled with polemics against the Roosevelt Administration,
and the parlors of the well-to-do often resounded with songs
of hate of That Man and of his wife.

Obeying a sudden mischievous whim, apparently, the
President dashed off a brief note inviting Smith to stay with

him in the White House when he came to Washington for
the dinner on January 23. (Roosevelt, it would seem, longed
for confrontation with his old leader, but when they did meet
they mostly exchanged jokes.) The invitation was politely
refused on the ground of a prior arrangement Smith had
made to be the guest of friends in Washington.

That dinner gathering, which many of America's rich sub-
scribed for and attended, was to be remembered afterward
as a sort of "Belshazzar's Feast" celebrated before the eve of
catastrophe for the Babylonians. It was to witness Smith's
last bid for a role in national politics, his last great charge.
The press had taken to singing his praises again; the radio
was to carry his big voice everywhere.

He began with the avowal that he was not a candidate for
any office anymore, "had no axe to grind, no personal feeling
. . . against anyone," and was happy in his present position
in life. He would speak, he said, for no special group, but
"for the best interests of the great rank and file of the American people, in which class I belong." The public heard him,
not for the first time, recapitulate his own Horatio Algeresque
rise from newsboy and fishmonger to the Governorship of
the greatest state in the Union. The heights of American
society had then, he pointed out, been open to all who had
the courage and will to fight their way up. But would this
be true in the future, under the tyrannical bureaucracy now
being imposed upon us? Here he uttered a fervent prayer
that his children and grandchildren might never find the
gates of freedom and opportunity closed to them. No, it was
not easy for one "born into the Democratic Party" to speak
against the present administration, but patriotism came before partisanship; the nation was in danger!

Now what are the dangers that I see? The first is the arraign-
ment of class against class . . .

The next thing that I view as being dangerous to national
well-being is government by bureaucracy instead of government . . . by law.

In a recent message to Congress President Roosevelt had
argued that his administration constituted always a "people's
government" and that its new instruments of public power
under such guidance presented no dangers. Smith, citing this
statement, exclaimed, "We don't want any autocrats . . . not
even a good one." The country must be returned to strict
constitutional rule, to the preservation of states' rights, to
the explicit Democratic platform of 1932, which Roosevelt
had repudiated. The government must save money, not
spend it wantonly, "the way they throw sawdust on a bar-
room floor." The President's error, in Smith's view, consisted
in his having allowed himself to be misled by his advisers.
Here Smith descended to a little coarse humor:

How do you suppose all this happened? The young Brain
Trusters caught the Socialists in swimming and they ran away
with their clothes . . . it's all right if they want to disguise themselves as Norman Thomas, or Karl Marx, or Lenin, or any of the
rest of that bunch. But what I won't stand for is allowing them
to march under the banner of Jefferson, Jackson, or Cleveland.

Smith concluded his speech with a highly emotional perora-
tion in which he warned his hearers that the country faced
a choice between "Washington and Moscow, [between] the
pure air of America or the foul breath of communistic Russia . . . the stars and stripes or the red flag of the godless . . .
Soviets." It was bizarre to see Smith wave the Bloody Shirt
of revolutionary Communism before his select audience, as if

seeking to raise up their visceral passions, their ancient xeno-
phobic hates of alien creeds and "secret conspirators." The
Ku Klux Klan had sought to arouse such irrational fears of
Smith himself and the alleged "international conspiracy" of
Rome in much the same manner. Smith's cries of warning
against the New Deal's trend to "communism" would echo
through the 1936 electoral campaign, and yet to no avail.
He had forgotten the multitudes of the ill-fed and ill-housed,
and forgotten that they were concerned with survival rather
than with constitutional dogmas.

The nation's press, eighty per cent anti-Roosevelt, warmly
applauded Smith's performance at the Mayflower Hotel, holding that he had dealt hard blows at the New Deal. *The New
York Times,* however, though opposed that year to Roosevelt's renomination, editorially voiced fears that Smith's extravagant terms would help rather than injure Roosevelt's
cause. The President's partisans retorted to Smith with gibes
and sneers all the angrier for their disappointment in the
liberal leader of former years. "Our knight of the brown
derby," said one leading journalist, had exchanged his old
headgear for a top hat. John L. Lewis vouchsafed the opinion
that Smith had doubtless been "well paid" for what he had
said by his present employers. Heywood Broun expressed
shock at the volte-face of the man he had so long admired.

In self-defense Smith permitted himself another thrust at
Roosevelt, explaining that he had gone into business "because I didn't have a rich aunt or a rich uncle to take care
of me." As to the New Deal partisans who denounced him as
a tool of Wall Street, he exclaimed:

> Unless you're ready to subscribe to the New Deal 100 per cent
> and sign your name on the dotted line, you're a Tory, you're
> a prince of privilege, you're . . . an economic Royalist . . . Well

anyone who has gone through what I went through in 1928 is not going to be worried by sneers and epithets.

On the day following the Liberty League dinner at Washington, Secretary Ickes, appearing at a public forum, took occasion to reply to Smith. He began by citing a speech of Herbert Hoover's in 1928 assailing Governor Smith as "socialistic" and "communistic" because he favored the development of public waterpower resources by the government. Then Ickes recalled Smith's own riposte to Hoover in which the old Governor declared that throughout his career he had found the spokesmen of our richest and most selfish corporations habitually attacking all measures of reform affecting their interests on the ground that they were "socialistic." Smith's red herring was disposed of in his own words of an earlier day.

Smith himself in a later statement a week before the November, 1936, election issued a correction of his earlier remarks, explaining that he had never intended to imply that President Roosevelt himself was either a Socialist or a Communist, but only that radical advisers had infiltrated his administration and led him astray. Smith mused, "There is some certain kind of foreign 'ism' crawling over this country; what it is I don't know."

The sponsors of the Liberty League, prior to the Democratic national convention, uttered threats that if President Roosevelt were renominated they might, as Al Smith phrased it, "take a walk" — that is to say, bolt their party. In June Roosevelt was renominated by acclamation, and he vowed that he would work in his next term for more reform and more social security and would spend more public money for the general welfare. Whereupon the Smith-Raskob-Shouse group carried out their threat, and gave their support to the

Republican candidate, Governor Landon of Kansas. In past times Smith would have considered the desertion of his party organization as something to be equated with a sin against the Holy Ghost, yet in the autumn of 1936 he brought himself to take the stump for the Republican nominee.

The citizens of the urban conglomerations of the Northeast, despite Smith's apostasy, voted en masse for Roosevelt. The bishops of the National Catholic Welfare Conference endorsed his candidacy. Under Roosevelt's egalitarian regime the mindless habit of ethnic and religious discrimination in public life in favor of the older American stocks was being largely overcome: the Roosevelt party made a great play for the Flynns and the Murphys and Corcorans, the Cohens and the Frankfurters, the Polettis and the Furcolos; hundreds of Catholics were named to high federal office and judgeships; some overtures were also made to Negroes. On election day the Roosevelt coalition carried the West as well as the Solid South, but the great strength of the revived Democratic Party was now rooted in the cities of the North and East which Smith had carried in 1928. The Democratic trend in the urban centers, so powerful in 1928 and 1932, became overwhelming in 1936. Smith himself had contributed greatly to the relocation of Democratic strength, which ensured the triumph of Roosevelt, his political heir, who no longer needed to depend on the old alliance with the South.

The Republicans sustained their heaviest defeat that year. Smith's wry comment on the results was "Well, the people don't shoot Santa Claus."

In a passage of one of Bourke Cockran's flowery orations, such as Smith in early life liked to memorize, there is a sad reflection on the destiny of fallen political leaders:

> Is the politician happy? Far from it. When the scepter of power finally drops from his nerveless fingers, he is condemned to an isolation the more unbearable because of the adulation to which he has become accustomed.

The aging Al Smith lived a life that was increasingly remote from the centers of public power, a life of a quietude he had never desired for himself. He was always blessed with affectionate and loyal friends, but to some of his visitors he seemed not only disillusioned, but almost misanthropic.

Norman Hapgood, his admiring biographer, called on him in the time of the first New Deal and, in friendly spirit, challenged his view that the nation was lost unless it could be won back to Jeffersonian individualism. Hapgood told Smith that he had recently interviewed the investment banker Otto Kahn (of Kuhn, Loeb & Company) on the subject of the new laws regulating the security exchanges, and that Kahn had roundly declared that they had not changed the real picture, that his fellow operators in Wall Street had learned nothing since the Great Crash and the coming of reform. Kahn predicted another and greater debacle in the future, after which the entire social structure would collapse. In view of Kahn's judgment would not Smith agree that regulation by the government was vital in such fields? Smith replied only that "he would rather go through another crash" on the constitutional principles that he advocated.

Emil Ludwig, author of many popular biographies of famous men, was in the United States at this time preparing to write a portrait of Franklin Roosevelt. His book, when published here in 1938, was of interest less for its knowledge of American political history than for its fresh insights by an observant man coming here from abroad. Late in 1937, he relates, he called on Alfred Smith at the Empire State Building to talk with him of the character and career of his former disciple. Ludwig noticed that, whereas Roosevelt's desk was cluttered with ship models, wooden donkeys, and other curiosa, Smith's desk was bare, save for a couple of heavy bronze tigers as paperweights, a large enameled cross, and a framed photograph of the Pope inscribed to him.

Ludwig began by broaching cautiously the question of whether Roosevelt's sacrifice of his friendship for Smith had not been "the first payment he had to make" for his own climb to power. On this point, Ludwig wrote, "Smith . . . refused in his gruff way to give me any information. I liked very much his avoidance of diplomatic trimmings."

The German author received the impression from what Smith or others said that after he had helped Roosevelt reach high office, he had "waited like a mother waiting for her married daughter to call her." But there was no word, there was no gratitude shown. Ludwig continues:

> The man in his middle sixties stirred in me a feeling of profound sympathy; political ambition had transformed a valiant and amazingly productive friend of man into an embittered misanthrope.
> . . . Now I found this disgruntled man at odds with himself and the world, not because he had lost the game, but because he felt he could no longer play it; an uncapped tower lifted against the sky, resenting that it lacked the anticipated spire to complete it, but not wise enough to understand that a fragment is often more beautiful than a completed structure.

As he spoke with Ludwig, Smith twisted his heavy cigar in his mouth; he seemed unhappy at the very thought of Mr. Roosevelt. To the visitor Smith in old age and defeat seemed wanting in that inner equilibrium that education and philosophy might have furnished. His faith should have consoled him, but Ludwig thought it did not. Suddenly the old Governor stood up, moved about restlessly like a younger man, and, brandishing a Democratic Party pamphlet that contained the platform of 1932, he began to thunder forth the dogmas of states' rights. The President had flouted the United States Constitution, he contended: "There he stood, a threatening figure, dark against the dazzling sunlight of the world city, with finger uplifted, invoking angrily the sanctity of the law."

More usually it was a smiling countenance he turned to the world. To New Yorkers strolling on Fifth Avenue he was a familiar and beloved figure for many years, as he walked toward the park with his Great Dane on leash, clad in elegant and conservative clothes, looking every inch a successful man in the most materialistic American sense of the term. On Sundays he was to be seen in morning costume and top hat setting off in his limousine with Kate to attend Mass at St. Patrick's Cathedral.

His daughter has told of how during the 1930's he became an Honorary Night Keeper of the Central Park Zoo. Since he lived close to the menagerie, Robert Moses had thought to confer upon him that whimsical appointment. Thus on occasion, armed with his special authority, he would conduct favored dinner guests at his Fifth Avenue apartment to the zoo across the street; at their head he would pass before the animal cages and stop before the old tiger, to whom he would mutter certain names. "La Guardia!" he would say, and the tiger would begin to roar, or sometimes he would pronounce the name "Roosevelt," and provoke renewed roars, to the vast amusement of Smith and his friends. On one occasion toward the end of his life, according to the New York newspapers, the Mall in Central Park was the scene of an informal barbershop chorus, in which the former Governor outdid all the other singers in volume and zest.

In the years as a private citizen he showed himself more deeply and seriously attached to his Church and its diocesan activities in New York than ever before. He came to be known as the leading Catholic layman in the United States; for many years he served as chairman of the Archbishop's Committee on the Laity, and his presence at important Church functions and his participation in its philanthropic work were a source of gratification to Cardinal Hayes, as later to Hayes's successor, Cardinal Spellman, who accorded him many honors for his charitable labors in the New York diocese. These associations too were not without influence on his thinking, for the Roman Catholic prelates of New York and Boston were strong conservatives, unlike Cardinal Mundelein of Chicago or Monsignor John A. Ryan of Wisconsin. In 1937, on his first and only trip to Europe, Smith was received in audience by the Pope, and to his joy was addressed by his Holiness as "my son." The following year he was named a Papal Chamberlain of the Cape and Sword.

In Rome he had also been received by Mussolini, who slyly prodded him on the possibility of Roosevelt's running for a third term; a few weeks later, in France, he paid his respects to President Lebrun and to Premier Léon Blum,

head of the Popular Front Ministry. Journeying on to England, he enjoyed a visit to the House of Commons while it
was in session and an afternoon with Winston Churchill at
his country house. His last stop in Europe was at Moate, the
village outside of Dublin where his grandmother had been
born. The former Governor, however, could make nothing of
rural Ireland, and like many American tourists he was never
so happy as when he set foot again on the dock in New York.
In a statement to ship reporters upon his return he said that
Europe was falling prey to dictators and he deplored the
spread of dictatorships of any kind.

And yet in this matter he was not entirely consistent. Since
the summer of 1936 a civil war had been raging in Spain,
where a democratically elected government was opposed by
a Fascist general with aspirations toward a dictatorship, but
Smith shared the views of the leaders of the Catholic Church
who were firmly aligned against the Loyalists in support of
Franco, thereby alienating himself further from his liberal
friends in America. On the other hand he had publicly denounced Hitler as early as 1934, when he appeared as the
principal speaker at an anti-Nazi rally at Madison Square
Garden attended by 20,000 New Yorkers. On this occasion,
whose object was to raise funds to help Jews suffering from
the new racial decrees in Germany, he called attention to the
injustice of exclusionist immigration laws in the United
States and to the reluctance of the State Department, even
under the Roosevelt Administration, to make exceptions in
favor of the victims of persecution. Not long afterward he
became one of the founders and sponsors of the Conference
of Christians and Jews, which aimed to eliminate misun-
derstandings between the three principal religious groups

in America, and served for several years on its directing
committee.

But the years were passing, and lengthening shadows
from across the world began to blur the differences between
the two great political adversaries. They even found areas
of agreement. When war threatened Europe in 1939, and
Roosevelt called on Congress to amend the Neutrality Act,
which prohibited the sale of arms to foreign countries, including potential allies, Smith put aside his disagreements
with the President and spoke over the radio warmly endors-
ing the proposed change. In response to this the President
wired him on September 29, "Very many thanks. You were
grand." Smith, to be sure, "took a walk" once more in 1940
in protest against a third term for Roosevelt, but after the
elections he spoke up in a public address broadcast by radio
in favor of the President's proposals for Lend-Lease in aid
of beleaguered England. This speech had a marked effect,
and again Roosevelt sent him a telegram of heartfelt thanks,
on May 29, 1941.

It was not until after the entry of the United States into
World War II, however, that the two men resumed communication on easy terms. In June, 1942, Smith wrote to the
President asking to see him "off the record." Roosevelt was
grateful for Smith's help not only in the matter of the Neutrality Act but particularly in regard to Lend-Lease, in which
the administration faced strong opposition, especially among
the Irish; moreover he must have been aware of Smith's
activities in various civilian defense committees in New York,
and that Smith's son Alfred, Junior, had gone into service as
an Army captain. He received Smith at the White House,

and the two men enjoyed a warm reunion, swapping stories of old times and old acquaintances in the political world. Smith was now a white-haired old party of sixty-nine, and the President too showed the wear of arduous years.

Roosevelt thought more often in those days of his place in history, and while biographers like Emil Ludwig had recently sung his praises, his ingratitude to Alfred Smith had also been remarked upon. The President, who like most politicians was somewhat thick-skinned, seems to have become aware of his past lapses, for his White House aides were henceforth alerted to remind him of little attentions that would give the old Governor pleasure. In February, 1943, on learning that Smith was under observation at St. Vincent's Hospital in New York, the President wired a kindly inquiry about his health. A month later they met again in private at the White House. When Smith celebrated his seventieth birthday on December 30, 1943, Roosevelt wrote him an affectionate letter of greeting on his having attained "the Scriptural Age." At this time he also imparted to Miss Tully some reminiscences concerning the former Governor's extraordinary personality and the "saga of success and service which made up Al's life."

In his last years, when the United States was on the verge of involvement in the war, Smith actively sponsored a series of large housing developments which were intended to eliminate the slums of the old East Side ghetto. His own preference was for privately financed constructions aided by reduced taxes and low interest rates. The raising of capital according to his scheme, however, proved difficult, and the sponsors of the project had to rely on financing by the State of New York. The first of these large low-rent developments was located near the East River, around the corner from Oliver Street where he had lived during his first fifty years, but it was not completed during his lifetime. In his honor the project was named the Alfred E. Smith Houses, and it remains one of the visible monuments to his glory. A far more imposing monument, as Mayor LaGuardia remarked later, was "written on the statute books of our State in the progressive welfare laws enacted during his time."

On April 5, 1944, Katherine Smith died after a lingering illness. Her husband, who had been distraught during the several weeks of her hospitalization, seemed inconsolable at the loss of his companion of nearly half a century. Five months later he himself went to St. Vincent's Hospital for a checkup. The doctors found that he was suffering from congestion of the lungs, and when he showed no improvement had him removed to the Rockefeller Institute Hospital for more intensive treatment. From Quebec, where he was then in conference with Winston Churchill, Roosevelt sent a last cheering message. On October 4, 1944, having received the apostolic benediction of the Pope, conveyed to him by Archbishop Spellman from Rome, and the last rites of the Church, the tired old warrior died.

The war in Europe was in its final phase, the war in the Far East was at its height, yet many of America's public men and women in Washington as in New York, out of sentiment for Alfred Smith, dropped whatever they were doing to attend the impressive funeral services at St. Patrick's Cathedral. There were 5000 mourners in the church, while in the streets and avenues surrounding it a huge throng of

200,000 New Yorkers prayed for him as the great bells tolled.

Secretary of Labor Frances Perkins was among the Washington contingent that came to New York to pay their last respects to Smith and she spoke with feeling of her old friend and of her sense of personal bereavement. "I do not think it is now generally realized that Al Smith was the man responsible for the first drift in the United States toward the conception that political responsibility involved a duty to improve the life of the people," she said to a reporter that day. And later, as she reviewed his characteristically American career, she found simpler and more poignant words to describe the man: "He could learn, he could remember, and he did the best he could at every level of his life."

NOTES

BIBLIOGRAPHY

INDEX

Notes

CHAPTER I: *Encounter at Albany*
(pp. 1–7)
This material is derived from Miss Perkins's manuscript.

CHAPTER II: *Origins and Childhood*
(pp. 8–32)
Martin Green's series of articles in the New York *Evening World*, "Fourth Ward Boy Who Became Governor" (beginning October 16, 1922, and continued in twelve installments), is particularly useful for this period of Smith's life, based as it is on interviews with the Governor and with many of his boyhood friends. In talks with Mrs. John Glynn, Smith's sister, Miss Perkins was able to learn details of his ancestry and early life that the Governor himself was ignorant of, or had forgotten. Miss Perkins also had studies made of the New York City Directories from 1842 to 1861, as well as of the New York State Census of 1855, for data on Smith's paternal grandparents. Smith's autobiography *Up to Now* and the books by Pringle and Hapgood and Moskowitz provide further details, while background material can be found in Campbell's *Darkness and Daylight*, Riis's *How the Other Half Lives*, and *Valentine's Manual*.

CHAPTER III: *Schooling*
(pp. 33–53)
Brother Angelus Gabriel's *The Christian Brothers in the United States* is informative about the kind of teachers Smith had in

school. Moskowitz's *Alfred E. Smith, An American Career* has a few facts not recorded elsewhere, but Martin Green and Smith himself are sources for most of the material on this period, while Mrs. Glynn's recollections, as given to Miss Perkins, are homely but apt. Smith's scrapbooks have many items connected with the St. James Literary Society. The Wagner quotation is found in *Current Biography*, 1941.

CHAPTER IV: *Ward Politics*

(pp. 54–69)
The conventional view of Tammany Hall in Smith's youth, conveyed by Parkhurst, Hodder, and Riordan, and documented by Werner, is softened in Smith's own recollections. Miss Perkins's anecdote about The McManus is contained in her Oral History Memoir. Hapgood and Moskowitz, and Smith's scrapbooks, supply details about the Governor's start in politics; Pringle tells of his conduct at the Commission of Jurors and his early political aspirations; Green describes his courtship.

CHAPTER V: *"My University"*

(pp. 70–100)
An excellent description of the history and architectural features of the Capitol in Albany is contained in *Capitol Story*, by Roseberry. For Smith's first years in the Assembly his autobiography, Pringle, and Green have been drawn upon. The text of his inaugural address in 1925 is in *Progressive Democracy*.

CHAPTER VI: *"He Read a Book"*

(pp. 101–117)
Miss Perkins's Oral Memoir provides information about her birth and early life. Material on her college career and the years following is found in the records of Mount Holyoke College, the college yearbook, the *Llamarada*, for 1902, and in letters she contributed to *The Class of 1902*, a booklet published privately from time to time, in the Mount Holyoke College library. Miss

Perkins's daughter, Mrs. Calvert Coggeshall, was also helpful. The Perkins file at the New York School for Social Work has documents on Miss Perkins's move from Philadelphia to New York in 1909. Brenner, Bruno, Chambers, Davis and Meier are useful for the history of the social worker movement. Josephine Goldmark's *Impatient Crusader* gives a vivid picture of Florence Kelley, and Miss Perkins's tribute to Mrs. Kelley in the *Social Service Review* is informative and affectionate.

CHAPTER VII: *New Directions*

(*pp. 118–144*)

The firsthand newspaper accounts of the Triangle Fire and its aftermath are reliable, though highly emotional. Leon Stein's book assembles all the relevant material and analyzes it with restraint and power. Rose Schneiderman's speech was reported in *The New York Times* and in *The Survey*. Some Factory Investigating Commission hearings were reported in the press; the Reports of the Commission are sources for all the formal hearings; Miss Perkins's Oral Memoir gives her personal impressions of the commission's travels about the state and tells of how this study contributed to Smith's education. The labor and safety measures passed as a result of the investigation are listed in the Legislative Manual. How the 54-hour Bill was passed is told in "Behind the Rail," in the *Metropolitan Magazine* for June, 1912.

CHAPTER VIII: *Growth in Leadership: 1912–15*

(*pp. 145–176*)

Smith's home life at this period is described by Emily Smith Warner in her biography of her father. The unfriendly reports of Smith's conduct as Speaker come from *Knickerbocker Press*, Albany, January 19, 1913, and *The New York Times*, March 29, 1913. The Sulzer impeachment and the Mitchel campaign were covered in the press. Smith's position in the Sulzer affair is discussed in the *Times*, March 29, 1913, as well as in Miss Perkins's Oral Memoir. His role in the Constitutional Convention is everywhere apparent in the official record of the proceedings. Martin

Green quotes his speech in defense of the Widows' Pension bill, also Foley's remark on Smith's political aspirations at the time. The New York *Evening World* of October 28, 1913, describes Smith's warm relations with his Fourth Ward constituents in "Al Smith Night in Old Oliver."

CHAPTER IX: *The First State Campaign*

(*pp. 177–209*)

Green's series in the *Evening World* gives anecdotes of Smith's years as Sheriff. Smith's comment on Mitchel appears in *Up to Now*. The Mitchel administration is described from an insider's point of view by Miss Perkins in her Oral Memoir; Mary Heaton Vorse's *A Footnote to Folly* has a memorable picture of the unemployed in New York in 1915. Smith's campaign for President of the Board of Alderman is told in Hapgood and Moskowitz; his relations with Hylan are dealt with there also, as well as in Pringle. Judge Proskauer in an interview gave details of the formation of the Independent Citizens' Committee, which was also reported in the press. Mrs. Moskowitz's part in the campaign is told in Miss Perkins's Oral Memoir; Carlos Israels, Mrs. Moskowitz's son, and Judge Proskauer gave further details. *The New York Times* of October 17, 1918, comments on Smith's attitude toward women voters and women in office. His reminiscent article, "Electioneering Old and New," in the *Saturday Evening Post*, August 30, 1930, is a lively account of his first campaign for Governor. The press covered the campaign, though scarcely with the attention they were to devote to Smith later in his career. The impression he made on his first installation as Governor is quoted from Hapgood and Moskowitz.

CHAPTER X: *Governor of New York*

(*pp. 210–241*)

Green's series in the *Evening World* deals in part with the home life of the Smiths in Albany; Emily Smith Warner and Frances Perkins, in her Oral Memoir, contribute many intimate observations. The press followed his appointments closely. An interview with Miss Perkins in the New York *Sun* of February 24, 1919, is interesting in connection with her appointment to the Industrial Commission, the story of how she joined the Democratic Party is taken from her Oral Memoir, as well as the account of the origins of the Reconstruction Commission. The Reconstruction Commission's Reports give the scope of its studies; Hapgood and Moskowitz discuss its operations at length. Miss Perkins's Oral Memoir is the source of the story of the Rome strike, corrected and amplified by contemporary accounts in the Rome *Daily Sentinel* and the Utica *Herald-Dispatch*. The anecdote about how Smith edited speeches written for him is told by Judge Proskauer; the Knapp story is recounted by Robert Moses. Smith's opinions on many public questions are set forth in *Progressive Democracy*.

CHAPTER XI: *The Duel with Hearst*

(pp. 242–279)

Swanberg's *Citizen Hearst* is an exhaustive study of the man and his works. The New York *American* and the *Evening Journal* give Hearst's side of the controversy with Smith; the *World* and *The Times* gave much space to Smith's answers to Hearst's attacks. In *Up to Now* Smith tells the story briefly. The origin of Smith's "War Board" was described in an interview with Judge Proskauer. Martin Green tells about the Governor's job at the United States Trucking Corporation; in his *A Tribute to Governor Smith* Moses describes Smith's real preoccupations at that time. Roosevelt's letter urging Smith to run again in 1922 and Smith's reply are in the Franklin D. Roosevelt Library at Hyde Park. The *World* carried a blow-by-blow account of the prenomination doings at Syracuse in 1922. The events of the campaign are taken from the New York press.

CHAPTER XII: *The Fighting Governor*

(pp. 280–317)

Hapgood and Moskowitz quote Smith on the effect Republican opposition had on his career. Proskauer's story about his appointment as judge was told in an interview. Miss Perkins's Oral

Memoir discusses Smith's policy on appointments and the changeover from the spoils system. The anecdote about the defeat of
the Eight-Hour Bill for Women was told by Rose Schneiderman
in an interview. The repeal of the Mullan-Gage Act is dealt with
in Hapgood and Moskowitz; the newspapers of the time followed
it closely. Roosevelt's attitude is shown in a letter to Smith quoted
by Burns, while Murphy's view is reported by Flynn. Miss Perkins's Oral Memoir has a detailed account of the administration
of the Labor Department; the report of the Moreland Act Commission to investigate the department is available in typescript at
the New York State Library in Albany. Two contemporary articles tell of Mrs. Moskowitz's role in Smith's political family, "The
Woman Political Strategist," by C. S. Hand in the New York
World, July 15, 1923, and "A Certain Person," by O. H. P. Garrett
in *The New Yorker,* October 9, 1926. The comment on the passing
of Murphy is attributed to Mrs. Moskowitz in "Friends of the
Governor," by Denis Tilden Lynch in the *North American Review,* June, 1928. Judge Proskauer is the source of the story about
Roosevelt's accepting the chairmanship of the Citizens' Committee for Smith in 1924. "Rural nativism" vs. "Urban rowdyism" is
quoted from Freidel's *Roosevelt.*

CHAPTER XIII: *Harvest: 1925–27*

(*pp. 318–349*)

Smith's comment on the death of Foley was quoted in *The New
York Times.* His differences with Hylan were reported at length
by Silas Bent in the New York *World,* May 10, 1925. Miss
Perkins's Oral Memoir treats the choice of Walker for Mayor;
Fowler's *Beau James* gives a graphic picture of the company
Walker kept. In *Up to Now* Smith dryly describes his method of
going to the people. The Mahti Latti case is given in some detail
by Miss Perkins in her Oral Memoir; it is also recorded in the
Bulletin of the New York State Industrial Commission; the Supreme Court decision in the case is found in *United States Re-
ports,* Volume 273, Cases Adjudged in the Supreme Court. Miss
Perkins describes Emily Smith's wedding at length, from the point

of view of a friend of the family; the press also carried a full account.

CHAPTER XIV: *The 1928 Campaign*

(pp. 350–400)

Tumulty's advice to Smith is cited in Handlin. Norris's statement in Smith's support was reported in *The New York Times*. Roosevelt's comment on Smith's attitude toward business appears in a letter to Ward Melville, September 21, 1928, at the Roosevelt Library, Hyde Park. The Lippmann quotation is from *Men of Destiny*. Moses described the Tiger Room in a letter to Miss Perkins, April 1, 1959, among the Perkins papers at Columbia University. Flynn's view of it is in *You're the Boss*. Senate Committee hearings on Smith's campaign funds were reported in *The New York Times*, also in an article by H. L. Mencken in the Baltimore *Sun* of May 17, 1928, quoted by Moses in *A Tribute to Governor Smith*. The Raskob article appeared in the *Ladies' Home Journal*, August, 1929. Lindsay Rogers, in an interview, recalled Smith's reaction to the Marshall letter. The 1928 correspondence between Smith and Roosevelt on this subject is at the Hyde Park Library. Emily Smith Warner's book tells how the Governor's answer to Marshall was drafted. Mrs. Kelley's view of the Governor's attitude toward legislation frowned on by the Church is reported by Miss Perkins; her Oral Memoir also tells how Smith resisted pressure from Cardinal O'Connell. Lippmann's comment appears in his *Interpretations*.

The 1928 convention was covered in full by the press; Lewis Gannett gives his strong sense of the crosscurrents at work there in "Big Show at Houston," in *The Nation*, July 11, 1928. Roosevelt's remarks on the choice of Raskob as chairman are quoted from Burns. The account of Smith's decision in the matter is based on the recollections of Judge Proskauer and Carlos Israels, son of Mrs. Moskowitz. The resentments of Tammany workers against Raskob were aired in the newspapers.

Tugwell describes his collaboration with Smith on the farm problem in *The Democratic Roosevelt*. The campaign speeches

were carried in the press, which dealt with the slanders of the
Smiths only charily; Moses gave further details on the defamatory
literature circulated at the time in an interview. Michelson tells
of how Smith revised his Oklahoma speech in *The Ghost Talks;*
Lehman's reaction to the speech is contained in Nevins's biog-
raphy. Mrs. Moskowitz's anxiety about the Oklahoma meeting is
recalled by Smith in *Up to Now*. Miss Perkins is authority for the
story of Smith's attitude toward western provincials, and her Oral
Memoir describes the women's campaign at some length. White's
The Making of the President points up the differences between
Smith and Kennedy in regard to the Catholic issue. Tucker's *The
Mirrors of 1932* has an account of the end of the 1928 campaign.
An excellent analysis of voting trends established in the 1928
election is in Lubell's *The Future of American Politics*.

CHAPTER XV: *The Unhappy Warrior*

(pp. 401–444)
Miss Perkins's Oral Memoir describes the scene when the Roose-
velt family replaced the Smiths in the Executive Mansion. Moses
gave details of his conflict with Howe, and thus with Roosevelt,
in an interview. Mrs. Sara Delano Roosevelt's attitude toward
Mrs. Moskowitz was described in an interview with Mrs. Henry
Goddard Leach, who was present at their meeting. Mrs. Franklin
Roosevelt's comment on Smith's frustration in 1929 is quoted from
This I Remember. The New York *Herald Tribune* obituary of
Mrs. Moskowitz cites her thoughts on retirement. Smith's move to
Fifth Avenue was explained by him at a Senate Finance Committee hearing, 72nd Congress, 2nd Session, cited in Schlesinger. The
story of his talk at Harvard is told by Emily Smith Warner in her
biography, which also describes his success with the Long Island
set. Lindsay Rogers related the anecdote about the visit to Senator Gerry's mansion in an interview. Smith's comments on his
job at the Empire State Building are in "Al Smith Talks as a Man
of Business," by S. J. Woolf in *The New York Times* Sunday
Magazine, October 6, 1929. The failure of the County Trust
Company was fully reported in the New York press, where the

career of Walker can also be followed. Correspondence between
Smith and Roosevelt at this period is at the Roosevelt Library at
Hyde Park. Smith's speech nominating Roosevelt for reelection
in 1930 is quoted in Tugwell's *The Democratic Roosevelt*. Miss
Perkins in her Oral Memoir describes Moses's methods of operation humorously, adding that she nevertheless always felt a strong
affection and regard for him. Her perceptive comments on the
temperamental differences between Smith and Roosevelt are also
drawn from her Oral Memoir. Roosevelt's letter of November 11,
1931, is among the Alfred E. Smith papers at the New York State
Library in Albany. Smith's hesitancy about running again for the
Presidency is discussed in Farley's *Behind the Ballots*, in Flynn,
and in Emily Smith Warner's biography. Farley's role is also
touched upon in "An Aid to the End," by Mary Dewson. The
letter from Clark Howell to Roosevelt of December 2, 1931, is at
the Roosevelt Library at Hyde Park. Mrs. Moskowitz's attempt to
reach Garner was described by her son in an interview with the
author. The Curry story is told in Handlin. Gerard Swope on
Mrs. Moskowitz is quoted by Ickes in *Secret Diary*.

CHAPTER XVI: *A Lost Leader*

(*pp. 445-471*)
Smith's changing views about the New Deal are found in his
articles in *The New Outlook*. The story of the Triborough Bridge
imbroglio is revealed in Ickes's *Secret Diary*. How Smith sold
space in the Empire State Building to the Roosevelt administration was told by Moses in an interview; in lesser detail it appears
in his *A Tribute to Governor Smith*. In the same interview Moses
disclosed how Smith acquired shares in the company. The story
of the financing of the Empire State Building appeared in the
press in 1939 and 1941. Smith's alleged envy of Roosevelt is suggested by Tucker. Frankfurter's comments on his visit to Smith
appear in his reminiscences. The meeting between Smith and
Churchill is described in Handlin. Smith's connection with the
Liberty League and comments on his change of attitude were
covered in the press. Heywood Broun wrote of his disillusion-

ment in *The Nation*. Bourke Cochran's speech is quoted by
Handlin. Hapgood's visit to Smith is described by Ickes in *Secret
Diary*. The impressions of Emil Ludwig are found in his book on
Roosevelt. Emily Smith Warner's biography portrays her father
in his declining years. Smith's denunciation of the Nazis was
published in Pierre Van Paassen's *Nazism: An Assault on Civili-
zation*. Miss Tully's recollections of the last meeting between
Roosevelt and Smith are contained in her *F.D.R., My Boss*.
Smith's funeral was described in the press and in Miss Perkins's
Oral Memoir.

Bibliography

THE PAPERS of Frances Perkins, deposited at Columbia University, are one of the principal sources of material bearing on the personality of Smith. Smith himself left disappointingly few personal papers, and it is told that he destroyed all but official correspondence just before he left office as Governor in 1928. Nevertheless his scrapbooks, in the possession of his daughter, Emily Smith Warner, offer insights into his early years and interests, and a few items at the New York State Library in Albany escaped the general holocaust. The Franklin D. Roosevelt Library at Hyde Park, New York, contains correspondence of exceptional interest for an understanding of the relations between the President and the Governor, as well as a manuscript memoir by Mary Dewson, "An Aid to an End," which throws light on relations between Roosevelt and some of Smith's former supporters. In addition to an extensive taped memoir by Frances Perkins, the Oral History Collection at Columbia University has memoirs by many other persons who knew Smith more or less well. For primary material on Frances Perkins the library of Mount Holyoke College and the Library of the New York School of Social Work have been helpful. The Arthur and Elizabeth Schlesinger Library at Radcliffe College is a source of much original material on the social workers. To the librarians of all these institutions many thanks are due for their cooperation and assistance.

NEW YORK STATE PUBLICATIONS

Bulletin of the New York State Industrial Commission
Constitutional Convention, 1915, Revised Record, Vols I–III

Factory Investigating Commission Reports, 1912–1915
Legislative Manual, 1906–1915
Moreland Commission Report (Preliminary), by Jeremiah F. Connor, March 26, 1919
Reconstruction Commission Reports (4 volumes)
Also:
Minutes of Hearings, before Governor Alfred E. Smith, January 22–23, 1924, unpublished typescript entitled "Investigation of Charges Made by Associated Industries of New York State, Inc., against the State Department of Labor."

NEWSPAPERS

New York *American*
New York *Herald* and *Herald Tribune*
New York *Evening Journal*
New York *Sun*
New York Times
New York *Evening World*
New York *World*
Rome (N.Y.) *Daily Sentinel*
Utica (N.Y.) *Herald Dispatch*
Albany (N.Y.) *Knickerbocker Press*

BOOKS AND PAMPHLETS

Addams, Jane, *Forty Years at Hull-house*. New York, 1935.
Allen, Frederick Lewis, *Only Yesterday*. New York, 1931.
Bard, Erwin Wilkie, *The Port of New York Authority*. New York, 1942.
Becker, Leona F., *Alfred E. Smith* (Thesis offered for a master's degree at the University of Chicago, 1938, unpublished).
Bird, Frederick L., *A Study of the Port of New York Authority*. New York, 1949.
Brenner, Robert H., *From the Depths: The Discovery of Poverty in the United States*. New York, 1956.

Bruno, Frank J., *Trends in Social Work, 1874–1956*. New York, 1957.

Burner, David, *The Politics of Provincialism: The Democratic Party in Transition, 1918–1932*. New York, 1968.

Burns, James MacGregor, *Roosevelt: The Lion and the Fox*. New York, 1956.

Campbell, Helen, *Darkness and Daylight, or Lights and Shadows of New York Life*. New York, 1891.

Chambers, Clarke A., *Seedtime of Reform: American Social Service and Social Action, 1918–1933*. Minneapolis, 1963.

Citizens' Union of New York Reports.

The Class of 1902, 1903, 1906, 1910, 1915, 1924. Privately printed by the Class of 1902, Mount Holyoke College.

Commons, John R., and others, *History of Labor in the United States*, 4 volumes. New York, 1935.

Consumers' League of New York Reports.

Costello, Jerry, *The Life of Alfred Smith* (told in forty-eight pictures). New York, 1928.

Current Biography, 1941.

Davis, Allen F., *Spearheads for Reform: The Social Settlements and the Progressive Movement*. New York, 1967.

Dickinson, Thomas H., *The Portrait of a Man as Governor*. New York, 1928.

Dreier, Mary E., *Margaret Dreier Robbins: Her Life, Letters and Work*. New York, 1950.

Duffus, R. L., *Lillian Wald, Neighbor and Crusader*. New York, 1938.

Ellis, David M., and others, *A Short History of New York State*. Ithaca, N.Y., 1957.

Farley, James A., *Behind the Ballots*. New York, 1938.

——, *Jim Farley's Story*. New York, 1948.

Feldman, M. I., *The Political Thought of Alfred E. Smith*. New York, 1963.

Flynn, Edward J., *You're the Boss*. New York, 1947.

Fowler, Gene, *Beau James*. New York, 1949.

Frankfurter, Felix, *Felix Frankfurter Reminisces*. New York, 1962.

Freidel, Frank Burt, *Franklin Roosevelt*, 3 volumes. Boston, 1956.

Gabriel, Brother Angelus, *The Christian Brothers in the United States, 1848–1948; a Century of Catholic Education.* New York, 1948.

Gilbert, Clinton Wallace, *The Mirrors of Washington.* New York, 1921.

Goldmark, Josephine, *Impatient Crusader: Florence Kelley's Life Story.* Urbana, Ill., 1953.

Graham, Frank, *Al Smith, American, An Informal Biography.* New York, 1945.

Handlin, Oscar, *Al Smith and His America.* Boston, 1957.

Hapgood, Norman, and Moskowitz, Henry, *Up from the City Streets.* New York, 1927.

Hodder, Alfred, *A Fight for the City.* New York, 1903.

Huthmacher, J. Joseph, *Senator Robert F. Wagner and the Rise of Urban Liberalism.* New York, 1968.

Ickes, Harold L., *Secret Diary,* 3 volumes. New York, 1954.

Linn, James Weber, *Jane Addams, a Biography.* New York, 1935.

Lippmann, Walter, *Interpretations.* New York, 1932.

———, *Men of Destiny.* New York, 1928.

Lubell, Samuel, *The Future of American Politics.* New York, 1952.

Ludwig, Emil, *Roosevelt, A Study in Fortune and Power.* New York, 1938.

Meier, Elizabeth G., *A History of the New York School for Social Work.* New York, 1954.

Michelson, Charles, *The Ghost Talks.* New York, 1944.

Moscow, Warren, *Politics in the Empire State.* New York, 1948.

Moses, Robert, *A Tribute to Governor Smith.* New York, 1962.

Moskowitz, Henry, *Alfred E. Smith, An American Career.* New York, 1924.

Nevins, Alan, *Herbert H. Lehman and His Era.* New York, 1963.

Nutt, Charles, *History of Worcester and Its People.* New York, 1919.

O'Connor, Edwin, *The Last Hurrah.* Boston, 1956.

Parkhurst, Charles H., *Our Fight with Tammany.* New York, 1895.

Patten, J. H., *"The Immigration Crew" on the New Deal "Railroad."* American Vigilant Intelligence Federation, Chicago, 1935.

Perkins, Frances, "After-care for Industrial Compensation Cases," in *Proceedings of the National Conference of Social Work,* 1921.

———, "The Factory Inspector," in Catherine Filene, editor, *Careers for Women.* Boston, 1920.

———, *People at Work.* New York, 1934.

———, *The Roosevelt I Knew.* New York, 1946.

———, "The Social and Human Cost of Fire," in *Proceedings of the 17th Annual Meeting, National Fire Protection Association.* New York, 1913.

Pringle, Henry F., *Alfred E. Smith, a Critical Study.* New York, 1927.

Proskauer, Joseph M., *A Segment of My Times.* New York, 1950.

Riis, Jacob A., *How the Other Half Lives.* New York, 1957.

Riordan, William L., *Plunkitt of Tammany Hall.* New York, 1963.

Roosevelt, Eleanor, and Hickok, Lorena A., *Ladies of Courage.* New York, 1954.

Roosevelt, Eleanor, *This I Remember.* New York, 1949.

Roseberry, Cecil R., *Capitol Story.* Albany, N.Y., 1964.

Schlesinger, Arthur M., *The Rise of the City: 1878–1898.* New York, 1933.

Schlesinger, Arthur M., Jr., *The Crisis of the Old Order, 1919–1933.* New York, 1957.

Schneiderman, Rose, with Goldthwaite, Lucy, *All for One.* New York, 1967.

Shannon, William V., *The American Irish.* New York, 1963.

Siegfried, André, *America Comes of Age.* New York, 1927.

Simkhovitch, Mary Kingsbury, *Neighborhood.* New York, 1938.

Smith, Alfred E.,

———, *Address . . . at the Lawyers' Club,* March 18, 1922.

———, *Addresses . . . Delivered at the Meetings of the Friendly Sons of St. Patrick, 1922–1944.* New York, 1945.

———, *Campaign Addresses.* Washington, D.C., 1929.

———, "The Challenge to America," in Pierre Van Paassen, *Nazism, An Assault on Civilization.* New York, 1934.

———, *Progressive Democracy; Addresses and State Papers.* New York, 1928.

———, *Up to Now.* New York, 1929.

Stein, Leon, *The Triangle Fire*. Philadelphia, 1962.

Sullivan, Mark, *Our Times*, 6 volumes. New York, 1926–35.

Swanberg, W. A., *Citizen Hearst*. New York, 1961.

Tucker, Ray, *The Mirrors of 1932*. New York, 1931.

Tugwell, Rex, *The Democratic Roosevelt*. New York, 1957.

Tully, Grace, *F.D.R., My Boss*. New York, 1949.

United States Reports, Volume 273, Cases Adjudged in the Supreme Court at October Term 1926. Washington, D.C., 1927.

Valentine's Manual of Old New York, Edited by Henry Collins Brown. New York, 1926.

Vorse, Mary Heaton, *A Footnote to Folly*. New York, 1935.

Warner, Emily Smith, with Hawthorne, Daniel, *The Happy Warrior*. New York, 1956.

Werner, M. R., *Tammany Hall*. Garden City, N.Y., 1928.

White, Theodore H., *The Making of the President, 1960*. New York, 1961.

MAGAZINES AND ARTICLES
OF SPECIAL INTEREST

American Mercury, June, 1928, "Fat Cats and Free Rides," by Frank R. Kent.

Atlantic Monthly, April and May, 1928, "Open Letter to Governor Smith," by Charles G. Marshall and Smith's reply.

Charities and the Commons. (Later *The Survey*.)

Collier's Magazine, May 19, 1928, "A Woman Looks at Smith," by Ida Tarbell.

The *Forum*, June, 1928, "Al Smith and a Catholic Party." A Three-Cornered Debate by Stanley Frost, Michael Williams, and William Bennett Munro.

Ladies' Home Journal, August, 1929, "Everybody Ought to Be Rich," an Interview with John J. Raskob by Samuel Crowther.

Llamarada, Yearbook of Mount Holyoke College, 1902.

Metropolitan Magazine, July, 1912, "Behind the Rail," by Leroy Scott.

The *Nation*, 1928–1933.

The *New Republic*, 1928.

New York History, October, 1964, "Al Smith in the Thirties," by Jordan A. Schwartz; October, 1965, "The Brown Derby Campaign," by David Burner.

New York Times Magazine, October 22, 1922, "Alfred E. Smith, a Personal Impression," by Ann O'Hagan Shinn; October 6, 1929, " 'Al' Smith Talks as a Man of Business," by S. J. Woolf.

The *New Yorker,* October 9, 1926, "A Certain Person," by O. H. P. Garrett.

North American Review, October, 1928, "Friends of the Governor," by Denis Tilden Lynch.

The *Outlook* and The *New Outlook,* 1928–1932.

Saturday Evening Post, February 27, 1932, "How Governor Smith Educated Himself," by Christian Gauss; August 30, 1930, "Electioneering Old And New," by Alfred E. Smith; May 24, 1930, "Spell-binding," by Alfred E. Smith; July 27, 1940, "Madame Secretary, A Study in Bewilderment," by Benjamin Stolberg.

Scribner's Magazine, September, 1926, "A Personal Portrait of Governor Al Smith," by James Kerney.

Social Forces, December, 1929, "A Measurement of the Factors in the Presidential Election of 1928," by William F. Ogburn and Nell Snow Talbot.

Social Service Review, Vol. XXVIII, 1954, "My Recollections of Florence Kelley," by Frances Perkins.

The *Survey,* February 1933, "Belle Lindner Moskowitz."

Index